Experience Music!

Experience Music!

Katherine Charlton
Mt. San Antonio College

Robert Hickok
Professor of Music Emeritus
University of California–Irvine

Boston   Burr Ridge, IL   Dubuque, IA   Madison, WI   New York   San Francisco   St. Louis
Bangkok   Bogotá   Caracas   Kuala Lumpur   Lisbon   London   Madrid   Mexico City
Milan   Montreal   New Delhi   Santiago   Seoul   Singapore   Sydney   Taipei   Toronto

The McGraw-Hill Companies

Higher Education

Published by McGraw-Hill, an imprint of The McGraw-Hill Companies, Inc., 1221 Avenue of the Americas, New York, NY 10020. Copyright © 2007. All rights reserved. No part of this publication may be reproduced or distributed in any form or by any means, or stored in a database or retrieval system, without the prior written consent of The McGraw-Hill Companies, Inc., including, but not limited to, in any network or other electronic storage or transmission, or broadcast for distance learning.

This book is printed on acid-free paper.

2 3 4 5 6 7 8 9 0 WCK/WCK 0 9 8 7 6

ISBN-13: 978-0-07-246244-9
ISBN-10: 0-07-246244-2

Editor in Chief: *Emily Barrosse*
Publisher: *Lyn Uhl*
Senior Sponsoring Editor: *Melody Marcus*
Executive Marketing Manager: *Suzanna Ellison*
Director of Development: *Lisa Pinto*
Editorial Coordinator: *Beth Ebenstein*
Project Manager: *Holly Paulsen*
Manuscript Editor: *Elaine Kehoe*
Design Manager: *Preston Thomas*
Text Designer: *Jeanne Calabrese*
Cover Designer: *Yvo Riezebos*
Art Editor: *Emma Ghiselli*
Illustrator: *Emma Ghiselli*
Photo Research Coordinator: *Nora Agbayani*
Photo Researcher: *Judy Mason*
Media Producers: *Shannon Gattens/Jocelyn Arsht*
Media Project Manager: *Marc Mattson*
Production Supervisor: *Tandra Jorgensen*
Composition: *10.5/12 Minion by Interactive Composition*
Printing: *45# Pub Matte, Quebecor World*

Credits: The credits section for this book begins on page 365 and is considered an extension of the copyright page.

Library of Congress Cataloging-in-Publication Data has been applied for.

www.mhhe.com

To my husband, Jeff Calkins, who likes music with tunes he can hum. —KC

To Roanne, who has lived and sung with me for fifty years. —RH

Brief Contents

Contents

List of Boxes

HEARING THE DIFFERENCE

THE LIVE EXPERIENCE

More than anyone else, students have shaped this book. In over twenty years of teaching music appreciation, I have learned as much from my students as I learned from my own teachers. The ways in which students respond to music, the questions asked, the elements that pique interest, and the many musical experiences that help to develop a lifelong appreciation—all of these came into play in the writing of this book.

One key goal I had in mind was to keep this book streamlined. Although it is comprehensive in teaching the fundamentals and the history of music, it is shorter than many music appreciation texts. I have attempted to clearly convey key concepts within an appealing narrative, asking myself as I wrote, "What do students really need to know?" My hope is that the resulting book will be flexible for a variety of teaching approaches and highly readable for students.

I wanted to support this approach with pedagogy that stimulates student interest, reinforcing listening skill development within the fascinating historical context of Western music. *Experience Music!* has an abundance of features to engage students. And so another question I asked was "How do students really learn?"

With these questions playing in my head, *Experience Music!* developed into a student-centered music appreciation text that I hope will give students an appreciation of music that endures for a lifetime.

Although *Experience Music!* is a first edition, it is not a completely new book. The foundations of this text are based on Robert Hickok's *Exploring Music,* a book that was highly regarded and widely used through five editions. I taught from that book for several years and always liked its warm, appealing tone and balanced coverage. I was very happy to be given the opportunity to propose ideas for a new version of the text that would build on the enduring strengths of Bob's text but also approach today's students in new ways.

Coverage

The first three chapters supply a very brief overview of the fundamentals of music. This information, the building blocks of music, is further reinforced and expanded with the *Experience Music Interactive!* student CD-ROM, through activities that enable students to learn about and experiment with elements such as rhythm, melody, harmony, and pitch. At the end of the discussion of each element, the CD-ROM includes a quiz that students can take. They can then print out their score or e-mail it to their instructor as evidence that the material has been studied and understood. Of course, this material can also be covered in class using the examples on the CD-ROM. The coverage of elements in the book and on the CD-ROM is thus flexible and oriented to a variety of learning styles. Icons throughout the book show where material on the CD-ROM supports the coverage in the book.

Chapters 4 through 29 follow the history of Western music from medieval Europe to the present. Chapters are short and are designed to be adaptable to a variety of syllabi while still offering comprehensive coverage of major topics and composers. I hope that instructors will find space available to personalize their course by adding favorite musical examples of their own. I always like to do things like add examples that were composed for instruments my students play, such as harp or classical guitar, to help the students feel that they are part of music history themselves.

Chapters 30 to 37 trace the development of American music, including more chapters on these topics than most other music appreciation books. While many colleges offer individual courses on these subjects, students may not be exposed to these forms of music or may not be planning to take courses in them. I hope that this book's introduction will stimulate some students to pursue further study of these areas. Chapter 38 discusses music in film, a topic that I find intrigues many of my students.

Chapters 39 to 41 explore international influences on music, including influences from Indonesia, China, India, Africa, and the Middle East. Finally, Chapter 42, "Fusion of Cultures," ties together these multicultural influences, exploring what they mean to today's—and tomorrow's—world of music.

What's Different about *Experience Music!*?

Listening is the key that unlocks a passion for music and an appreciation for how it enhances our lives. While the overall chapter structure will be familiar to instructors, *Experience Music!*'s features and pedagogy are uniquely designed to help students become skillful, enthusiastic listeners.

Listening Introductions, Listening Guides, and Finales

Listening to music is a skill that must be exercised in order to develop. *Experience Music!* provides the equipment needed to build that skill in an enjoyable, affirming way with a three-part listening experience:

- The **Listening Introduction** at the beginning of every chapter asks students to listen to a piece of music and guides their attention with simple questions such as "Can you determine the meter?" and "What is the general mood of the piece?" When the piece chosen for the Listening Introduction is on the two-CD set that comes with the book, students can do the listening and answer the questions on their own. When the introductory piece is on the optional three-CD set and the students have not purchased that set, the questions may be answered in class. The Listening Introduction can become a class project for students to work on individually or in groups.

- Each **Listening Guide** walks students step-by-step through key works discussed in the book. This guided listening experience trains the listener's ear by pointing out meaningful elements, themes, and instrumentation in key works.

- After reading the chapter, students return to the piece of work they encountered in the Listening Introduction and respond to similar questions in the **Finale.**

Students improve their listening skills faster by listening to an individual recording several times, and these features give them a guided way to listen repeatedly to the same piece of music. Students also feel a sense of affirmation when they see how much more skillful they are at *hearing* the music when they reach the end of the chapter. This pedagogy is reflected and reinforced in the student CD-ROM, *Experience Music Interactive!* The CD-ROM includes interactive versions of the Listening Introduction, Listening Guides, and Finale for each chapter, which students can use in conjunction with their audio CDs. *Experience Music Interactive!* is uniquely crafted to guide and support students' listening skill development.

Preludes

Preludes, which precede groups of chapters, give historical, social, and cultural background to the various periods of music. They provide needed context on the essentials required to understand something about how people lived in that era and how music was part of their lives.

Hearing the Difference

Hearing the Difference boxes emerge directly from my teaching experience. I find that some students who study and try to listen carefully still have trouble correctly identifying particular works on exams. Now that my teaching practice has students compare pieces of music, they are much more successful on exams. I select works that are somewhat similar (both played by an orchestra, for example) and play both, having the students concentrate on particular characteristics of each recording, such as instruments or rhythms. The Hearing the Difference feature helps students do this comparison on their own when the works are on recordings they have, or they can become class projects with students checking off characteristics listed as they hear them when the music is played. The level of listening skill builds throughout the book, and students hone their ability to discern different styles.

The Live Experience

Students are probably unaware of how the questions they ask in class can prompt the teacher to see the subject in some new way. For example, students who have asked me questions like "What does the conductor do?" gave me the idea of writing The Live Experience boxes in this book. Like many music professors, I have always taken for granted what a conductor does, but with these boxes I open the door for students to the experience of being a musician—a singer, a composer, or an instrumentalist, for example—and how performers' work affects our concert experience.

Student Resources

Experience Music! contains a wealth of resources for students.

Audio CDs

Two audio CDs are provided with every copy of *Experience Music!* and the guided listening for these selections is in the Listening Guides, which students can use on their own. (Three additional CDs are also available for optional purchase.)

Experience Music Interactive! CD-ROM

Experience Music! is packaged with an interactive CD-ROM entitled *Experience Music Interactive!* This carefully crafted study tool was developed by McGraw-Hill with Steven Estrella, an experienced music educator, and a professional software development team. It contains a wide range of support for the student:

- **Explore** activities for each chapter illuminate concepts in a highly engaging and interactive way. Icons placed throughout the textbook indicate where materials on the CD-ROM support a concept being learned. The elements chapters in particular contain a wide range of Explore materials. Each chapter after the elements chapters contains at least one Explore activity. Some Explore activities have students directly manipulate musical elements. Others incorporate animation, quizzes, performance or interview video clips, Web research, and listening activities.

- Each **Listening Introduction** in the text is repeated on the CD-ROM, and the students may make notes in the associated notepad.

- **Listening Guides** on the CD-ROM take students through the musical selection step-by-step, with key terms defined in context.

- The **Finale** at the end of the text chapter is repeated on the CD-ROM, again with the opportunity for students to make notes and then compare them with their notes from the Listening Introduction so that they can see how much they have learned over the course of the chapter. The Finale closes with a brief quiz that can be e-mailed to the instructor if he or she so requests.

Online Learning Center

The Online Learning Center (OLC) that accompanies this text can be found at http://www.mhhe.com/experiencemusic. It provides students with an abundance of additional resources such as multiple-choice questions, listening quizzes, projects, and links to useful Web sites. All material on the OLC is available in a cartridge for WebCT and Blackboard for use in online courses or course Web sites.

Instructor Resources

McGraw-Hill provides unparalleled support for the music appreciation instructor.

Instructor's Resource CD-ROM

For the instructor we offer an Instructor's Resource CD-ROM that includes the following elements:

- An **Instructor's Manual,** by David H. Evans of Henderson State University, with comprehensive teaching suggestions for each chapter.

- Approximately 450 **PowerPoint slides,** also by David H. Evans, that highlight key lecture points and Listening Guides.

- A **Test Bank,** by Janice Dickensheets of the University of Northern Colorado, with 30–40 questions for each chapter.

- McGraw-Hill's **EZ Test,** a flexible and easy-to-use electronic testing program that allows instructors to create tests from book-specific items. It accommodates a wide range of question types, and instructors may add their own questions. Multiple versions of the test can be created and any test can be exported for use with course management systems such as WebCT, Blackboard, or PageOut. EZ Test Online is a new service and gives you a place to easily administer your EZ Test–created exams and quizzes online. The program is available for Windows and Macintosh environments.

▌ The **Classroom Performance System,** or CPS, by eInstruction, with content prepared by Ronald Garber of Butler Community College, allows instructors to gauge immediately what students are learning during lectures. Instructors can ask questions, take polls, host classroom demonstrations, and get instant feedback. In addition, CPS makes it easy to take attendance, give and grade pop quizzes, or give formal, paper-based class tests with multiple versions of the test using CPS for immediate grading. Visit www.mhhe.com/cps for more information.

Instructor's Edition/Online Learning Center

The **Online Learning Center** at www.mhhe.com/experiencemusic includes a separate, password-protected Instructor site with a wide range of resources for instructors, including the Instructor's Manual and PowerPoint slides in PDF format. The Online Learning Center also contains

▌ Listening quizzes with streaming music, prepared by Gregory Carroll of the University of North Carolina at Greensboro.

▌ Image Library with links to sites containing fine art appropriate to each chapter in the book, prepared by Cathryn Wilkinson.

▌ Student Projects associated with each Prelude, prepared by Richard Perkins of Anoka-Ramsey Community College.

▌ Chapter-by-chapter links to appropriate Web resources, prepared by Gregory Jones of Truman State University.

Acknowledgments

I acknowledge with gratitude the many reviewers who took the time to read and critique the manuscript.

Kevin Bartram, *Mary Washington College*

Mary Dave Blackman, *East Tennessee State University*

Andra C. Bohnet, *University of South Alabama*

Dana Brown, *Kent State University*

Gregory Carroll, *University of North Carolina, Greensboro*

Henrietta Carter, *Golden West College*

Christopher Chaffee, *Wright State University*

Jonathan Chenoweth, *University of Northern Iowa*

Richard Cole, *Virginia Polytechnic Institute*

Laura Dankner, *Southeastern Louisiana University*

Seth Davis, *Kingwood College and Alamo CCD*

Marc Dickman, *University of Northern Florida*

Hollie Duvall, *Westmoreland County Community College*

David H. Evans, *Henderson State University*

Richard Allen Fiske, *Shasta College*

Sheila Forrester, *Santa Fe Community College*

Cliff Ganus, *Harding University*

Ron Garber, *Butler Community College*

Richard Greene, *Georgia College & State University*

David Haas, *University of Georgia*

Edward Hart, *College of Charleston*

Kristin Hauser, *Tennessee Technological University*

Michael Hillstrom, *Heartland Community College*

David Johansen, *Southeastern Louisiana University*

Gregory Jones, *Truman State University*

Laura J. Keith, *Claflin University*

Sandra Kipp, *California State University–Northridge and Moorpark College*

Orly Krasner, *City College/CUNY*

Aaron Liu-Rosenbaum, *The City College of New York*

William Malone, *Pikes Peak Community College*

Grant Manhart, *Northern State University*

Alan Mason, *Barry University*

Brian Mason, *Morehead State University*

Charlotte Mueller, *Lee College*

Mikylah Myers McTeer, *Fort Lewis College*

Tom Noonan, *Front Range Community College*

Patricia Nuss, *Middle Georgia College*

Debra O'Dell, *North Idaho College*

Jay O'Leary, *Wayne State College*

Jill O'Neill, *Winthrop University*

Stephanie Berg Oram, *Red Rocks Community College*

Richard J. Perkins, *Anoka-Ramsey Community College*

Pamela J. Perry, *Central Connecticut State University*

Clark Potter, *University of Nebraska–Lincoln*

Alan Rawson, *Minnesota State University–Moorhead*

Anthony Scelba, *Kean University*

David Schiller, *University of Georgia*

William Shepherd, *University of Northern Iowa*

Matt Shevitz, *Harold Washington College*

Mark L. Singer, *Morgan State University*

Floyd Slotterback, *Northern Michigan University*

Frederick Key Smith, *Santa Fe Community College*

Wayne C. Smith, *Spokane Falls Community College*

Ron Stinson, *Johnson County Community College*

Virginia Stitt, *Southern Utah University*

Karla J. Stroman, *North Hennepin Community College*

James Syler, *University of Texas at San Antonio*

John F. Vallentine, *University of Northern Iowa*

Beverly Vaughn, *The Richard Stockton College of New Jersey*

Cathryn Wilkinson, *Concordia University*

Dieter Wulfhorst, *California State University–Fresno*

I want to express my particular gratitude to these professors whose valuable suggestions were incorporated into the text:

Patrice Ross, *Columbus State Community College*

Dale A. Scott, *Oklahoma State University*

I have many people to thank for their help in the writing of *ExperienceMusic!* First, of course, is my co-author, Robert Hickok. Although he has been retired from his position as Dean of the School of the Arts at the University of California at Irvine for some years, Robert was very helpful to me in every step of this new project and we have become very good friends during the process. His book dedication is to his lovely wife, Roanne, who has also been very supportive of our work. My dedication is to my husband, Jeffrey Calkins, for many reasons. He has done a lot of proofreading, but he has also spent many an evening coming home from his job as a research attorney at the California State Court of Appeals to end up cooking dinner and calling me away from my computer when it was ready. Now that the book is finished, I will have to learn how to cook all over again. In addition to being a brilliant attorney, Jeff is a political scientist who was very helpful in making suggestions to improve the Preludes in the book.

Colleagues who helped me with their suggestions and proofreading include Gary Toops and Kevin Wiley. Gary is an organist who also teaches music appreciation at my college and was very helpful in suggesting additions that enriched the book. He also provided wonderful insights when I wrote The Live Experience box called "Playing the Organ." Kevin is an accompanist and librarian in my department, and he assists me in many of my duties as department chair, something I particularly needed while writing this book. I also received some much appreciated advice on both world and film music from another colleague in my department, Joseph LoPiccolo. Marjie Toops teaches Spanish at University High School in Irvine, and I appreciate her help in giving me both the Spanish text and the English translation for "Saeta." Other colleagues who advised and encouraged me in various ways include Bill McIntosh and Scott Zeidel. One of my former teachers, Dr. Robert Stewart, was also very encouraging. I learned more about contemporary music from him than from any other source, and I constantly find myself quoting him when I teach the subject. Dr. Larry Timm, author of *The Soul of Cinema: An Appreciation of Film Music,* is an old friend of mine and was very helpful in making suggestions to improve the chapter on music in film.

I'm grateful to McGraw-Hill sales representative Lorraine Zielinski, who suggested to the company that I would be right for this project. Justyn Baker and Luis Lange, from the NAXOS Record Company, were most helpful in providing me with recordings to use in the book, getting permissions to use the recordings I needed that NAXOS did not have, and then putting together the audio CD set that is used with the book. I appreciate the work of the many McGraw-Hill editorial, media, marketing, and production staff members and freelancers who were involved in this book. In addition to those who are listed on the copyright page, I would like to acknowledge the work of Carol Einhorn, Nadia Bidwell, Chris Narozny, Teresa Nemeth, Barbara Gerr, Beth Ebenstein, and Nicole Caddigan.

As I indicated earlier, the most important people who guided my choices and attitudes about this book were the many students I have had over the years. I hope that the students who use this book enjoy it, learn from it, and feel encouraged to ask questions in class. After all, we teachers and writers work for them.

Preface for the Student: A Guided Tour

Learning to appreciate music is a skill. This book will help you develop that skill with a variety of features and resources. The guided tour describes the organization of the chapters and the special features of your text, allowing you to make the most out of your study time.

---

20 | The Concert Overture

Music is a code that opens a door to a world everybody interprets differently because our aesthetic and sensory values are different and each generation has to discover its own.
—CELLIST YO-YO-MA (BORN IN 1955)

Listening Introduction

Listen to the example of music that represents this chapter, the *Romeo and Juliet* overture, by Tchaikovsky, and make notes about what you hear. Give some attention to the following:

▪ Can you guess at the tempo?

▪ Can you detect the meter?

▪ This is a rather long composition. Listen carefully to the first nine minutes, and then see if you hear any repetition of those melodies later in the work. Do any repeat?

▪ What kind of contrasts do you hear between or among the themes (melodies) that are played during the nine-minute exposition?

▪ If you know the story of Romeo and Juliet, can you connect the sounds of the main themes to people or events in the story?

Keep these notes to compare with your impressions about the music after you study the information in this chapter.

Listening Introduction

Experience music at the very beginning of each chapter with a Listening Introduction that asks you to listen to a piece of music and guides your attention with questions such as "What is the general mood of the piece?"

Listening Guide

Each Listening Guide leads you step-by-step through key musical selections discussed in the book. This guided listening experience trains your ear by pointing out meaningful aspects of the selections.

Listening Guide
Romeo and Juliet Overture PETER ILYICH TCHAIKOVSKY

CD 4
Tracks 9–15

Year: 1870
Tempo: Slow introduction, faster with some variation later
Meter: Quadruple
Form: Sonata with an introduction
Instrumentation: Two flutes (piccolo), two oboes, two clarinets, one English horn, two bassoons, four horns, two trumpets, three trombones, one tuba, timpani, cymbals, bass drum, harp, first violins, second violins, violas, cellos, double basses
Duration: 18:53
Special feature: Notice how well the themes fit the characters or emotions in the play: The Friar Laurence theme is serious and sounds like it might be played in a church, the feud theme sounds like a street fight, and the love theme is beautiful and gentle.

Timing		What to listen for
Introduction		
9	0:00	*Friar Laurence*	Hymnlike, homophonic theme softly in clarinets and bassoons
	0:31		Foreboding fragments begin in low strings, build gradually to winds with harp
	1:54		Strings pizzicato, Friar Laurence theme more agitated in woodwinds
	2:24		Foreboding music returns, then with harp arpeggios
	3:44		Timpani roll introduces intense, threatening motives climaxing in loud, fast passage
	4:15		Timpani, threatening motives: woodwind-string echoes build directly to:
Exposition		
10	4:59	*Theme 1: Feud*	Agitated feud theme in orchestra; strings rush up and down; agitated feud theme; rising three-note motive tossed between strings and winds
	5:22		Fragments of feud theme and rushing strings combined, developed with three-note motive; full orchestra with cymbal crashes in loud chords and rushing strings build to climax
	6:01		Feud theme explodes in full orchestra; transition with rushing strings; feud theme builds to close
	6:22	*Bridge*	Energy released in woodwind development of three-note motive; low strings take over
11	7:06	*Theme 2: Love*	Flowing love theme in English horn and muted violas, pulsating horns accompany
	7:22		Harp arpeggio introduces muted strings with tender love music
	8:03		Flutes and oboes surge upward to love theme with countertheme in French horn creating a love duet; greatly extended with lush orchestration
	9:05	*Closing*	Harp chords and soft tones in strings and winds subside to restful close
Development		
12	10:08		Fragments of feud theme; fast scales in strings accompany Friar Laurence theme intoned softly in horn; theme extended and developed
	11:22		Three-note motive interrupts in cellos and basses, with fragments of feud theme; downward rushing strings added and build to climax
	11:38		Cymbal crash, full orchestra develops feud theme fragment; Friar Laurence theme combined forte in trumpet; rushing strings with loud chords in orchestra lead directly into:

continued

Timing		What to listen for
Recapitulation		
13	12:12	*Theme 1*	Agitated feud theme in full orchestra with cymbal crashes; strings rush downward
14	12:35	*Theme 2*	Tender love music in oboes and clarinets; intensity grows as other winds enrich the sound; strings rise intensely upward into:
	13:13		Love theme soars in strings and flute with countertheme in horn and throbbing woodwind accompaniment; grows to full, rich orchestration
	14:18		Love theme fragment in cellos answered by flute; extended with fragments and horns answered by flute and oboe; strings begin love theme but it dissolves
15	14:55	*Coda*	Fragments of feud and love themes vie with each other in full orchestra; feud theme emphatically takes over, then combines with Friar Laurence theme in brass; extended development as feud music takes over; furious activity decreases to ominous timpani roll
	16:12		Drumbeat continues as in a funeral march; fragments of love theme sound brokenly in strings, drumbeat ceases as woodwinds answer with a variation of tender love music; rising harp arpeggios signal union of the lovers, strings yearningly sing fragment of love theme
	18:31		Drum roll crescendo to strong final chords, recalling the feud theme

Summary

The romantic era gave rise to a new type of overture, one that did not introduce a longer work but was instead a self-contained work in one movement, intended for performance in the concert hall. The concert overture, exemplified by Tchaikovsky's "Romeo and Juliet," often had programmatic elements but retained the sonata form of organization.

New People and Concepts

concert overture

fantasy overture

incidental music

Peter Ilyich Tchaikovsky

Finale

Listen again to the *Romeo and Juliet* overture by Tchaikovsky and compare your impressions now with your notes from your first listening. Do you hear more now than you did before? You should now be able to answer the following questions:

▪ What is the tempo and what happens to it during the mood changes in the work?

▪ What is the meter?

▪ Do any themes from the beginning repeat later?

▪ What kind of contrasts do you hear among the three main themes?

▪ How do those themes fit the story of Romeo and Juliet?

Finale

After reading the chapter, you return to the piece you encountered in the Listening Introduction and respond to similar questions in the Finale. Having studied the piece in the chapter, you will see how much more you are now able to hear in the same piece of music.

HEARING THE DIFFERENCE
Mozart's "Non più andrai" and Schubert's "Erlkönig"

These two works are quite different from one another in that Mozart's is an aria from an opera accompanied by a full orchestra and Schubert's is an art song accompanied by piano. The two are not compared here for those obvious differences, but rather for the very classical formal structure of one and the very romantic structure and content of the other.

	Non più andrai	Erlkönig
Historical period	Classical	Romantic
Tempo	Vivace (fast and lively)	Fast
Meter	Quadruple	Quadruple
Performers	Bass/baritone singer accompanied by full orchestra	Mezzo soprano singer accompanied by piano
Language	Italian	German
Form	ABACA-Coda, a symmetrically balanced form often used in the classical period	Through-composed, to have the melody that is sung continually change to suit the ongoing story
Mood	Very jovial and teasing. The aria is sung to a young man who has just been told that he must enter the military.	Very intense. A fearful child is tempted by the Elf King and the father tries to calm him. The ending is very sad, as the listener learns that the child has died. The sense of mystery, and even the presence of the Elf King spirit, are subjects that some Romantics particularly enjoyed.

as in music. He had studied music as a child but began his university education majoring in law. He gave up the study of law to concentrate on music and, in 1830, began taking lessons from a well-known piano teacher in Leipzig, Friedrich Wieck.

Wieck had many students, but his primary concentration was on his extremely talented daughter, Clara, who was eleven years old when she first met Robert Schumann. By that age, **Clara Wieck** had performed many times in Leipzig, and within the next two years she gave concerts across Europe to Paris and back to Germany. She had composed many small pieces for the piano and undertook her largest composition, a Concerto for Piano and Orchestra in A Minor, op. 7, in 1836. Clara had not studied orchestration, but Robert Schumann had. The two had become friends, and Clara asked Robert to help her in writing the orchestral parts. He did that, and Clara premiered the work in November of 1835 with Felix Mendelssohn conducting the Gewandhaus orchestra in Leipzig. She joined Mendelssohn and another pianist in the performance of a concerto for three keyboard instruments by J. S. Bach on that same concert program. In the next few years, Clara continued to perform her concerto in concerts all over Germany and Austria. The work was published in 1837. It was performed by other pianists throughout the 1800s.

Hearing the Difference
This box compares works that share certain features so that you can discern different styles of music. For example, here you compare key characteristics of music of the baroque and romantic eras.

Prelude | The Triumph of the Baroque Style

(two notes played back and forth very quickly). Stark contrasts between light and dark in paintings are common in much baroque art. In music, we will also hear dramatic contrasts between dynamic levels, in which one musical phrase will be played loud, followed by another that is much softer, almost like an echo of the first.

We can see these striking contrasts between light and shadow, as well as vigorous action and realism, in Caravaggio's (1573–1610) painting *The Conversion of St. Paul* (1600–1601). The biblical story shown is that of Saul of Tarsus, who had been a Christian persecutor but who was instantly converted to Christianity on the road to Damascus by a vision of Jesus that temporarily blinded him. The painting captures the very moment of the blinding and conversion, which is typical of the type of action seen in much baroque art.

Of course, there are many other artists whose works display similar activity and contrast. The sculptor Gianlorenzo Bernini's (1598–1680) *David Slaying Goliath* (1623) serves as a good example of baroque style when compared with Michelangelo's depiction of the same biblical personality (see page 47). David was the young future king of Israel (ca. 1000–ca. 960 BCE), who used a slingshot to slay a Philistine giant named Goliath who had challenged the Jews. Bernini's *David* is seen in the actual act of throwing the stone, whereas Michelangelo's

David Slaying Goliath by Bernini (1598–1680). This sculpture shows the kind of activity often portrayed in baroque art.

sculpture shows a more sedate, relaxed pose. Neither sculpture is more religious nor more representative of the story than the other. They are just concentrated on different times in the story, chosen by the popular style of the period.

Music continued to play an important role in the life of the churches, as it had in the Renaissance. Sounds, perhaps more than the visual arts, could move, elevate, and involve a congregation and thus intensify the spiritual experience. Whereas Protestants were skeptical of visual displays and the veneration of images, they warned to the use of music in church services. In the seventeenth century, major Protestant churches began to form orchestras and choirs, to have large organs built for their churches, and to hire organists, soloists, and music masters. The greatest baroque church musician was Johann Sebastian Bach, who spent a major part of his career at Leipzig, leaving a vast treasure of sacred music, vocal and instrumental, at the time of his death in 1750.

The concentration of baroque art and architecture was not exclusively religious. In France monumental art was used to enhance the position of Louis XIV and his court. The efforts of architects, stonemasons, sculptors, painters, furniture makers, and gardeners were carefully coordinated to remake the royal palace at Versailles in the

latter half of the seventeenth century. By 1700, a visitor to Paris would have been overwhelmed by French monuments to the power of the Crown. In the eighteenth century, Paris replaced Rome as the leader in European culture and design.

The grandeur of baroque style reflected the tastes of the church and the ruling class. Most people were, of course, farmers who never even saw the great cities of Rome or Paris. In the cities lived many workers and artisans who constructed and decorated the great

61

Peasant Family by Louis Le Nain (1603–1648). The Louvre, Paris. Most peasants worked many hours just to live and had no way of appreciating the grandness of baroque style.

He Revels from *The Rake's Progress* by William Hogarth (1697–1764). Well-to-do nobles and merchants enjoyed public gatherings such as the one portrayed in this painting.

monuments of the period. The average worker worked about sixteen hours a day, six days a week, and families looked much like the one depicted in the painting *Peasant Family* by Louis Le Nain. Entertainment for the lower classes included visits to alehouses, where musicians, storytellers, and gambling were available. Some common spectator sports such as cockfighting were very violent and bloody. Stealing, swindling, and murder were common and were punished by whipping, branding, having a body part cut off, or death.

There was not a very large middle class, but there were well-to-do nobles and merchants who had much better lives than the poor workers. They enjoyed hunting, gambling, and various types of ball and board games, as did the aristocracy. Educated people learned to play musical instruments or sing, and enjoyed performing with or for friends in their homes. Public entertainments such as plays, balls, and masques (skits based on allegorical stories performed with elaborate staging and costumes) were popular. An engraving of *He Revels* (*The Orgy*) from the series *The Rake's Progress*, 1735, by William Hogarth displays some of this type of lifestyle. Opera, eventually, was added to the list of possibilities for entertainment for those who could afford to attend. By the baroque period, the New World products of coffee, chocolate, and tobacco were easily available and enjoyed

Prelude
This section precedes groups of chapters, providing background to the various periods of music. It gives you some context on the essentials required to understand how people lived in that era and how music was part of their lives.

THE LIVE EXPERIENCE
Playing the Organ

The organ is a unique instrument because it can make a great many different types of sounds. The console at which the player sits is connected to several or many sets of pipes, each of which has its own tone quality. Although electronic versions of the organ are available today, real pipe organs have air pushed through the pipes by a series of bellows. The console has two or more keyboards that the player can connect with the sets of pipes. Organs can actually play what sounds much like bowed strings, woodwind, or brass instruments, and some even have percussion sounds, allowing the organ to sound like a full orchestra.

In addition to the keyboards, the organ console has a full display of buttons and knobs, called **stops**, that the organist sets to assign the pipes for each keyboard to play. Before the organist plays a piece of music, he or she has to decide what pipes to play in what parts of the music and then set the stops to allow for that. This is called setting the **registration** for the piece. One organist might make very different decisions about registration from another, giving the organist even more control of the sound than a player of any other musical instrument.

One reason that the sounds on the organ vary as much as they do is that the pipes vary in size, from thirty-two (or more) feet long for very low tones to pencil-sized ones that sound very high. These sets of large to small pipes with many sizes in between can be made of wood, metal, or other material, giving each set its own particular tone quality. Some pipes even have reeds attached to them to make them sound much like woodwind instruments with reeds.

Pipe organs have to be built specifically for the church or concert hall in which they are to be used, because some sets of pipes take up quite a bit of space. Also, because the different sets of pipes are often spread around the front, sides, and back of the space for the congregation or audience, the particular acoustics of the building need to be taken into consideration so that the instrument can achieve the best possible sound.

In addition to playing several sets of pipes on several different keyboards, the organist has a full keyboard of pedals to play with his or her feet. This **pedal board** is most often used to play bass notes, such as the lowest lines we heard in Bach's Fugue, but it is also possible to play higher melodies and even chords on the pedals.

Dynamic levels on some organs are changed by use of a swell box with shutters that open to let out as much sound as possible or close to soften the sound. The swell box is controlled by pedals above the pedal board that look like the accelerator pedal on a car or bus.

Organs like this one from the baroque period often have elaborate, magnificent sets of pipes.

The Live Experience

This box focuses on the experience of being a musician—a singer or a composer, for example—and how performers' work affects our concert experience.

Musicians on Musicians

A quote at the beginning of each chapter points out something insightful, or sometimes just humorous, about music.

---

14 | Classical Vocal Music

It's people like that who make you realize how little you've accomplished. It is a sobering thought, for example, that when Mozart was my age—he had been dead for two years!
—SINGER/SONGWRITER TOM LEHRER
(BORN IN 1928)

Listening Introduction

Listen to the example of music that represents this chapter, "Non più andrai" ("No more will you") from Mozart's opera *Le Nozze di Figaro (The Marriage of Figaro)*, and make notes about what you hear. Give some attention to the following:

- Can you tell the gender of the singer?
- Can you tell what instruments are used to play the accompaniment?
- Can you detect the meter?
- Can you tell the language of the text?
- What is the general mood of the aria? Can you guess what it might be about?

Keep these notes to compare with your impressions of the music after you study the information in this chapter.

Composers of the classical era tended to concentrate more on instrumental music than on vocal music. The lieder (songs) written by Haydn, Mozart, and Beethoven are considered a relatively secondary part of their compositional efforts. The operas composed by Haydn to entertain the guests at the Esterházy palace were popular in their day but are not performed today. Beethoven wrote only one opera, *Fidelio*. The age was not, however, completely without significant and lasting achievements in the area of vocal music. Some of the large choral works of Mozart, Haydn, and Beethoven, and many of Mozart's operas, made lasting contributions to vocal literature.

Haydn's Vocal Music

Opera was a highly important part of musical activity at the Esterházy palace, and for a long time Haydn was quite proud of his more than twenty stage works. Austrian Empress Maria Theresa reputedly said, "If I want to hear a good opera, I go to Esterházy." However, when Haydn became familiar with Mozart's incomparable genius for opera composing, he realized that his own works were of lesser quality. Today they are all but forgotten.

Haydn composed Masses based on the same religious texts as those discussed in Chapter 4. Those Masses and his oratorios present a different story. The last six of his twelve Masses, composed between 1796 and 1802, are his crowning achievement as a church composer. One of those, his *Missa in Angustiis (Mass in Time of Peril)*, was composed as a tribute to a naval battle. It is also called the

---

Summary

Ludwig van Beethoven expanded nearly every aspect of classical composition. His works are longer and larger in scale than those of his contemporaries and predecessors. Beethoven's compositions place great emphasis on developmental procedures and use such effects as dynamics to reach new heights of expressiveness. Beethoven often used a lively scherzo rather than a minuet in third movements of multi-movement works. He also used a single theme or motive in more than one movement to unify longer

works. He used this idea in his Fifth Symphony when the rhythm of three short notes, followed by a long note, was featured in all four movements.

Improvements in instruments and instrumental techniques directly influence Beethoven's compositions. He increased the size of the orchestra from that used by Mozart and Haydn. He was a virtuoso pianist, and his piano works fully exploited the new brilliance and power that the newer pianos of his time were capable of achieving.

New People and Concepts

allegro assai	legato	pianoforte
allegro con brio	Ludwig van Beethoven	theme and variations form
andante con moto	orchestration	
cyclic form	piano	

Finale

Listen again to Symphony no. 5, first movement, by Beethoven, and compare your impressions now with your notes from your first listening. Do you hear more now than you did before? You should now be able to answer the following questions:

- What is the meter?
- When do you hear the first theme return later in the movement?
- When does the exposition repeat?
- When does the second theme appear and then repeat?
- What is the tempo?

Characteristics of Classical Music

Texture	Largely homophonic, but flexible, with shifts to polyphony
Tonality	Major-minor system with frequent modulations to related keys; heavy dependence on tonic-dominant relationship
Rhythm	Variety of rhythmic patterns within a work
Melody	Composed of short, balanced phrases; melodic phrases often contrasted with each other
Mood	Expression of variety of moods within a work and sudden changes of mood
Dynamics	Gradual dynamic changes
Large works	Sonata, symphony, concerto, string quartet, Mass, oratorio, opera
Musical instruments	Piano and violin favored for solo concerto; makeup of orchestra becomes standardized; development of orchestra favors growth of symphonic works
Formal structures	Sonata principle (multimovement structure for long pieces); single-movement sonata form; rondo; minuet and trio; scherzo and trio; theme and variations; cadenza and double exposition used in concertos
Symphonic style	Follows four-movement plan, with first movement in sonata form; each movement self-contained; clarity and balance are major stylistic features

---

Review Table

For each period, a table calls out key characteristics of a period of music, serving to review the content of several chapters.

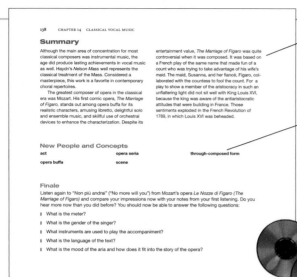

138 CHAPTER 14 CLASSICAL VOCAL MUSIC

Summary

Although the main area of concentration for most classical composers was instrumental music, the age did produce lasting achievements in vocal music as well. Haydn's *Nelson Mass* well represents the classical treatment of the Mass. Considered a masterpiece, this work is a favorite in contemporary choral repertoires.

The greatest composer of opera in the classical era was Mozart. His first comic opera, *The Marriage of Figaro*, stands out among opera buffa for its realistic characters, amusing libretto, delightful solo and ensemble music, and skillful use of orchestral devices to enhance the characterization. Despite its

entertainment value, *The Marriage of Figaro* was quite controversial when it was composed. It was based on a French play of the same name that made fun of a count who was trying to take advantage of his wife's maid. The maid, Susanna, and her fiancé, Figaro, collaborated with the countess to fool the count. For a play to show a member of the aristocracy in such an unflattering light did not sit well with King Louis XVI, because the king was aware of the antiaristocratic attitudes that were building in France. Those sentiments exploded in the French Revolution of 1789, in which Louis XVI was beheaded.

New People and Concepts

act   opera seria   through-composed form

opera buffa   scene

Finale

Listen again to "Non più andrai" ("No more will you") from Mozart's opera *Le Nozze di Figaro (The Marriage of Figaro)* and compare your impressions now with your notes from your first listening. Do you hear more now than you did before? You should now be able to answer the following questions:

▮ What is the meter?

▮ What is the gender of the singer?

▮ What instruments are used to play the accompaniment?

▮ What is the language of the text?

▮ What is the mood of the aria and how does it fit into the story of the opera?

Summary

A summary at the end of each chapter provides an overview of the key points presented.

New People and Concepts

When a new term is introduced, it is boldfaced and defined immediately. The terms are listed in New People and Concepts at the end of each chapter.

Audio CDs

Two audio CDs are packaged with your copy of the text. The CDs contain many of the works discussed in the Listening Guides. Another set of three CDs is available for optional purchase at your instructor's discretion.

OLC Web Site

The Online Learning Center Web site features additional chapter-related resources including listening-based quizzes for self-assessment and web-based activities to help you practice your listening skills.

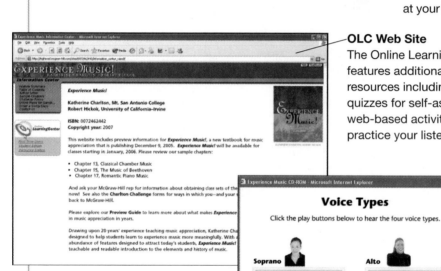

Experience Music Interactive! CD-ROM

Icons in the text direct you to the CD-ROM packaged with your text. All content on the CD-ROM is organized like the book, to make it a natural extension of your studies. *Explore* activities present—via video, animation, or engaging interactions—key concepts in the chapters. The CD-ROM also provides support for the listening activities in the text. *Listen* activities are interactive versions of the Listening Guides in the textbook, and they work with the music audio CDs.

Katherine Charlton Calkins is chair of the music department at Mt. San Antonio College in Walnut, California, where she has taught full-time since 1974. During a sabbatical in 1990, she taught music history at the American Institute for Foreign Study at the University of London. She holds degrees in classical guitar performance and music history and she has performed on medieval gittern, Renaissance lute, and baroque guitar with her late first husband, Andrew Charlton, who was well known in the field of early music. In addition to performing early music, she has played percussion in the California University at Fullerton Wind Ensemble and toured Japan with the group. Charlton developed a class in the history of rock music and wrote the best-selling text on that subject, *Rock Music Styles: A History*, currently in its fourth edition and published by McGraw-Hill.

Robert Hickok is a Professor Emeritus from the University of California at Irvine where he was the Dean of the School of the Arts and founder/conductor of the Irvine Camerata. His position at Irvine was preceded by advanced training at Yale University School of Music, where he was a pupil of Paul Hindemith. Hickok's long and successful career includes faculty positions at the Brooklyn College of the City University of New York, where he was the founding Dean of the Brooklyn College School of Performing Arts. He later headed the choral department of the Manhattan School of Music, where he regularly conducted major works from the baroque through the romantic eras. He founded and conducted the Janus Chorale of New York, which performed in New York City's Town Hall, Carnegie Hall, and Alice Tully Hall in Lincoln Center. He was a frequent guest conductor of the New Jersey Pro Arte Chorale and the Washington Orchestra. From 1977 to 1985, Hickok was the Dean of the School of Music at the North Carolina School of the Arts, and Director of its International Music Program, where he conducted performing groups that toured annually in Germany and Italy.

Experience Music!

The London Philharmonic Orchestra in concert

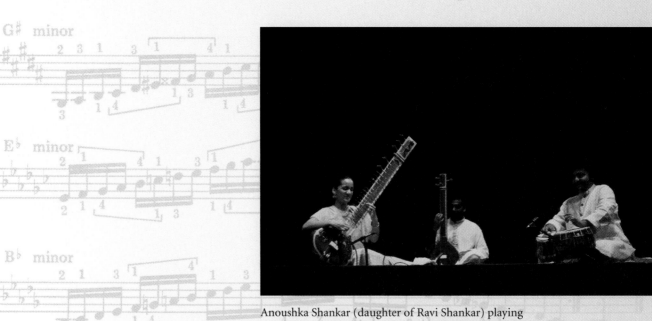

Anoushka Shankar (daughter of Ravi Shankar) playing
the sitar, accompanied by men playing a tambura and
tabla (drums)

Prelude | The Fundamentals of Music

By the time you have finished reading this text you will have listened to a wide range of works, including symphonies, chamber music, opera, jazz, and rock. Despite their apparent differences, these works are all made from the same component parts: sound, rhythm, melody, and harmony. Before you can begin a serious study of music, you need to understand its most basic elements, and you need to understand how those elements combine to form individual pieces. In addition, for a full appreciation of music, it is helpful to be familiar with the orchestra and various musical instruments. The following chapters will give you the fundamental vocabulary necessary to study music of all kinds.

A ballerina from the Bulgarian National Opera & Ballet School

1 | Elements of Music: Sound, Rhythm, Melody, and Harmony

The man that hath no music in himself, nor is not moved with concord of sweet sounds, is fit for treasons, stratagems and soils . . . let no such man be trusted.

—WILLIAM SHAKESPEARE (1564–1616)

Music is built from elements that we describe using a particular vocabulary. After you have studied that vocabulary, you will be in a much better position to discuss a piece of music with a friend, write a report that describes music you have listened to, and understand what someone else has written about music. For example, a review that criticizes a conductor for not using enough dynamic contrasts or says that an opera singer had problems maintaining good tone quality in certain pitch ranges will make more sense to you when you know what dynamics, tone quality, and pitch ranges are. Without knowing those terms, you might still understand that the reviewer did not like everything about the performance, but the musical vocabulary communicates more than that simple fact.

Sound

Chapter 1 Activity

What Is Sound?

Music is an art based on the organization of sounds in time. A sound, any sound, is the result of vibrations in the air set in motion by the activation of a sounding body—the slamming of a door, the ringing of a bell, or the playing of a musical instrument. In the case of a *musical* sound, the vibrations are so definite and steady that they produce what is called a *tone* (also referred to as a **note**), the highness or lowness of which is called the **pitch.**

Chapter 1 Activity

Pitch

The precise pitch is determined by the *frequency,* as measured in cycles per second, of its vibration—the *faster* the frequency, the *higher* the pitch, and, conversely, the *slower* the frequency, the *lower* the pitch. When music is written down, the higher pitches are represented by notes that are higher (toward the top of the page) on the **staff:** the set of five horizontal lines on or between which the notes are placed. That staff helps us measure how much higher or lower one note is from another. The following is an example of the contour (or high and low shape) of pitches (without the staff) for the beginning of "The Star-Spangled Banner."

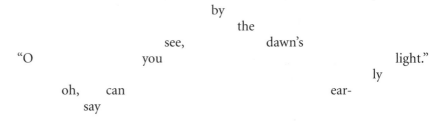

Chapter 1 Activity

Interval of an Octave

The distance between two pitches is called an **interval.** The smallest interval that occurs when two identical pitches are played one after the other is called a **unison.** Another interval, called an **octave,** is that between notes of the same name, for example, one C and the next C above it. They will sound similar to one another because the higher pitch is produced by exactly double the number of

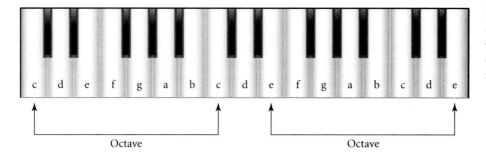

FIGURE 1.1
Piano keyboard with one
octave from C to C and
another octave from E to E
marked.

vibrations that it takes to produce the lower pitch. For example, the words *say* and *see* in "The Star-Spangled Banner" are separated by an octave. Between the two notes that mark an octave, there are eleven other notes and many intervals possible among them.

As you look at the piano keyboard, you should notice that the black keys are grouped in patterns of twos and threes. Each note looks different from any other depending on where it fits within those groupings. Any note on the white key just to the left of a set of two black keys, for example, will be the note C. If you play one C and then the next higher or lower C, you have played an octave. If you play the notes on the white keys from one C to the next, you are playing a C **major scale,** sometimes referred to as the "do-re-mi" scale because those syllables are used to identify the notes as follows: C = do, D = re, E = mi, F = fa, G = sol, A = la, B = ti. If you were to continue on and play the notes up to the next higher C, you would be playing what is called a two-octave scale. The two-octave scale has a greater **pitch range** than the single-octave scale. The distance between the lowest and the highest notes an instrument or a voice can produce is referred to as the instrument's or voice's *pitch range.*

Another important aspect of musical sound is **dynamics,** or levels of loudness and softness. Sometimes musicians use a variety of dynamic levels when playing a single piece of music. If the musician wants to emphasize one note over the others, he or she can **accent** it by playing it louder. *Piano,* which means soft, and *forte,* which means loud, are Italian terms used by musicians to notate dynamic levels. Extremes of those dynamic levels are written by adding the suffix "*issimo.*" In other words, *piano* is soft and *pianissimo* is softer yet. *Forte* is loud and *fortissimo* is even louder. *Mezzo* means medium, so *mezzo piano* is medium soft and *mezzo forte* is medium loud. Sometimes letters are used as an abbreviation of the full dynamic terms. To abbreviate the "issimo" terms, simply double the letters (*pianissimo* is notated as *pp,* and *fortissimo* as *ff*). "Mezzo" is represented by an *m,* so *mp* is medium soft and *mf* medium loud. The following is a list of these dynamic levels, from the softest to the loudest:

pianissimo	*pp*
piano	*p*
mezzo piano	*mp*
mezzo forte	*mf*
forte	*f*
fortissimo	*ff*

Other terms are used to indicate a gradual change in dynamic levels. **Decrescendo** (or **diminuendo**) indicates that the music is getting softer, which can often give the effect of a calming of tension, and **crescendo** indicates that it is getting louder, which can express exuberance.

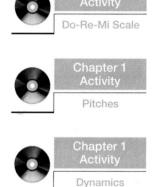

Chapter 1
Activity
Do-Re-Mi Scale

Chapter 1
Activity
Pitches

Chapter 1
Activity
Dynamics

Chapter 1
Quiz
Pitch
Discrimination

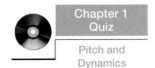

Different instruments and voices each have their own distinct kind of sound. A melody played on the flute sounds different from the same melody played on the clarinet because the sound quality of the clarinet is clearly different from that of the flute. The distinctive sound quality of an instrument is called tone color, or **timbre** (pronounced *tam-bur*).

Rhythm

Rhythm is the ordered flow of music through time. The regular, recurrent pulsation in most music is called the **beat.** Perhaps the beating of our own hearts is the most basic beat we feel. In some music the beat is pounded out by a drum or other instrument and is consequently so clear that you may find yourself clapping along. That steady beat helps us measure musical time, but the word *rhythm* refers to much more than that. Rhythm includes the way music flows even between the beats. Although the presence of a steady beat is common, in some music the beat is not clear at all, perhaps because the composer wished to evoke a smooth or even "floating" effect. We can see such an effect in nature if we watch waves washing up on a beach. The waves do not pound away at any steady sort of beat, but the effect they create is indeed very rhythmic. It is rhythmic because of the sense of flowing motion they create. In other words, the word *beat* refers to the steady pulse you might hear in music, whereas the word *rhythm* covers much more about musical time. A beat can be part of rhythm, but musical rhythm can exist without a beat.

Sometimes individual notes are played on each beat, but notes can also be held for more than or less than a whole beat. In the first phrase of "America," observe the notes that are longer than one beat—the note for the word *'tis,* for example. Also notice that the longer notes are followed by notes that are held for less than one beat, such as the note on *of.* The word *liberty* has three notes of varying lengths, and *sing* is held for a full three beats.

"My country 'tis of thee, sweet land of li- berty. Of thee I sing."
Beats: / / / / / / / / / / / / / / / / / /

Against this background of regularly occurring beats or pulsations, notes of varying lengths make some beats sound more prominent—or "heavier"—than others. That does not necessarily mean that those notes should be played louder; they usually stand out because of the patterns of long and short notes. In the case of "America," the first of every three beats is given more weight. The following example groups the beats into patterns of three.

"My country 'tis of thee, sweet land of li- berty. Of thee I sing."
Meter: **1** 2 3 **1** 2 3 **1** 2 3 **1** 2 3 **1** 2 3 **1** 2 3

This organization of beats into regular groups is called **meter,** and the units themselves are called **measures.** Different types of meters are defined by the number of beats in the measure. The example we heard in "America" is called **triple meter,** because it consists of three beats per measure. The first beat of each group, the one that carries more weight, is called the **downbeat.** On the CDs that came with your book, the recording of "When I am laid in earth" from Purcell's opera *Dido and Aeneas* is in triple meter. Listen to it and see if you can hear the meter.

When music has two beats in each measure, which means an accent on every other beat, we say it is in **duple meter.** "Mary Had a Little Lamb" is in duple meter.

"Mar-y had a little lamb, little lamb, little lamb, Mar-y had a little lamb, Its fleece was white as snow.
Meter: 1 2 1 2 1 2 1 2 1 2 1 2 1 2 1 2

On the CDs that came with your book, the recording of the first movement of Mozart's Symphony no. 40 is in duple meter. Listen to it and see if you can hear the meter.

Music played to a four-beat measure is in **quadruple meter,** which can sound a lot like music in duple meter because the groups of four beats are usually also two groups of two beats. There is, however, a difference: in duple meter, every other beat is a downbeat, but this is not the case in quadruple meter. The four beats of quadruple meter begin with a strong downbeat followed by a weaker second beat. The third beat is stronger than the second or fourth beats, but not as strong as the downbeat. The following example of quadruple meter also has a short note before the downbeat. That short note is called an **upbeat.**

Chapter 1 Activity

Quadruple Meter

"Mine eyes have seen the glory   of   the   coming of the Lord.   He has . . ."

Meter: **1**   2   **3**   4   **1**   2   **3**   4

On the CDs that came with your book, the recording of "Comfort ye" from Handel's *Messiah* is in quadruple meter. Listen to it and see if you can hear the meter.

Another common meter, called **sextuple,** has six beats in each measure. The six beats are usually divided into two sections of three beats each. The accents fall on beats one and four (**1** 2 3 **4** 5 6). The following example, "Silent Night," is in sextuple meter:

Chapter 1 Activity

Sextuple Meter

"Si-   lent Night,   Ho-   ly   Night!   All   is   calm,   all   is   bright"

Meter: 1   2   3   4   5   6   1   2   3   4   5   6   1   2   3   4   5   6   1   2   3   4   5   6

On the CDs that came with your book, the recording of "America" from Bernstein's *West Side Story* is in sextuple meter. It is also accented to sound like triple meter at times, however, making it an interesting combination of meters. Listen to it with meter in mind and you will hear that "I want to be in A-" is sextuple and then the rest of the word, "-merica" sounds triple. Actually, what Bernstein has done is accent the sextuple meter **1** 2 3 **4** 5 6 for "I want to be in A-" and then accent it **1** 2 **3** 4 **5** 6 on "-merica."

Other meters, such as **quintuple,** with five beats per measure, and **septuple,** with seven, are not nearly as common as those we have discussed, though composers of the twentieth century and beyond, particularly jazz and art-rock musicians, have used them with some frequency. In many cases in which those unusual meters are used, the musicians are trying to give an effect that noticeably counters the meters we are accustomed to hearing. If you have ever heard the song "Money" by the rock band Pink Floyd, for example, the lyrics are about money-grubbing people who care only for themselves. The song's meter is septuple, making it seem a bit odd and difficult to dance or tap your foot to. The music, in other words, is just as uncomfortable as the subject of the song and therefore supports the lyrics very effectively. If you listen to the recording, the repeating bass line, which outlines the seven beats, should help you follow the meter.

Earlier in this chapter, we touched on the term *accent.* Ways of accenting a note include playing it louder, longer, or higher or lower than its surrounding notes. Accents cause notes to stick out and grab our attention. Sometimes composers accent notes that are played between, rather than directly on, the steady beat. This effect is called **syncopation.** The beginning of Stephen Foster's song "Camptown Races" is syncopated: both times "dah" is sung, it comes before the beat, though the listener most likely expects to hear it on the beat. You could sing the song with the "dah"s exactly on the second beats, but the effect would lack

Chapter 1 Activity

Accent and Syncopation

the energy added by the syncopation. The lyrics and beats follow:

Camptown ladies		sing this		song,		doo dah,		doo dah
Beats: 1		2		1		2		1	2	1	2

Chapter 1
Activity

Tempo

All aspects of rhythm are very much affected by the **tempo,** or pace, of the music. The tempo is the rate or speed of the beat. If the beat is quick, the tempo is *fast;* if the beat is long, the tempo is *slow.* Indications concerning tempo are usually given in Italian and most often appear at the beginning of the piece, though they may also appear in other sections, particularly if the tempo changes abruptly:

Very slow:	***Largo*** (broad)
	Grave (grave, solemn)
Slow:	***Lento***
	Adagio (leisurely; literally, at ease)
Moderate:	***Andante*** (at a walking pace)
	Moderato
Fast:	***Allegretto***
	Allegro (faster than allegretto; literally, cheerful)
Very fast:	***Vivace*** (vivacious)
	Presto (very quick)
	Prestissimo (as fast as possible)

These basic terms are often accompanied by the following modifiers: *molto* (very), *meno* (less), *poco* (a little), and *ma non troppo* (not too much). For example, *allegro molto* is very fast; *poco adagio* is somewhat slow; and *allegro non troppo* is fast but not too fast. *Accelerando* (getting faster) and *ritardando* (becoming slower) indicate gradual changes in tempo. To reestablish the original tempo, the term *a tempo* is used.

Tempo can be altered in other ways. The term **rubato** indicates freedom to move ahead and fall behind the tempo, and the symbol ⌒ (**fermata**) tells the performer to hold the note longer than its normal time value—momentarily suspending the meter and tempo. As was the case with dynamic indications, tempo indications are approximate and relative, leaving a great deal of discretion to the performer.

Melody

Whereas rhythm measures the flow of music in time, **melody** fits into a given rhythm by adding a series of pitches that we might enjoy humming along with. We often will remember the melody—whether it is sung with words or played instrumentally—better than any other aspect of the music.

We can define a melody as a series of notes that add up to a recognizable whole. Melody gives music a sense of physical movement as it progresses forward in time. Different melodies follow different patterns of movement. Those that move from one note to another in a major scale (*do* to *re* in the *do-re-mi* scale, for example) move by steps. When the notes of a melody skip notes (or steps) of the scale (from *do* to *mi* or some other note in the scale), they are moving by leaps.

Melody also comprises the way in which notes connect with one another. If the notes seem to flow naturally and smoothly from one to the next, we say the melody is played or sung **legato.** If the notes sound "choppy," that is, short and detached from each other, we say the melody is played or sung **staccato.** We will hear many examples of each of these effects as we follow the musical examples in this book.

Melodies are often made up of shorter sections called **phrases.** When a phrase or a melody ends with a sense of finality, that resting point is called a **cadence.** In the song "Row, Row, Row Your Boat" (see below), for example, the two phrases are equal in length, with the second phrase sounding like a completion of the first. The phrases are identified by letters of the alphabet—"a" for the first phrase and "b" for the second. When you sing the song, notice that the end of the "a" phrase does not sound complete, but rather sets us up to expect the "b" phrase. That type of seemingly incomplete ending is called an *incomplete cadence.* The entire melody ends with a complete cadence.

phrase "a"	"Row, row, row your boat gently down the stream,
phrase "b"	Merrily, merrily, merrily, merrily, life is but a dream."

Sing the melody to "Row, Row, Row Your Boat" again and notice that there is a sense of energy on the first "merrily." This energy is created by the fact that that note is the highest note in the melody. Such a melodic high point is called the *climax.*

When a melody is made up of two very similar phrases, we do not use the letter "b" for the second phrase. Instead, we identify it as a varied version of the first phrase by calling it "a′." Such is the case with the song "Mary Had a Little Lamb."

phrase "a"	"Mary had a little lamb, little lamb, little lamb,
phrase "a′"	Mary had a little lamb, its fleece was white as snow."

Of course, many melodies are much more complicated than the two we have cited. Some melodies are made up of phrases of unequal lengths. Sometimes, too, we find melodic patterns repeated at different pitch levels. This is called a **sequence.** The song "America" uses a sequence. The words "Land where my fathers died" and "Land of the Pilgrim's pride" are sung to the same melodic pattern, but the second phrase is sung at a lower pitch than the first.

The melody is an extremely important part of any piece of music. In a long composition, some melodies assume greater importance than others. A melody that serves as the starting point for an extended work is called a **theme.** In the course of a musical composition, important themes may be stated and restated in many different forms.

Harmony

If melody is the "horizontal" aspect of music, **harmony** is the "vertical." That is, instead of sounds in succession, harmony involves notes sounding at the same time. Most Western music depends on harmony to help enhance its expressiveness.

We have defined the term *interval* as the distance between two notes in a melody, but we can also use it to refer to the distance between notes that are sounded together to make harmony. Thus harmony is a composite sound made up of two or more notes of different pitches that are played or sung simultaneously. The smallest harmonic unit is one consisting of two notes, but we usually have three or more notes played or sung together to create harmony. Those groups of notes make up what we call **chords** (pronounced "cords"). A series of chords is called a **progression.**

An important quality of a given harmony is its degree of consonance or dissonance. A combination of notes that is considered stable and without tension is called a **consonance.** A combination of notes that is considered unstable and tense, so much so that they sometimes sound as if they are fighting with one another, is called a **dissonance.** Dissonance adds variety and a sense of forward motion to music. Dissonance usually occurs as a transient tension in a harmonic progression. Resolution usually refers to a dissonant chord moving to a consonant chord. The movement from dissonance to consonance can give a sense of dramatic or psychological resolution, like seeing the villain get what's coming to him or her in a movie.

The general character of most pieces is consonant, even though they may feature some dissonance. Haydn's String Quartet, op. 33, no. 3 is a good example. Listen to its fourth movement on the CDs that accompany your book and notice that the music sounds as though the notes all fit together into a pleasing harmonic unit. Other works are predominantly dissonant, such as Cage's Sonata V from *Sonatas and Interludes* for prepared piano. When you listen to Cage's work, you will hear many groups of notes that clash against one another, creating much tension. As we move through music history from century to century, we find that the relationship of consonance and dissonance begins to change, with a gradual increase in the importance or prevalence of dissonance as we approach the twentieth century.

The simplest chord is the **triad.** It is made up of three notes that are usually spaced one note apart—*do, mi,* and *sol* in the *do-re-mi* (major) scale, for example. The first note of any scale—in this case, *do*—is called the **tonic** note. The triad built on the notes beginning with *do* is, therefore, called the *tonic chord.* Tonic chords sound very stable and are traditionally played at the end of a musical composition in order to supply a sense of conclusion to the harmonic progression.

Chords can be broken up so that their notes are played one at a time instead of all together. This is called an **arpeggio.** Arpeggios can be used to accompany melodies or they can create a melody themselves. The melody to the words "Oh say can you see" from "The Star-Spangled Banner" is composed out of an arpeggio because all of the notes come from a single, in this case tonic, chord.

Chapter 1
Activity

The Triad

Chapter 1
Activity

Arpeggios

Chapter 1
Quiz

Harmony

Summary

Music is made up of many different, and simultaneously present, elements. When we listen to a melody, we are also listening to the rhythm upon which that melody is based. That rhythm can be a steady beat, and it may or may not fall into a particular meter (pattern of accented notes). The melody itself is composed of a series of pitches that might fall in a very narrow range of notes (close to one another), or the melody might jump around from very high to very low notes. Either way, listening for both melody and rhythm adds to the enjoyment of music.

Tempo is an important part of rhythm. Many longer pieces of music are made up of several sections of contrasting tempos. One section might be fast and lively, whereas the following section is slow and smooth sounding. Another fast section might follow to add contrast and balance.

A single piece of music might vary in dynamic levels. A melody might create a sense of tension by beginning softly and then gradually reaching a crescendo. Dynamic contrasts add to the expressiveness of music in much the same way that a "dynamic" speaker might shout part of the time and speak slowly, softly, and directly at other times.

Harmony is the vertical aspect of music—the notes that are played together to accompany the melody. Harmonies can be consonant (sounding as though they fit well together and create a sense of relaxation), or they can be dissonant (sounding as though the notes are all fighting one another). Most music includes both consonances and dissonances.

New Concepts

accent	harmony	quadruple meter
adagio	interval	quintuple meter
allegretto	*largo*	rhythm
allegro	legato	rubato
andante	*lento*	septuple meter
arpeggio	major scale	sequence
beat	measures	sextuple meter
cadence	melody	staccato
chord progression	meter	staff
consonance	*mezzo forte mf*	syncopation
crescendo	*mezzo piano mp*	tempo
decrescendo	*moderato*	theme
diminuendo	note	timbre
dissonance	octave	tonic
downbeat	phrase	triad
duple meter	*pianissimo pp*	triple meter
dynamics	*piano p*	unison
fermata	pitch	upbeat
forte f	pitch range	*vivace*
fortissimo ff	*prestissimo*	
grave	*presto*	

2 | Elements That Structure Music—Key, Texture, and Form

Music gives soul to the universe.
—PLATO (CA. 427–CA. 348 BCE)

We have seen that combinations of individual types of sounds produce the basic elements of music: sound, rhythm, melody, and harmony. In this chapter we explore the ways in which these elements combine to give structure to complete pieces of music. Our discussion of sound described pitches that came together to form scales, which are the basis of many melodies. We now expand the idea of the scale into an overall sense of a key, or tonal, center for an entire musical composition. When we discussed melody, we dealt with single melodies. Now, we discuss music that has more than one melody at one time, creating a denser texture. Our discussion of melody also showed how melodies are often made up of phrases that repeat or contrast with one another. When we view a complete composition, we see how melodies are sometimes repeated and contrasted to give the music a sense of structure that we call *form*.

Key

One of the fundamental characteristics of Western music is its reliance on **tonality** as an organizing element. *Tonal music* is characterized by the presence of the "tonic," the central note around which a specific musical composition is organized, and of a chord built on that note, called the *tonic chord* (discussed in Chapter 1). The tonic chord acts as the musical center of gravity, a kind of "home base" in that when it is played it can give a sense of completion to the music. If the tonic note is C, we say that the melody is in the **key** of C. In other words, *key* refers to the central note, scale, and chord. Another word for key is *tonality*.

Melodies are usually based on the notes in a particular scale. The notes from one C to the next C on the white keys of the piano make up the C **major scale.** The C major scale has a particular sound because of the placement of the black keys between the white ones on the keyboard (see Figure 1.1). When two adjacent white keys have a black key between them, they are a whole step apart. When two adjacent white keys have no black key between them, they are a half step apart. The distance between any note and the next possible note, black or white, is also a half step. A whole step is made up of two half steps, represented by the black key between the two white ones that are a whole step apart. The major scale (*do-re-mi* scale), then, is made up of the following pattern of whole and half step intervals: w - w - h – w – w – w - h.

Another common type of scale is the **minor scale,** which resembles the major scale but has a number of lowered notes. When a note is lowered, it is played on the black key to the left of the white one, lowering its pitch by one half step. The notation of a flat sign (♭) indicates the notes that are lowered. This lowering of some notes gives a minor melody a different sort of psychological effect than a major melody. The lowered notes can sound a bit sadder than the ones in a major scale, although that is certainly not always the case.

To this point, we have been basing our scales on the C tonic, but other notes can be tonic notes, too. If we start a major scale on the note D and use it as the basis of our music, we say that the music is in the key of D major. Conversely, if we base our music on a minor scale that begins on the note D, our music will be in the key of D minor. Compositions can be found in major or minor keys based on every tonic note we have.

Chapter 2
Activity

Scale: Major &
Minor

When we notate music in different keys, we use the flat sign (♭) to lower a note a half step (move it down to the next possible note, usually the next black key to the left) and the sharp sign (#) to raise it a half step (move it up to the next possible note, usually the next black key to the right). If our entire composition is going to need certain notes to be flatted or sharped all the way through, we indicate that at the beginning of each line of music instead of putting the signs in front of each note. This indication is called a **key signature.** When we play a D major scale, for example, we have to raise (sharp) all of the F and C notes for the scale to sound major (like the *do-re-mi* scale). Because the key signature is printed at the beginning of every line of music, the player knows to sharp all of the necessary notes (F and C in this case) as he or she plays the music. If the composer wants to cancel one of the sharps or flats, a natural sign (♮) is placed before the note.

A scale that includes all notes (on both black and white keys played in order on the piano) is called a **chromatic scale.** This scale is not the basis of a particular key because all of the notes are just one half step apart and no single note sounds like "home base." In fact, a chromatic scale does not have to start or end on any particular note. Because a chromatic scale includes all notes, including many that are dissonant with one another, composers can use it to create dissonance and tension not present in a standard major or minor scale. Composers often use that dissonance for special, dramatic effects.

Chapter 2
Activity

Scale: Major,
Minor,
Chromatic

Sometimes, for variety, longer pieces of music change from one tonal center, or key, to another during the flow of the music. The shift from one key to another within the same composition is called **modulation.** No matter how many times a piece of music modulates, it usually ends by going back to the tonic key with which it began, making use of the sense of "home base" the tonic creates. In other words, a piece in the key of D major will begin and end with D as its tonic, even though many other keys might have been played in the middle of the piece.

Chapter 2
Activity

Dominant to
Tonic Cadence

Chapter 2
Quiz

Key

Texture

Like cloth, music is woven of horizontal and vertical strands. We think of melody as moving horizontally, because one note follows the next along the flow of time. We describe harmony as vertical because it is based upon sounds that occur simultaneously and in combination with one another. **Texture** describes the way the vertical and horizontal strands of melody are interwoven. In this sense, texture combines both melody and harmony. In addition to strands of melody, the term *texture* can refer to how many different layers of sound are heard at the same time. There are three basic musical textures commonly found in Western music: **monophony, polyphony,** and **homophony.**

The simplest musical texture is monophony, which literally means "one sound," although in music it means one melodic line with no accompaniment. (You can hit two rocks together and create one sound, but that would not create monophonic texture.) If you sing or hum by yourself, you are creating monophonic music. Music is also monophonic if a single melodic line is performed by more than one instrument or voice at the same time. In that case, we say that the instruments or voices are playing or singing in unison. We have used the term *unison* before to describe the interval when two identical pitches are played one after the other. Here, the two pitches are played or sung together. Even if men and women sing the same melody at the same time, with the women singing an octave higher than the men, the texture is monophonic.

On the CDs that came with your book, the recording of the "Salve Regina" chant is an example of monophonic texture. Listen to it and notice that it is sung as a single-line melody with no accompaniment.

When two or more melodies of equal interest are performed at the same time, the texture is polyphonic ("many sounds"). In discussing texture, we often call a single line of music a "voice" because it is a melody that one person could sing. Independence and equality of voices are the defining characteristics of polyphony. Independence refers to a voice's ability to compete with other melodic strands for the attention of the listener.

In polyphonic music we need to listen carefully to the relationship between or among the independent, simultaneous melodies. Our attention will shift from one melodic line to another, depending on which is most prominent at any given moment. The melodic lines thus enhance and enrich each other, contributing to the expressiveness of the overall sound. The technique of combining several melodic lines into a meaningful whole is called **counterpoint.** The term *contrapuntal texture* is sometimes used in place of the term *polyphonic texture* because notes (points) of each melody tend to move in different directions, countering one another.

Sometimes in polyphonic music we hear one melodic idea presented by one singing voice or instrument and then hear it restated immediately by another voice or instrument. This is called **imitation** or *imitative polyphony* because the second voice sounds like an imitation of the first. Several voices can enter the music one after the other, each imitating the first melody.

If you listen to the beginning of *Ave Maria* by Josquin on the CDs that came with your book, you will hear an example of the type of gentle beauty and sense of unity of purpose that imitative polyphony can create.

Chapter 2 Activity

The Round

Imitative polyphony, in which all of the voices play the exact same melody all the way through with no variation, is called a **round** or a **canon.** A round is an example of what we could call *strict imitation*. In performance, a first voice begins alone, and when it gets to a particular part of the melody, a second voice starts at the beginning. Similarly, other voices enter one at a time, each singing the same melody from the beginning. Once the earlier voices finish the melody and drop out, the last voice finishes alone, giving a round a very simple beginning and ending with much imitative polyphony in between. The songs "Row, Row, Row Your Boat" and "Three Blind Mice" are both examples of rounds.

On the CDs that came with your book, the recording of Billings's "When Jesus Wept" is a round. Listen to it and make note of the imitation as new voices enter. Notice that when more than one voice sings, the texture is polyphonic.

Chapter 2 Activity

Homophonic Texture

In homophonic ("same sound") music, a *single* melodic line predominates, while the other voices or instruments provide an accompanying harmony. The listener's attention is focused on the melody; the harmonic accompaniment is heard as a kind of musical background. Harmonic accompaniment to the melody can take various forms—from the simple strumming of chords on a guitar to a full orchestra playing music that supports, but does not get in the way of, the melody.

On the CDs that came with your book, the recording of Beach's "Ah, Love, but a Day" is an example of homophonic texture. Listen to it and notice that the primary single melody is sung with piano accompaniment.

Another type of homophonic texture occurs when several melodies are played together in the same rhythm. That rhythm may include the presence of a steady beat or meter, or it may flow gently without a beat but with all of the melodies staying together. Because the voices are all following the same rhythm patterns, the lower melodies do not stand out as separate from the highest melody, which usually dominates the listener's attention. This type of texture occurs when several people sing a hymn tune or praise song in church. It is sometimes called *homorhythmic texture* because of the similar rhythms in all of the parts.

Actually, much music employs both polyphonic and homophonic textures. Frequently, a piece of music alternates between or among textures. An essentially homophonic section, for example, may be followed by a polyphonic one. What is important here is that you understand what the textures are in their clearest examples and then listen for them in the more complex music you will listen to later.

On the CDs that came with your book, Farmer's "Fair Phyllis" uses a combination of textures. Listen to it and note that the phrase "Fair Phyllis I saw sitting all alone" is monophonic. The song then turns polyphonic until the last phrase, "Oh, then they fell a-kissing," which is homophonic, with all voices singing in the same rhythm.

Chapter 2 Activity

Texture Lab

Chapter 2 Quiz

Textures

Form

The organization of musical ideas (which are usually melodies but can be some other combination of sounds) in time is called **form.** Sustaining the listener's interest in music depends on the presence of two essential factors: unity and variety. Unity is usually achieved through **repetition** of musical ideas, and variety through the introduction of new, often contrasting musical ideas. Repetition of musical ideas provides an overall sense of unity by engraving an important melody or other musical idea, such as a very distinctive rhythm pattern, in the mind of the listener. An important and returning melody in a musical composition is called a *theme.* When a theme is played at the beginning of a piece of music and returns at the end, it gives the music a feeling of balance and symmetry.

In addition to repetition and **contrast, variation** is often an important element in the form of a piece of music. Composers vary themes in any number of ways, but all variation retains some features of the original musical idea. For example, you might hear a piece of music that begins with a melody and simple accompaniment followed by a variation of the melody, or theme. In the variation you will probably still be able to pick out the notes of the melody, but you might hear some of those notes changed, or you might hear them with a different kind of accompaniment. Some very interesting pieces of music are based on a theme and a series of varied versions of that theme. The form of this type of piece is called **theme and variations.**

There are many different organizational forms, but two of the most common are the three-part form, called **ternary form,** and the two-part form, called **binary form.** The three parts of ternary form include a beginning section, a contrasting middle section, and then a repeat of the beginning. Binary form has only two parts. Letters are often used to describe these forms. For example, ternary form is usually shown by the letters ABA. The first A represents the section of music at the beginning; the B represents a contrasting section. The repeat of the letter A indicates that the beginning music returns or is repeated. The second A section does not have to be as long as the first, but it must include the same theme or themes to be considered a return of A. Sometimes the second A has the same themes as the first, but there are some changes in the way they are presented: for example, they might be played on different instruments. When that is the case, we diagram the form as ABA'. The A' stands for "A with some changes." The B section includes different themes from those in A.

Chapter 2 Activity

Form: Contrast and Return

Chapter 2 Activity

Form: Unequal Phrases

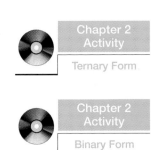

Chapter 2 Activity

Ternary Form

Chapter 2 Activity

Binary Form

Chapter 2 Quiz

Form

Binary form consists of a beginning section followed by a contrasting second section. The two sections can be of equal or unequal length and may or may not be repeated. The simplest example of binary form is diagrammed as AB. Notice that this is different from ternary form because the *A* section, or beginning music, does not come back at the end of the piece. With repetitions, binary forms can include AABB or AAB or ABB.

Summary

The melody, rhythm, and/or harmony in music discussed in the previous chapter are held together by an overall structure. Much music we hear today is tonal, which means that the melodies and harmonies fall into a particular key, or tonal center. Long or short sections of the music sometimes change to a new key, although the key of the beginning of a piece of music usually returns at the end to create a sense of balance and finality for the overall composition.

The relationship between the horizontal (melody) and vertical (harmony) aspects of music comes together through texture. A composition's texture is created by a layering of sound. A single melody played or sung alone creates a monophonic texture. Two or more melodies played at the same time, each sounding independent of the other(s), creates polyphonic texture. One melody played with an accompanying harmony is homophonic in texture. Many pieces of music change from one texture to another, and listening for those changes adds to our appreciation of the music.

Most compositions have sections that repeat music that was heard before. It is also common to hear music that contrasts or creates a variation on music heard earlier. We determine the form of music by listening for repetition, contrast, and variation. Some forms are easier to hear and recognize than others, but once you learn to listen for repetition, contrast, and variation, you will begin to recognize the composition's larger structure.

New Concepts

binary form	key	repetition
canon	key signature	round
chromatic scale	major scale	ternary form
contrast	minor scale	texture
counterpoint	modulation	theme and variations
form	monophony	tonality
homophony	polyphony	variation
imitation		

3 | Musical Instruments and Ensembles

The flute is not an instrument with a good moral effect. It is too exciting.
—ARISTOTLE (384–322 BCE)

The great variety of musical instruments available to the composer or performer today offers a tremendous range of qualities of sound. Instruments are usually categorized into what we refer to as *families*. The standard families are voices, strings, woodwinds, brasses, percussion, keyboard, and electronic. In this chapter we discuss the most commonly used instruments in each of these families. We concentrate on modern instruments; however, most modern instruments have early predecessors, and a few of those predecessors are mentioned in this chapter. We use the year 1750 to mark the break between the use of old and modern instruments because it roughly dates the time period in which some of the older instruments dropped out of favor, the piano came into common use, and the orchestra that we know today began to develop.

Voices and Vocal Ensembles

Because it is part of the human body, the voice is in many respects our most fundamental musical instrument. The expressive qualities of the voice are greatly enhanced by its ability to combine music and words. Individual voices vary in pitch range, but male and female voice types are generally divided into high, middle,

English Essex University Choir rehearsing

and low registers. Arranged from highest to lowest pitch register, the basic vocal categories are:

Female (or boys with unchanged voices):   **Soprano**

Mezzo soprano

Alto (also called *contralto*)

Male   **Tenor**

Baritone

Bass

These vocal types are often written by the first letter of the name: for example, a mixed **choir** that includes both women and men is often called an *SATB choir* because the four voices are soprano, alto, tenor, and bass. A women's choir is often referred to as an *SSA choir* because it includes first and second sopranos and altos. If the music is composed for two sections of sopranos and two of altos, it is called an *SSAA choir*. A men's ensemble is often referred to as *TTBB* for first and second tenors and two basses. We discuss different types of solo singing styles in later chapters.

Stringed Instruments

Chapter 3
Activities

Strings

Stringed instruments can be played by plucking, striking, or bowing the strings. The earliest stringed instruments were plucked or struck, but the sound of a plucked or struck string decays (softens and fades) very quickly. The invention of the bow allowed the instruments to sustain their sound and play smooth and connected melodies. Strings can be made of gut (animal intestines that are dried and twisted), silk, plastic, nylon, metal, or metal wound around nylon centers. Each type of material produces its own distinctive tone quality. Some materials lend themselves better to plucking or striking, and others to bowing. Silk, plastic, and nylon are so smooth that they do not catch the hairs of the bow very well and therefore are more commonly found on plucked or struck stringed instruments. Gut and metal-wound strings tend to be used for bowed instruments.

Plucked Stringed Instruments

Prior to 1750, the most popular plucked stringed instruments included the *lute* (a halved-pear or bowl-shaped body with a fingerboard), *psaltery* (a flat wooden box with strings across it that were either plucked or struck with hammers, much like the *hammered dulcimer* still in use today), and the *harp* (strings stretched across a triangular frame). All of these instruments were small enough to be held in the lap of an individual player, and they all sounded at a very soft dynamic level. They were used to accompany solo singers, to play in small instrumental ensembles, or to take part in mixed **consort**s (groups of different types of instruments playing together).

Today, the most common plucked stringed instruments are the guitar and the harp. They can be played both as solo instruments and in ensembles.

Guitar—the acoustic guitar has a figure-8-shaped hollow body and a fingerboard. Electric guitars can have hollow or solid bodies.

Harp—strings stretched across a triangular frame with a hollow side to resonate the sound. Harps are often used as part of an orchestra.

Bowed Stringed Instruments

Three families of bowed stringed instruments were in common use before 1750: the *viol* family (with fat bodies, flat backs, and fingerboards), the *rebec* family (bowl-shaped body with a fingerboard), and the *violin* family (thinner body with a shaped back and a fingerboard). The word *family* is used for each of these types of instruments because they were made in many sizes. The same names we use for voices are used to describe the pitch range of the instruments: soprano, alto, tenor, and bass. A viol consort (group of instruments of the same type, in this case, viols) might include a soprano viol, an alto viol, a tenor viol, and a bass viol.

Of these three historical bowed stringed families, the violin family is most commonly used today. From highest to lowest in pitch range, the bowed stringed instruments include:

Violin—the neck is held with the left hand, and the tail rests beneath the player's chin.

Viola—held in the same way as the violin, but it is larger and produces a lower and somewhat more somber tone quality.

Cello—much larger and deeper sounding than the violin or viola, played upright with the body held between the player's knees.

Double bass—also called a *string bass,* the largest and lowest member of the family. Because of its size, the player sits on a stool or stands.

A woman playing the harp

Jennifer Pike (BBC Young Musician of the Year 2002) playing the violin

A man playing the cello

The double bass section of the Bournemouth Symphony Orchestra rehearsing

These instruments are called *bowed* because their strings are normally played by drawing a bow (a stick with horsehair, which has tiny barbs that catch the string being bowed, attached at both ends) across the string or strings. They can also be plucked by the player's finger, a technique called **pizzicato.** For special effects, they can even be played by striking the strings with the bow, but that is rather rare.

A variety of musical effects can be achieved by using different bowing techniques:

Legato—smooth and connected up-and-down strokes of the bow

Staccato—short and detached strokes of the bow

Tremolo—fast, repeated notes played by very rapid strokes of the bow

The tone quality of each instrument can be made richer or warmer by the use of **vibrato:** rapid vibration of the left hand while pressing the string against the fingerboard. A subdued, velvety tone is produced by the use of a **mute,** a device clamped onto the bridge (across which the strings are stretched) to soften the sound.

Woodwinds

Woodwind instruments produce sound when air is blown through the tubelike body of the instrument. The length of the vibrating air column is controlled by opening or closing small holes along the side of the instrument with fingers or pads activated by a key mechanism. In closing or opening the *finger holes,* the player lengthens or shortens the air column, thereby lowering or raising the pitch of the notes produced.

Woodwind instruments in common use before 1750 had few, if any, keys. They included the *transverse flute* (side blown), the *recorder* (a whistle-type instrument blown from the mouthpiece at the end), and instruments such as the *crumhorn, shawm,* and *bagpipes,* often called "the buzzys" because they had double reeds that buzzed against each other, creating a slightly nasal tone quality. Bagpipes also have an air bag and a pipe that plays a continuous note while the other pipes play melodies. That continuous note is called a **drone.** You might think of bagpipes as purely Scottish, but they were in common use all over Europe during the Medieval and Renaissance periods.

The following woodwind instruments are used in modern orchestras:

A woman playing the flute

Piccolo—a small, high-pitched flute.

Flute—side blown and made out of metal, although early flutes were made from wood.

Oboe—played with a double reed of two pieces of thin cane that vibrate against the player's lips.

Clarinet—end blown with a single reed on the mouthpiece.

English horn—a lower-pitched version of the oboe.

Bassoon—also a double-reed instrument, but bigger and lower pitched than the oboe or English horn.

Bass clarinet—a larger and lower-pitched clarinet.

Contrabassoon—a larger and lower-pitched bassoon.

The **saxophone** was invented in the mid-nineteenth century by Adolphe Sax (1814–1894) of Brussels. Although it is made of metal and does not look like a woodwind instrument, a single-reed mouthpiece places it in the woodwind family.

Robert Plane (BBC National Orchestra of Wales) playing the clarinet

Jaroslaw Augustyniak (BBC National Orchestra of Wales) playing the bassoon

A woman playing the trumpet

A woman playing the trombone

Brasses

Brass instruments are identified by their cup mouthpiece, against which the player buzzes his or her lips. Early brass instruments were sometimes made from animal horns or carved from wood, though today they are generally made out of metal. Brass instruments in common use before 1750 include the *cornett* and *serpent,* both of which were carved out of wood and covered with black leather. Metal brass instruments of early times included the *trumpet, slide trumpet,* and the *sacbut.* The valves (a set of keys that open or close parts of the instrument's tubing, allowing for easy changes from note to note) we see on many brass instruments today were not invented until 1815. Players of early brass instruments changed notes by adjusting the tension of their lips against the mouthpiece, although they could also cover and open finger holes to help adjust pitches. Players of the slide trumpet and the sacbut changed notes by moving a slide that effectively shortened or lengthened the instrument, thereby raising or lowering the pitch of the note being played.

Brass instruments in common use today include the following (from highest to lowest pitched):

Trumpet—the modern trumpet uses valves to move from note to note.

French horn—the modern horn also uses valves to change notes.

Trombone—a slide is used to change notes by adjusting the length of tubing.

Tuba—a very large and low-pitched instrument that uses valves to change notes.

Other brass instruments, such as the *cornet* (similar to the trumpet) and the *euphonium* (of the tuba family) are used in both concert and marching bands. Both the trumpet and trombone are popular jazz instruments.

Percussion Instruments

Whereas the stringed, woodwind, and brass instruments we have discussed have become standard members of the modern symphony orchestra, percussion instruments—those that produce sounds when struck, shaken, or scraped—vary greatly from ensemble to ensemble and from composition to composition. Essentially, percussion instruments fall into two categories: those that produce *definite* pitch or pitches and those that produce a sound without a definite pitch.

Percussion instruments in common use before 1750 included *bells, cymbals* (two metal disks that are hit against one another), *triangles, nakers* (two drums tied around the player's waist and hit with sticks), the *tabor* (a single drum), and *timpani* (large kettle-shaped drums). Of those, the bells, cymbals, and triangles were made of metal. Bells often came in sets of different sizes and produced definite pitches, which meant that they could be used to play melodies. Cymbals and triangles had no definite pitch. Nakers, the tabor, and timpani were drums with animal skins stretched and tightened across them. Nakers and the tabor were not tuned to any particular pitch, although they could produce high or low tones depending on their size. A small naker would sound higher than a larger one. Timpani had screws around the edges that allowed the player to tighten or loosen the drum head in order to raise or lower its pitch, making it one of the few early drums that produced a definite pitch.

The most common percussion instruments found in a modern orchestra include the following:

Definite Pitch

Timpani—also known as *kettledrums*. Usually found in sets of from two to five drums of varying sizes. Modern timpani are tuned by pedals that are easier to adjust than the old screws.

Glockenspiel—two rows of steel bars, each producing a definite pitch. A crisp bell-like sound is produced by striking the bars with mallets (sticks with padded tips).

Celesta—a glockenspiel with a keyboard that makes it look something like a small upright piano.

Xylophone—made of tuned wooden bars that produce a hollow sound when struck by mallets.

Marimba—a xylophone with resonators under each bar of the instrument.

Chimes—a set of tuned metal tubes suspended vertically in a frame. They are played with one or two mallets, and their sound resembles that of church bells.

The *vibraphone* has metal bars arranged similarly to the keyboard of a piano and an electrical mechanism that produces the instrument's characteristic vibrato (fluctuation of pitch) effect. Vibraphones are popular in jazz but are not common orchestral instruments.

The percussion section of a youth orchestra

Indefinite Pitch

Percussion instruments of indefinite pitch include just about anything that can be struck, scraped, or manipulated in some other fashion to produce a sound. Those used most commonly today include the following:

Bass drum—a large, deep-sounding drum with two heads.

Side (or snare) drum—a drum that has two drum heads. The top head is hit with sticks; the bottom head is rigged with metal wires that vibrate against it when the top head is struck.

Tambourine—a circular wooden frame, usually with a single head, and metal discs that jingle when the instrument is shaken or struck.

Triangle—a triangle made of a bent metal rod, struck with a metal beater.

Cymbals—metal disks that ring when they are hit against one another.

Gong—also called a *tam-tam,* usually a large suspended metal disk that is struck with a padded mallet.

Tom-toms—cylindrical drums with two heads but no snares. Tom-toms are made in many sizes and are played with sticks, mallets, and brushes for different effects.

Bongos—a pair of attached small drums, each with one head, played with the hands.

Congas—a tall drum with a single head played with the hands.

Percussionists in modern orchestras also have a host of handheld instruments such as the *cowbell,* the *ratchet, sleigh bells,* the *whip* (two pieces of wood that sound like a whip when hit against one another), *castanets,* and many others. Some of these instruments have sounds that relate to familiar images, such as sleigh bells for music depicting a winter scene or castanets to create a Spanish character.

Keyboard Instruments

Chapter 3
Activities

Keyboards

Keyboard instruments are played with the hands and can produce many notes at one time. They function well as both solo and accompaniment instruments because they can play both melodies and chords. Several types of keyboard instruments were in use before 1750. One type had strings that were plucked, struck, or even bowed when the player pushed the keys, and the other had pipes through which wind blew when the player opened them by pushing the keys. Those whose strings were plucked belonged to the *clavier* family, including the *harpsichord* and the *virginal.* A small and very soft keyboard instrument that had metal tangents to strike the strings was called the *clavichord.* The *hurdy-gurdy*'s strings were bowed by a wooden wheel that the player cranked with one hand while playing a keyboard with the other. It also had drone strings that played without the keyboard, giving it an almost bagpipe-like sound.

Keyboard instruments with pipes fall into the general category of *organs.* Organs had bellows to push air through the pipes in much the same way that wind players blew into their flutes, oboes, or other instruments to allow them to sound. Organs varied greatly in size. Little portative organs had short keyboards that the player played with one hand while pumping the bellow with the other. The large organs we find in churches often have many sets of pipes and consequently make a great variety of sounds available to the player. Some organ pipes even have double reeds, giving them a buzzy tone quality.

The most common keyboard instruments in use today are the piano and the organ:

Piano—a keyboard instrument developed during the mid-eighteenth century. Hammers hit the strings when the keyboard is played. The hammer mechanism allows the player to vary the dynamic level of the music. It was originally called a *fortepiano* or a *pianoforte;* both terms refer to the dynamic levels of *piano* (soft) and *forte* (loud).

Organ—originally wind instruments played with a keyboard, though today they often produce their sound electronically.

A man playing the piano

Electronic Instruments

One of the most powerful and far-reaching forces in music in the twentieth century has been the application of electronics to the performance, reproduction, and creation of sound. Electronic instruments fall into two general categories: (1) instruments that produce acoustic sounds that are modified electronically and (2) instruments that generate sounds using electronics. Electronically modified acoustic instruments include, among others, guitars, keyboards, or woodwind instruments that are amplified by the use of a pickup or a microphone.

Electronics are used both to modify the tone quality of the instruments and to make them louder. The tone can be altered by pushing the sound through an amplifier that adds qualities such as vibrato or fuzztone to the sound. The "wa-wa" pedal, used to give music an undulating dynamic, became popular during the 1960s.

There were obviously no electronic instruments before 1750; however, the first electronic instrument was invented much earlier than you might think. In 1860, Hermann Ludwig Ferdinand von Helmholtz (1821–1894), a German physicist, invented the "Helmholtz Resonator," which used electromagnetically vibrating metal resonating spheres to produce complex sounds. The Helmholtz Resonator was followed by other inventions, including a tone wheel in which a disk rotating through a magnetic field created a tone. The tone wheel principally influenced the development of the Hammond organ in the 1950s.

A vacuum tube capable of amplifying radio signals was invented in 1906. This not only made radio broadcasting possible but also was used in early televisions and computers. Vacuum tubes are still sometimes used to transmit extremely high frequencies, and some audiophiles still prefer the sound of amplifiers with vacuum tubes to solid-state circuitry. The transistor, which can be used for amplifying as well as generating sounds, was invented in 1947. Small transistor radios became very popular in the early 1960s. Transistors allowed for the invention of several types of music **synthesizers.** A synthesizer can imitate natural acoustic sounds, or it can design new sounds. Some early synthesizers were played by keyboards and others by touch-sensitive contact pads. The earliest synthesizers could produce only one note at a time, so it took the mixing of several recordings to produce music with full chords or multiple melodies.

Much electronic music is recorded—rather than played live—because composers like to experiment with various sounds and then mix the ones they want to create the final composition. In recent years, composers have used computers to create just about any sound or effect they desire. Those sounds imitate the tone qualities of natural, acoustic instruments, or they create completely new combinations of sounds.

Instruments in Non-Western Cultures

When we discuss instruments used in non-Western cultures, we generally categorize them differently than those used in Western cultures. For example, instead of dividing the two groups of woodwind and brass, we put all non-Western wind instruments into one category. We also separate percussion instruments differently than into the pitched and nonpitched groups we discussed earlier. The following categories are generally used in discussions of non-Western instruments:

> **Chordophones**—all stringed instruments, including those that are plucked, struck, or bowed.
>
> **Aerophones**—wind instruments of all kinds.
>
> **Idiophones**—solid instruments that are hit, struck together, shaken, scraped, rubbed, or have a hard extension (such as a piece of metal attached to the instrument) that is plucked to produce their sounds.
>
> **Membranophones**—drums that produce their sounds by the vibration of a membrane that is stretched across all or part of the instrument.

The music of non-Western cultures is a study in itself; in fact, it is very difficult to cover more than a few areas of the world in a course or book that is completely devoted to that field. In this book on Western music, we discuss non-Western music as it influenced Western music of the twentieth century, when music and instruments from several non-Western cultures became a very important source of new ideas for Western composers.

Instrumental Ensembles

Chamber Ensembles

Chapter 3
Activity

Tone Color
Mixer

Chamber music is a general term for small groups of instruments in which each player plays his or her own part. Chamber groups are small enough for the players to hear one another, so they do not need a conductor to keep them together. There are many different names for chamber groups; some names give a clear indication of the instruments in the group, and others do not. A *string quartet*, for example, is a group of four players of bowed stringed instruments, but a *piano trio* is not necessarily composed of three pianos, although it might be. Usually a piano trio is made up of one violin, one cello, and one piano. A much more complete discussion about chamber music is presented in Chapter 13, in which we listen to a movement from a string quartet by the classical composer Joseph Haydn.

Chapter 3
Activity

Instrument Lab

The Orchestra

Chapter 3
Activity

Britten's Guide
to Orchestra

An **orchestra** is a group of instruments from different families. The orchestra began to develop during the seventeenth century, when several bowed stringed

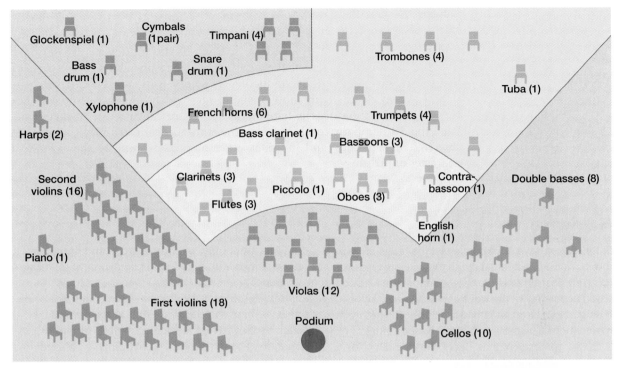

FIGURE 3.1
Distribution of musicians in an orchestra.

instruments played together with whatever woodwind and/or brass instruments the composer chose to include. These early orchestras usually made use of a keyboard instrument such as a harpsichord or an organ.

In the middle of the eighteenth century, the orchestra became more standardized. The strings remained dominant, but the woodwind and brass instruments took on an increasingly important role. Timpani were also added, often to play in support of the very majestic sounding brass instruments.

In the early nineteenth century, many inventions helped to expand the range of woodwind and brass instruments and make them easier to play in tune. By the second half of the nineteenth century, the orchestra grew extensively in both size and makeup and included many more percussion instruments than it had in past centuries. Today's symphony orchestra consists of a nucleus of as many as one hundred players, with additions and subtractions made to suit the requirements of individual pieces. The players are distributed according to the plan in Figure 3.1.

The Wind Ensemble

Wind ensembles (also called *concert bands* or *symphonic bands*) are made up primarily of woodwind, brass, and percussion instruments. The only bowed string instrument used in most wind ensembles is the double bass. Although a great body of music has been composed expressly for wind ensemble, much orchestral music has also been arranged to be played by wind ensembles. It can be quite interesting to hear the same piece played by an orchestra and then by a wind ensemble.

The Conductor

Large ensembles such as orchestras, wind ensembles, and choruses require the leadership of a **conductor.** Standing in front of the musicians, usually on a podium, the conductor directs the ensemble and is responsible for all aspects of the performance. The craft of conducting is a complex one, and conducting techniques and styles are highly individual and vary widely. In general, the conductor's right hand indicates the tempo and basic metrical structure of the music. With the left hand, the conductor cues the entrances of instruments, guides the shadings or dynamics, and indicates other nuances relating to the expressive character of the music.

Summary

In this chapter we have discussed the types of instruments we will be hearing in the musical discussions to follow. Instruments are categorized by families or types according to the ways in which they produce their sound. Common families include stringed instruments (both plucked and bowed), woodwinds, brasses, percussion (both pitched and unpitched), keyboard, and electronic. Voices are categorized by their vocal ranges, from high voices to low. These ranges include soprano, mezzo soprano, alto, tenor, baritone, and bass.

A great number of combinations and groupings are common with both instrumental and vocal music. Chamber ensembles include trios, quartets, and a number of other small groups, with usually one voice or instrument assigned to a part. Larger groupings, such as the orchestra, wind ensemble, or chorus, often have several voices or instruments performing a single part.

New Concepts

aerophones	conductor	legato
alto	congas	marimba
baritone	consorts	membranophones
bass	contrabassoon	mezzo soprano
bass clarinet	cymbals	mute
bass drum	double bass	oboe
bassoon	drone	orchestra
bongos	English horn	organ
celesta	flute	piano
cello	French horn	piccolo
chamber music	glockenspiel	pizzicato
chimes	gong	saxophone
choir	guitar	side (snare) drum
chordophones	harp	soprano
clarinet	idiophones	staccato

synthesizer	tremolo	vibrato
tambourine	triangle	viola
tenor	trombone	violin
timpani	trumpet	wind ensemble
tom-toms	tuba	xylophone

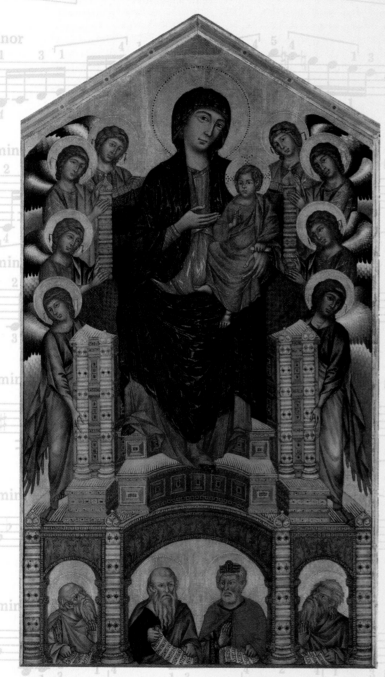

Madonna Enthroned by Cimabue (1240–1302). The stiff formality of this painting makes it more symbolic than realistic.

The Medieval Period (476–1450)

The medieval period (the "Middle Ages") in music history lasted about one thousand years (476–1450 CE) and served as a bridge between the ancient and modern worlds in Europe. One of the cultures of the ancient world that had a great deal of influence on the modern world was that of classical Greece (fifth century BCE). The Greeks idealized the human body in their artworks, as seen in the statue of *Poseidon* (page 31). They also stimulated independent thought through their philosophical writings and plays and encouraged their citizens to strive to develop skills through competition in their Olympic games. Rome conquered Greece in 146 BCE and took much of Greek culture and made it part of its own, as you can see in the Roman copy of a Greek sculpture of *The Apollo Belvedere* (page 31).

After the fall of the Roman Empire in 476 CE, the Christian church gained power. During the approximately one thousand years of the medieval period, people in Europe followed church doctrine that encouraged them to concentrate on living for the afterlife instead of celebrating their lives and experiences on earth. *Madonna Enthroned* by Cimabue illustrates this new focus. This cultural shift came full circle with the invention of the printing press with movable type in 1450, which made books less expensive and which spread literacy and independent thought to more Europeans than had been

The Culture of the Medieval Period

possible before. A new attitude about life that was thought to resemble that of the ancient Greeks resulted, ending the medieval period and ushering in the modern world.

The fifth century might seem terribly late to begin a study of the history of music when one considers how very many songs and musical instruments are mentioned in the Old Testament of the Bible and other writings from ancient times. Certainly,

many artworks from ancient Greece are full of portrayals of people singing, playing, and dancing to music. The Greeks studied music as a science, and some, such as Plato, thought that music controlled people's moods. The reason our detailed study of music is skipping all of this ancient history and beginning with the medieval period is that we cannot read the limited types of music notation from those periods and, therefore, do not

know for certain what the music sounded like. The notation we can read developed around the twelfth century, and that is the music with which we will begin our study.

Medieval Culture

Once Christianity was accepted by Roman leaders, it began to spread across the massive expanse of land that was to become Europe. Church monasteries, particularly before the development of towns in the twelfth century, were the principal patrons

Bronze statue of Poseidon, c. 460–450 BCE. The Greeks idealized the human body in sculptures such as this.

The Apollo Belvedere. This Roman copy of a Greek sculpture also idealized the human form.

of art and architecture. They were the vehicles for the preservation of literacy and of great literary works. In the monasteries, music became inextricably tied to important written works. Music in the form of liturgical chants was used in the recitation of religious texts, and monks composed new music for feast days. Books of these texts were copied by hand. Music notation was developed in order to preserve the traditional chants and distribute them to new monasteries in distant places. See the illustration on page 34 in which the Holy Spirit (a dove) is singing a chant to Pope Gregory, who in turn dictates it to a scribe.

Between the seventh and twelfth centuries, Europe turned into a mosaic of self-sufficient farms and manors that were controlled by secular lords or by the church. Average people worked on land under the protection of the lord or church, and the goods they produced were shared by the other workers and the protectors. Mobility was difficult, and people would generally live their lives never traveling beyond the valley in which they were born.

By the eleventh and twelfth centuries, interregional trade became more common. Villages developed into towns and cities, and major universities were established at Paris and Bologna. Bishops, using cities as administrative centers for a wealthy and powerful church, built great cathedrals that in the later medieval period replaced monasteries as the focal buildings of Europe.

Artists generally did not think that their abilities or achievements were anything more than a gift from God, and most did not sign their works for that reason. In many cases we have names of composers only because church records indicate the name of the person who was employed to write music around the time a piece was composed. Artists, including composers, created their works out of devotion to God, not to draw attention to themselves. This intention is clear in the art of the period. Look at the painting of *Madonna Enthroned* (page 30). Notice the stiff portrayal of Mary and the stiff, even adult look of the Christ child. As was often the case, religious figures are shown with large, unrealistic gold halos around their heads—more symbolic than human looking.

Few people outside of the church had learned to read because hand-copied books of text, and music as well, were very difficult and expensive to obtain. Music was sung from very large, shared books of chant notation and sung by members of the clergy. The congregations did not take part in the singing.

Once most people settled in towns and cities, they could practice trades and exchange goods with one another, making them more independent than the average person had been in the early part of the period. Men were generally in charge of families, and most community and church leaders were male. Marriages were arranged by

parents. The oldest male child in a family would often grow up to inherit what his parents owned, and other children would have to begin their own careers or dedicate their lives to the church. Women were trained to do jobs such as spinning, weaving, dyeing, and sewing. They also spent many hours preparing and preserving food. Women were not necessarily limited to such duties, however. They were able to own and run businesses, manage estates, and, if they could afford it, be educated. Although only men performed in plays or musical presentations in public, many men and women wrote poetry and songs to play and sing for their own or their friends' or families' enjoyment in their homes.

Some women chose, or their fathers chose for them, lives dedicated to the church and joined convents. The musical activities of women were somewhat restricted because of biblical verses that commanded that women be silent in church. (The sources of that view can be found in 1 Corinthians 14:34–35 and 1 Timothy 2:11–12.) Accordingly, the big city cathedrals were off-limits to women as far as music making was concerned. Convents were bound by different rules, however, and women were active participants in musical services and as composers for them.

In our study of the medieval period we will listen to examples of both secular and sacred music.

4 | Medieval Music

Sumer is icumen in, Lhude sing cuccu! (Modern English: "Summer is coming in, loudly sings the Cuckoo!")

—ANON. SONG TEXT (CA. 1250)

Listening Introduction

Listen to the recording of "Salve, Regina" and make notes about what you hear. Give some attention to the following:

▍ Can you tap your foot to a steady beat in the music?

▍ How many notes are being sung to each syllable of text? (Not exactly how many, but do you hear one, a few, or many?)

▍ Does the piece have a general mood that might give you a hint about the situation in which it was performed? What is that situation?

▍ Can you tell how many singers would be necessary to sing the piece?

▍ Can you determine the language of the text?

Keep your notes from this listening session to compare with your impressions about the piece after you study the information in this chapter.

Medieval Sacred Music

As the early Christian church grew, music played a major role in its ceremonies, and the body of music developed to accompany religious rites expanded enormously. At first, this music was not written down but was passed on by oral tradition to the monks, priests, and nuns of succeeding generations.

Pope Gregory I, who served as pope from 590 to 604, has generally been given credit for having ordered the simplification and cataloging of music assigned to specific celebrations in the church calendar. Many experts in medieval music today believe that it was really Pope Gregory II, who ruled from 715 to 731, who deserves this credit. Regardless of which pope really made the order, this decree resulted in the development of a standardized system of musical notation and the preservation of one of the greatest bodies of musical literature in the history of Western civilization. We call this music **Gregorian chant.**

Gregorian Chant

The chants, also known as *plainsong* or **plainchant,** are monophonic in texture (single-line melodies). Their texts are in Latin, and many are derived from the Bible, particularly the Book of Psalms.

The rhythm of the chants is unmeasured (nonmetric, no regular pattern of beats or accents), and the tempos are flexible. The melodic material is based on a system of scales now referred to as **church modes.** They are similar to the major and minor scales used today, but their half steps fall in different places so that

This is Pope Gregory I, who is generally credited with the cataloging of church music.

they do not express as strong a tonal center (tonic) as do today's scales. If one plays only on the white keys of the piano, the major scale goes from C to C and the natural minor scale from A to A. Other modes used in the Middle Ages can be played by playing from D to D, from E to E, from F to F, and so on.

The chant melodies achieve their aesthetic beauty with the most modest means. They have an undulating, wavelike quality and a simplicity that is wholly in keeping with their religious intent as a functional part of worship. Generally, chant melodies follow the implied inflections of the text, with its stressed and unstressed syllables.

"Salve, Regina" is a chant that was sung as part of evening worship (vespers). The first line of both the medieval notation of the chant and a modern transcription are included here, along with a recording of the entire chant. It is not necessary to be able to read the music as a performer would; simply follow the text and watch the notes go higher or lower as you hear them in the recording. The medieval notation is different in many ways from the modern notation, but you might be able to see how the two examples follow the same melody. The point is that, by this time in the medieval period, music notation had developed enough that we can be fairly certain about how it sounded. The chant is made up of six sections. The first

Gregorian and modern notation.

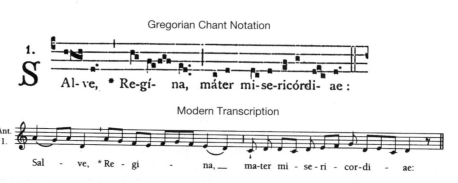

section consists of a melodic phrase and its immediate repetition with different words. Each subsequent section consists of a line of text with its own individual melody. Two types of text settings are employed: **syllabic,** in which each syllable of the text is given one note, and **melismatic,** in which a single syllable is spread over several notes. The concluding section is of particular interest because of the expressiveness resulting from the extended phrases on "O," the last of which is the longest **melisma** (one syllable spread over several notes) in the entire piece.

Chapter 4
Activity

Chant

Listening Guide

"Salve, Regina" ("Hail, Holy Queen") ANONYMOUS

CD 1
Track 1

Texture: Monophonic

Number of voices: Several men and boys, all singing the same melody together

Meter: Nonmetric

Duration: 2:35

Latin text	English translation
1 Salve, Regina, mater misericordiae:	Hail, Holy Queen, Mother of mercy
Vita, dulcedo, et spes nostra, salve.	Our life, our sweetness, and our hope, hail!
Ad te clamamus, exsules, filii Hevae.	To thee do we cry, poor banished children of Eve.
Ad te suspiramus, gementes et flentes	To thee do we send up our sighs,
in hac lacrimarum valle.	mourning and weeping in this valley of tears.
Eia ergo, Advocata nostra, illos tuos	Turn then, most gracious Advocate,
misericordes oculos ad nos converte.	thine eyes of mercy toward us;
Et Jesum, benedictum fructum ventris	and after this our exile, show unto us
tui, nobis post hoc exsilium ostende.	the blessed fruit of thy womb, Jesus.
O clemens: O pia: O dulcis Virgo Maria.	O merciful: O loving: O sweet Virgin Mary!

Hildegard of Bingen

As was discussed in the Prelude, the medieval church followed Biblical instructions and required women to be silent in the cathedrals. In convents, however, where there were only women, they were very active in musical activities. One of the best known of the female composers of sacred music in the medieval period was **Hildegard of Bingen (1098–1179).**

Hildegard was the tenth child born of noble parents in a small village near Rheinhessen, Germany. When she was eight years old, she was given to the Church to be raised and educated. She became a Benedictine nun at age fifteen, and the nuns elected her abbess of the convent when she was thirty-eight years old. After eleven years in that position, Hildegard moved herself and her nuns to a new convent in Bingen, Germany. From that place she became known as Hildegard of Bingen.

Throughout her life she claimed to have received visions that gave her insights from God. She began to write about her beliefs and completed the work *Scivias* (Know the Ways of God) in 1151. The book included some of the songs she had composed. It was well received by many who were able to get copies, and it gave Hildegard an opportunity to be known by and to correspond with several powerful people of her time, including the Pope, King Henry II of England, and Henry's wife, Eleanor of Aquitaine. Hildegard later wrote other major works, such as *Causae et Curae* (Causes and Cures), in which she reported various

A sculpture of Hildegard of Bingen

medical practices and remedies used by people of her time. A cure for baldness in her book involved making a paste of ash from burned wheat and bear's fat and putting it on the bald spot.

Hildegard's best-known musical works are a collection of sacred songs, *Symphonia* (Symphony of the Harmony of Heavenly Revelations) and the musical play *Ordo virtutum* (Play of Virtues). The Play of Virtues is the earliest complete morality play we have from the medieval period, and it must have been a fascinating production to see with Hildegard's nuns singing the roles of the virtues (Charity, Humility, Chastity, Fear of God, etc.), the soul who needs direction, and the Devil who tempts the soul (a spoken role).

Hildegard's music is different in many ways from the preexisting Gregorian chant repertoire. Her melodies tend to be freer and less controlled in range from high to low notes. They are still, however, monophonic and are written with unmeasured rhythms. In modern performances of her music, instrumentalists often add accompaniments to her songs.

On her death at age eighty-one, Hildegard's followers considered her a saint and applied to the pope for her canonization. No official documents were ever filed, but she is still thought of by many in modern Germany as Saint Hildegard.

Listening Guide

"Ave, Generosa" ("Hail, Noble One") HILDEGARD OF BINGEN

**CD 3
Track 1**

Texture: Monophonic

Number of voices: A group of female singers

Meter: Nonmetric

Duration: 6:27

Latin text

1
Ave, generosa,
gloriosa et intacta puella,
tu pupilla castitatis,
tu materia sanctitatis,
que Deo placuit.
Nam hec superna infusio
in te fuit,
quod supernum verbum
in te carnem induit.
Tu candidum lilium,
quod Deus ante omnem creaturam
inspexit.
O pulcherrima et dulcissima;
quam valde Deus in te delectabatur!

English translation

Hail, noble one,
shimmering and unpolluted,
you model of chastity,
you essence of holiness,
which was pleasing to God.
For this Heavenly infusion
was placed in you,
because the word from above
took on flesh within you.
You are the gleaming lily,
which God knew
before all other creatures.
O most fair and most sweet
how much did God delight in you!

Latin text	**English translation**
cum amplexione caloris sui	when he placed the embrace
in te posuit	of his warmth on you
ita quod filius eius de te lactatus est.	so that his son might be suckled by you.
Venter enim tuus gaudium habuit,	For your womb had joy,
cum omnis celestis symphonia	when the harmony of all Heaven
de te sonuit,	sounded out from you,
quia, Virgo, filium Dei portasti	because, Virgin, you carried the son of God
ubi castitas tua in Deo claruit.	when your chastity shone on God.
Viscera tua gaudium habuerunt,	Your flesh had joy,
sicut gramen super quod ros cadit	like the turf on which dew falls
cum ei viriditatem infudit:	when it instills it with greenness;
ut et in te factum est.	so also it was done with you,
o mater omnis gaudii.	mother of all joy.
Nunc omnis ecclesia in gaudio rutilet	Now let the whole church shine with joy
ac in symphonia sonet	and sound in concert,
propter dulcissimam Virginem	on account of the sweetest Virgin,
et laudabilem Mariam	and praiseworthy Mary,
Dei genitricem. Amen.	mother of God. So be it.

The Mass

The **Mass** is the most solemn service of the medieval Christian church. It is the commemoration and symbolic reenactment of the Last Supper of Christ. The **liturgy** of the Mass, the prescribed ceremony, is divided into two parts: the **Ordinary** (using those texts that do not change from day to day) and the **Proper** (using those texts that vary according to the religious nature of the specific day in the church year). The Mass service combines and sometimes alternates items from the Ordinary and the Proper.

Composers who wrote music for the Mass generally composed music to be sung to the texts from the Ordinary, because that would allow their music to be performed whenever the Mass was celebrated, regardless of the time of year. The titles of the texts from the Ordinary that came to be favored for musical settings were the Kyrie, Gloria, Credo, Sanctus, Benedictus, and Agnus Dei; you can make out these words as you listen to many Gregorian chants. Works based on those texts have been a source of inspiration for many famous composers, including Bach, Mozart, Beethoven, and Stravinsky. Today, these works are more often performed in concert halls than in church services because they have become major parts of classical repertoire.

Polyphony and Measured Rhythm

Music remained monophonic and unmeasured until the tenth century, when two or more voice parts began appearing in combination. This new method of composition went through a number of stages over a long period of time. The development of polyphonic music from the twelfth to the fourteenth centuries was centered in northern France and was dominated by the Notre Dame school under the leadership first of **Léonin** (fl.c. [flourished about] 1163–1190) and then his successor, **Pérotin** (fl.c. 1190–1225). The earliest **polyphonic** (a texture with more than one melody line) works were called organa (singular, **organum**).

The rhythm of early organa was unmeasured, as it was just two melodies moving at the same time. Eventually, the voice parts assumed rhythmic independence. Léonin approached this by taking a preexisting chant as a low part and slowing it down into very long held notes. He then composed a faster-moving melody to be sung above that slow chant, so that his music was really two melodies being sung at the same time but not moving to the same rhythm pattern. For this new music, a new type of notation was developed in which the relative time values of notes in the melody were indicated with precision (measured)—a technique called **mensural notation.** Pérotin further complicated his compositions by adding two or three newly composed melodies above a slow-moving chant melody.

The independence of simultaneous melodies that moved in different directions *melodically* and at different times *rhythmically* resulted in what became known as polyphony. Thus two major developments in Western music took place: (1) the change from monophony to polyphony and (2) the change from unmeasured, relatively free rhythm to **measured rhythm,** in which precise time values were related to each other. Polyphony and measured rhythm were fully developed in the polyphonic setting of the Mass and the motet. We discuss the motet form later in this chapter.

Guillaume de Machaut

One of the most important composers of the fourteenth century was **Guillaume de Machaut** (c. 1300–1377). His name means "William of Machaut." Machaut is a town in northern France, just northeast of Rheims. Most of the extant records about Machaut's life are connected with his education and work in Rheims, a city with a beautiful and important cathedral where much music was sung. Machaut took holy orders but never became a priest. By the end of his life he had advanced to the position of canon, a clergyman who practices the rules of the church but who has not taken the full vows of a priest, and who lives outside a monastery.

Machaut was one of the most literary men of his time and was employed as a scribe and private secretary by several aristocrats. He also became friends and shared some of his musical compositions with Charles V, King of France. Although we are studying Machaut's importance as a composer, he was perhaps better known in his own time as a poet who wrote many poems about his work with these important men.

In addition to large quantities of secular music and motets, Machaut wrote the earliest polyphonic setting of the entire Ordinary of the Mass, *Messe de Nostre Dame (Mass of Our Lady)*. Before Machaut, different composers wrote each section of a Mass, creating an inconsistent overall style. Machaut's Mass was beautifully constructed and represented the most advanced compositional techniques of his time, including four voices with more ornamentation and contrary motion than had been common in earlier three-voiced works. After you have studied the "Agnus Dei" from the Ordinary of that Mass, turn to Hearing the Difference: "Salve Regina" and Machaut's "Agnus Dei." Machaut was buried in the cathedral at Rheims, where his music has often been performed.

Listening Guide

"Agnus Dei" ("Lamb of God") from *Messe de Nostre Dame (Mass of Our Lady)*
GUILLAUME DE MACHAUT

CD 1
Tracks 2–4

Texture: Polyphonic

Number of voices: Four

Meter: Triple

Duration: 3:41

	Timing	Latin text	English translation	Musical characteristics
2	0:00	Agnus Dei, qui tollis peccata mundi: Miserere nobis.	Lamb of God, who takest away the sins of the world: Have mercy upon us.	"**A**" section with more rhythmic motion in the upper two parts.
3	1:08	Agnus Dei, qui tollis peccata mundi: Miserere nobis.	Lamb of God, who takest away the sins of the world: Have mercy upon us.	"**B**" section with new music, also most motion in upper parts.
4	2:25	Agnus Dei, qui tollis peccata mundi: Dona nobis pacem.	Lamb of God, who takest away the sins of the world: Grant us peace.	Repeat of the music for the "**A**" section, but with new text at the end.

HEARING THE DIFFERENCE
"Salve, Regina" and Machaut's "Agnus Dei"

So far, we have studied three pieces of sacred music from the medieval period. They were all in Latin, the language of the church. The "Salve, Regina," by an anonymous composer, and Hildegard of Bingen's "Ave, Generosa" are somewhat similar to one another in style, but Machaut's "Agnus Dei" represents several new developments in the composition of sacred works during the medieval period. In order to appreciate how very advanced Machaut's composition is beyond the early chant style, listen again to these two works, back to back, and see if you can discern the following differences:

	Salve, Regina	Agnus Dei
Texture	Monophonic	Polyphonic
Number of voices	Several men and boys singing the same melody together	Four separate voices singing different melodies at the same time
Meter	Nonmetric	Triple meter
Flow of text	Rhythms flow with inflections of the text	Rhythms seem to be imposed on rather than flowing with the text
Overlap of voices	All singers sing the same words at the same time	Voices tend to move independently of one another, causing the different words to be sung at the same time. The text and rhythms come together at the beginnings and endings of phrases.
Form	There is very little repetition of sections of the melody	The form is ABA. The return of the beginning melody at the end creates a sense of balance.
Performance situation	A church or cathedral during an evening service	A church or cathedral as part of the Ordinary of the Mass

Medieval Secular Music

In addition to the music of the church, the medieval period witnessed the growth of a rich tradition of nonreligious, or **secular,** music. Gregorian chants used Latin, but secular texts came to be written in the **vernacular** (everyday) language of the country of origin. Like today's popular music, these texts often concerned the subject of love. Some texts were humorous and some were quite bawdy; others treated political subjects or told stories of vagabonds.

The most important early secular vocal music was created and performed by poet-musicians, called ***trouvères*** in northern France, ***troubadours*** in southern France, and ***minnesingers*** in Germany. These poet-musicians were generally members of the nobility, even kings, who would not have performed in public but instead would have sung their songs to their families and friends in their own homes or at royal courts. Sometimes they would give their songs to lower-class musicians to perform in public. Those traveling street performers were called ***minstrels*** or ***jongleurs.*** Frauenlob, a German poet-composer, was a *minnesinger.*

The number of musical and poetic works created by these poet-musicians is enormous. The melodies of their songs, like the melodies of chant, were monophonic and simple in design. The songs mainly paired one note of music

German poet-composer Frauenlob (c. 1255–1318) with musicians.
Frauenlob is an example of a *minnesinger.*

with one syllable of text, with occasional ornamental melismas. In the case of the *trouvères* and troubadours, the form of their pieces was rather free, often including a **refrain**—a recurring line of words and its distinctive melody. Many of the songs were **strophic** in form, with each verse of text being sung to the same melody.

Improvised Accompaniment to Monophonic Songs

The song manuscripts written by medieval poet-musicians are all in monophonic notation. On the other hand, drawings, paintings, and other artistic portrayals of the time show people singing and playing instruments. Some modern performers of medieval music take the manuscripts as they are and sing the music monophonically without accompaniment. Many other modern-day performers assume that instruments originally accompanied the songs, as portrayed in medieval artworks, and add instruments to their performances. No one can be certain exactly what the instruments should play, but we do know from written descriptions of music of the time that instrumentalists did a lot of improvisation around existing melodies. Drones were popular on instruments such as the bagpipe and the hurdy-gurdy, so instruments playing dronelike long-held notes might be acceptable as accompaniments.

Instruments not only accompanied songs but also played an important role in the accompaniment of dances. Many types of instruments were employed, including the harp, the vielle (a precursor of the modern violin), the psaltery (a kind of zither played by striking or plucking its strings), lutes, horns, drums, trumpets, a variety of wind instruments and bells, and portable organs. Medieval and Renaissance dance music is discussed in Chapter 5.

Beatriz of Dia

Beatriz of Dia was a troubadour in the late twelfth century. She was a countess, married to Guillem (William) of Poitiers. Several of her poems were directed to another man whom she took as a lover, rather than to her husband. Because marriages were generally arranged by parents during the medieval period, it was common for husbands and wives to live together for practical purposes but to take lovers when they became so attracted. Beatriz's lover was the nobleman and troubadour Raimbaut d'Orange (of Orange, a town in southern France).

Beatriz of Dia, both countess and troubadour

As a noblewoman, Beatriz was well educated. She could read and write both words and music. A woman of her social rank would not have sung her songs for anyone she did not know, but she might well have written them to sing for her own pleasure, or for the pleasure of her husband, lover, and friends.

Most of Beatriz's songs exist only as poems, and because the lines of each poem tend to scan similarly, it could be assumed that she sang the poems to preexisting melodies. She also might have composed melodies, but if so, the musical notation has been lost. Her one song that has survived with its melody is "A Chantar" ("It Is Mine to Sing"). We will discuss this song in the next Listening Guide, and will then compare it to the "Salve, Regina" chant that we have heard several times before.

Listening Guide

"A Chantar" ("It Is Mine to Sing") BEATRIZ OF DIA

CD 1
Track 5

Texture: Monophonic

Meter: Nonmetric, but with a sense of a regular beat

Voices: Solo female singer without accompaniment

Text setting: Syllabic

Language: French

Duration: 1:03

(first verse only; later verses are sung to this same melody)

French text	English translation
5 A chantar m'er de so qu'eu no volria	I must sing of that which I would rather not;
tant me rancor de lui cui sui amia	I am so aggrieved by him whose lover I am,
Car eu l'am mais que nulha ren que sia	for I love him more than anything that exists,
Vas lui no.m val merces ni cortezia	Pity and courtliness do not help me with him,
Ni ma beltatz ni mos pretz ni mos sens,	Nor my beauty, nor my worth, nor my intelligence
Qu'atressi.m sui enganad' e trahia	For also I am deceived and betrayed
Com degr' esser s'eu fos desavinens.	As I would deserve to be if I were loathsome.

The Motet

Much as the organa had added an independent line of music to the chant, the **motet** added a second set of words (the name *motet* comes from the French word *mot,* meaning "word"). Originally a form of religious music, the motet grew out of the two-part organa in the thirteenth century. As the motet form evolved, the upper voice began to sing in the vernacular. The subject matter was usually secular. Gradually, composers added a third and even a fourth voice part. Most medieval motets were, therefore, a combination of the sacred and secular. With the original chant in Latin on the lower (or lowest) part and the secular text(s) in French above that, many of the motets were *polylingual,* or sung in multiple languages. When they had two or three parts added above the chant, those parts each had their own separate texts and separate rhythms, making the music *polytextual.* With two or three independent melodies being sung at the same time, motets were also polyphonic in texture.

By the fourteenth century, the motet had increased in length and had become more elaborate in its melodic and rhythmic structure. But even with the increased number of melodic lines and texts, the range of voices remained narrow, and the chant was almost always retained in some form in the lowest voice part. By the fifteenth century, the motet had evolved full circle. Once again it became

HEARING THE DIFFERENCE
"Salve, Regina" and Dia's "A Chantar"

Of the two works we listened to in the previous "Hearing the Difference" comparison, "A Chantar" does not have more in common with Machaut's "Agnus Dei" than Machaut's "Agnus Dei" did with "Salve, Regina." Comparing "Salve, Regina" and "A Chantar," however, allows us to hear two songs that are both monophonic with unmeasured rhythms, but are different from one another in several other ways. "Salve, Regina" represents the style of sacred music that was composed early in the medieval period and "A Chantar" is a secular song composed during the late 1100s. As you listen to both works again, pay attention to the following differences (some similarities are listed here as well):

	Salve, Regina	**A Chantar**
Texture	Monophonic	Monophonic
Number of voices	Several men and boys	Solo female singer
Meter	Nonmetric	Nonmetric, but with a sense of a regular beat, if not a specific meter
Text setting	Syllabic and melismatic	Mostly syllabic, with occasional places where two or three notes are sung on a single syllable
Form	Very little repetition of sections of the melody	Strophic (although we heard only one verse, the song includes many other verses intended to be sung to the same melody)
Language	Latin (the language of the church)	French (the language Beatriz of Dia spoke every day)
Performance situation	A church or cathedral during an evening service	Beatriz of Dia's home or other non-public place; sung to her lover, friends, or relatives. The song might have also been performed by others in similar situations.
Possible accompaniments	None; the singers would have sung without instrumental accompaniment	It is extremely likely that musical instruments would have been added to the performance of the song. The singer could strum or pluck a lute or harp, for example. Other instruments could join in adding a drone or other improvised accompaniment.

primarily a religious form, using one text for all voices. The text was almost always taken from the Bible. The motets of the Renaissance developed from these late medieval ones.

Summary

Western music grew out of the religious music of the medieval period. The liturgy of the Mass is divided into the Ordinary and the Proper. The Kyrie, Gloria, Credo, Sanctus, Benedictus, and Agnus Dei became the parts of the Ordinary most favored for musical settings. Chants, closely allied with the Roman Catholic liturgy, were codified and compiled during the time of Pope Gregory (I or II), and a system of music notation was developed to preserve them. In the following centuries the simple, monophonic form of these chants evolved into the more complex, polyphonic forms of organa, polyphonic settings of the Mass, and the motet. The motet of the medieval period generally included secular verses in the vernacular, along with chant melodies with Latin texts.

Secular music was also developing at this time. Early vocal music was performed by *trouvères* in northern France, troubadours in southern France, and *minnesingers* in Germany. Their songs were sung in the vernacular and were sometimes quite bawdy. The songs of these poet-musicians were monophonic, but instruments were probably used to accompany them.

New People and Concepts

Beatriz of Dia	melisma	polyphonic
church modes	melismatic	**Proper**
Gregorian chant	mensural notation	refrain
Guillaume de Machaut	*minnesingers*	secular
Hildegard of Bingen	*minstrels*	strophic
jongleurs	motet	syllabic
Léonin	Ordinary	*troubadours*
liturgy	organum	*trouvères*
Mass	**Pérotin**	vernacular
measured rhythm	plainchant	

Finale

Listen again to the recording of "Salve, Regina" and compare your impressions now with your notes from your first listening. Do you hear more now than you did before? You should now be able to answer the following questions:

▌ Does the music have a beat or meter?

▌ Are the text settings syllabic, melismatic, or both?

▌ What is the situation in which the piece would have originally been performed?

▌ What is the texture?

▌ What is the language of the text?

Characteristics of Medieval Music

Texture	Chants and songs were monophonic; later Masses and motets employed polyphony
Tonality	Church modes
Rhythm	Chants employed unmeasured rhythm; later sacred music and secular music employed measured rhythm
Singing style	Sacred music: solemn, expressive, small voice range
	Secular music: often more rhythmic than sacred music
Large vocal works	None
Small vocal works	Chant, organum, motet
Musical instruments	Instruments accompanied songs and dances
Instrumental music	Dances and other secular compositions

***Madonna del Granduca* by Raphael (1483–1520).** Like Raphael and other Renaissance painters did in their art, Josquin des Prez depicted an idealized Virgin Mary in his music.

Although medieval Europe idealized meditative withdrawal from worldly concerns, the Renaissance (1450–1600) stressed activity and worldly excellence. *Renaissance* is the French word for "rebirth," and what was reborn in 1450 was the kind of pride in being a fully realized human being that was common in ancient Greece. With the invention of the printing press and, in turn, the spread of literacy, education in all fields expanded. Reason began to replace faith as the intellectual norm. In the new climate, portraiture and the ideal nude—kinds of art that had vanished since the fall of Rome—again became the fashion. Look carefully at the statue of *David* by Michelangelo on page 47 and notice the sense of pride in the human body and spirit it portrays. Similarly, Renaissance portrayals of the Madonna and Child, such as Raphael's *Madonna del Granduca* (left), show the Christ child to be much more human and vulnerable than had the medieval ones.

Interest in exploration of the world outside of Europe increased during the Renaissance, and that exploration opened up many new cultures, attitudes, and goods to Europeans. After Columbus discovered the New World, such items as coffee, tobacco, and chocolate became part of Europeans' experience. Other explorers ventured to Asia and Africa, in addition to continuing to explore the American continent. In Britain and on the continent of Europe, mail service began during the Renaissance,

Prelude | The Renaissance: The Rebirth of Humanism

David **by Michelangelo (1475–1564).** This is one of many Renaissance sculptures that display the same sense of pride in the human body that we see in Greek and Roman sculptures such as *Poseidon* (page 31) and *The Apollo Belvedere* (page 31).

greatly aiding communication over great distances.

Literacy and a well-rounded education became so important that we sometimes use the term "Renaissance man" to credit a person who was well educated and talented in many fields. That term is still used today, but the most famous example of such a person in the Renaissance was Leonardo da Vinci (1452–1519), who was a painter, sculptor, architect, engineer, scientist, poet, and musician.

In a different kind of shift away from the dominance of the Roman Church, Martin Luther (1483–1546) and the Christians he led in Germany broke away on the grounds of corruption within the church and disagreement with doctrine. He ignited a firestorm of conflict in which Protestants saw themselves as individually responsible for their spiritual destinies, not subject to papal authority. John Calvin and several other religious leaders followed Luther in forming new Protestant religions that are still in existence today. The Roman Catholic Church reevaluated itself after having lost the allegiance of so many Christians and made reforms in some areas of its practices. One primary reform required composers to simplify sacred music so that the liturgical text would be better understood.

The lives of average people during the Renaissance were much like those in the late medieval period, except that an increase in trade and business caused more men to concentrate on their status and power in ways that women could not. Women lost much of the independence they had had in the medieval period and were seen primarily as assistants to their husbands, working alongside them to earn a living. Most women could not attain the Renaissance ideal of multiple skills because education was not as available to women as to men. The daughters of aristocratic families learned Latin and Greek, which allowed them to read religious literature and classic texts. Some of these educated women became writers, but female artists and composers were rare.

The more worldly outlook of the Renaissance influenced the music of the period. No longer required to reflect the meditative simplicity of medieval styles, composers could develop the old religious chants into longer, more complex, multivoiced works. New secular vocal and instrumental dance music also emerged.

The printing press with movable type was applied to music, and printed music became more available. With the ability to purchase music by a variety of composers, an average educated person with no talent for composition could learn to read, sing, and play music along with family members and friends. Performers could make a good living by giving music or dance instruction to members of wealthy families. They were also often hired to entertain for more formal parties.

The medieval attitude of living primarily to glorify God and to reach the afterlife did not allow for the kinds of societal advancements that began in the Renaissance. In general, the Renaissance is considered the beginning of the modern world, because Renaissance attitudes of humanism, respect for the individual and for independent thought, and interest in learning about the world through scientific investigation led directly to the sciences, arts, and philosophies we have today. The Renaissance's more humanistic outlook altered European art for the next several hundred years.

5 | Renaissance Music

The better the voice is, the meeter it is to honor and serve God therewith: and the voice of Man is chiefly to be employed to that end. Since singing is so good a thing, I wish all men would learn to sing.

—ENGLISH COMPOSER WILLIAM BYRD (1543–1623)

Listening Introduction

Listen to the recording of Josquin des Prez's "Ave Maria" and make notes about what you hear. Give some attention to the following:

▌ Can you tell the meter?

▌ Does the piece have a general mood that might give you a hint about the situation in which it was performed?

▌ Can you tell the number of singers that would be necessary to sing the piece?

▌ Can you tell the texture and notice if and when it changes?

▌ Can you determine the language of the text?

Keep your notes from this session to compare with your impressions about the piece after you study the information in this chapter.

Renaissance Sacred Music

The Renaissance in literature and the visual arts began in the 1300s and was centered in Italy. The Renaissance in music began around 1450 in what is today northern France, Holland, and Belgium. The style that developed in these countries spread to all parts of Europe.

The composers of this northern style, sometimes referred to as "Franco-Flemish," most often wrote music in four voices. For many of their Masses and motets, they continued to use chant melodies as one of the voices, but for the first time they did not keep the chant in the bass. They composed new bass lines and placed the chant in another voice above it. They sometimes even abandoned chant melodies altogether, creating completely new compositions. Occasionally, Renaissance composers used a secular tune as one of the voices in their religious compositions, something that composers of the medieval period would not have thought appropriate. This music is performed **a cappella,** or without instrumental accompaniment.

The polyphonic style of these Franco-Flemish composers emphasized the true independence of each of the four voices in their works. **Imitation** was common. At the beginning of "Ave Maria," you will hear imitation when a melodic fragment is stated in one voice and is then repeated or imitated by another voice a measure later. Each voice comes in one at a time, imitating the melody

Chapter 5
Activity

Homophony
and Polyphony

that was sung first. The imitation does not continue throughout the composition, but it creates an effective beginning that composers often used in the Renaissance.

Josquin des Prez

Josquin des Prez, Renaissance composer

IOSQVINVS PRATENSIS.
(circa 1450—1521.)

The composer of "Ave Maria," **Josquin des Prez** (c. 1450–1521), was one of the most influential composers of the Renaissance; his style was copied by many other composers. It is not known exactly where Josquin des Prez was born, but it is generally assumed to be somewhere in what is today northern France or Belgium. The year of his birth is sometimes given as 1440, but that date is uncertain.

Josquin was a member of the choir at the court of the Duke Galeazzo Maria Sforza in Milan in 1474. When the Duke was assassinated in 1476, Josquin went to Rome, where he got a job singing at the chapel of Cardinal Ascanio Sforza. While in Rome, Josquin also spent some time singing in the papal choir. In 1501 Josquin went to France and spent two years singing at the court of Louis XII. He moved on to the Italian court at Ferrara but left there after only one year to avoid an outbreak of the plague. That was a smart move on his part, because his successor died from the plague. Josquin spent his last years singing at a cathedral in Condé, France.

Throughout his life Josquin composed music and taught students while making his primary living as a singer. He was well aware of his talents and often demanded higher pay than was common for his colleagues. He did not put dates on his compositions, and his name was so well known in his own time that some other composers put his name on their works to sell them. All of this causes some confusion in the collection and evaluation of his work. Josquin left many motets, many Masses, and a considerable amount of secular music. He was also a gifted teacher, and many of his pupils became outstanding figures in the next generation of composers.

As we discussed in the last chapter, medieval motets had a sacred Latin chant as the lowest voice with secular texts in the vernacular (everyday language) above them. In some cases, there were two or three melodies with secular texts (different texts on each part) above the sacred one. The texture was polyphonic and a listener would have a very difficult time understanding any of the texts, particularly the sacred one. By the Renaissance, motets dropped the secular influences and became sacred, with one Latin text for all voices. Josquin's "Ave Maria" is a good example of a Renaissance motet.

In the motet discussed in the next Listening Guide, notice the changes from polyphonic to homophonic (all voices are sung to the same rhythm) textures and notice when each is used. Sometimes the homophonic texture calls attention to the text because it is easier to understand the words, if one knows Latin. Homophonic texture is used at the beginning of the section in triple meter, helping to stress the new meter. Because of the importance of the Holy Trinity (Father, Son, and Holy Ghost) in Christianity, triple meter is sometimes used to signify purity. Is there anything particularly significant about the text in the triple-meter section that the new meter might have been intended to stress? Notice that the three beats of the triple-meter bars are fit into the same amount of time as two beats of the rest of the motet, which is in duple meter. When Renaissance music changes from duple to triple meter, it is typical to have the notes in the triple section speed up to keep a constant pulse for each bar.

Listening Guide

"Ave Maria" ("Hail, Mary") JOSQUIN DES PREZ

CD 1
Tracks 6–7

Year: 1470s

Texture: Polyphonic and homophonic

Number of voices: Four

Meter: Duple, with one section in triple meter

Duration: 4:45

	Timing	Latin text	English translation	Features
6	0:00	Ave Maria, gratia plena, Dominus tecum, Virgo serena.	Hail, Mary, full of grace, the Lord be with you, fair Virgin.	Polyphonic texture with much imitation
	0:49	Ave cujus conceptio, Solemni plena gaudio,	Hail to you whose conception, full of solemn joy,	Homophonic texture
	1:12	Coelestia, terrestria, Nova replet laetitia.	fills heavenly and earthly beings with new gladness.	Polyphonic texture
	1:28	Ave cujus nativitas Nostra fuit solemnitas,	Hail to you whose nativity was our solemn feast,	Polyphonic with voices paired
	1:51	Ut lucifer lux oriens Verum solem praeveniens.	indeed was the morning star rising preceding the true sun.	Imitative polyphony
	2:18	Ave pìa humilitas Sine viro foecunditas	Hail, holy humility, fruitful without man,	Homophonic with paired voices
	2:30	Cujus annunciatio Nostra fuit salvatio.	whose annunciation was our salvation.	More polyphonic with paired voices
7	2:49	Ave vera virginitas, Immaculata castitas, Cujus purificatio Nostra fuit purgatio.	Hail, true virginity, undefiled chastity, whose purification was our cleansing.	Triple meter stressed by a homophonic beginning, then somewhat polyphonic
	3:14	Ave praeclara omnibus Angelicis virtutibus, Cujus fuit assumptio Nostra glorificatio.	Hail, to you, admirable in all angelic virtues, whose assumption was Our glorification	Return to duple meter Polyphonic texture
	4:10	O Mater Dei, Memento mei. Amen.	O, Mother of God, remember me. Amen.	Homophonic texture

Giovanni Pierluigi da Palestrina

One of the most distinguished of Josquin's successors was **Giovanni Pierluigi da Palestrina** (1525–1594), who spent the greater part of his life as choirmaster of St. Peter's in Rome. Palestrina's great contribution was to return church music to the simplicity and purity of earlier times. Although his motets are masterpieces of composition, his Masses constitute his most important work.

Palestrina lived and worked during the **Counter-Reformation,** the reaction by the Catholic Church to the spread of **Protestantism.** Central to this reaction was the **Council of Trent,** which met from 1545 to 1563 to formulate and execute the means by which church reform could be accomplished. The Council investigated every aspect of religious discipline, including church music. It was the opinion of the Council that sacred music had become corrupted by complex polyphonic devices that obscured the text and diverted attention from the act of worship. To remedy this situation, the Council called for a return to a simpler vocal style, one that would preserve the sanctity of the text and discourage displays of virtuosity by singers. In addition to this, the council objected to the use of loud instruments such as sacbuts (early trombones) in indoor church services and banned all secular melodies from the composition of Masses. They also decided to continue to perform their services in Latin instead of changing to the vernacular, as the Protestant churches had done.

Legend has it that in order to prevent the Council from abolishing the polyphonic style entirely, Palestrina composed a Mass of such beauty and simplicity that he was able to dissuade the cardinals from taking this drastic step. Palestrina composed many other Masses that are equally beautiful, and we don't know exactly how close the Council was to abandoning polyphony, but the story is that this particular Mass, *Pope Marcellus Mass* (1567), saved polyphony for the Roman Catholic Church. You will hear the Kyrie from that Mass in class. The Kyrie is the only section of the traditional Mass that is written not in Latin but in Greek. The Kyrie is Greek. The text and translation are given in the following Listening Guide.

Listening Guide

"Kyrie" ("Lord") from *Missa Papae Marcelli* (the *Pope Marcellus Mass*)

GIOVANNI PIERLUIGI DA PALESTRINA

CD 3	Year: 1567
Tracks 2–4	Texture: Polyphonic a cappella voices
	Meter: Duple, but with little accent on the beats. It flows much like medieval chant.
	Voices: Six (soprano, alto, two tenors, and two basses)
	Duration: 4:33

	Timing	Greek text	English translation
2	0:00	Kyrie eleison.	Lord, have mercy upon us.
3	1:32	Christe eleison.	Christ, have mercy upon us.
4	3:17	Kyrie eleison.	Lord, have mercy upon us.

As you listen to the Kyrie, notice that it sounds thicker and fuller than Josquin's "Ave Maria." The reason is that Palestrina used six, instead of four, voices. The six parts are also particularly heavy on the low voices, with parts for one soprano, one alto, two tenors, and two basses. Something you might notice about the text is that it is in three sections, representing the Trinity.

Renaissance Secular Music

In addition to being a time of great piety, the sixteenth century was also a period of bawdy earthiness, irreverent humor, and celebration of sensual love. The same composers who created works "for the greater glory of God" also wrote compositions of this character. In Italy and England, the principal form of secular vocal music was the **madrigal;** in France, it was the **chanson;** in Germany, the **lied.**

The Madrigal in Italy

The Renaissance madrigal is a poem set to music. It had its beginnings in the fourteenth century among the aristocrats of the small Italian courts. The texts, written in the vernacular, were often twelve-line poems whose subjects were sentimental or erotic. The early madrigal was written in a predominantly homophonic style. It was usually in three, but sometimes four, parts, and its expressive qualities were subdued and restrained. The madrigal of the mid-sixteenth century was written usually for five and sometimes for four or six voices. Its texture was more polyphonic than that of the early madrigal, and a greater attempt was made to capture in the music the expressive possibilities of the words.

The final flowering of the madrigal took place during the closing decades of the sixteenth century. The late madrigal was an elaborate composition, invariably not strophic, with a mixture of homophonic and polyphonic textures. It used chromaticism (the inclusion of notes that create tension through the use of dissonance) for bold effects, often to express sadness. The compositions also used coloristic and dramatic effects. One of the most interesting elements of the madrigal style was **word painting,** which meant that the melody was written to represent the literal meaning of the text being sung. For example, on the word *heaven,* the melody would ascend, or on the word *water,* it would rise and fall in a wavelike motion. On the word *death,* the music might become very chromatic, creating dissonance and tension.

Many Italian composers wrote madrigals, not the least of whom was **Claudio Monteverdi** (1567–1643), who published eight books of madrigals. Monteverdi was an active composer of the late Renaissance who changed his style to that of the next period, the baroque, in approximately 1600. His early madrigal books are wonderful examples of the madrigal of the Italian Renaissance, and his late ones represent the new style. We will study Monteverdi as an early opera composer in the next chapter. Other major Italian madrigal composers include Adrian Willaert, Carlo Gesualdo, and Luca Marenzio. "The Live Experience: Madrigal Singing in Homes" discusses the use of this form of music in personal life.

As was said earlier, there were many fewer women composers during the Renaissance than men, but one deserves mention here. Maddalena Casulana was one of the first women composers to consider herself a professional musician. She was an active singer, lutenist, and music teacher who composed and published three volumes of madrigals in addition to other individual works. Her books were so popular that the first was reprinted twice. The dedication in her first book says "to show the world . . . the futile error of men who believe themselves patrons of the high gifts of intellect, which according to them cannot also be held in the same way by women." She must have been quite a feminist for her time.

Songs accompanied by the lute was also a popular form of entertainment during the Renaissance.

The Madrigal in England

Around the middle of the sixteenth century, the Italian madrigal was brought to England. There it flourished under a variety of names in addition to *madrigal: song, sonnet, canzonet,* and *ayre.* William Byrd (1543–1623) and his student

THE LIVE EXPERIENCE
Madrigal Singing in Homes

The invention of movable type made printed music readily available to people outside of the church. Given that the Renaissance took place hundreds of years before the invention of radios or televisions, people could have music in their lives only if they played or sang it themselves, hired people to entertain them, or went out to a place where music was performed. It became a standard part of a good education for people to learn to **sight sing** from music notation or to play an instrument. In England, books of madrigals were often handed out to people after dinner in expectation that all would participate in singing the madrigals. The madrigal composer Thomas Morley told of this practice in his *Plaine and Easie Introduction to Practicall Musicke,* first published in 1597: "But supper being ended and music books (according to the custom) being brought to the table, the mistress of the house presented me with a part earnestly requesting me to sing; but when, after many excuses, I protested unfeignedly that I could not, everyone began to wonder; yea, some whispered to others demanding how I was brought up." The story might well be one that Morley made up in order to encourage more

people to buy and sing his music, but the practice of group singing after dinner was very common in wealthy, noble, and royal households, including those of King Henry VIII and his daughter, Queen Elizabeth I.

Today, re-creations of the Renaissance practice of singing around the dinner table have become increasingly popular, usually around Christmastime. Early music societies, churches, or schools sometimes put on "madrigal dinners," in which a madrigal group dressed in Renaissance costumes sits at the "royal" table in the front of the dining room and the guests are served dinner while being entertained by the singing. In more elaborate dinners of this type, the entertainment will also include actors, jugglers, dancers, or other types of performers. Attending the dinners can be lots of fun for the guests who, today, are not generally required to participate in the singing. Many of the places that put on such meals do so for fund-raising purposes and advertise through local newspaper ads or even on the Internet. To find one on the Internet, you can type "madrigal dinner" and your city and state, and treat yourself to an evening in the Renaissance.

Thomas Morley were the first English composers to cultivate the genre. Morley wrote simplified versions of the madrigal, known as **balletts.** Adapted from the Italian *balletti,* they were usually characterized by a *fa-la-la* refrain of the type that appears in the English carol "Deck the Halls." Enlivened by accents and a regular beat, the music was largely homophonic.

The madrigal "Fair Phyllis" was composed by **John Farmer.** Not a lot is known about Farmer's life. His birthplace and year are not known for certain, but around 1595 he was employed as an organist and choral director of Holy Trinity (now Christ Church) Cathedral in Dublin, Ireland. He was in London by 1600 and is assumed to have spent the rest of his life there. He is best known for his four-part settings of biblical texts from the Psalms and also for his four-part madrigals. Listen to the piece, then see "Hearing the Difference: Josquin's 'Ave Maria' and Farmer's 'Fair Phyllis.'"

Listening Guide

"Fair Phyllis" JOHN FARMER

CD 1
Track 8

Year: 1599

Texture: Mostly polyphonic with a homophonic ending

Number of voices: Four

Meter: Duple

Timing: 1:52

Text	**Examples of word painting**
Fair Phyllis I saw sitting all alone,	Sopranos sing this line alone.
Feeding her flock near to the mountainside.	More voices join as Phyllis is joined by her flock.
The shepherds knew not whither she was gone,	Polyphonic texture as if singers were looking for her.
But after her lover Amyntas hied.	
Up and down he wandered whilst she was missing;	"Up" is sung to higher notes than "down."
When he found her, O then they fell a-kissing.	Homophonic texture as the two lovers kiss.

The Chanson in France

In the sixteenth century, the *chanson* (the French word for "song") was to France what the madrigal was to Italy and England. Chansons modified the motet style with strong accented rhythms, frequent repetitions, and short phrases ending simultaneously in all parts. They were usually sung by three, four, or five voices, and sections of simple imitation alternated with sections that were essentially homophonic. Word painting occurred frequently in the early chansons, as it had in madrigals.

The Lied in Germany

In Germany, the counterpart to the French chanson was the *lied,* also meaning "song." The lied (plural, *lieder*) dates from the middle of the fifteenth century, when both monophonic melodies and three-part settings appeared. The early lieder, which were heavily influenced by the Netherlands' polyphonic style, later provided the Lutheran Church with many melodies for **chorale** tunes (sacred songs).

In the sixteenth century, Germany looked to Italy and France for musicians to staff its courts and municipalities. As a result, lieder composers began to write in a style more typical of the chanson and madrigal, with various melodies set in imitative counterpoint.

Renaissance Instrumental Music

Although most of the music of the Renaissance was written for voices, the role of instrumental music should not be underestimated. Instruments were used in church, at many festive and social occasions, as part of theatrical productions, and in private homes.

The earliest music played on instruments was sacred or secular vocal music. During the Renaissance, some music was written specifically for instruments. Most of it was dance music, because dancing was an important part of Renaissance social life. A fairly large collection of this music has been preserved, but apparently much of it was improvised on well-known tunes or harmonic bass patterns, as jazz is today.

HEARING THE DIFFERENCE
Josquin's "Ave Maria" and Farmer's "Fair Phyllis"

So far, we have studied three pieces of music from the Renaissance. In order to take notice of some basic differences between sacred and secular music of the era, we will now listen to and compare one of the sacred works, Josquin's "Ave Maria," with the secular one, Farmer's "Fair Phyllis." In both recordings we will hear mostly syllabic text setting and a cappella singing (no instrumental accompaniment). Listen again to these two compositions, back to back, and see if you can discern the following differences:

	"Ave Maria"	**"Fair Phyllis"**
Type and mood	A sacred motet sung in a serious and gentle mood	A secular song about love sung in a playful spirit
Language	Latin, the language of the church	English, the everyday language
Texture	Mostly polyphonic, with some homophonic sections	Begins monophonic, but becomes mostly polyphonic, with a homophonic ending
Meter	Duple with one section in triple meter	Duple throughout
Performance situation	Performed in a church or other religious setting. For that reason, the four vocal parts would all have been sung by men.	Performed in a noble or royal household, probably by family members after dinner. The highest two parts would have been sung by women, since there was no restriction against women singing in their own homes, and the lowest two parts would have been sung by men.

The most popular instrument of the 1400s and 1500s was the lute, a plucked string instrument with a bowl-shaped body and fingerboard. The earliest lute music consisted of transcriptions (a **transcription** is an arrangement of a composition for a medium other than that for which it was originally written) of vocal pieces and dance music, but in the sixteenth century, composers began to write original pieces for the lute. These *ricercari,* or **fantasias,** were elaborate polyphonic pieces that demonstrated the virtuosity of the performer, who was often also the composer. Beginning in the early sixteenth century, volumes of solo music for the lute were published in Italy, France, Germany, England, and Spain.

Keyboard instruments, especially the clavichord, harpsichord, and organ, were also popular during the Renaissance. Keyboard music evolved through the same phases as lute music, from vocal music to dance music and then to original compositions that, in some cases, were quite complex.

Small chamber music ensembles, called *consorts,* were favored among those who performed music in their homes. When the consort was made up of all instruments of the same family, it was called a whole consort. Whole consorts could be made up of viols (bowed stringed instruments) or woodwind instruments,

A lutenist accompanying dancers, illustrated in Book of Hours, Tours, France, 1530–1535.

such as recorders. Sometimes consorts would include a mixture of instruments of different types. Those consorts were called broken consorts. Music for brass and reed instruments was popular for outdoor occasions, for festive church ceremonies, and for dancing.

We will listen to three dances composed by **Michael Praetorius** (1572–1621), a German composer of the late Renaissance. Although Praetorius began his musical career as a church organist and organ consultant, he moved on to become a court musician for a duke in Wolfenbūttel, near Braunschweig, Germany. In addition to working at the duke's court, he also composed for and conducted a variety of musical ensembles in other parts of Germany. His works include many settings of Lutheran chorales, including some large-scale polychoral works. These ballets were published in a set of 312 dances called *Terpsichore* (1612). Although this set of dances was composed when the next style period in music history, the Baroque, was beginning in Italy, the collection of dances is very Renaissance in style.

Listening Guide

Three Dances from *Terpsichore* MICHAEL PRAETORIUS

CD 1
Tracks 9–12

Year: 1612

Texture: Polyphonic

Meter: Duple

Number of voices: Four melodic instrumental lines plus percussion

Duration: 3:16

	Timing	Dance	Instrumentation
9	0:00	Ballet des Baccanales	SATB recorders, lute, and tambourine
10	1:26	Ballet des Feus	SATB brass instruments and drum
11	2:06	Ballet des Matelotz	SATB bowed string instruments with low brass and drum
12	2:37	Ballet des Matelotz	**Tutti** (all instruments in the ensemble)

T H E   L I V E   E X P E R I E N C E
Renaissance Dances

It was as important for an educated person of the Renaissance to be able to dance as it was for him or her to be able to sing, because dancing was a popular social activity. Many books were published giving information about dance steps and proper behavior for dancing. In 1594 a German writer, Johann von Munster, wrote:

> Once the order for the dance has been given to the wind and string players the dancer comes forward in a splendid, graceful, delightful and superb manner and chooses from amongst the ladies and girls present a partner for whom he feels particular affection, and asks her, with a bow, removing his hat, kissing her hands, bending his knee, with kind words and other ceremonies, if she is willing to share a

happy and honest dance with him. Once her consent is obtained, both move forward holding hands and kissing each other—even on the mouth—and demonstrate mutual friendship by words and gestures. Then when they reach the dance, they begin with a certain gravity, without that disturbing agitation which is permitted in the second part of the dance, where more freedom is allowed. Conversation is best employed during the first part of the dance than in the second, where tight hand holding, secret taps, jumps, peasant screams and other improper things take place. Once the dance is over, the dancer escorts his partner back to her place and, with a bow, he either takes his leave of her or else he sits on her lap and talks to her.

A set of dances like the one we just heard would have been played and danced to at a royal court such as the one at which Praetorius was employed. Renaissance musicians generally **embellished** (added to or changed notes of the melody) the music when they repeated any section, allowing the composition to be extended without sounding too repetitious to the dancers. "The Live Experience: Renaissance Dances" illustrates how these dances were performed.

Summary

Sacred music of the Renaissance was primarily vocal, polyphonic with occasional homophonic sections of pieces, and performed a cappella. Motets and movements of the Mass Ordinary were the primary types of compositions performed in the churches. With the exception of the Kyrie, which was in Greek, the language of the Roman Catholic Church and of sacred works written for it continued to be Latin. Protestant churches broke away from that tradition and used the vernacular.

Secular music became very popular for performance in noble, royal, or other wealthy and educated people's homes during the Renaissance.

Secular music was sung in the vernacular so that the fun and sometimes quite bawdy texts could be appreciated by the singers. Common secular forms were the madrigal in Italy and England, the chanson in France, and the lied in Germany.

Instrumental music of the Renaissance evolved from vocal music to dance music and then to more complex original compositions. The most popular Renaissance instrument was the lute, with keyboard music and chamber consorts also coming into use. Dancing was an important social activity, providing musicians with steady employment at the homes and palaces of the wealthy.

New People and Concepts

a cappella	embellished	Michael Praetorius
balletts	fantasia	madrigal
chanson	Giovanni Pierluigi da Palestrina	Protestantism
chorale	imitation	sight sing
Claudio Monteverdi	John Farmer	transcription
Council of Trent	Josquin des Prez	tutti
Counter-Reformation	lied	word painting

Finale

Listen again to the recording of Josquin des Prez's "Ave Maria" and compare your impressions now with your notes from your first listening. Do you hear more now than you did before? You should now be able to answer the following questions:

▌ What is the meter?

▌ What is the situation in which the piece would have originally been performed?

▌ How many singers would be necessary to sing the piece?

▌ What is the texture and when does it change?

▌ What is the song about?

Characteristics of Renaissance Music

Texture	Mostly polyphonic
Tonality	Church modes
Rhythm	Measured
Singing style	Four-part singing common, some virtuoso singing; late madrigal and chanson used word painting
Large vocal works	Polyphonic Mass
Small vocal works	Motet, madrigal, chanson, lied
Musical instruments	Whole and broken consorts, solo instrumental works
Instrumental music	Ricercari, fantasias, dances

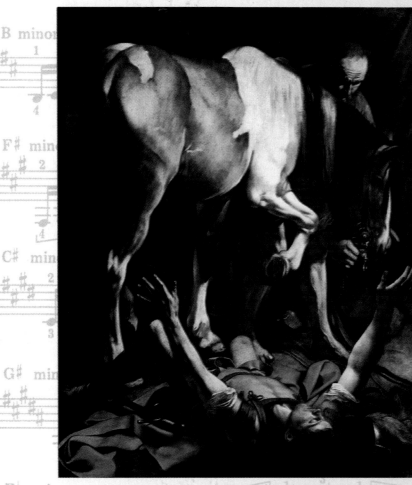

The Conversion of St. Paul by **Caravaggio (1573–1610).**
This dramatic painting shows the stark contrasts between dark and light that are common in much baroque art.

The early baroque period is best reflected in Italian art and shows the recovery of the Roman Catholic Church after the Protestant challenge of the sixteenth century. As part of the Counter-Reformation, the Catholic Church had reexamined its rituals and established the Jesuit order as an international force for teaching, missionary work, reconversion, and protection of the faith. By the seventeenth century, those efforts had paid dividends: Most of Europe remained bound to Catholicism and Rome.

After 1600, the arts were used by the Italians to celebrate the power and glory of the church. New churches and palaces were decorated with rich gilding and ornamentation. Rome became an unparalleled cultural center where artists from many different countries came to admire the classical ruins and modern wonders of the city. Pilgrims and noblemen visited Rome and returned home with marvelous tales of "the first city of the world." The new Roman style rapidly spread to the rest of Europe and became international.

Style changes were generally reflected in all of the arts. The rich gilding and ornamentation that decorated churches and palaces were reflected in paintings and sculpture through very active and dramatic scenes and figures. Baroque music often has a fairly constant sense of motion and much melodic decoration, with the addition of ornaments such as trills

Prelude | The Triumph of the Baroque Style

(two notes played back and forth very quickly). Stark contrasts between light and dark in paintings are common in much baroque art. In music, we will also hear dramatic contrasts between dynamic levels, in which one musical phrase will be played loud, followed by another that is much softer, almost like an echo of the first.

We can see these striking contrasts between light and shadow, as well as vigorous action and realism, in Caravaggio's (1573–1610) painting *The Conversion of St. Paul* (1600–1601). The biblical story shown is that of Saul of Tarsus, who had been a Christian persecutor but who was instantly converted to Christianity on the road to Damascus by a vision of Jesus that temporarily blinded him. The painting captures the very moment of the blinding and conversion, which is typical of the type of action seen in much baroque art.

Of course, there are many other artists whose works display similar activity and contrast. The sculptor Gianlorenzo Bernini's (1598–1680) *David Slaying Goliath* (1623) serves as a good example of baroque style when compared with Michelangelo's depiction of the same biblical personality (see page 47). David was the young future king of Israel (ca. 1000–ca. 960 BCE), who used a slingshot to slay a Philistine giant named Goliath who had challenged the Jews. Bernini's *David* is seen in the actual act of throwing the stone, whereas Michelangelo's

sculpture shows a more sedate, relaxed pose. Neither sculpture is more religious nor more representative of the story than the other. They are just concentrated on different times in the story, chosen by the popular style of the period.

Music continued to play an important role in the life of the churches, as it had in the Renaissance. Sounds, perhaps more than the visual arts, could move, elevate, and involve a congregation and thus intensify the spiritual experience. Whereas Protestants were skeptical of visual displays and the veneration of images, they warmed to the use of music in church services. In the seventeenth century, major Protestant churches began to form orchestras and choirs, to have large organs built for their churches, and to hire organists, soloists, and music masters. The greatest baroque church musician was Johann Sebastian Bach, who spent a major part of his career at Leipzig, leaving a vast treasure of sacred music, vocal and instrumental, at the time of his death in 1750.

The concentration of baroque art and architecture was not exclusively religious. In France monumental art was used to enhance the position of Louis XIV and his court. The efforts of architects, stonemasons, sculptors, painters, furniture makers, and gardeners were carefully coordinated to remake the royal palace at Versailles in the

***David Slaying Goliath* by Bernini (1598–1680).** This sculpture shows the kind of activity often portrayed in baroque art.

latter half of the seventeenth century. By 1700, a visitor to Paris would have been overwhelmed by French monuments to the power of the Crown. In the eighteenth century, Paris replaced Rome as the leader in European culture and design.

The grandness of baroque style reflected the tastes of the church and the ruling class. Most people were, of course, farmers who never even saw the great cities of Rome or Paris. In the cities lived many workers and artisans who constructed and decorated the great

Peasant Family **by Louis Le Nain (1603–1648).** The Louvre, Paris. Most peasants worked many hours just to live and had no way of appreciating the grandness of baroque style.

He Revels from ***The Rake's Progress*** **by William Hogarth (1697–1764).** Well-to-do nobles and merchants enjoyed public gatherings such as the one portrayed in this painting.

monuments of the period. The average worker worked about sixteen hours a day, six days a week, and families looked much like the one depicted in the painting *Peasant Family* by Louis Le Nain. Entertainment for the lower classes included visits to alehouses, where musicians, storytellers, and gambling were available. Some common spectator sports such as cockfighting were very violent and bloody. Stealing, swindling, and murder were common and were punished by whipping, branding, having a body part cut off, or death.

There was not a very large middle class, but there were well-to-do nobles and merchants who had much better lives than the poor workers. They enjoyed hunting, gambling, and various types of ball and board games, as did the aristocracy. Educated people learned to play musical instruments or sing, and enjoyed performing with or for friends in their homes. Public entertainments such as plays, balls, and masques (skits based on allegorical stories performed with elaborate staging and costumes) were popular. An engraving of *He Revels (The Orgy)* from the series *The Rake's Progress,* 1735, by William Hogarth displays some of this type of lifestyle. Opera, eventually, was added to the list of possibilities for entertainment for those who could afford to attend. By the baroque period, the New World products of coffee, chocolate, and tobacco were easily available and enjoyed by the noble and royal classes, although they were still unavailable to the average person.

Marriages were still arranged by parents, and there was little chance of ending a marriage. Even separations were next to impossible because the running of a home absolutely required people in both roles of husband and wife. Yet romantic affairs were common and accepted for the upper classes.

As was the case for the music we studied from the medieval and Renaissance periods, the music that is available for us to study was composed for and played by or for the upper and royal classes. The types of songs and dances that were enjoyed in the alehouses or other types of street entertainments were not usually notated in music notation, and we can only guess what they sounded like. We begin our study of baroque music with opera, one of the grandest of the arts and one that was born at the beginning of the baroque period.

6 | Baroque Opera

An opera begins long before the curtain goes up and ends long after it has come down. It starts in my imagination, it becomes my life, and it stays part of my life long after I've left the opera house.

—OPERA SINGER MARIA CALLAS (1923–1977)

Listening Introduction

Listen to the example of music that represents this chapter, "When I am laid in earth," and make notes about what you hear. Give some attention to the following:

▌ Can you detect the meter?

▌ Can you tell the number and gender of the singer(s)?

▌ Can you tell what instruments are used to play the accompaniment?

▌ Can you hear a repeated melody in the bass?

▌ Can you identify the language of the text?

▌ Does the piece have a general mood that supports the meaning of the text?

Keep these notes to compare with your impressions about the music after you study the information in this chapter.

The Birth of Opera

A whole new relationship between words and music began in Florence, Italy, around 1600. A group of scholars and musicians calling themselves the *camerata* (Italian for "a society of friends") sought to recapture the spirit of Greek drama by writing melodies for the actors to sing as they played their dramatic roles. Greek scholars today are certain that the actors of ancient Greece did not sing their roles, but it is a wonderful accident of history that the camerata thought that they might have, because their sung dramas developed into the grand art of **opera.** Because the words of the plays had to be clearly understood by audiences, a new vocal style called **monody** was born. In monody, a solo singer provided the predominant sound. The rhythmic flow of the singer's melody followed the accented patterns the text would have if it were spoken. The singer was accompanied by harmonies played by a combination of instruments called **basso continuo.** Monodic texture is homophonic because it includes only a single prevailing melody with accompaniment.

Basso continuo literally means "continuous bass," but it was really more than that. The composer wrote a bass line with a kind of musical shorthand, called **figured bass,** under some of the notes. The notes of the bass line, along

The Royal Theater in Turin, Italy, was a showcase for baroque opera, like the one being performed in this painting.

with the shorthand, told a player of a chordal instrument such as a lute, a harpsi-chord, or an organ what chords to play and improvise on to provide a simple accompaniment to the vocal line. The bass line was also played by a melodic bass instrument such as a cello or bassoon.

Although the basso continuo (or simply **continuo**) originated to accompany singer/actors in early baroque operas, it came to be applied to virtually all music throughout the period, both vocal and instrumental. So prevalent was the continuo practice that the baroque period was later nicknamed the "continuo period."

Chapter 6 Activity

Monody and Basso Continuo

Baroque Vocal Styles

Recitative is a kind of combination of singing and speech that served as dialogue in baroque operas and other related works. Like monody, its musical rhythm was flexible and dictated by the natural inflection of the words. The tempo was slowed down or speeded up according to the singer's interpretation of the text.

When it was accompanied by basso continuo instruments alone, it was called *secco recitative* ("dry" singing). In some more dramatic situations, recitative singing could be accompanied by continuo, along with other instruments, even a small orchestra, in which case it was called *accompanied recitative.* In either case, recitative was intended to be clear to allow audiences to understand the text.

A more lyrical style of singing in early operas was that of the **arioso,** which was a more melodic and expressive type of recitative. The **aria** was an expansion of arioso-styled singing. Very early baroque operas were all or mostly recitative, but once the aria developed, it became the focal point of vocal expressiveness. Arias were usually composed to be able to stand apart from the story of the operas as complete songs. They were often symmetrically balanced in a three-part form, ABA. The first section is represented by the letter A, the B represents a contrasting section, and the return of A indicates that the singer ends the aria by repeating the first section. An aria in this form is called a **da capo aria** because the words *da capo,* which mean "the head" in Italian, are written into the music to tell the singer to repeat the beginning (head) section of music. Singers usually embellished the repeated "A" section in order to display their vocal skills.

When the story of an opera included a group of people, such as citizens of the town in which the action was taking place, the opera included a **chorus,** or group of singers. Composers tended to handle texts differently for choruses than they did for solo singers because it was more difficult for audiences to understand the words when they were sung by several singers together. For that reason, operatic choral singing is much more homophonic in texture than was typical for much Renaissance group vocal music. Operatic choral texts also had more repetition of important sections of words than was common in earlier music. Again, the primary goal was to be understood by the audience. "The Live Experience: Opera Singers of the Baroque" discusses some of the types of performers who sang in operas.

The earliest surviving opera was written by a member of the camerata named Jacopo Peri (1561–1633), whose *Eurydice* dates from the year 1600. Based on the Greek legend of Orpheus and Eurydice, it consists almost entirely of secco recitative. In accordance with the principles of the camerata, Peri wrote in the foreword to his opera that its style was intended to "imitate speech in song." The development of the arioso and aria made operatic singing more expressive than secco recitative and contributed to the expanding popularity of opera.

The first woman known to have composed an opera, Francesca Caccini, might have performed in Peri's *Eurydice,* as did her father, Giulio Caccini. In addition to being a talented singer, Francesca played the harpsichord and the lute and became a court composer for the Medici family in seventeenth-century Florence. The opera for which she is best known is *La Liberazione di Ruggiero* (1625). The Medici family had her compose the opera to be performed for the visiting Prince Wladislaw Zygmunt of Poland. The prince enjoyed its performance so much that he took a copy of it back to Poland with him and had it translated into Polish and performed there. It is famous for being the first opera to be performed outside of Italy.

Claudio Monteverdi

Claudio Monteverdi

The first master of operatic composition was the Italian Claudio Monteverdi (1567–1643). Monteverdi's life spanned across the change of style from the Renaissance into the baroque. His early madrigals are wonderful examples of

THE LIVE EXPERIENCE
Opera Singers of the Baroque

Because operas were dramatic works, they generally told stories that included roles for both men and women. In earlier times, it had not been thought appropriate for women to perform for the general public, but by the baroque period, most of Europe had dropped that restriction, allowing women to sing female operatic roles. In some parts of Italy and a few other areas of the continent, however, it was still not considered respectable for a woman to perform in public situations. In those places, female roles were sung by high-voiced male singers known as *castrati.*

A **castrato** was a man who was castrated before puberty. When the castrato grew up, his voice did not change to a lower pitch, and yet it did mature. The castrato voice was, therefore, high, clear, and strong. The castrato voice was commonly heard in churches, where no women were allowed to sing and the castrato's strength was needed to balance with men on the lower musical parts. When opera began, castrati were used not only for female roles in places that did not allow women singers but also, commonly, for heroic male roles. In some cases a castrato could become an international star. The most famous castrato was Carlo Broschi (1705–1782), known as **Farinelli.** A film, *Farinelli,* was made about his life in 1994. The film director kept his speaking voice that of a "normal sounding" man, then electronically combined the voices of a female soprano and a boy to create his singing voice. The real Farinelli would have had a high speaking, as well as a high singing, voice. The film drama-tized Farinelli's operatic career from his begin-nings in Italy through his stardom in England. The English did not approve of the Italian practice of castration, but they were willing to hire and enjoy some of the best of the Italian castrati who traveled to England.

After women became more accepted as performers and noncastrated men with tenor

Farinelli (Carlo Broschi) was the most famous castrato.

voices were accepted in heroic operatic roles, castrati were still hired by the Roman Catholic Church in Rome to sing sacred works in the church. The last castrato was named Alessandro Moreschi (1858–1922). He was actually recorded in 1902 and 1904, but his vocal style was not operatic, so it gives us little clue as to what Farinelli or other popular castrati of the baroque period sounded like.

The practice of using castrati in baroque operas creates a problem for modern-day productions. With no castrati around, either female sopranos or

continued

men who have specially trained themselves to sing high, called **counter tenors,** sing the heroic roles that were composed for castrati. Sometimes directors attempt to rewrite the music so that a normal-voiced tenor or baritone can sing it. A major problem is that when the singer taking the lowered castrato part has to sing with another singer, the other part must also be changed. The result is a far from accurate performance.

Even with the problems involved in producing a modern performance of a baroque opera, some opera companies occasionally attempt them. George Frideric Handel, whom we will study as the composer of the **oratorio** *Messiah,* composed some wonderful operas while he was in London, and some of those have had modern performances.

Chapter 6
Activity

Sopranos and
Counter tenors

music in the Italian Renaissance. His operas, however, represent the new style of the baroque. Monteverdi's treatment of the legend of Orpheus and Eurydice, *Orfeo* (Italian for Orpheus), marks the beginning of opera as a major art form. First performed in Mantua in 1607, *Orfeo* had elaborate costuming, staging, and lighting, an instrumental ensemble of forty players, and a chorus of singers and dancers.

In the Greek legend of Orpheus and Eurydice (Orfeo and Euridice, in Italian), a messenger approaches Orpheus to give him the sad news that his wife, Eurydice, died from a snake bite while avoiding the advances of another man. Devastated by the news, Orpheus made his way into the underworld to find Eurydice and bring her back to life. His beautiful playing of a lyre convinced the king of the underworld to allow Eurydice to follow Orpheus back to the upper world if he would trust that she was following him and not look back at her until they were out. Orpheus made the mistake of looking back, and as a result Eurydice returned to the world of the dead. When back in the upper world, Orpheus refused to have anything to do with other women. He must have been quite attractive, because the women were so upset that he ignored them that they actually tore his body to pieces. His body parts were buried at the foot of Mt. Olympus, and his head was thrown into the sea, where it floated to Lesbos and became an oracle (fortune teller).

The **libretto** (text) for Monteverdi's *Orfeo* changed the Greek legend to be more suitable for the Christian beliefs of his time. The opera began with Orfeo and Euridice singing of their love for one another. Later, Orfeo received a messenger, who told him that Euridice died from a snakebite while out picking flowers. Orfeo had to have God's help to be able to enter the world of the dead, where he was finally able to get permission to bring his wife back to life. The condition of not looking back at her was given and, as in the Greek version of the story, he did just that and lost her as a result. To create a happy ending, Monteverdi's Orfeo then called on his divine father, Apollo, who allowed Orfeo to ascend into heaven, where he could see Euridice for eternity.

Many librettists have changed opera plots to fit the tastes of their audiences. In a later version of *Orfeo* by Christoph Willibald Gluck (1714–1787), Orfeo was completely forgiven for looking back, and Euridice returned to a happy life with her husband.

An excerpt from Monteverdi's *Orfeo* follows. This is a section from Act 2 in which Orfeo receives the news of Euridice's death and vows to go into the underworld to get her back.

Listening Guide

Excerpt from Act 2 of *Orfeo* CLAUDIO MONTEVERDI

CD 3
Track 5

Year: 1607

Texture: Homophonic

Instrumentation: Solo voice with continuo that includes
   harpsichord, a small organ, chitarrone (a large, lute-like plucked
   string instrument with a finger board), cello, and viola da gamba.

Meter: Nonmetric recitative

Voices: One messenger (a soprano), three shepherds (one
   countertenor and two tenors), and Orfeo (a tenor)

Duration: 7:57

Timing	Italian text	English translation
	MESSAGGIERA	MESSENGER
0:00	A te ne vengo, Orfeo,	I come to you, Orpheus,
	Messaggiera infelice	unhappy messenger
	Di caso più infelice e più funesto.	of a happening more unhappy and more dreadful.
	La tua bella Euridice . . .	Your fair Eurydice . . .
	ORFEO	ORPHEUS
0:30	Ohimè che odo?	Alas, what do I hear?
	MESSAGGIERA	MESSENGER
0:39	La tua diletta sposa è morta.	Your beloved bride is dead.
	ORFEO	ORPHEUS
0:52	Ohimè!	Alas!
	MESSAGGIERA	MESSENGER
1:00	In un fiorito prato	In a flowery meadow
	Con l'altre sue compagne	with her other companions
	Giva cogliendo fiori	she went picking flowers
	Per farne una ghirlanda alle sue chiome;	to make a garland for her hair,
	Quand'angue insidioso,	when a deceitful snake
	Ch'era fra l'erbe asconso,	that was hidden in the grass,
	Le punse un piè con velenoso dente.	bit her foot with poisoned fang.
	Ed ecco immantinente	And lo immediately
	Scolorirsi il bel viso e ne' suoi lumi	her fair face grew pale and in her eyes
	Sparir que' lampi, ond'ella al sol fea scorno.	that light that outshone the sun faded.
	Allor, noi tutte sbigottite e meste,	Then we all, appalled and sorrowing,
	Le fummo intorno, richiamar tentando	gathered round her, trying to recall
	Gli spiriti in lei smarriti	her spirits that grew faint,
	Con l'onda fresca e co' possenti carmi,	with fresh water and with powerful charms,
	Ma nulla valse, ahi lassa,	but to no avail, ah alas,
	Ch'ella i languidi lumi alquanto aprendo	for she opened her failing eyes a little,
	E te chiamando, Orfeo,	and calling you, Orpheus,

continued

Timing	Italian text	English translation
	Dopo un grave sospiro	after a deep sigh,
	Spirò fra queste braccia; ed io rimasi	she died in these arms; and I remained,
	Piena il cor di pietrade e di spavento.	my heart full of pity and of fear.
	PASTORE	SHEPHERD
4:00	Ahi, caso acerbo, ahi, fato empio e crudele,	Ah, bitter mischance, ah, wicked, cruel fate,
	Ahi, stelle ingiuriose, ahi, ciel avaro.	Ah, hurtful stars, ah, envious heaven!
	PASTORE	SHEPHERD
4:30	A l'amara novella	At the bitter news
	Rassembra l'infelice un muto sasso	the unhappy man seems like a speechless rock
	Che per troppo dolor non può dolersi.	And through too much grief cannot grieve.
	PASTORE	SHEPHERD
4:52	Ahi, ben havrebbe un cor di tigre o d'orsa	Ah, he would have the heart of a tiger or bear
	Chi non sentisse del tuo mal pietae	that did not feel pity at your misfortune,
	Privo d'ogni tuo ben, misero amante.	deprived of every happiness, wretched lover.
	ORFEO	ORPHEUS
5:20	Tu se' morta, mia vita, ed io respiro?	You are dead, my life, and do I breathe?
	Tu se' da me partita	You are gone from me
	Per mai più non torrare, ed io rimango?	never to return, and do I remain?
	No, che se i versi alcuna cosa ponno,	No, for if my verses can do anything,
	N'andrò sicuro a' più profondi abissi,	I will go surely to the deepest abysses,
	E, intenerito il cor del re de l'ombre,	and, having softened the heart of the King of Shades,
	Meco trarrotti a riveder le stelle:	I will bring her back to see again the stars:
	O, se ciò negherammi empio destino,	Oh, if wicked destiny refuses me this,
	Rimarrò teco, in compagnia di morte.	I will stay with you in the company of death.
	Addio, terra, addio cielo e sole, addio.	Farewell earth, farewell heaven and sun, farewell.

As was the case with *Orfeo*, baroque operas were generally based on Greek legends or, in some cases, Roman history. It was thought that opera was such a grand art form that it should not be wasted on stories of contemporary lifestyles or events. The earliest operas were performed for gatherings of aristocrats, but the appeal of music and drama together was so great that by 1637 public opera houses were built, and operas became a popular form of entertainment for the middle class, as well as aristocrats.

Opera Outside of Italy

During the baroque period, the popularity of opera spread throughout Europe. Because of the need for audiences to understand the text, operas were often composed in the vernacular, although there are many examples of operas being composed and performed in Italian outside of Italy. The English composer **Henry Purcell** (1659–1695) based his opera *Dido and Aeneas* on a Roman legend adapted from the first and fourth books of Virgil's epic poem, *Aeneid* (19 BCE).

English composer Henry Purcell

The plot of the opera was based fairly closely on the original story, which likely would have been familiar to educated people of Purcell's time. The story of the opera opened at the royal palace of Carthage, where the widowed queen, Dido, expressed her love for the Trojan hero, Aeneas, who has been shipwrecked on her shore. Aeneas returned her love, but could not stay in Carthage with Dido because he was destined to sail on to Italy, where he was to become the founder of the great city of Rome. A fire had been built on the shore to help Aeneas and his sailors see their way out of the harbor. As he left, Dido stood by the fire and sang her funeral song, "When I am laid in earth," after which she threw herself into the flames. The opera ended with the singing of a chorus of cupids who came down from the sky to spread roses on Dido's body.

Listening Guide

"When I am laid in earth" from *Dido and Aeneas* HENRY PURCELL

CD 1
Track 13

Year: 1689

Texture: Homophonic

Meter: Triple

Form: Binary (AABB)

Voices: One female singer accompanied by four bowed
    stringed instruments

Language: English

Duration: 3:54

Special feature: A five-measure **ground bass** line is played
    alone at the beginning and repeats throughout the aria.
    Dido sings her first note when the last note of the ground
    bass is played. The ground bass line is played nine times
    before and during Dido's aria and then repeats two more
    times during the instrumental closing.

Text

[13]   When I am laid, am laid in earth,
    May my wrongs create no trouble, no trouble in thy breast.
    (repeat)
    Remember me! Remember me! But ah! Forget my fate.
    Remember me! But ah! Forget my fate.
    (repeat)

Dido and Aeneas was Purcell's only real opera, although he composed other theater music, as well as works for chamber ensembles and organ and many anthems for the Church of England. He was close to the English court and composed funeral music after the death of Queen Mary (1694). He served as the principal organist at the Chapel Royal and also at Westminster Abbey in London.

HEARING THE DIFFERENCE
Dia's "A Chantar" and Purcell's "When I am laid in earth"

These two songs are being compared to display how much the baroque operatic style of the seventeenth century had advanced beyond the simple secular song of the medieval period. Of course, the medieval song might have been accompanied by instruments and certainly such songs did have instrumental accompaniment during the Renaissance, but the accompaniment in "When I am laid in earth" is more structured than was usual for earlier song accompaniments. The bass line is generally very important in baroque music, and in "When I am laid in earth" we hear a repeating bass line (ground bass) that adds to the tension of the aria and Dido's impending suicide.

	A Chantar	When I am laid in earth
Historical period	Medieval (late 1100s)	Baroque (1689)
Texture	Monophonic	Homophonic
Meter	Nonmetric, but with a sense of a beat	Triple meter
Voices	Solo female singer without accompaniment	Solo female singer accompanied by four bowed stringed instruments the lowest of which plays a constantly repeating bass line called a ground bass
Language and text	French, a secular song, sung by a woman about her lover who has deceived her	English, an aria in an opera in which the singer is about to kill herself because her lover is leaving her

During the latter part of the baroque period, Italian opera spread throughout Europe, reaching its heights in the Italian operas of Handel in England. The Italian style had less influence in France, where the composer Jean-Baptiste Lully (1632–1687), ironically an Italian, headed the group that created and supported French opera. In his operatic style, Lully concerned himself with the text and composed arias that were much like recitative. He added musical interest with choruses, dances, and instrumental pieces when he could fit them into the story.

Summary

The baroque era began in Italy around the year 1600. Fundamental style changes were brought about by a reaction against Renaissance vocal polyphony and a desire to make music serve and reflect the mood and meaning of the words. This attitude resulted in the monodic style, in which a single voice is accompanied by a group of instruments called basso continuo.

Many new vocal forms developed during the baroque period, notably the speechlike recitative and the lyrical arioso. The da capo aria is an expansion of the arioso and is characterized by an ABA form. The opera is an elaborately staged dramatic form based on secular themes. The first great opera was *Orfeo,* written by the Italian Claudio Monteverdi.

The popularity of opera spread all over Europe. Some of the greatest operas of the baroque era are those that Handel (whose oratorio, *Messiah,* we will study) composed in the Italian style while he was in England. In France, Jean-Baptiste Lully developed his own style of opera that included more dance and simpler arias than had the Italian operas.

New People and Concepts

aria	counter tenor	libretto
arioso	da capo aria	monody
basso continuo	Farinelli	opera
castrato	figured bass	oratorio
chorus	ground bass	recitative
continuo	Henry Purcell	

Finale

Listen again to "When I am laid in earth" and compare your impressions now with your notes from your first listening. Do you hear more now than you did before? You should now be able to answer the following questions:

▌ What is the meter?

▌ What is the gender of the singer?

▌ What instruments are used to play the accompaniment?

▌ Can you hear the repeated melody in the bass?

▌ What is the language of the text?

▌ What is the mood of the aria and how does it fit into the story of the opera?

7 | Cantata

The miracle of Bach has not appeared in any other art. To strip human nature until its divine attributes are made clear, to inform ordinary activities with spiritual fervor, to give wings of eternity to that which is most ephemeral; to make divine things human and human things divine; this is Bach, the greatest and purest moment in music of all time.
—CELLIST PABLO CASALS (1876–1973)

Listening Introduction

Listen to Bach's "Bereitet die Wege, bereitet die Bahn!" ("Make ready the ways, make ready the path!"), from Cantata no. 132, and make notes about what you hear. Give some attention to the following:

▌ Can you detect the meter?

▌ Can you tell the gender of the singer and the language of the text?

▌ Can you tell what instruments accompany the singer?

▌ Can you hear any section of the music that repeats to the point that you might be able to guess at the form?

▌ Does the music create a mood that allows you to guess what the song is about and where it might have been performed?

Keep these notes to compare with your impressions about the music after you study the information in this chapter.

A **cantata** is a dramatic work for solo voices, sometimes a small chorus, and either basso continuo or a small orchestra. The same types of vocal styles we heard in opera were used in cantatas, including recitative to provide clear dialogue, arioso, and aria. Baroque cantatas were quite different from operas, however, in that they were short—usually not more than twenty minutes long—and they were not performed with scenery, costuming, or stage action. Like operas, they needed to be understood by their audiences and were generally composed in the vernacular. Secular cantatas were performed in palaces or wealthy people's homes, as well as in town halls for gatherings of prominent citizens. Sacred cantatas were performed in churches, often as part of a service that could be as long as three hours, the cantata being only a short episode somewhere in the middle. Because they were not staged, cantatas were much less expensive to produce than operas, and they were very popular during the baroque period.

The Secular Cantata

The secular cantata was a popular form of musical entertainment in baroque Italy. Prominent composers such as Giacomo Carissimi (ca. 1605–1674) and Antonio Cesti (ca. 1623–1669) wrote numerous cantatas for performance at social gatherings in the homes of wealthy aristocrats. The earliest secular cantatas

Court Concert at Prince Bishop of Luettich at Seraing Palace by **Paul Joseph Delcloche (1716–1759).** Court concerts like the one depicted here were popular forums for performances of the cantata.

had several contrasting **movements** but were comparatively short and consisted of recitatives, ariosos, and arias.

One of the most prolific composers of secular cantatas was Barbara Strozzi (1619–ca. 1664). Between 1644 and 1664, Strozzi published eight volumes of vocal works containing a total of about one hundred pieces, most of which were individual arias and secular cantatas for soprano and basso continuo. The texts of many of her cantatas centered on stories about unrequited love, a favorite theme among seventeenth-century composers. In all probability, Strozzi performed these pieces for the *Accademic degli Unisoni,* a Venetian fellowship of poets, philosophers, and historians who met in the home of her father.

Johann Sebastian Bach (1685–1750) was well known for his sacred cantatas, but he also composed some wonderfully entertaining secular ones. One fun example is his "Schweigt Stille, Plaudert Nicht," also known as the "Coffee Cantata." This cantata was composed in 1734 for performance in a coffeehouse that was regularly visited by musicians and music students, including two of Bach's sons. It consisted of ten movements for three soloists: a soprano, a tenor, and a bass. The tenor sang the role of narrator, the bass the role of the father, and the soprano the role of a coffee-addicted young daughter. In the story, the father tried to get his daughter to stop drinking so much coffee by threatening not to allow her to marry until she gave up the habit. She promised, but while the father was out finding an appropriate husband, the daughter spread the word all over town that she would consider no husband who would not allow her to drink coffee whenever she wanted. The "Coffee Cantata" is only a little over twenty-five minutes long, and it was probably not performed with staging, but it was about the closest Bach ever came to composing in the secular dramatic form of opera.

The Chorale

Of the different Protestant religions that broke away from the Roman Catholic Church during the Renaissance, both Martin Luther (1483–1546) and John Calvin (1509–1564) shared the belief that it was important for their churches to

THE LIVE EXPERIENCE
Basso Continuo Players

As was discussed in the chapter on baroque opera, basso continuo was a type of accompaniment that was improvised from a bass line with figurations indicating what chords should be played. It generally took two instruments to play a basso continuo (continuo) part, one playing a chordal instrument and one playing a bass instrument. Composers seldom indicated what instrument they wanted a continuo part to be played by, so it was usually dependent on what musicians were available. The most common chordal instruments used were keyboard instruments, particularly harpsichord or organ, or plucked stringed ones such as lute, guitar, or even harp. A cello, a bassoon, or even a sackbut (early form of the trombone) could be used for playing the bass line.

The art of playing continuo developed out of the medieval and Renaissance practice of instruments improvising accompaniments for monophonic songs. Of course, we do not know exactly what those improvisations were, but the new monodic style of the baroque probably simplified the accompaniments. Basso continuo automatically puts a stress on the bass line, which was probably not there in Renaissance accompaniments.

Some early baroque publications included a preface that told continuo players how to read the figured bass parts. The figurations told players what chords to play, but that still left many choices up to the player about exactly how to play them. For example, the player had to decide whether the chords should be played with all notes together exactly in rhythm with the bass notes or whether to spread out the notes of the chords by playing them one after the other as arpeggios. The baroque writers asked players to know the meaning of the text they were accompanying so that they could dramatize their playing to fit it. One important writer, Quantz, warned continuo players not only to be sure to do nothing that might obscure the vocal part but also to emphasize dissonances when the text calls for tension. The baroque interest in activity and ornamentation called for soloists to add faster note passages and ornaments to their performances, but continuo players had to avoid such decoration. Again, the idea was to provide an accompaniment but to stay out of the way.

Baroque musicians were trained in basso continuo playing from figured bass lines, but only a few early-music specialists in our own time have learned to do that. In order to allow twenty-first century musicians to play baroque music, many modern publications include **realizations** (completely notated music meant to stand in for a section that would have been improvised during the baroque period) of chordal parts. The realizations have to be written for specific instruments, and many are available today for keyboard instruments or for classical guitar. If we buy music or see program notes that have credits given, we sometimes will see "Keyboard part realized by . . ." to let us know who provided the music for the performer to play. The performer would have been the person responsible for the part in the baroque period. The painting on page 75 shows a harpsichordist and a cellist playing basso continuo for the singers.

have music that the congregations could sing together. They wanted the music sung in church to be simple and in the vernacular language so that everyone in the congregation could be part of the musical performance and understand what they were singing. They based their songs on melodies from Gregorian chants, secular tunes, and newly composed songs. These *chorales* or *hymns* were single melodies sung in monophonic texture at first. Simple parts were eventually added below the main melodies to give the music a fuller sound. Luther himself composed many such chorale melodies.

By the baroque period, more than one hundred years after the Renaissance, many of Luther's chorale melodies were very well-known by the members of German Lutheran churches. The famous German composer Johann Sebastian Bach (1685–1750) enhanced the music by resetting the chorale tunes into more complex compositions. Many of Bach's chorales not only functioned as the basis for congregational singing but also provided a rich body of materials from which larger and more complex vocal and instrumental musical structures such as sacred cantatas could be built.

Chapter 7
Activity

Bach Chorale

The Sacred Cantata

Like opera, the cantata went through considerable transformation from early to late baroque, reaching its height in Germany in the works of Dietrich Buxtehude (ca. 1637–1707) and Johann Sebastian Bach. By Bach's time, the sacred cantata often included the standard baroque elements of recitative, aria, chorus, and instrumental ensemble. Cantatas generally included several movements that featured a variety of solo singers, and they usually concluded with a four-part setting of a chorale melody.

Sacred cantata texts related to specific feast days of the church year, and for church musicians such as Bach, the writing of cantatas was a routine professional obligation. Between 1704 and 1740, Bach composed cantatas on a regular basis for the churches he served. He is believed to have written more than 300, although only 195 have been preserved.

Bach's Cantata no. 132 was composed for the fourth Sunday in Advent. Advent means "the coming to" and is a period of four weeks just before Christmas. Bach composed this cantata in 1715, when he was working as court organist and composer for the chapel of the Duke of Weimar. The cantata was scored for two oboes, two violins, viola, and basso continuo with four soloists, a soprano, an alto, a tenor, and a bass. It concluded with a four-part chorus that might have been sung by the four soloists, who could also have been joined by other singers or the congregation. The aria is in da capo (ABA) form and serves as a beautiful opening for the cantata.

"The Live Experience: Basso Continuo Players" discusses an important type of accompaniment in baroque music.

Listening Guide

Cantata no. 132: "Bereitet die Wege, bereitet die Bahn!" ("Make ready the ways, make ready the path!") JOHANN SEBASTIAN BACH

CD 3
Tracks 6–8

Year: 1715

Meter: Sextuple

Voice: Soprano

Instruments: Two oboes, two violins, viola, and basso continuo
    played by organ, cello, and double bass

Form: Da capo aria (ABA)

Duration: 5:54

continued

	Timing	German text	English translation	Form
6	0:00	Bereitet die Wege, bereitet die Bahn!	Make ready the ways, make ready the path!	A
		Bereitet die Wege, bereitet die Bahn!	Make ready the ways, make ready the path!	
		bereitet die Bahn!	make ready the path!	
		Bereitet die Wege, bereitet die Bahn!	Make ready the ways, make ready the path!	
		bereitet die Bahn!	make ready the path!	
		Bereitet die Wege, bereitet die Bahn!	Make ready the ways, make ready the path!	
7	2:20	Bereitet die Wege	Make ready the ways	B
		und machet die Stege	and make smooth the road	
		im Glauben und Leben	in faith and life	
		dem Höchsten ganz eben	for the highest,	
		im Glauben und Leben	in faith and life	
		im Glauben und Leben	in faith and life	
		dem Höchsten ganz eben	for the highest	
		Bereitet die Wege	Make ready the ways	
		und machet die Stege	and make smooth the road	
		Messias kömmt an!	The Messiah comes!	
		Bereitet die Wege	Make ready the ways	
		und machet die Stege	and make smooth the road	
		im Glauben und Leben	in faith and life	
		im Glauben und Leben	in faith and life	
		dem Höchsten ganz eben	for the highest	
		Bereitet die Wege	Make ready the ways	
		und machete die Stege	and make smooth the road	
		Messias kömmt an!	The Messiah comes!	
		Messias kömmt an!	The Messiah comes!	
8	3:26	(Repeat of A section)		A

The Passion

A **Passion** was a musical setting of the story of the suffering and crucifixion of Jesus Christ as told in the Bible by the Gospels. Passions were usually identified by the particular gospel writer whose text was used. The Passion was often performed during Holy Week (leading up to Easter), especially on Good Friday, when the crucifixion was remembered. The early settings of the Passion text—for instance, those of the great German master of the early baroque, Heinrich Schütz (1585–1672)—employed only the biblical text with an introductory and concluding chorus. By Bach's time, musical settings of the Passion had expanded to include nonbiblical texts in the form of commentary about the events described in the Gospel.

In Bach's monumental (over two and a half hours long) *Passion According to St. Matthew,* the Gospel account of the betrayal, arrest, trial, and crucifixion of Christ was told by soloists in recitative, secco for all characters except for Christ, who was accompanied by a string quartet. The chorus assumed various roles, such as the crowd and the disciples. The nonbiblical contemplations were interspersed between sections of the Gospel story in the form of da capo arias sung by soloists and numerous chorales in which the congregation joined the choir and orchestra.

Johann Sebastian Bach

Johann Sebastian Bach was one of the most prolific composers of the baroque period. He came from a family of musicians that reached back four generations before him and that was carried forward by three of his sons. His father, Johann Ambrosius, was a musician in service to the town council of Eisenach in eastern Germany. Bach's father was an excellent violinist and taught him to play stringed instruments.

German composer Johann Sebastian Bach

Orphaned when he was only ten, Bach was sent to live with his eldest brother, Johann Christoph, an organist at the nearby town of Ohrdruf. He remained there five years, taking organ and harpsichord lessons from his brother, earning some money as a soprano, and studying at the town's famed grammar school. He did so well at the school that he was offered a scholarship to St. Michael's, a secondary school in Lǘneburg, a city in northern Germany.

In 1703 Bach obtained his first musical position, as a violinist in the small chamber orchestra of the ducal court of Weimar, but when a post as church organist became available in Arnstadt in August of 1703, he accepted the position. Dissatisfied with working conditions in Arnstadt and the poor state of the church choir, Bach left in 1707 to become organist at the church of St. Blasius in the Free Imperial City of Mühlhausen. In that same year he married a cousin, Maria Barbara Bach.

Soon entangled in disagreements over the type of music that the congregation wanted to hear as opposed to what Bach wanted to write, Bach left Mühlhausen in 1708 to become court organist, and later concertmaster, in the ducal chapel of Weimar. His nine years in Weimar constituted his first major creative period. There he composed a number of cantatas and some of his greatest organ works.

Because of his evident talents as a composer, performer, and conductor, Bach expected to be offered the top position of *Kapellmeister* (chapelmaster) at Weimar when it became available in 1716. However, he was passed over in favor of another composer. The following year he accepted the position of court conductor to the small principality of Anhalt-Cöthen.

Bach enjoyed a growing reputation as an organist and composer of church cantatas, and he made annual performing tours to important centers such as Kassell, Leipzig, and Dresden. His duties at Cöthen were marred by the death of his wife in 1720. Bach soon remarried, however, and his new wife, Anna Magdalena, proved to be a hardworking, cheerful companion who raised Bach's four children by Maria Barbara along with her own. Anna gave birth to thirteen children in all, six of whom survived.

In 1723 Bach was offered the position of kantor (director of music) at St. Thomas Church in Leipzig, one of the most important musical posts in Protestant Germany. However, it was not a completely auspicious beginning for Bach, as the city council turned to him only after it had received refusals from two other composers. His duties included composing cantatas for St. Nicholas Church, as well as for St. Thomas Church, supervising the musical programs in all the municipal churches, and teaching Latin in the St. Thomas choir school.

Despite the irksome nature of some of his duties and his uneasy relationship with the Leipzig town council, Bach remained in Leipzig for the rest of his life. He personally supervised the musical education of his most gifted sons, Wilhelm Friedemann, Carl Philipp Emanuel, and Johann Christian, and saw them embark on promising musical careers. Though, like Handel, he went blind in old age, his creative powers remained undimmed. His last composition, dictated to a son-in-law a few days before his death, was a chorale prelude, "Before Thy Throne, My God, I Stand,"

Summary

Cantatas were multiple-movement dramatic works for one or several solo singers accompanied by basso continuo or by a small orchestra. They were different from operas in that they were not staged with costumed singers or action and they were usually not longer than twenty minutes. Secular cantatas were performed in the palaces or homes of the wealthy classes, as well as in more public places, such as town halls or coffee-houses. Sacred cantatas were usually performed in churches, at times as part of a three-hour or longer service.

The Passion was a musical setting of the story of the suffering and crucifixion of Jesus Christ as told in the Bible by the Gospels. Early in the baroque period, Passions were short and performed as part of church services during the week before Easter. By the late baroque, however, they became monumental compositions to be performed independently of a religious service.

New People and Concepts

cantata	movement	realizations
Johann Sebastian Bach	Passion	

Finale

Listen again to Bach's "Bereitet die Wege, bereitet die Bahn!" ("Make ready the ways, make ready the path!"), from Cantata no. 132, and compare your impressions now with your notes from your first listening. Do you hear more now than you did before? You should now be able to answer the following questions:

▌ What is the meter?

▌ What is the gender of the singer and the language of the text?

▌ What instruments accompany the singer?

▌ Can you hear the music from the beginning return at the end (ABA form)?

▌ Does the music sound like it fits the sacred text?

I should be sorry, my Lord, if I had only succeeded in entertaining them; I wished to make them better.
—COMPOSER G. F. HANDEL (1685–1799) AFTER
MESSIAH WAS PERFORMED IN LONDON IN 1743

Listening Introduction

Listen to "Hallelujah" and make notes about what you hear. Give some attention to the following:

▌ Can you detect the meter?

▌ Can you tell or guess the gender(s) of the singers?

▌ Can you tell what instruments are used to play the accompaniment?

▌ Can you tell the language of the text?

▌ What is the general mood of the piece?

Keep these notes to compare with your impressions about the music after you study the information in this chapter.

Oratorio

An oratorio is a dramatic work for chorus, solo voices, and orchestra. Unlike opera, it does not include scenery, costuming, or stage action. It is similar to the cantata in many ways except that it is longer and is performed on a much larger scale. The oratorio developed as part of the Roman Catholic Church's efforts for reform after the Protestant Reformation. In order to reach out to as many community members as possible, the Congregation of the Oratory built buildings close to churches that were used for talks, lectures, and musical performances through which religious subjects could be taught outside of the liturgical services offered by the church. Because they were intended to teach, the earliest oratorios were often based on Bible stories and had a singing narrator to explain what was happening before and between the other musical sections. The stories were then enhanced by a series of arias, recitatives, choral movements, and instrumental sections. Some churches in Rome had oratorios with Latin texts, but most were in Italian so that the citizens could easily understand them. When oratorios were composed in other countries, the text was in the vernacular of that country for the same reason.

Oratorios take as long as two hours or more to perform. In Italy, they were particularly popular during Lent, when theatrical performances such as operas were banned. The oratorio rose to its height in England in the monumental works of **George Frideric Handel** (1685–1759).

George Frideric Handel

George Frideric Handel was born in Halle, Germany, a trading center some eighty miles southwest of Berlin, the son of a prosperous barber-surgeon attached to the court of the Duke of Saxony. His father had in mind a legal career for the boy but did allow him to begin music study at age eight with the organist of the town's principal Lutheran church. Aside from learning to play the organ, harpsichord, violin, and oboe, young Handel also studied composition, writing church cantatas and numerous small-scale instrumental works.

Out of respect for his father's wish, Handel enrolled at the University of Halle in 1702. At the end of his first year, however, he withdrew from the university and went to Hamburg to pursue his interest in music. Musical activity in Hamburg, as in most cosmopolitan cities of the time, centered on the opera house, where Italian opera thrived. Soon after Handel arrived in Hamburg in 1703, he obtained a position as violinist in the theater orchestra and industriously set about learning the craft of opera composition. His first opera, *Almira* (1704), reflected the curious mixture of native German and imported Italian musical styles then prevalent in Hamburg; the recitatives were set in German, the arias in Italian. The work was a popular success, and three other operas soon followed. In 1706, feeling that he had learned all that Hamburg had to offer, Handel decided to go to Italy.

His three-year stay in Italy was amazingly successful. Traveling back and forth between Florence, Venice, Rome, and Naples, he met many of Italy's greatest composers and was the frequent guest of cardinals, princes, and ambassadors. Much of his popularity stemmed from the success of his operas, *Rodrigo* (1708) and *Agrippina* (1709).

Through one of the friends he made in Italy, Handel obtained the position of musical director to the Electoral Court of Hanover, Germany. He had just taken up his duties in 1710, however, when he asked permission from Elector Georg Ludwig to visit London. Italian opera was then in great vogue with the English aristocracy, and the success of his opera *Rinaldo* (1711) led Handel to ask permission for another leave of absence the following year. By promising to return to Hanover "within a reasonable time," Handel stretched out his second London visit indefinitely.

George Frideric Handel, composer of one of the most famous baroque oratorios, *Messiah*

Because European kings and queens had to be of royal blood and because England's Queen Anne died with no English heir, Handel's former employer from Hanover, Elector Georg Ludwig, ascended to the British throne as King George I. How Handel settled the embarrassing problem of his long-neglected contract with the Electoral Court is unknown. But the annual pension Queen Anne gave him was continued and even increased by George I, and within several years he was in high favor at the royal court.

Handel became an English citizen in 1726. He continued to compose operas that were very successful, including some for the Royal Academy of Music, organized by British nobility under the sponsorship of the king. During the academy's eight-year existence (1720–1728), Handel's career as an opera composer reached its highest point.

Chapter 8
Timeline

Handel

The popularity of Handel's operatic style received a blow, however, in 1728, when John Gay's *The Beggar's Opera,* which had spoken dialogue instead of recitative, short catchy songs instead of arias, and a story about dishonest businessmen and thieves, pleased large audiences in new ways. A parody of Italian style, *The Beggar's Opera* was widely imitated, and a new form of light, popular musical entertainment was created and sung in English.

Though Handel continued to compose Italian operas for more than a decade after the appearance of *The Beggar's Opera,* he turned increasingly to the oratorio. His first English oratorio, *Haman and Mordecai* (later revised and renamed *Esther*), was composed in 1720. Others followed during the 1730s, but it was not until 1739, with the completion of *Israel in Egypt* and *Saul,* that he seemed to sense the full musical and dramatic possibilities of this form. Neither of these works was an immediate success, but others that followed were. In 1741, Handel was invited to conduct several oratorios in Dublin, Ireland, during Holy Week, when operatic theaters were closed. He decided that a new oratorio based on the birth, death, and significance of Jesus Christ would make for a successful ending to the series. Proceeds from the performance were to be given to charity. He composed that oratorio, *Messiah,* in just over three weeks, earning a large sum for charity and even more esteem for himself.

In his last years, Handel was universally recognized as England's greatest composer. His popularity with all segments of English society steadily grew, and the royal patronage of George I was followed by that of George II. Despite declining health and the eventual loss of his eyesight, Handel continued to maintain a heavy schedule of oratorio performances, which he conducted himself from the keyboard. While attending a performance of *Messiah* on March 30, 1759, he suddenly grew faint and had to be taken home. He died two weeks later and was buried with state honors in London's Westminster Abbey. His will revealed that he had accumulated a substantial private fortune, which was dispersed—along with his music manuscripts—among friends.

Today the fame of George Frideric Handel rests largely on his oratorios (particularly *Messiah*), some of his operas, and a variety of instrumental works. The bulk of Handel's oratorios are dramatic, with singers taking the roles of specific characters. *Messiah* is a nondramatic oratorio in which the chorus dominates, narrating and describing the events. The solo voices do not represent specific characters as they would in a dramatic oratorio. Instead, they complement and act as a foil for the chorus.

Messiah

Chapter 8
Video

Messiah

Messiah is based on the life of Christ. Although we might expect that the text for this oratorio would come from the Gospels of the New Testament, in which the life of Christ is recorded, Handel chose to take the bulk of the libretto from prophetic passages in the Old Testament. The opening texts we will hear are from Isaiah 40:1–5.

Messiah was composed in only twenty-four days. It was a success in Handel's lifetime and has become one of the most loved and popular pieces of music in the history of Western civilization. At its first London performance in 1743, King George II was so moved by the opening of the "Hallelujah" chorus that he stood during its performance, a precedent that most audiences follow still.

All together, *Messiah* represents about two and one-half hours of music for four solo voices (a soprano, an alto, a tenor, and a bass), a four-part chorus, and an orchestra. The oratorio is structured in three parts and comprises fifty-three

King George II set a precedent when he rose to his feet during the "Hallelujah" chorus at this early performance of *Messiah.*

movements. The movements include arias, recitatives, choruses, and orchestral sections. Part I deals with the prophecy of the coming of the Messiah and his birth; Part II, the sacrifice of Jesus and the salvation of humanity through his suffering and death; Part III, redemption through Christianity. An **overture,** sometimes called a **sinfonia,** introduces the work.

The overture to *Messiah* is structured according to what is generally called the **French overture.** Needless to say, this form was first popular in France, but it worked so well as a dramatic introduction for large-scale works of all kinds that it was used by many baroque composers. The idea behind the French overture is simple. It has two sections that contrast in style. The first section uses stately rhythms based on a pattern of long followed by very short notes, one after the other. The flow of "long, short, long, short, long, short" note values creates a rather crisp, even majestic effect. Musicians use the term "dotted rhythms" to describe this rhythmic pattern. The dotted first section of a French overture is followed by a faster section that has one melody after another following in imitation. Some French overtures end with a return to the dotted style of the beginning. Handel used the French overture style to introduce many of his operas, as well as this oratorio.

In this and many other dramatic works, the overture functions to set the mood for the story. The following Listening Guides include the overture, a recitative, an aria, and a chorus from *Messiah.*

Listening Guide

Overture from *Messiah* GEORGE FRIDERIC HANDEL

CD 3
Tracks 9–10

Year: 1742

Texture: Homophonic first section and polyphonic second section

Meter: Quadruple

Form: French overture

Instrumentation: Small string orchestra and continuo (cello and harpsichord)

Duration: 3:09

	Timing	What to listen for
9	0:00	Grave introductory section featuring dotted rhythms and a sense of majesty.
	0:37	Repeat of what was just played.
10	0:14	Allegro moderato (faster) section that starts with a single melody that is imitated in other voices in a fugal style.
	2:55	Return to the tempo and homophonic texture of the first section.

Listening Guide

"Comfort ye," an accompanied recitative from *Messiah* GEORGE FRIDERIC HANDEL

CD 1
Track 14

Texture: Homophonic

Meter: Quadruple

Voice: Solo tenor

Language: English

Duration: 3:07

Special feature: The voice is accompanied by two violins, viola,
    and continuo (cello and organ).

Text (Note: The singer repeats several phrases of text.)

14
Comfort ye, comfort ye my people,
saith your God.
Speak ye comfortably to Jerusalem,
And cry unto her, that her warfare,
her warfare is accomplish'd,
That her iniquity is pardon'd.
The voice of him that crieth in the wilderness:
Prepare ye the way of the Lord,
Make straight in the desert a highway for our God.

Listening Guide

"Ev'ry valley," an aria from *Messiah* GEORGE FRIDERIC HANDEL

CD 1
Track 15

Texture: Homophonic

Meter: Quadruple

Voice: Solo tenor

Language: English

Duration: 3:34

Special feature: The vocal melody often displays the text using
    word painting.

Text

15
Ev'ry valley, ev'ry valley shall be exalted,
shall be exalted, shall be exalted,
shall be exalted,

and ev'ry mountain and hill made low,

Word painting

The word "exalted" is stretched out over
    several bars of exuberant and highly
    decorated melody.
"Mountain" is begun on a high note and
    finished on a low one, just as the shape
    of a mountain.
The melody on "hill" has a little rise and fall.
The word "low" is sung to a low note.

continued

Text	Word painting
the crooked straight,	"Crooked" is sung to two notes that go back and forth as if they were crooked, and "straight" is held on a long note as if it were straight.
and the rough places plain,	"Plain" is on a long note.
the crooked straight,	
the crooked straight,	
and the rough places plain,	
and the rough places plain.	
Ev'ry valley, ev'ry valley shall be exalted,	"Valley" starts on a high note and ends on a low one.
	"Exalted" is again stretched out over an exuberant melody.
ev'ry valley, ev'ry valley shall be exalted,	
and ev'ry mountain and hill made low,	
the crooked straight, the crooked straight,	"Crooked" has notes that jump around, "straight" is long held.
the crooked straight,	
and the rough places plain,	
and the rough places plain,	
and the rough places plain,	
the crooked straight, and the rough places plain.	

Listening Guide

"Hallelujah" from *Messiah* GEORGE FRIDERIC HANDEL

CD 1
Track 16

Texture: Polyphonic and homophonic

Meter: Quadruple

Voices: SATB chorus (sopranos, altos, tenors, and basses), also called a "mixed" chorus

Language: English

Duration: 3:37

Features: Sections of text repeat several times.

Text	Features and textures
	Instrumental introduction
16 Hallelujah!	Homophonic texture
for the Lord God omnipotent reigneth;	Monophonic
Hallelujah!	Homophonic and finally polyphonic
The kingdom of this world is become	Homophonic
the Kingdom of our Lord and of	
His Christ;	
and He shall reign for ever and ever,	Monophonic, then polyphonic with imitation
King of Kings, and Lord of Lords,	Homophonic with interruptions of "for ever
for ever and ever, Hallelujah,	and ever" and "Hallelujah"
Hallelujah!	Homophonic

HEARING THE DIFFERENCE
Josquin's "Ave Maria" and Handel's "Hallelujah Chorus"

These two choral works are being compared because they are both representative of the periods in which they were composed and, therefore, they display several basic differences between choral music of the Renaissance and that of the baroque. Both pieces are very religious, but the first thing you will probably notice in comparing them is the very different attitude toward religion each one displays. "Ave Maria" is gentle and yet respectfully serious. "Hallelujah" is exuberant with a full chorus and orchestra all joined together in celebrating the joy of acknowledging Christ as the Messiah. Other comparisons follow:

	Ave Maria	Hallelujah
Historical period	Renaissance	Baroque
Texture	Mostly polyphonic with some homophonic sections	Texture changes from polyphonic to homophonic fairly often
Meter	Duple, with one section in triple	Quadruple
Performers	Four-part male choir, a cappella	Four-part mixed chorus, accompanied by an orchestra with basso continuo
Language and text	A sacred motet set to a prayer to the Virgin Mary, taken from Luke 1:28–1:42, in Latin, the language of the Catholic Church	A choral movement from an oratorio. The text is taken from Revelation 11:15, in English, the language used in the Church of England
Mood	Serious and gentle	Exuberant and joyful
Performance situation	A church or other religious setting	Can be performed in a church, concert hall, or anywhere else that is large enough for a choir, orchestra, and audience

Messiah is often performed today, but the entire work is very long for some types of seasonal concerts. The length is often cut down for those performances. At Christmastime, many churches or schools perform only Part I, about the birth of Christ, and then end by skipping to the famous "Hallelujah" chorus from Part II. At Easter, one can hear many performances of the opening overture, followed by Parts II and III of *Messiah* without any of Part I. Either way, the famous "Hallelujah" chorus is part of the performance, and most audience members still stand up through it as did King George II in 1743.

Summary

An oratorio is a large-scale dramatic work for chorus, solo voices, and orchestra that is performed without scenery, costuming, or stage action. Most oratorios are based on biblical texts and were intended to both instruct and entertain audiences. George Frideric Handel, a German composer who studied opera composition in Italy and then spent most of his life in England, composed some of the most popular of all oratorios. The most often performed of those was *Messiah,* based on the birth and death of Jesus Christ and on the redemption offered by his sacrifices. *Messiah* features soprano, alto, tenor, and bass soloists, as well as a large choir and orchestra. It is still performed often during the Christmas and Easter seasons.

New People and Concepts

French overture   **overture**   **sinfonia**

George Frideric Handel

Finale

Listen again to "Hallelujah" and compare your impressions now with your notes from your first listening. Do you hear more now than you did before? You should now be able to answer the following questions:

▌ What is the meter?

▌ What are the genders of the singers?

▌ What instruments are used to play the accompaniment?

▌ What is the language of the text?

▌ What is the general mood of the piece?

Baroque Solo and Chamber Music

So you want to write a fugue, You have the urge to write a fugue, You have the nerve to write a fugue, So go ahead.
—PIANIST GLENN GOULD (1932–1982) WITH FULL AWARENESS OF HOW DIFFICULT IT CAN BE TO WRITE A COMPOSITION AS COMPLEX AS A FUGUE

Listening Introduction

Listen to the example of music that represents this chapter, "The Little Fugue in G Minor," and make notes about what you hear. Give some attention to the following:

▐ Can you detect the meter?

▐ Can you tell the number of melodies that play at the same time in different sections?

▐ Can you tell what instrument(s) is/are being played?

▐ Can you hear a melody from the beginning that comes back later in the piece?

▐ Can you hear anything like the imitation we heard in some Renaissance vocal music?

Keep these notes to compare with your impressions about the music after you study the information in this chapter.

The baroque era was not just a period of magnificent achievement in vocal composition; it also saw the gradual development of a significant body of instrumental music. The baroque was the age of the great violin makers, among them the members of the Stradivari family. Improvements were made in the construction of virtually every wind and brass instrument, and the organ and the harpsichord became the basic keyboard instruments. By the end of the baroque era, instrumental music had gradually equaled or surpassed vocal music in importance.

Keyboard Music

A large body of music for keyboard instruments—the organ and harpsichord—was written during the baroque period. We will see the piano take over in importance in later periods, but it was just being invented in the late baroque. These keyboard pieces appeared with various titles—**fantasia, prelude, toccata**—all of which were fairly free in structure.

The term *toccata* derived from the Italian verb *toccare* ("to touch") and implies a piece full of scale passages, rapid runs and trills, and massive chords. The *fantasia* was a piece characterized by displays of virtuosity that made it seem to the listener that the music was spontaneously flowing from the player at the moment it was being played. The *prelude* was also generally free in form and improvisatory in style. It customarily introduced another piece or group of

89

pieces. The prelude, fantasia, and toccata were often used as an introduction to a **fugue,** one of the great intellectual musical structures of the baroque era.

Fugue

A **fugue** is based upon the polyphonic development of a melody called the **subject.** Fugues are composed for a certain number of "voice" parts. These voice parts are not necessarily sung by singers, although they can be. They are melodies that are often played by individual musical instruments or by a single instrument such as a keyboard or lute that can play several notes and melodies at the same time. It is essential that each voice maintain its musical independence from the other voices. The precise manner in which the subject is developed among these voice parts varies from piece to piece. However, the initial section of virtually every fugue follows a plan that is more or less standard. This section is called the **exposition.**

The exposition begins with a single voice stating the subject. As the subject ends, the second voice enters in imitation, stating the subject while the first voice continues with a contrasting melody called the **countersubject.** The countersubject *counters,* or is played along with, the imitation of the subject. This process of imitative entrances of each voice in turn continues until all voices have stated the fugue subject, at which point the exposition has been accomplished. Without pause, the piece continues with a number of sections that function either as new statements of the fugue subject or some variation of it, or as transitions between statements of the subject. The transition sections are called **episodes.** Although the exposition is part of virtually every fugue, what follows the exposition is quite free and varies greatly from fugue to fugue.

The primary musical interest of the fugue lies in remembering the subject when you first hear it and then recognizing it when it is played or sung again throughout the course of the composition. Sometimes, the subject is presented in slower or faster versions than it had been at the beginning, but that does not happen in the fugue we will be listening to. This fugue was composed by the unchallenged master of the baroque fugue, Johann Sebastian Bach. We heard an aria from a cantata by Bach in Chapter 7. Bach composed works in every form of musical composition prevalent in the baroque period with the exception of opera.

Listening Guide

"The Little Fugue in G Minor" JOHANN SEBASTIAN BACH

CD 1
Track 17

Year: 1709

Texture: Polyphonic

Meter: Quadruple

Form: Fugue

Voices: Four

Duration: 4:20

Special feature: Notice that the subject is played through in its entirety before it is imitated in other voices. That is different from the imitation at the beginning of most Renaissance vocal works, such as Josquin's "Ave Maria" in Chapter 5, in which each voice entered before the beginning melody was completed.

Timing	What to listen for
0:00	The first playing of the subject in the highest (soprano) voice.
0:18	The imitation of the subject in the next lower (alto) voice, while the soprano voice continues by playing the countersubject.
0:41	The imitation of the subject in the next lower (tenor) voice, while the soprano and alto voices continue playing.
0:59	The imitation of the subject in the lowest (bass, played on the pedals) voice, while the soprano and tenor voices continue to play.
1:16	Episode (transition during which the subject is not played).
1:26	The tenor voice begins the subject and the soprano picks it up and finishes it.
1:47	Episode.
1:56	The alto voice plays the subject.
2:12	Episode.
2:24	The bass voice plays the subject.
2:40	Episode.
2:59	The soprano plays the subject.
3:17	Episode.
3:48	The bass makes the final statement of the subject.

[17]

In addition to being fun to listen to, this little fugue illustrates a major stylistic feature of much baroque instrumental music in that it features an unbroken, uninterrupted, steady flow of music from the first note to the last chord. Quite unlike later styles, in which sections of music are separated by pauses, the polyphonic instrumental style of the baroque is characterized by continuous motion and progression from beginning to end. We mentioned this feature in the prelude to the baroque period, in which we pointed out the general sense of activity seen in much baroque art. Music remains constantly active, just as the art did.

Chapter 9
Activity

Bach Fugue

"The Live Experience: Playing the Organ" explains how organists achieve rich and varied sounds on this instrument.

Baroque organ literature included many works intended for performance in conjunction with religious ceremonies, and many of these pieces were based on chorale melodies. For instance, as an introduction to the service, the organist would play a work based on the particular chorale tune appropriate for the specific day in the church year, and that piece would be called a **chorale prelude.** Many of Bach's chorale preludes introduced the same chorale melody that was used later in the same service as the basis of a cantata.

Suite

Another type of composition popular among baroque composers was the **suite.** Unlike the fugue, which is a piece of music that can stand by itself or be paired with some type of introductory piece such as a prelude or toccata, suites are multimovement works. Most suites are comprised of a series of movements, each based on a particular dance rhythm and style. A typical suite included the German **allemande,** the French **courante,** and the **sarabande** (originally a rather erotic dance from Spain but changed to a slow, courtly dance by the French and Germans), and ended with the English or Irish **gigue** (jig). Many suites also included the French **gavotte** and, at times, nondance movements such as an introductory prelude. Baroque suites were not intended for dancing, as were the pairs or sets of

THE LIVE EXPERIENCE
Playing the Organ

The organ is a unique instrument because it can make a great many different types of sounds. The console at which the player sits is connected to several or many sets of pipes, each of which has its own tone quality. Although electronic versions of the organ are available today, real pipe organs have air pushed through the pipes by a series of bellows. The console has two or more keyboards that the player can connect with the sets of pipes. Organs can actually play what sounds much like bowed strings, woodwind, or brass instruments, and some even have percussion sounds, allowing the organ to sound like a full orchestra.

In addition to the keyboards, the organ console has a full display of buttons and knobs, called **stops,** that the organist sets to assign the pipes for each keyboard to play. Before the organist plays a piece of music, he or she has to decide what pipes to play in what parts of the music and then set the stops to allow for that. This is called setting the **registration** for the piece. One organist might make very different decisions about registration from another, giving the organist even more control of the sound than a player of any other musical instrument.

One reason that the sounds on the organ vary as much as they do is that the pipes vary in size, from thirty-two (or more) feet long for very low tones to pencil-sized ones that sound very high. These sets of large to small pipes with many sizes in between can be made of wood, metal, or other material, giving each set its own particular tone quality. Some pipes even have reeds attached to them to make them sound much like woodwind instruments with reeds.

Pipe organs have to be built specifically for the church or concert hall in which they are to be used, because some sets of pipes take up quite a bit of space. Also, because the different sets of pipes are often spread around the front, sides, and back of the space for the congregation or audience, the particular acoustics of the building need to be taken into consideration so that the instrument can achieve the best possible sound.

In addition to playing several sets of pipes on several different keyboards, the organist has a full keyboard of pedals to play with his or her feet. This **pedal board** is most often used to play bass notes, such as the lowest lines we heard in Bach's Fugue, but it is also possible to play higher melodies and even chords on the pedals.

Dynamic levels on some organs are changed by use of a swell box with shutters that open to let out as much sound as possible or close to soften the sound. The swell box is controlled by pedals above the pedal board that look like the accelerator pedal on a car or bus.

Organs like this one from the baroque period often have elaborate, magnificent sets of pipes.

The organ is sometimes called the "King of Instruments" because it can fill a church or concert hall with the most majestic of sounds, and yet it can also play very gentle and soft music.

Depending on the pipes connected to it, the organ's range of high to low notes can be greater than that of an orchestra, making it the most versatile of all single instruments.

dances of the Renaissance, but the collection of dances in most suites provided interesting contrasts in meter, tempo, and texture.

Suites were composed for almost any solo instrument or group of instruments, including orchestras. Bach's orchestral suites and Handel's *Water Music* remain popular today. The next Listening Guide is based on a sarabande from a suite for harpsichord by a very talented female composer of the baroque, **Elisabeth-Claude Jacquet de la Guerre** (1665–1729).

Elisabeth-Claude Jacquet de la Guerre

Elisabeth's father, Claude Jacquet, was a musician who taught his daughter from an early age to play music. A child prodigy, she was performing on the harpsichord as young as age five. The family lived in Paris and when King Louis XIV heard her play he not only praised her performance, but he hired her to entertain himself, his mistress, and their guests on a regular basis. He also supported her musical education and attended many of her concerts. She, in return, dedicated many of her compositions to him.

Elisabeth married another musician, Marin de la Guerre, in 1684. The couple had one son, who was only ten years old when he died. Living through the loss of her son and then her father and her husband in 1702 and 1704 respectively, she managed to continue her career. She performed at public recitals and composed extensively through the end of her life. Her works include songs, cantatas, operas, and sonatas for chamber groups. Her publications sold well, and she was a very successful performer as both a harpsichordist and singer. This sarabande is from the first of two books of harpsichord music she published.

We have previously heard a harpsichord as accompaniment to the voice in "Comfort ye" and "Ev'ry valley" from *Messiah*. The instrument was often part of baroque orchestras, but it was also a very popular solo instrument, and one on which Elisabeth-Claude Jacquet de la Guerre excelled. Before listening to the sarabande it might be helpful to understand something about the instrument.

A harpsichord is shaped something like a small grand piano and, like the piano, has metal strings that run parallel to the long side of the body of the instrument. What makes it different from the piano is that its strings are plucked instead of being hit with hammers. That plucking action gives the harpsichord a very crisp tone quality that worked well in baroque orchestras because it could cut through the sound of the other instruments and still be heard. The plucking also sounds at the same dynamic level, no matter how hard or lightly the keys are played. Some harpsichords have two manuals (keyboards) that each pluck a different set of strings. The player can "couple" the keyboards so that playing on one will cause both keyboards to work and sound both sets of strings together. That makes the sound of the instrument much louder than it would be if either keyboard was played by itself. It is also possible to play using a "lute stop," which deadens the strings to make them sound more like a lute. There are many sizes and types of harpsichord or related instruments that were used throughout the baroque period.

Harpsichords, like the one being played in this depiction, were well-suited for much of the music from the baroque period.

Listening Guide

"Sarabande" from Suite no. 1 from *Pieces for Harpsichord*

ELISABETH-CLAUDE JACQUET DE LA GUERRE

CD 3
Track 11

Year: 1707

Texture: Mostly homophonic

Meter: Triple

Form: Binary

Duration: 2:10

Special features: The music is highly ornamented. The composer wrote in signs to tell the player to add such ornaments as trills and other fast, decorative note patterns. The player also often arpeggiates chords (spreads out the notes in time, rather than playing all notes together) and plays fast-note runs with a somewhat free sense of rhythm.

	Timing	What to listen for
11	0:00	A section of the form
12	0:19	Repeat of the A section
13	0:38	B section of the form
14	1:22	Repeat of the B section
	2:09	Final cadence

Baroque Sonata

In the beginning of the baroque period, the term **sonata** was applied to instrumental pieces that varied greatly in structure, character, and the number and type of instruments. Usually it was a multimovement work, but the number of movements varied from piece to piece.

Gradually there developed a distinction between the sonata written to be played in a church, the **sonata da chiesa,** and that intended to be played in a chamber or room in a home or palace, the **sonata da camera.** The sonata da camera became essentially a dance suite, and the sonata da chiesa a four-movement work in which the movements alternated in tempo: slow-fast-slow-fast.

Toward the latter part of the baroque period, three types of sonatas were predominant: the sonata for unaccompanied instrument; the **solo sonata,** for one solo instrument (usually the violin) and continuo; and the **trio sonata,** usually employing two violins for the upper voices with a cello and keyboard instrument for the continuo. Corelli, Vivaldi, Handel, and Bach all made important contributions to the sonata literature.

Summary

The baroque era saw the rise of instrumental music due in part to the development and improvement of existing instruments.

The harpsichord and the organ were the chief keyboard instruments of the baroque period. Single-movement works written for these instruments include the fantasia, the prelude, and the toccata. Chorale tunes were an important part of literature written for the organ. The suite is an example of the multimovement keyboard form that became popular for other solo instruments and ensembles. The fugue, in which a melodic subject is presented and developed in a variety of ways, is one of the most significant forms of the baroque period. Fugues often appeared in keyboard, instrumental, and vocal works.

The baroque sonata is a multimovement work for one or more instruments. Two of its early forms are the sonata da camera and the sonata da chiesa. Later developments include the sonata for unaccompanied instrument, the solo sonata, and the trio sonata.

New People and Concepts

allemande	fugue	sonata da camera
chorale prelude	gavotte	sonata da chiesa
countersubject (of a fugue)	gigue	stops (on an organ)
courante	pedal board	subject (of a fugue)
Elisabeth-Claude	prelude	suite
Jacquet de la Guerre	registration (on an organ)	toccata
episode	sarabande	trio sonata
exposition	solo sonata	
fantasia	sonata	

Finale

Listen again to "The Little Fugue in G Minor" and compare your impressions now with your notes from your first listening. Do you hear more now than you did before? You should now be able to answer the following questions:

▌ What is the meter?

▌ How many separate melodies often play at the same time?

▌ What instrument is being played?

▌ Do you hear the subject returning several times during the piece?

▌ Do you hear the subject being imitated in each voice after its initial complete statement?

10 | The Baroque Orchestra

All in all, Vivaldi composed about 450 concertos of one sort or another. People who find his music too repetitious are inclined to say that he wrote the same concerto 450 times. This is hardly fair: he wrote two concertos, 225 times each.
—MUSIC JOURNALIST DAVID W. BARBER
(BORN IN 1958)

Listening Introduction

Listen to the example of music that represents this chapter, "Spring," first movement, from *The Four Seasons,* and make notes about what you hear. Give some attention to the following:

▌ Can you detect the meter?

▌ Can you hear the melody that the orchestra plays at the beginning come back later in the movement?

▌ Can you tell what instrument is featured as a soloist accompanied by the orchestra?

▌ Can you hear basso continuo as part of the orchestra?

▌ Does the piece have a general mood that fits the title, "Spring"?

Keep these notes to compare with your impressions about the music after you study the information in this chapter.

Concerto

The first orchestras were used to accompany singers in baroque operas, cantatas, and oratorios. The rich orchestral sound was so pleasing that it did not take long for royal or other wealthy families to hire musicians, along with a composer/conductor, to come to their palaces or estates and provide instrumental music for themselves and their guests. Many of these court orchestras at first were made up only of bowed stringed instruments, though woodwinds and others were gradually added.

The pitting of soft sounds against loud ones fit the interest in contrasts central to the arts of the baroque period. **Concertos** developed out of this interest. The term *concerto* comes from the Latin word *concertare,* which means to fight or contend. In music, that idea was applied to the joining together of dissimilarly sized groups, or a solo instrument with an orchestra, to "oppose" one another to provide an interesting and harmonious, but contrasting, sound. The two types of concertos we discuss are the **concerto grosso,** in which a small solo group plays "against" the orchestra, and the **solo concerto,** in which the relatively soft sound of an individual solo instrument is pitted against that of an orchestra.

The two concerto movements we will listen to are in what is known as **ritornello** form. *Ritornello* is Italian for "return" or "repetition." As we will hear in our examples, short sections of orchestral music return later during the movements.

THE LIVE EXPERIENCE
Playing Solos in Baroque Music

As we discussed in Chapter 7, basso continuo players had quite a bit of freedom when they performed because both players had only one figured bass line provided by the composer. The ways of playing the chords were mostly improvised. Baroque musicians who played or sang solos were also given a great number of choices about exactly how to play or sing their music. In a practice that dated back to improvised playing in the medieval and Renaissance periods, the music that a composer notated was almost more of a guide as to what melody should be played than an exact instruction. Particularly in slow movements, solo parts sometimes were notated in long notes that would sound quite uninteresting if played exactly as written. In such cases, the composer's long notes were no more than an indication of what note fit the accompaniment and the composer expected the player to improvise other notes around that written note. Of course, some parts that were notated to be played fast had little room for added notes, and strictly

organized music such as that in a fugue had to be played the way it was written, but the practice of players adding to the music was still very common. The term for such additions is **embellishment.**

Binary form was commonly used for dances, sonatas, and other single movements during the baroque period. Because a movement in binary form has two sections, each of which is repeated (AABB), players generally embellished the repeats with extra fast notes, runs, or ornaments. This was one way in which individual musicians who were not necessarily composers themselves had an opportunity to display their talents and attract listeners to their performances.

When one listens to baroque music that is played well (played with a certain amount of improvised embellishment added to the music), noticing what happens on repeated sections can be very interesting. This improvisational practice adds much to the energy and drive we hear in baroque music.

This form is very easy to listen to because the constant return of the usually energetic introductory orchestral melody provides the listener with a sense of unity for the entire movement. "The Live Experience: Playing Solos in Baroque Music" illustrates how musicians inserted their own personalities into their performances.

Concerto Grosso

Chapter 10
Activity

Concerto
Grosso

The concerto grosso is a multimovement work in which a small group of solo instruments, called the **concertino,** and the full orchestra, called the **ripieno** (Italian for "full"), are contrasted. The basic structure and number of movements of the concerto grosso varied, with the three-movement structure (fast-slow-fast) the most commonly used outline.

J. S. Bach, whom we discussed earlier as a cantata composer, spent time providing music for court orchestras, particularly when he was employed at Cöthen. The instrumentation for his orchestras varied according to what players he had available and what sort of event the music was to be part of. Some of his orchestral works were composed for fairly large ensembles that included several violins, a viola, two or three oboes, one bassoon, two or three trumpets, two timpani, and harpsichord with cello and double bass as continuo instruments.

J. S. Bach completed six works dedicated to Christian Ludwig, the Margrave (a hereditary title given to some German princes) of Brandenburg, in 1721. Although Bach referred to these pieces as "concertos for several instruments," they have come to be known as the Brandenburg Concertos. Three of them (nos. 2, 4, and 5) follow the tradition of the contrasting concertino and ripieno groups mentioned earlier. By his choice of instruments for the concertino, Bach created a contrast in timbre *within* the solo group, as well as *between* the solo group and the ripieno. In the fifth Brandenburg, for example, the three members of the concertino—the violin, the flute, and the harpsichord—all have quite different tone qualities.

Listening Guide

Brandenburg Concerto no. 5, first movement JOHANN SEBASTIAN BACH

CD 3
Tracks 15–17

Year: 1721

Tempo: Fast

Meter: Quadruple

Form: Ritornello (The ritornello theme, or part of it, returns constantly with contrasting sections between)

Concertino: Flute, violin, and harpsichord

Ripieno: String orchestra with continuo

Duration: 10:38

Special Feature: Although the concertino group includes three instruments, the end of this movement features the harpsichord as a solo instrument for a **virtuoso** to play.

Timing	What to listen for
15 0:00	**Ritornello theme (Ripieno),** complete statement of vigorous melody that surges upward, setting rhythmic drive in motion
0:23	**Contrasting section (Concertino),** fragments from ritornello theme; imitation between flute and violin, with harpsichord an independent third part in constant motion
0:51	**Ritornello theme,** partial statement from beginning of theme
0:55	**Contrasting section,** continued imitation between flute and violin
1:18	**Ritornello theme,** partial statement, begins where last ritornello left off
1:25	**Contrasting section,** harpsichord enters; flute and violin echo in single notes, then develop other fragments
1:48	**Ritornello theme,** partial statement, taken from where the last ritornello left off
1:55	**Contrasting section,** interplay between violin and flute; fast notes, virtuosic display draw attention to harpsichord
2:40	**Ritornello theme,** partial statement from middle of theme
2:47	**Contrasting section,** figures tossed back and forth between flute and violin; new melodic fragment introduced and developed; extended length; final trills lead to:
4:35	**Ritornello theme,** partial statement from beginning of theme

continued

Timing	What to listen for
4:40	**Contrasting section,** continued imitation between violin and flute
5:29	**Ritornello theme,** full statement of theme
5:41	**Contrasting section,** continued imitation between flute and violin moving smoothly into:
6:11	**Ritornello theme,** continued imitation between flute and violin moving smoothly into:
6:20	**Contrasting section,** the longest contrasting section; virtuosic display draws attention to harpsichord; flute and violin drop out, leaving harpsichord, with trills and passage work, leading to the return of:
10:09	**Ritornello theme,** complete statement of the theme

[16] is to the left of the 5:29 row. [17] is to the left of the 6:20 row.

Solo Concerto

The concerto grosso and another type of concerto called the ripieno concerto, in which the ripieno group plays without a solo instrument or instrumental group, were popular throughout the baroque period, but eventually the desire for more contrast led to the development of the solo concerto.

Antonio Vivaldi

One of the most prolific composers of baroque solo concertos was the Italian composer **Antonio Vivaldi** (1678–1741).

Vivaldi was the son of a violinist who played as part of the instrumental ensemble at St. Mark's Cathedral in Venice. His father taught him to play the violin, but when he was young he was more interested in becoming a priest. For whatever reason, possibly his ill health, Vivaldi turned his attention from religion to music. He obtained a job as a violin teacher and composer at a girls' orphanage. Because he had red hair, which was not all that common in Italy, and was also a priest, he became known as the "Red Priest."

Orphanages not only took care of girls who had no parents, but they also taught the girls a trade so that they could one day support themselves. The orchestra at the orphanage in which Vivaldi taught became famous enough that it was hired to perform at courts and general city functions, entertaining any number of important visitors. By such performances, the girls earned some of their support, and Vivaldi earned a great deal of recognition. He composed concertos, particularly solo concertos, to display the talents of girls who played particularly well.

Of all Vivaldi's concertos, the group called *Le Quattro Stagione (The Four Seasons)* is perhaps the most interesting because of the extramusical basis of its inspiration. Vivaldi was one of the first to try to depict through music the feelings and sounds of the changing seasons. These four violin concertos are an

Antonio Vivaldi, composer of many solo concertos, including *The Four Seasons*

early example of baroque descriptive or **program music,** and the music for the solo violin, which calls for virtuoso playing, demonstrates Vivaldi's skill at writing for the instrument. In spite of their descriptive intent, all of the concertos follow the three-movement formal outline—fast, slow, fast.

Each of the four concertos bears the title of one of the seasons—spring, summer, fall, and winter—and each is preceded by a sonnet, which may or may not have been written by Vivaldi, describing that particular season. For instance, the first movement of the concerto entitled "Spring" has the following introduction:

> Spring has come, and the birds greet it with happy songs, and at the same time the streams run softly murmuring to the breathing of the gentle breezes.

> Then the sky being cloaked in black, thunder and lightning come and have their say; after the storm has quieted, the little birds turn again to their harmonious song.

The poem depicted in the second and third movements continues to portray aspects of the spring season:

> Second movement: "Here in a pleasant flowery meadow, the leaves sweetly rustle, the goatherd sleeps, his faithful dog at his side."

> Third movement: "Nymphs and shepherds dance to the festive sound of the pastoral musette under the bright sky that they love."

Listening Guide

"Spring," first movement, from *Le Quattro Stagione* (*The Four Seasons*) ANTONIO VIVALDI

CD 1 Tracks 18–22	Year: 1725
	Tempo: Allegro (fast)
	Meter: Quadruple
	Form: Ritornello
	Concertino: Solo violin (joined occasionally by two more solo violins)
	Ripieno: String orchestra with continuo
	Duration: 3:26
	Special feature: The music is composed to sound like birds singing, streams murmuring, and thunder and lightning from a storm in order to fit the poem.

	Timing	What to listen for
18	0:00	**Ritornello,** orchestra, first phrase of optimistic spring theme stated forte, echoed piano
	0:15	Second phrase of spring theme, stated forte; echoed piano
19	0:31	**Contrasting section,** three solo violins, high pitch, trills, suggest bird calls
	1:06	**Ritornello,** orchestra, second phrase of spring theme, forte

continued

Timing	What to listen for
[20] 1:14	**Contrasting section,** orchestra, smoothly flowing, soft note pairs suggest streams and breezes
1:37	**Ritornello,** orchestra, second phrase of spring theme
[21] 1:44	**Contrasting section,** forte **tremolo** (fast, repeated notes) in orchestra for thunder, scales rushing upward for lightning; solo violin added with new lightning theme, tremolo continues in orchestra
2:12	**Ritornello,** orchestra, second phrase of spring theme
[22] 2:20	**Contrasting section,** three solo violins suggest bird calls; sustained note in bass
2:37	Orchestra, forte, ritornello-related theme
2:48	Solo violin with continuo, passage work
3:01	**Ritornello,** orchestra states second phrase of spring theme forte; echoed softly to conclude

Summary

The orchestra began in the baroque period. Baroque orchestras varied in size and instrumentation, and several types of works were composed for them. The concerto grosso is a multimovement work that pits a small group, the concertino, against the full ensemble, the ripieno. A solo concerto differs from the concerto grosso in that the concertino is reduced to a single instrument. The three-movement pattern of the concerto (fast-slow-fast) and the use of the ritornello form in the first movement were common.

New People and Concepts

Antonio Vivaldi	**embellishment**	**solo concerto**
concertino	**program music**	**tremolo**
concerto	**ripieno**	**virtuoso**
concerto grosso	**ritornello**	

Finale

Listen again to "Spring" and compare your impressions now with your notes from your first listening. Do you hear more now than you did before? You should now be able to answer the following questions:

▌ What is the meter?

▌ How many times does the ritornello return after its initial introduction?

▌ What solo instrument is featured?

▌ What instruments play the basso continuo part of the orchestra?

▌ What sounds that are mentioned in the poem are depicted by the music?

Characteristics of Baroque Music

Texture	Homophonic, polyphonic
Tonality	Major-minor system with dissonance used for special effects
Rhythm	Measured
Singing style	Monody, recitative, aria, arioso, large-scale choral works
Large vocal works	Opera, oratorio, Passion, Mass
Small vocal works	Cantata
Dynamics	Terraced
Musical instruments	Harpsichord, organ, lute, orchestras made up of bowed strings with some woodwinds and/or brass instruments with basso continuo
Solo instrumental music	Fantasia, prelude, toccata, fugue, suite
Group instrumental music	Sonata da chiesa, sonata da camera, concerto grosso, solo concerto
Other features	Activity, contrasts, and much improvised embellishment to decorate the musical lines

The Bathers by **Jean-Honoré Fragonard (1732–1806).** Paintings such as this one display the elegance, delicacy, softness, and playfulness of the French rococo style.

The classical era in the arts lasted from about 1750 to about 1800. This fifty-year period was highlighted by the American Revolution (1775–1783) and the French Revolution (1789–1799), both of which shocked conventional attitudes about governmental monarchies and the citizens they ruled. Intellectuals of the age perceived themselves as living in an age of enlightenment and reason. They believed in human control over a rational universe that had been created by a God who was more of a great watchmaker than a Father or Judge. Denis Diderot (1713–1784) and other French philosophers compiled the first encyclopedia. It

was a set of twenty-four books that put into writing all of the knowledge the writers were aware of from the past into the present. Intellectuals of the late eighteenth century glorified the power of the individual to control and order the world, a viewpoint that nurtured both economic growth and the notion that governments should reflect the will and interests of the people. That attitude is reflected in both the American and French revolutions.

A very popular artistic style of prerevolutionary France, known as the "rococo," lasted well into the classical period. The name of the style came from the French word *rocaille,* which means "a shell, or

Prelude | The Classical Era: Reason and Revolution

shell work." The rococo style emphasized elegance, delicacy, softness, and playfulness but retained much of the ornamentation of the baroque. The tastes of the period can be seen in the work of painters such as Jean-Honoré Fragonard, as well as in the interiors of aristocratic French palaces, which were decorated with beautiful gold-and-white curved woods, crystal chandeliers, and gilt ceilings.

Two of the most important rococo composers were Francois Couperin (1668–1733) and Jean-Philippe Rameau (1683–1764). Their music has many of the characteristics of the baroque, including the use of basso continuo in chamber or orchestral works. It tends to be even more highly decorated with ornaments and embellishments than was common in most Baroque music, however. The extreme amount of ornamentation quite fits with the gold gilded interiors just mentioned.

A word associated with French rococo dress is *macaroni.* It meant the ultimate in French fashion at the time. Think of the pancake makeup, long brocaded coats, and pompadour wigs that you often see in movies showing the period, such as the 1984 Academy Award–winning movie, *Amadeus.* In its day, though, "macaroni" was the height of style. British soldiers fighting Americans in the Revolutionary War made fun of their adversaries by casting them as country bumpkins in the song "Yankee Doodle." Yankees were so

An eighteenth-century French interior

unsophisticated that they thought that merely sticking a feather in their caps would qualify as "macaroni." Clearly, it took more than a mere feather to project the French style.

The style that foreshadowed the classical period in Germany and Austria was known in its day as *Empfindsamkeit,* or "sensitive style." It sharply contrasted with the rococo music of France by using more simple melodies and less ornamentation. Carl Philipp Emanuel Bach (1714–1788), son of Johann Sebastian Bach, was one of its primary composers.

This German-Austrian "sensitive style" eventually became known as "neoclassicism" or "classicism"

because it derived its primary inspiration from the clean lines and balanced forms of art and architecture of ancient Greece and Rome. Just as rococo music corresponded with the ornate interiors of French palaces, the classical style had its parallel in many buildings all over Europe and even in America that looked like Greek temples had been stuck on them. The "Georgian" style of architecture—named for the Georges who were the kings of England in the 1700s—with its columns that seem to be copied from Greek temples developed during this time. That influence was also exemplified in the American colonies, where many wealthy Americans, particularly in the South, were devoted to Greek art and literature. Compare the photo of the Parthenon, built in 448–432 BCE in Athens, Greece, with that of the rotunda of the University of Virginia at Charlottesville (page 109).

An artistic example of classicism can be seen in the works of Jacques-Louis David (1748–1825), a painter whose style avoided the "capricious ornament" of the rococo. Instead, in such works as *The Death of Socrates,* he built solemn scenes of noble sacrifice and great historical moments in a clear, balanced, linear style. Again, an interest in ancient Greece is reflected

here. Socrates (ca. 470–399 BCE) was an ancient Greek philosopher who was convicted of not believing in the gods of Athens and of corrupting his students. He was forced to commit suicide by drinking poisonous hemlock. In the picture, he is surrounded by his students, who grieve for him.

The two composers most commonly associated with the style are two Austrians, Wolfgang Amadeus Mozart (1756–1791) and Franz Joseph Haydn (1732–1809). Both depended on commissions for most of their careers—Mozart as a concertmaster to the Archbishop of Salzburg and then later a composer and music teacher in Vienna, and

Haydn as a music director for a series of four Hungarian princes in the Esterhazy family.

The rococo era in France would come to an abrupt end with the French Revolution. In July of 1789, a mob of angry French citizens stormed the Bastille, which was the state prison in Paris. This was the first of a series of attacks on the government that developed into the French Revolution. An Assembly of these revolutionaries wrote a *Declaration of the Rights of Man,* as well as a new constitution that limited the control of the monarchy. They presented it to their king, Louis XVI (1754–1793), who claimed to accept it but then fled the country.

The French Revolution was a particularly bloody affair. The king was brought back to Paris as a prisoner, tried for treason, and beheaded by a guillotine in a public ceremony in 1793. Later in the same year his wife, Marie Antoinette (1755–1793), and many other members of the aristocracy were also beheaded. The revolution led to the revolutionary French army engaging in a series of battles with the armies of France's more monarchial neighbors. From these contests emerged a new French hero and leader—Napoleon Bonaparte (1769–1821). By 1799, Napoleon had enough power to take over the French government. In the next fifteen years he came to control almost all of Europe, then lost it.

One of the effects of the French Revolution was the discrediting of

The Death of Socrates by Jacques-Louis David (1748–1825).
This painting of the Greek philosopher Socrates drinking the poison hemlock is a good example of the kind of clear and balanced artistic style that was popular during the classical period in Europe.

Napoleon Bonaparte, the French military hero and self-proclaimed king.

the ideals of rationality and order that had dominated the 1700s. Those ideals had, in the minds of many people, led to the bloodshed of the French Revolution and the rise of Napoleon's despotism. Clothing became much more simple, corresponding to the orderly simplicity of the music of Mozart and Haydn. Beau Brummel, an English style setter, omitted the needless ornamentation and frills that had dominated the rococo style in fashion in the 1800s and adopted more simple cuts that still influence clothing today.

The classical style would linger a little longer, and its transition to the next major era, the romantic, as well as that era's rejection of classicism, can be seen in the works of the German composer Ludwig van Beethoven (1770–1827). Beethoven initially felt a great amount of admiration for Napoleon Bonaparte, who was only one year his senior. He gave tribute to Napoleon by originally naming his third symphony "Bonaparte." That respect and admiration was crushed, however, in 1804, when Napoleon proclaimed himself the new king of France. When Beethoven heard that news, he tore up the title page of his yet unpublished symphony and renamed it the *Eroica,* "heroic symphony." Beethoven would even go so far as to write a piece celebrating "Wellington's Victory" over Napoleon at Waterloo. Beethoven serves as our best example of the transition from the classical period to the romantic period, as can be heard by listening to his works. Many of his earlier ones do not sound too much different from those of Mozart. His later ones would exhibit the great emotional flourishes and periods of quiet and crescendo that we associate with the romantic era, as is discussed in Prelude: Music of the Romantic Era.

11 | The Classical Symphony

*Mozart is just God's way of making the rest of us
feel insignificant.*

—MUSIC JOURNALIST DAVID W. BARBER
(BORN IN 1958)

Listening Introduction

Listen to the example of music that represents this chapter, Mozart's
Symphony no. 40, first movement, and make notes about what you hear. Give
some attention to the following:

▌ Can you detect the meter?

▌ Can you hear any melodies from the beginning that come back later in the
movement?

▌ Can you hear if there are any repeated sections?

▌ Can you hear any contrasting melodies (secondary melodies that are
different in character from the opening melody)?

▌ What would you guess the tempo to be?

Keep these notes to compare with your impressions about the music after you
study the information in this chapter.

The term *classical* is applied to music in several different ways. In one sense, we
speak of a "classic" as any work of lasting value. "Classical" sometimes designates
so-called *serious* or concert music, as opposed to *popular* music. In such an instance,
the term is applied without regard to historical or stylistic factors, so that composers
of different style periods—Bach, Beethoven, and Tchaikovsky, for example—may
all be considered "classical" composers. In a narrower and more accurate sense,
the term is applied to European music from about 1750 to about 1800, particularly
the works of Haydn, Mozart, and, to an extent, Beethoven and Schubert. Beethoven
and Schubert were transitional in that their compositions were based in classicism
but also contained elements of the coming romantic period.

As we discussed in Chapter 6, the style of the baroque period began as a
reaction against the vocal polyphony of the late Renaissance. Gradually, the
homophonic style of early baroque music was transformed into a new kind of
polyphony based on the major-minor harmonic system.

Similarly, the style of the classical era was the result of a reaction to the
instrumental polyphony of the late baroque period, particularly in the music of
Johann Sebastian Bach. Actually, J. S. Bach's music was considered old fashioned
by the end of his life, and it was not often played or commonly respected until
the mid-nineteenth century, when composers such as Mendelssohn rediscov-
ered him.

The Parthenon in Athens (left, 448–432 BCE) and the rotunda at the University of Virginia (right, 1819–1826) are both examples of classical architecture.

The new "classical" style was essentially homophonic rather than polyphonic; it was based on the idea of successive *contrasting* melodies rather than the contrapuntal expansion of *one* melody. In general, classical music tends to be structured in clear sections with clear divisions, even occasional pauses. Baroque music tends to flow without pauses and stopping points from the beginning to the end of individual pieces or movements.

Although the basso continuo was gradually abandoned in the classical era, composers continued to use the major-minor tonal system. That type of tonality, homophonic texture, and contrasting melodies are all common in the sonata style of the classical period.

The Form of the Classical Sonata

The meaning of the word *sonata* varies from age to age in music history. Originally, it meant something to be *played,* as opposed to a *cantata,* which was to be *sung.* The term had various applications throughout the baroque period. We studied several types of sonatas in Chapter 9. In the classical era the term *sonata* took on a very specific and important meaning.

The classical **sonata** is a multimovement work in one of two schemes, either of which has three or four movements: The forms listed for each individual movement indicate the basic structure the music most often follows. We discuss the details of each form later in this chapter and in the following chapters. The names are given here now just to make the outlines complete.

Three-movement plan

First movement	*Second movement*	*Third movement*
Fast tempo	Slow tempo	Fast tempo
Sonata form	Sonata, theme and variations or other form	Rondo, sonata, or other form

Four-movement plan

First movement	*Second movement*	*Third movement*	*Fourth movement*
Fast tempo	Slow tempo	Minuet and trio	Fast tempo
Sonata form	Sonata, theme and variations or other form	or scherzo and trio form	Rondo, sonata, or other form

In both plans, the first movement is invariably cast in what has become known as **sonata form.** Sonata form is based on the overall plan of the statement of two contrasting melodies, or **themes,** the manipulation of those themes, and the restatement of these themes. This general plan is realized in three specific sections of the movement: (1) the exposition, (2) the **development,** and (3) the **recapitulation.**

Exposition

The exposition introduces themes, usually two, that form the basis of the entire movement. In Mozart's works particularly, the first theme is usually fairly energetic, and the second theme contrasts with it by being more lyrical. These themes are connected by a **bridge.** The first theme establishes the tonality for the movement; the second theme is always in a different key. The bridge serves the function of modulating from the key of the first theme to the new key of the second theme. Usually there is a clear and definite cadence, pause, or both separating the bridge and the second theme. Frequently, a short section called a **codetta** is employed after the second theme to bring the exposition to a close. In almost all cases the exposition is repeated to help the listener remember the themes and recognize them when they reappear later in the movement.

Development

The development concentrates on the themes that were presented in the exposition and manipulates them in a variety of ways. The themes may be fragmented into small melodic or rhythmic **motive**s (short themes or parts of themes). These motives can be expanded, or the themes or parts of them might be repeated at different pitch levels. Changes in timbre, rhythm, and dynamics are among the many devices that may be employed. No two development sections are the same; however, what is common to all of them is the process of **modulation,** or the frequent changing of tonal centers.

Recapitulation

The recapitulation is a restatement of the whole exposition, with one important change—the second theme appears at the pitch level of the home key (the tonal center of the overall movement) rather than in a contrasting key, as it did in the exposition. The reaffirmation of the tonic key and the return of the themes of the exposition create a sense of unity and balance for this formal structure. In some pieces, the **coda** ("tail") is added as an extended conclusion of the movement.

Occasionally a movement in sonata form is preceded by a slow introduction. The introduction, however, is not part of the form and is not usually included in the repetition of the exposition or in the recapitulation.

Sonata form is outlined below:

Exposition	Development	Recapitulation
Theme I (tonic)	Transformation of themes from the exposition	Theme I (tonic)
Bridge (modulates to new key)		Bridge (extended)
		Theme II (tonic)
Theme II (new key)	Rapid modulations	Coda
Codetta to cadence		Final cadence
Exposition repeated		

Another form, or structure for an individual movement, is the **minuet and trio.** This form is most often used for the third movement of a four-movement work. Styled after the minuet dance, it is written in triple meter. The minuet and trio follows a ternary form as outlined below:

A	B	A
Minuet	Trio	Minuet

The term *trio* for the middle section is a carryover from the 1600s, when the second of two alternating dances was often scored for three instruments. In the classical sonata, the trio is rarely a three-voice piece but does contrast with the minuet in a variety of ways.

Beethoven experimented with the minuet and trio a great deal and eventually adopted, in place of the minuet, a much faster type of piece known as a **scherzo** and trio. As we shall see, the scherzo and trio became a movement of great power and drama in his works.

The Classical Orchestra

In the baroque era, instrumental music became an independent idiom, and a vast literature for instrumental ensembles was produced. But the baroque orchestra, aside from the usual complement of strings, had no fixed makeup.

In the classical era, the composition of the orchestra became standardized to a great extent, largely due to the work of **Johann Stamitz** (1717–1757), a violinist, composer, and conductor of the orchestra at the German city of Mannheim. Under his direction, the Mannheim orchestra developed into the most celebrated musical ensemble in Europe. The excellence of its playing was praised by the leading composers of the day.

By baroque standards, the Mannheim orchestra was of large dimensions. In 1756 it consisted of twenty violins divided into two sections (first violins and second violins), four violas, four cellos, and four basses. The wind section included four horns in addition to pairs of flutes, oboes, clarinets, and bassoons. Trumpets and timpani were also used, usually together. The German poet and musician D. F. D. Schubert (1739–1791) recorded his impressions of the orchestra in his *Essay on Musical Esthetics:*

> No orchestra in the world ever equaled the Mannheimers' execution. Its forte is like thunder, its crescendo like a mighty waterfall, its diminuendo a gentle river disappearing into the distance, its piano is a breath of spring. The wind instruments could not be used to better advantage; they lift and carry, they reinforce and give life to the storm for violins.

"The Live Experience: The Duties of the Conductor" discusses the importance of the conductor to the sound of the orchestra.

Although we will concentrate on Mozart in this chapter and on Haydn in Chapter 13, "Classical Chamber Music," the point needs to be made here that it was Franz Joseph Haydn who did so much to develop both the classical **symphony** and the string quartet forms that he is often called the "Father of the Symphony" and the "Father of the String Quartet." As we discuss in greater detail later, Haydn was responsible for producing music for a series of princes who wanted new symphonies and string quartets, often in order to entertain their guests or to enjoy playing themselves. As he composed one work after another, Haydn devised ways of getting a fuller and fuller sound out of the orchestra or quartet, something that was well liked by his listeners and copied by other composers, including Mozart.

THE LIVE EXPERIENCE
The Duties of the Conductor

In many ways an orchestral **conductor** "plays" the orchestra as if it were his or her instrument. Of course, the orchestra is not a single instrument, and the conductor faces many challenges in making the collection of musicians play together as one. Small orchestras of the classical period were sometimes led by the first violinist. In those cases, many of the duties conductors perform today were left to chance. Orchestras led by a conductor who does not need to play part of the music soon became the standard, as it is today.

The conductor brings the various parts of the orchestra together to create one, cohesive sound.

The conductor's most obvious duty is that of establishing, maintaining, and making whatever changes might be appropriate to the tempo. Orchestral conductors usually use a baton, which they wave in particular patterns that follow the meter of the piece. The speed at which they make those movements establishes the tempo at which the entire orchestra plays.

The musicians need more than just the setting of a tempo, however, to know how to play. Musicians on one side of the orchestra cannot hear those on the other, so they must rely on the conductor to tell them how loud or soft to play in order to balance with the other instruments. At times, one part needs to be emphasized so that the audience will hear it over the rest of the ensemble, and the conductor has to let the musician know exactly how to do that.

Sometimes individual musicians do not play through long sections of the music, and it is important that the conductor let the players know exactly when to come in. The players have the music and it tells them how long to wait before playing, but over a longer rest they could easily get lost and come in at the wrong time without the help of the conductor.

Some conductors perform from memory, but most use a score. A conductor's score is quite different from the music that each individual player has because the conductor must have all of the players' parts on one page. Individual players need only their own parts. The conductor's score has the parts notated so that all are lined up vertically, allowing the conductor to see exactly who should be playing when.

Beyond the practical details of keeping the players together and well balanced, the conductor is the one who leads the **phrasing** (the degree to which lines are played smoothly, detached, or in some combination of those), **articulation** (the way a musician starts and stops the tone quality of each note he or she plays), and other details of musical interpretation for the group. Composers often indicate the phrasing and articulation they desire for a given piece, but the degree to which those are followed is up to the conductor. Conductors can be quite autocratic about this, and a musician who refuses to follow direction might find him- or herself out of a job.

When a concert is over, you might notice that the conductor acknowledges the first violinist (the concert master or mistress), who has been responsible for the bowing of the string parts and for overseeing the tuning of the orchestra. He or she will also acknowledge any musicians who played solo parts, to allow the audience to give them special applause. Of course, it is the conductor who takes most of the credit for the quality of sound the orchestra produces.

Wolfgang Amadeus Mozart

The first major composer of the classical period we will study is **Wolfgang Amadeus Mozart** (1756–1791). Mozart was born in Salzburg, Austria, and began his musical career as one of the most celebrated child prodigies in eighteenth-century Europe. His father, Leopold, a highly respected composer and violinist, recognized his son's extraordinary talent and carefully supervised his musical education. Mozart began harpsichord lessons when he was four and wrote his first compositions when he was five. At the age of six, he and his older sister, Maria Anna ("Nannerl"), were taken by their father on a concert tour of Munich and Vienna.

Austrian composer
Wolfgang Amadeus Mozart

Up to age fifteen Mozart was almost constantly on tour, playing prepared works and improvising. Although the harpsichord and later the piano remained Mozart's principal instruments, he also mastered the violin and the organ. In addition to keyboard pieces, he wrote church works, symphonies, string quartets, and operas. In 1769, on a long trip to Italy, Mozart was commissioned to compose his first major opera, *Mitridate*, which was performed in Milan in 1770. His success in Italy, as triumphant as Handel's had been some sixty years earlier, brought him a number of commissions for operas.

His father, Leopold, court composer and vice chapelmaster to the Archbishop of Salzburg, obtained a position for his son as concertmaster in the archbishop's orchestra. But the new Archbishop of Salzburg, installed in 1772, failed to appreciate Mozart's genius. Relations between the haughty churchman and the high-spirited young composer steadily deteriorated until, in 1781, despite his father's objections, Mozart quit his position and settled in Vienna.

The first years in Vienna were fairly prosperous. Mozart was in great demand as a teacher; he gave numerous concerts, and his German **Singspiel**—a German comic opera with spoken dialogue—*Die Entführung aus dem Serail (The Abduction from the Seraglio, 1782)* was a success. He married Constanze Weber, a woman he had met several years earlier on a concert tour. Overall, the marriage was a happy one, but Constanze was a careless housekeeper, and Mozart was a poor manager of finances. He never achieved a permanent post at the court. Public taste changed, and his teaching began to fall off. Except for occasional successes—his opera *Le Nozze di Figaro (The Marriage of Figaro, 1786)* and the Singspiel *Die Zauberflöte (The Magic Flute, 1791)*—the last ten years of his life were spent, for the most part, in poverty.

In 1788 Mozart gave up public performances, relying on a meager income from teaching and loans from various friends to sustain himself and his family. He was Catholic but also a member of the Freemasons, a secret society that believed in brotherhood and helping one another. He gave credit to the aid he received from his Mason friends by including many Masonic symbols and practices in his last opera, *Die Zauberflöte (The Magic Flute)*. In spite of his troubles, he continued to compose, but his health began to decline. When he died in 1791 at the age of thirty-five, he was buried in an unmarked grave in a part of the cemetery reserved for the poor.

Unlike the meticulous Haydn, who kept a chronological list of all his compositions, Mozart never bothered to organize his musical papers in any consistent fashion. In the nineteenth century, Ludwig von Köchel compiled a roughly chronological listing of Mozart's music (numbering up to 626 pieces). This catalogue, along with substantial revisions and additions by later musicologists, remains in use today, the number of each work being preceded by "Koch" or the initial "K" for the man who did the organization.

Mozart was able to carry around finished compositions in his head, once re-marking that "the committing to paper is done quickly enough. For everything is already finished, and it rarely differs on paper from what it was in my imagination." His instrumental music includes forty-one symphonies, twelve violin concertos, over twenty-five piano concertos, some fourteen concertos for other instruments, twenty-six string quartets, seventeen piano sonatas, over forty violin sonatas, and numerous other chamber music works. All of this is in addition to a large amount of vocal music, which we discuss in Chapter 14.

Chapter 11
Activity

Mozart
Symphony

We discussed the classical sonata earlier. Symphonies are often constructed in a similar way. Some early symphonies followed the three-movement plan, but most symphonies of the classical period have four movements. Of the four standard movements in Mozart's Symphony no. 40, we will hear the first and third movements. The first is in sonata form, and the third is in minuet and trio form.

In accordance with the four-movement sonata plan, the second movement contrasts with the first. It is slower in tempo (andante, a walking pace), different in meter (sextuple), and in a contrasting key. Like the first movement, it is cast in sonata form, yet it differs strongly in content and mood. A discussion of the third movement follows as an example of minuet and trio form. "Hearing the Difference: Vivaldi's 'Spring' from *The Four Seasons* and Mozart's Symphony no. 40, first movement" will help you compare these works.

Listening Guide

Symphony no. 40 in G Minor, first movement WOLFGANG AMADEUS MOZART

CD 1
Tracks 23–28

Year: 1788

Texture: Homophonic

Tempo: Allegro

Meter: Duple

Form: Sonata form

Instrumentation: Orchestra consisting of one flute, two oboes, two clarinets, two bassoons,
   two horns, and strings

Duration: 7:28

	Timing		**What to listen for**
	Exposition		
23	0:00	Theme 1	Violins play bouncing theme 1; agitated accompaniment in violas
	0:30	Bridge	Theme 1 restated; orchestra plays forte (loud), rushing strings, emphatic close
24	0:47	Theme 2	Violins play floating theme 2, answered by woodwinds
	1:08		Strings take over, crescendo, build twice to high point; soft descending scale
	1:19		Rhythmic motive from first theme traded among woodwind instruments and strings alternating soft and loud
	1:37	Closing	Rushing downward string scales, emphatic closing chords

(The exposition is repeated)

Timing		What to listen for
Development		
[25] 3:44		Piano, theme 1 in violins, new harmonies
3:58		Sudden forte, theme 1 traded between low strings and violins
4:25		Soft, static version of phrase traded between violins and woodwinds
4:35		Woodwind answer reduced to three-note motive
4:40		Sudden forte, three-note motive traded between violins and low strings
4:48		No strings, flute and clarinets trade three-note motive descending into:
Recapitulation		
[26] 4:53	Theme 1	Violins; woodwinds answer; loud chords
5:14		Violins begin theme again
5:22	Bridge	Forte, upward-leaping motive in violins, then low strings back and forth
5:30		Rushing string scales, emphatic close
[27] 6:02	Theme 2	Flowing theme 2 in violins; woodwind answer
6:23		Strings take over, crescendo, build twice to high point; soft descending scale
6:39		Rhythmic motive from theme 1 traded among woodwind instruments and strings alternating soft and loud
[28] 6:57	Coda	Rushing string scales, build to woodwind chord
7:07		Violins begin theme 1, answered by violins, violas, woodwinds; sudden forte, emphatic closing chords

Listening Guide

Symphony no. 40 in G Minor, third movement WOLFGANG AMADEUS MOZART

CD 3
Tracks 18–20

Texture: Homophonic

Tempo: Allegretto

Meter: Triple

Form: Minuet and trio form

Duration: 4:37

Timing		What to listen for
[18] 0:00	**Minuet (A)**	First phrase played by orchestra, forte; first phrase repeated
0:34		Second phrase, more dissonant; moves directly into repeat of first phrase, varied
1:08		Repeat of second phrase and varied first phrase
[19] 1:41	**Trio (B)**	Relaxed, lyrical phrase in strings, woodwinds, then strings; lyrical phrase repeated
2:33		Lower strings begin, answered by woodwinds; woodwinds complete the phrase; horns join strings in varied return of lyrical phrase; phrase completed by horns with woodwinds, then strings
3:08		Strings and woodwinds repeat second phrase; horns with strings, then woodwinds, repeat varied return of first phrase
[20] 3:42	**Minuet (A)**	First phrase, forte
3:59		Second phrase and return of first phrase repeated; soft ending in woodwinds

HEARING THE DIFFERENCE

Vivaldi's "Spring," first movement, from *The Four Seasons,* and Mozart's Symphony no. 40, first movement

In comparing these two compositions, we will concentrate on some basic differences in the sound of the orchestras of two different style periods, the baroque and the classical. The most obvious of those is the presence of the harpsichord in Vivaldi's "Spring," but the added presence of woodwind and brass instruments in Mozart's symphony creates a fuller and more colorful effect that is typical of the sound of the classical orchestra. Additionally, "Spring" was composed to describe the visions of springtime in the poem that Vivaldi wrote to go with it, and Mozart's symphony was composed to appreciate as pure music with no storyline association. The violin soloist stands out in "Spring," since it is a violin concerto.

	"Spring," first movement, from *The Four Seasons*	**Symphony no. 40, first movement**
Historical period	Baroque	Classical
Tempo	Allegro	Allegro
Meter	Quadruple	Duple
Form	Ritornello (notice that the opening theme returns often throughout the movement, with contrasting sections between the returns).	Sonata (exposition, development, recapitulation, and coda). The opening themes do return in the recapitulation, but not so constantly as they would in ritornello form.
Instrumentation	Solo concerto for violin and string orchestra with harpsichord continuo.	Classical symphonic orchestra with flute, oboes, clarinets, bassoons, and horns in addition to the string section.
Story behind the compositions	Themes composed to fit the bird song, stream, and storm sections of the poem, "Spring." The term for this is *program music.*	Themes composed to contrast with one another and no intention of the portrayal of nonmusical subjects. The term for this is ***absolute music.***

Summary

The classical period in music history lasted from about 1750 to about 1800. German and Austrian composers such as Haydn, Mozart, and Beethoven organized their compositions according to the same sense of balance and symmetry common in artworks of the "classic" civilizations of ancient Greece and Rome. Such organization included three- or four-movement works with each movement following a balanced formal structure.

One of the most popular ways of structuring a first or other movement was the sonata form. It featured an exposition that "exposed" two themes on which the rest of the movement would be based. That was repeated to allow for the listeners to hear the themes enough times to remember them. The next section was the development, during which the composer varied the themes or parts of them. The idea of balance was created by the next section of the form, the recapitulation, in which the themes return to remind the listener where the movement began. A coda sometimes brings the movement to a conclusion.

One of the most prolific and brilliant composers of the classical period was Wolfgang Amadeus

Mozart. He was a child prodigy who was trained by his composer father and who composed music in every genre (type of work) of the classical era.

New People and Concepts

absolute music	Johann Stamitz	Singspiel
articulation	minuet and trio	sonata
bridge	modulation	sonata form
coda	motive	symphony
codetta	phrasing	theme
conductor	recapitulation	Wolfgang Amadeus Mozart
development	scherzo	

Finale

Listen again to Symphony no. 40, first movement, and compare your impressions now with your notes from your first listening. Do you hear more now than you did before? You should now be able to answer the following questions:

▮ What is the meter?

▮ When do you hear the first theme return later in the movement?

▮ When does the exposition repeat?

▮ When does the second theme appear and then repeat?

▮ What is the tempo?

12 | The Classical Concerto

There is no shadow of death anywhere in Mozart's music. Even his own funeral was a failure. It was dispersed by a shower of rain; and to this day nobody knows where he was buried or whether he was buried at all or not. My own belief is that he was not. Depend on it, they had no sooner put up their umbrellas and bolted for the nearest shelter than he got up, shook off his bones into the common grave of the people, and soared off into universality.
—MUSIC CRITIC GEORGE BERNARD SHAW
(1856–1950)

Listening Introduction

Listen to the first movement of Piano Concerto no. 23 in A Major by Mozart and make notes about what you hear. Give some attention to the following:

❚ Can you detect the meter?

❚ Can you guess at the tempo?

❚ Can you tell what instruments are playing?

❚ Can you hear any melodies at the beginning that are played again later in the piece?

❚ Can you hear any section of the music where a single instrument plays without the orchestra?

Keep these notes to compare with your impressions about the music after you study the information in this chapter.

During the baroque era, the term *concerto* referred to both the concerto grosso (Bach's Brandenburg Concerto no. 5) and the concerto for solo instrument and orchestra (Vivaldi's *The Four Seasons*). In the classical era, composers continued to develop the solo concerto, while the concerto grosso fell into disuse. The violin and piano were the favored solo instruments, but solo concertos were also written for other instruments, such as the cello, trumpet, bassoon, horn, and clarinet. Typically, the classical concerto follows the three-movement sonata plan outlined in Chapter 11 and consists of a fast-slow-fast movement sequence *without* a minuet and trio.

Chapter 12
Activity

Mozart
Concerto

The contrast between the solo instrument and the orchestra was an essential element in the concerto, and the formal structure of each movement was planned to give the soloist an opportunity to be featured along with or apart from the orchestra at several important places. As we discussed in Chapter 11, the conductor is the person who, among other things, is in charge of the dynamic levels of the orchestra, which sometimes means quieting them down to allow the soloist to be heard. "The Live Experience: Concerto Soloists" describes the soloist's responsibilities.

THE LIVE EXPERIENCE
Concerto Soloists

Large concert halls such as those we have today did not exist in the eighteenth century, and yet members of the growing middle class wanted to hear music. Public concerts were usually held in theaters or in halls that had been constructed for other uses. Most of the halls held no more than a few hundred listeners seated in chairs. Admission prices were fairly expensive, and admission was limited to subscribers, so the audiences were fairly certain to be knowledgeable about music and interested in what they were going to hear. On the other hand, they were much larger and less exclusive audiences than were common in palaces. Performers whose incomes depended on their being popular enough to be invited to perform again had plenty of incentive to please their listeners. Concerto soloists were no exception.

Many composers were also concerto soloists and so wrote music to showcase their musicianship and technical ability. Much of the rest of the time, composers wrote concertos for their students or for musicians who could afford to commission (pay for) works. Johann Joachim Quantz (1697–1773), for example, composed about 300 concertos for flute and orchestra, which both he and his patron, Frederick the Great, King of Prussia (1712–1786), performed. Frederick the Great would not have performed in public houses, but he enjoyed playing in his own chambers. Quantz performed the works both in the king's chambers and for the public.

Generally, when performing a concerto, the soloist sits or stands to the left of the conductor, in front of the orchestra. When the music features the soloist, attention is drawn to him or her. Many concertos include a special time for the soloist to showcase his or her skills in what is called a **cadenza.** Cadenzas are often placed somewhere toward the end of fast movements. Right before a cadenza, the orchestra usually sustains a chord and then stops playing completely, allowing the soloist to take over. Classical cadenzas were usually improvised by the soloist, and even the length was not dictated by the composer. Soloists were free to play using whatever techniques they thought would please the audience, though they usually related their playing to the themes of the preceding movement. When they felt their solo drawing to a close, they used the playing of a **trill** (two notes played back and forth very fast) to indicate to the conductor that it was time to bring the orchestra back in.

Today, musicians who play classical music are seldom taught to improvise, and famous soloists have composed suggested cadenzas that are published and often used by other players. If you attend a concert or buy a CD of a classical concerto performance, you will often see the words "cadenza by . . . ," giving credit to the person who composed it. By the next period in music history, the romantic period, it became more common for composers to write out the cadenzas because they wanted more control of what was played under their names. Mozart, always ahead of his time, frequently composed suggested cadenzas. This is the case for the concerto we will listen to, Mozart's Piano Concerto no. 23 in A Major.

Double-Exposition Sonata Form

First movements of classical concertos were based on the single-movement sonata form discussed in Chapter 11. The form was handled somewhat differently, however, when it was used in concertos. Where the standard sonata

A Keyboard Concerto, 1777.

form repeated the exposition so that the listeners would be able to remember the themes, the concerto exposition was not repeated. Instead, concerto composers wrote the themes out two or more times so that both the soloist and the orchestra had an opportunity to play them. Because the themes were written out at least twice, this version of the sonata form is called "double-exposition sonata form."

As in all movements in sonata form, a development section followed the exposition. In the development the composer had much freedom to switch from the orchestra to the soloist and back whenever he or she desired.

The recapitulation followed, again presenting the main themes to allow the listeners to hear them return much the way they were played in the exposition. The cadenza was usually fitted in somewhere toward the end of the recapitulation (although it could be elsewhere, even at the end of the development). Wherever the cadenza was placed, the full orchestra was brought back to end the movement.

Listening Guide

Piano Concerto no. 23 in A Major, first movement WOLFGANG AMADEUS MOZART

CD 3
Tracks 21–29

Year: 1786

Texture: Homophonic

Tempo: Allegro

Meter: Quadruple

Form: Double-exposition sonata form

Instrumentation: Solo piano, flute, two clarinets, two bassoons, two French horns, and strings

Duration: 10:24

Special feature: The cadenza was composed by Mozart.

Timing		What to listen for
First Exposition		
0:00	Theme 1	Strings play the theme; winds repeat the opening; strings and then winds return
0:31	Bridge	Full orchestra plays bridge theme; violins play fast phrase
0:53	Theme 2	Violins play theme 2 softly
1:09		Theme repeated by violins and bassoon, flute enters at repeat
1:28		Full orchestra; high woodwinds; pause

Track markers: 21 (at 0:00), 22 (at 0:53)

Timing		What to listen for
Second Exposition		
23	2:01	Theme 1	Piano solo accompanied by strings; piano varies the theme on repeat
	2:28	Bridge	Orchestra plays bridge theme
	2:36		Piano, accompanied by strings and **staccato** (short, detached) winds
24	2:56	Theme 2	Piano plays second theme; violins and flute repeat it
	3:24		Piano and orchestra
	4:04		Full orchestra; pause
Development		
25	4:15		Strings and piano introduce new theme
	4:38		Clarinet, then piano with strings
	4:45		Flute, then piano with strings
	4:53		Woodwinds, piano, then strings
	5:37		Solo piano, orchestra leading to:
Recapitulation		
26	5:53	Theme 1	Theme 1 played by strings, then woodwinds
	6:07		Piano with woodwinds
	6:20	Bridge	Orchestra plays bridge theme
	6:28		Piano with strings; staccato violins and woodwinds
27	6:47	Theme 2	Solo piano plays theme 2; winds repeat, piano joins
	7:14		Piano with orchestra
	7:45		Solo piano plays theme from development; woodwinds repeat theme
	8:24		Orchestra plays bridge and development themes, then holds chord and pauses
Cadenza		
28	8:52		Piano solo, ends with long trill
Coda		
29	9:55		Full orchestra, **cadence** (final-sounding ending)
	10:08		Woodwinds; orchestra; flutes and violins trill

Summary

Classical concertos were usually solo concertos for violin, piano, or other instruments with orchestra. They most often followed the three-movement sonata plan, with fast-slow-fast tempos for the movements. The primary element of a concerto is the soloist contrasting with the orchestra, with each having an opportunity to be featured.

The primary opportunity for the soloist to showcase his or her talents came in the cadenza, a solo section toward the end of most fast concerto movements. Though composers sometimes wrote them out, cadenzas were most often improvised by the players. Today, soloists can improvise their own cadenzas or use cadenzas that were written and published by composers or other soloists. Improvised cadenzas end with a trill to let the conductor know that it is time to bring back the orchestra.

First movements in concertos follow the double-exposition sonata form. "Double exposition" indicates that the themes are written out for both the orchestra and the soloist and are not repeated as they would be in a standard symphonic sonata form. After the double exposition, the concerto form has development and recapitulation sections similar to those in the standard sonata form, although these sections allow time for the concerto soloist to be featured along with the orchestra.

New People and Concepts

cadence   staccato   trill

cadenza

Finale

Listen again to the first movement of Piano Concerto no. 23 by Mozart and compare your impressions now with your notes from your first listening. Do you hear more now than you did before? You should now be able to answer the following questions:

▌ What is the meter?

▌ What is the tempo?

▌ What instruments are playing?

▌ Where do melodies at the beginning return later in the piece?

▌ Where does a single instrument play without the orchestra?

13 | Classical Chamber Music

Haydn had neither the flashy individuality of Mozart nor the brooding, romantic passion of Beethoven. He was more of a middle-management type.

—MUSIC JOURNALIST DAVID W. BARBER (BORN IN 1958)

Listening Introduction

Listen to the example of music that represents this chapter, String Quartet op. 33, no. 3 ("The Bird"), fourth movement, by Haydn, and make notes about what you hear. Give some attention to the following:

▌ Can you guess at the tempo?

▌ Can you detect the meter?

▌ Can you tell what instruments are playing?

▌ Can you hear a melody at the beginning that returns later?

▌ Can you hear anything that caused people to call the piece "The Bird"?

Keep these notes to compare with your impressions about the music after you study the information in this chapter.

Chamber Sonatas

Despite the popularity of the orchestra, music for smaller ensembles continued to thrive as wealthy patrons commissioned works to be performed in their palaces for private audiences. We call music for small ensembles **chamber music.** Most chamber music is composed for from two to nine instrumentalists. The pieces are often titled according to the number of players as follows: **duet** (2), **trio** (3), **quartet** (4), **quintet** (5), **sextet** (6), **septet** (7), **octet** (8), and **nonet** (9). Sometimes the names of the works make it obvious what instruments are needed to play them. For example, a guitar duet is a work for two guitars. In other cases, the titles are not so telling. A **piano trio** is written for violin, cello, and piano; a **piano quartet** is written for violin, viola, cello, and piano; and a **piano quintet** is for string quartet and piano. Sometimes chamber works are given titles such as sonata followed by the names of the instruments needed to play them.

Normally, chamber music is performed with one player on each part, but occasionally string players double or triple up on the parts to create a chamber orchestra. Mozart's "Eine kleine Nachtmusik" ("A Little Night Music"), for example, was composed for a string quintet (five players), but it is often performed by a string orchestra. Such a change does not require any revision to the music; the sound is just much fuller.

One of the great beauties of chamber music is its intimacy. No conductor is needed because the musicians can communicate among themselves about such things as when to start or what tempo to use. A mere nod or two from one of the players is enough to tell the group to begin. Chamber music is often referred to

THE LIVE EXPERIENCE
The Performance of Chamber Music

Because chamber music is performed with a single player on each part and by groups of no more than nine musicians, a conductor is not necessary to determine the tempo, keep the players together, balance the dynamics, indicate when musicians should come in, or direct the phrasing. Similarly, a concertmaster/mistress is not needed to "bow" string parts or oversee tuning. The bowing of string parts involves deciding when the players should play up or down with the bow. Because down bows tend to sound a bit heavier than up bows, their use greatly affects the phrasing.

As is also the case with orchestras, the real work in chamber music happens during rehearsal sessions. A chamber group will often use their first rehearsal to simply "read through" the music they will perform, playing the music to give the musicians an idea about what the composer intended and how they will eventually interpret it. Depending on how comfortable each player feels with his or her part and what ideas come up in discussions about the music, further rehearsals will be planned as necessary. Players responsible for particularly difficult sections will take their music home to practice their own part so they will be ready for the next rehearsal. Difficult or awkward sections of the music will often be practiced through many times until the entire group is comfortable with the way they play together. Typically, musicians who have performed together before need less rehearsal time than those who are unfamiliar with one another's playing styles.

Chamber music sometimes begins with a single musician playing solo, which makes it easy for the others to join in where appropriate. Often, however, all of the musicians begin playing at the same time,

and that requires some planning. Because the musicians will have agreed on the exact tempo they will use, it usually takes only a single nod from the assigned musician to have them all start together. That same player will often nod in tempo at other times when he or she wants the group to gradually slow down, speed up, or make any other changes to the speed of the beat at which the group is playing.

Unlike members of a large orchestra, chamber musicians can easily hear one another in both rehearsals and performances. This allows them to balance dynamics to make certain that all players are heard equally or to have one or more players to stand out while they are playing. Because chamber musicians each play their own part with no other member of the group playing the same notes, they can each phrase their part themselves up to a point. In rehearsal, the group will decide together how crisply they want to play the staccato (detached) notes or how smoothly they want to play a legato (connected notes) phrase and will pencil those indications into their music. Orchestral musicians do this too, but the directions are given to them by the conductor.

At a chamber music concert, the audience generally applauds when the musicians walk out on stage. They will bow, take their seats, check their tuning, and look at the group member who will give the nod to begin. One might question the need for tuning the instruments in front of the audience since the instruments have surely been tuned before. The last-minute tuning is necessary because stage lights tend to be very hot and heat affects an instrument's pitch. If there is a keyboard instrument included in the group, the other musicians will tune to that.

as the music of friends because of the close proximity of the players and the fact that each player can be heard clearly within the group sound.

The multimovement sonata structure that we encountered was also used in chamber music for a wide variety of instrumental combinations. The **string quartet,** consisting of a first and second violin, a viola, and a cello, became in the classical era the most important chamber music medium. Its popularity continued well into the twentieth century in the works of Bartók, Hindemith, and others. "The Live Experience: The Performance of Chamber Music" discusses this type of music in detail.

Franz Joseph Haydn

Franz Joseph Haydn (1732–1809) was the first great master of string quartet composition. Haydn was born in Rohrau, a small Austrian village located near the Hungarian border southeast of Vienna. His parents, both of peasant stock, seem to have encouraged their son's musical ability and entrusted his earliest musical training to a relative, Johann Franck, a schoolteacher and choirmaster in the nearby town of Hainburg. At age six, Haydn was already singing in Franck's church choir and had begun playing the **clavier** (a generic name for a keyboard instrument) and violin.

In 1740, the composer and choirmaster at St. Stephen's Cathedral in Vienna stopped in Hainburg to recruit singers for his choir. Impressed with the eight-year-old's voice, he arranged to take the young boy back with him to Vienna.

For the next nine years, Haydn was employed as a Catholic choirboy. He received a smattering of elementary education at St. Stephen's choir school and continued with violin and voice lessons, but his training in composition and theory was so erratic that he was largely self-taught. In 1749, when his voice began to mature, Haydn was dismissed and had to find work outside the church.

The following years were hard ones. At first Haydn made his living teaching clavier by day and playing in street bands and serenading parties by night. His reputation as a teacher and vocal accompanist, however, gradually spread, and he started serious composition. In 1759, he was appointed *Kapellmeister* (conductor) and chamber composer to a Bohemian nobleman, Count Morzin. He composed his first symphonies for the count's small orchestra.

Franz Joseph Haydn. The composer is depicted here directing a string quartet rehearsal.

Esterházy Palace in Fertod, Hungary, was where Haydn composed and debuted much of his work.

The year 1761 proved to be good for Haydn. He was hired as assistant music director to Prince Paul Anton Esterházy, head of one of the most powerful and wealthy Hungarian noble families. Haydn's contract stipulated that he was to compose whatever music was required of him (which would become the property of his patron), keep the musical instruments in good repair, train singers, and supervise the conduct of all of the musicians.

Despite the rigid and burdensome requirements of his contract, Haydn enjoyed his work and was to say later, "My prince was pleased with all my work, I was commended, and as conductor of an orchestra I could make experiments, observe what strengthened and what weakened an effect and thereupon improve, substitute, omit, and try new things; I was cut off from the world, there was no one around to mislead and harass me, and so I was forced to become original."

Haydn remained in the employ of the Esterházy family for almost thirty years, serving first Prince Paul Anton and then his brother, Prince Nikolaus. Despite his isolation at their country estate, his fame gradually spread throughout Europe. He was able to work on commissions from other individuals and from publishers all over the continent.

Prince Nikolaus loved music and invited many important guests to his palace to hear Haydn's compositions. These included symphonies; chamber works of all kinds, particularly string quartets; and operas. The prince played a cello-like bowed string instrument called the baryton and enjoyed playing with Haydn and other musicians in the privacy of his own quarters. Haydn also provided the music for those sessions.

Haydn's music has a wonderful sense of humor and, although he was a hired servant, he had a good relationship with the prince. Both his humor and his ability to communicate with the prince are evidenced in his Symphony no. 45, the *Farewell* (1772). It was composed after a long summer during which Prince Nikolaus had entertained hundreds of guests and had required much music for their entertainment. It was the time of year for the musicians, who did not live at the summer palace full-time, to go back to their primary residences and be with their families. Not able to directly tell the prince that the musicians needed leave, Haydn composed Symphony no. 45 to communicate the message for him.

During the last movement, one or two of the musicians at a time stopped playing, snuffed out their candles, and left the room. Only two violinists, the concertmaster and Haydn, were left to finish the symphony. The prince was confused at first, but then got the point and allowed them to go home for their winter break.

When Prince Nikolaus died in 1790, Haydn was retained as nominal *Kapellmeister* for the Esterházy family, but he was now independent. Moving to Vienna, he resumed his friendship with Mozart, whose talent he had admired since their first meeting in 1781. Haydn also gave lessons to a young, rising composer named Ludwig van Beethoven. He made two successful trips to London (1791–1792, 1794–1795), where he conducted a number of his own symphonies, written on commission for the well-known impresario Johann Salomon. After his second London visit, he ceased writing symphonies, turning instead to the composition of Masses and oratorios. After 1800, his health began to fail, and he lived in secluded retirement. He died in 1809 at the age of seventy-seven.

Haydn's **opus** (work number within the collected works of a particular composer) 33 is a set of six string quartets. The set is sometimes called the Russian Quartets, because the audience for their **première** performance included the Russian Grand Duke Paul (later Tsar Paul II) and his wife, who were visiting Vienna. Number 3 is nicknamed "The Bird" because of the birdlike trills and ornaments in the first, second, and fourth movements. We will listen for bird sounds in the fourth movement.

This movement introduces a form we have not heard before, the **rondo.** A rondo is an extended alternating form in which the first theme, "A," returns several times with contrasting music (represented by letters B and C) between the A's. Using letters to identify the order in which the themes appear, the most common rondo is ABACA or ABACABA. The rondo we will listen to differs slightly from the norm in that it has two sections of development, in which the themes are tossed around and reduced to two notes. Because development sections are usually part of the single-movement sonata form, this form combines the two names and is called a **sonata rondo.** Listen, then see "Hearing the Difference: Mozart's Symphony no. 40, first movement, and Haydn's String Quartet op. 33, no. 3, fourth movement."

Chapter 13
Activity

Beethoven
Rondo

Listening Guide

String Quartet op. 33, no. 3 ("The Bird"), fourth movement FRANZ JOSEPH HAYDN

CD 1
Tracks 29–36

Year: 1781

Texture: Homophonic with some polyphony in the first
development section and a monophonic repeated note in the
second development

Tempo: Presto (very fast)

Meter: Duple

Form: Sonata rondo (AB-development-AB-development-A)

Instrumentation: Two violins, one viola, one cello

Duration: 2:46

Special feature: Bird calls are imitated in some melodies.

continued

	Timing	Form	Instrumentation
29	0:00	**A**	Bouncy theme, staccato, repeated
	0:13		Repeated-note bird calls, motive from bouncy theme accompanies; repeated, clear stop
30	0:35	**B**	More flowing theme, repeated; goes directly into:
		Development	
31	0:57		Opening motive of bouncy theme and repeated-note fragment developed in rapid-fire polyphony; four-note motive tossed back and forth, reduced to two-note motive; sudden pause
32	1:25	**A**	Bouncy theme
	1:32		Repeated-note theme, goes directly into:
33	1:42	**B**	Flowing theme, goes directly into:
		Development	
34	1:54		Long notes in first violin, bouncy theme motive accompaniment; flowing theme motive repeated, reduced to repeated monophonic note, transition back to:
35	2:08	**A**	Bouncy theme
	2:14		Repeated-note theme, clear stop at end
36	2:25	**Coda**	Two-note motive and bouncy motive tossed back and forth, move quickly to pause; moves further to apparent emphatic closing; piano (soft), bouncy motive and repeated-note motive to actual quiet close.

HEARING THE DIFFERENCE
Mozart's Symphony no. 40, first movement, and Haydn's String Quartet op. 33, no. 3, fourth movement

	Symphony no. 40, first movement	String Quartet op. 33, no. 3, fourth movement
Tempo	The tempo is fast, allegro	The tempo is very fast, presto
Meter	Duple meter	Duple meter
Form	Sonata form (exposition, development, recapitulation, coda)	Sonata rondo form (AB-development-AB-development-A)
Sound	Full orchestral sound	A much lighter sound of only four string instruments
Themes	Themes repeat and contrast but are not composed to represent anything other than music.	The second, repeated-note, theme is reminiscent of a bird call.

Summary

Chamber music is usually composed for from two to nine instrumentalists, each playing his or her own distinct part. Classical composers wrote chamber works for any number of combinations of instruments, their choices often being dictated by their patron or their knowledge of what instrumentalists were available. String quartets were among the most popular of the chamber ensembles.

Franz Joseph Haydn was a master of string quartet composition. His primary patron, Prince Nikolaus Esterházy, played the cello and an instrument similar to the cello, the baryton. The prince enjoyed playing music himself, and many of Haydn's string quartets or chamber works for baryton were composed for his patron.

The string quartets in Haydn's opus 33 are called the Russian Quartets because they were first performed for an audience that included the Russian Grand Duke Paul (later Tsar Paul II) and his wife, who were visiting Vienna.

New People and Concepts

chamber music	piano quartet	septet
clavier	piano quintet	sextet
duet	piano trio	sonata rondo
Franz Joseph Haydn	première	string quartet
nonet	quartet	trio
octet	quintet	
opus	rondo	

Finale

Listen again to String Quartet op. 33, no. 3 ("The Bird"), fourth movement, by Haydn, and compare your impressions now with your notes from your first listening. Do you hear more now than you did before? You should now be able to answer the following questions:

- What is the tempo?

- What is the meter?

- What instruments are playing?

- Can you hear a melody at the beginning that returns later?

- What caused people to call the piece "The Bird"?

14 | Classical Vocal Music

It's people like that who make you realize how little you've accomplished. It is a sobering thought, for example, that when Mozart was my age—he had been dead for two years!

—SINGER/SONGWRITER TOM LEHRER

(BORN IN 1928)

Listening Introduction

Listen to the example of music that represents this chapter, "Non più andrai" ("No more will you") from Mozart's opera *Le Nozze di Figaro (The Marriage of Figaro),* and make notes about what you hear. Give some attention to the following:

▌ Can you tell the gender of the singer?

▌ Can you tell what instruments are used to play the accompaniment?

▌ Can you detect the meter?

▌ Can you tell the language of the text?

▌ What is the general mood of the aria? Can you guess what it might be about?

Keep these notes to compare with your impressions of the music after you study the information in this chapter.

Composers of the classical era tended to concentrate more on instrumental music than on vocal music. The lieder (songs) written by Haydn, Mozart, and Beethoven are considered a relatively secondary part of their compositional efforts. The operas composed by Haydn to entertain the guests at the Esterházy palace were popular in their day but are not performed today. Beethoven wrote only one opera, *Fidelio.* The age was not, however, completely without significant and lasting achievements in the area of vocal music. Some of the large choral works of Mozart, Haydn, and Beethoven, and many of Mozart's operas, made lasting contributions to vocal literature.

Haydn's Vocal Music

Opera was a highly important part of musical activity at the Esterházy palace, and for a long time Haydn was quite proud of his more than twenty stage works. Austrian Empress Maria Theresa reputedly said, "If I want to hear a good opera, I go to Esterházy." However, when Haydn became familiar with Mozart's incomparable genius for opera composing, he realized that his own works were of lesser quality. Today they are all but forgotten.

Haydn composed Masses based on the same religious texts as those discussed in Chapter 4. Those Masses and his oratorios present a different story. The last six of his twelve Masses, composed between 1796 and 1802, are his crowning achievement as a church composer. One of those, his *Missa in Angustiis (Mass in Time of Peril),* was composed as a tribute to a naval battle. It is also called the

Haydn is shown here conducting a performance of his oratorio *The Creation* in Vienna, 1808.

Nelson Mass, because it was written in 1798 during the naval Battle of the Nile in which Lord Nelson led the British fleet to defeat Napoleon. Martial fanfares in the Benedictus (second part of the Sanctus in the mass ordinary) served to represent that victory. When Lord Nelson visited the Esterházy castle at Eisenstadt in 1800, this mass was among the works performed in his honor.

The orchestration of Haydn's Masses varied from work to work according to the instruments and players available to him at the time. The *Nelson Mass* is scored for a comparatively small orchestra consisting of three trumpets, timpani, organ, and strings, together with four solo voices (SATB) and an SATB chorus.

Stimulated by Handel's oratorios, some of which he had heard during his London visits, Haydn produced three of his own. One of the most widely performed today is the *Creation.* It depicts the story of the creation of the world. From the overture (Representation of Chaos) to the final triumphant chorus, Haydn uses soloists, chorus, and orchestra to impart the story vividly and dramatically. Together with his Masses, Haydn's oratorios constitute his most important contribution to vocal music.

Classical Opera

The greatest composer of opera in the classical era was Wolfgang Amadeus Mozart, who, with his finest works, took each type of operatic form to its epitome. Each type of opera composed during the classical period can be illustrated by Mozart's most famous works:

Opera seria (serious opera)

   Idomeneo, 1781

Opera buffa (Italian comic opera)

   Le Nozze di Figaro (The Marriage of Figaro), 1786

THE LIVE EXPERIENCE
Classical and Romantic Opera Singers

By the classical period, most female operatic roles were sung by women and most male roles by men. Castratos were still occasionally used for heroic or youthful roles, but that practice was in decline. Mozart included castratos in two of his operas, *Idomeneo re di Creta* (Idomeneo, King of Crete) and *La Clemenza di Tito (The Clemency of Titus)*. One of the most famous examples of a castrato role in the classical period is that of Orfeo (Orpheus) in the opera *Orfeo ed Euridice* by the German composer Christoph Willibald Gluck (1714–1787). The Greek myth that served as the basis of the story of this opera involves Orpheus journeying into the underworld to bring his dead wife, Eurydice, back to life; Orpheus promises not to look back but ultimately does. The original version of Gluck's opera was composed in Italian and performed in Vienna in 1762 with a castrato singing as Orfeo. French audiences had never warmed to the use of castrati, and when Gluck revised the opera for performances in France he had to replace the castrato voice with a male tenor.

In the classical period, one other type of gender exchange—often referred to as a "pants role"—was used in opera. "Pants" indicates that a female singer, usually a mezzo soprano, sings the part of a young man. It was thought that "real men," even tenors with high voices, did not have light enough voices to sound as if they were in their teens or barely beyond. In Mozart's opera *Le Nozze di Figaro (The Marriage of Figaro),* the role of Cherubino is a pants role. Other famous pants roles include Ottavian in Strauss's *Der Rosenkavalier (The Knight of the Rose),* Siebel in Gounod's *Faust,* and Hänsel in Humperdinck's *Hänsel and Gretel.*

However, it was still most common for men to sing male roles and women to sing female roles in classical and later operas. Operatic voice types developed to be quite specialized. Soprano voices were broken into categories such as *coloratura soprano,* which describes a very florid and high voice; *lyric soprano;* which describes a smooth and melodious sound, and *dramatic soprano,* which describes a heavier tone than the other soprano

types. Sopranos were generally given the female lead roles. Because of their deeper tone quality and lower pitch ranges, mezzo sopranos were often typecast into roles as older women who were not given the primary attractive or sympathetic roles. Like sopranos, tenor voices broke down into particular types—including *lyric tenor* and *dramatic tenor*—according to the range and character of their voices. Baritones had medium-range male voices that were occasionally given lead roles. Figaro, in Mozart's *Le Nozze di Figaro (The Marriage of Figaro),* is a baritone or a bass-baritone. The lowest male voices were sometimes used in light character roles called *basso buffo,* but they also sometimes took serious, mature sounding roles called *basso profundo.*

What does this all mean for opera singers? It means that their voices are specialized and they can only sing roles that are particularly suited to them. Singers know this and they generally study with teachers who begin by testing for their natural abilities and then train them to develop their voices to fit vocal types such as those just mentioned. If a soprano has a naturally high voice and has been trained to take advantage of it, she will not likely sing a role that was composed for a dramatic soprano: She will sing coloratura roles.

Have you ever heard of a *diva*? "Diva" means "goddess," and divas are sopranos who are so accustomed to singing lead roles that they collectively have developed a reputation for having very big egos. Perhaps the most famous diva was Nellie Melba (1861–1931), who sang for London's Covent Garden opera company for thirty years. She always insisted that she be paid more than any other singer the company hired, including the famous tenor Enrico Caruso (1866–1953), and she refused to allow any other singer to use her dressing room— even on nights when she was not singing. Male lead roles tend to be given to tenors and as a result they often have the same reputation as diva sopranos. Of course, not all sopranos and tenors deserve such a reputation, but the "diva" stories are part of the color of opera as a dramatic art form.

Don Giovanni, 1787

Così fan tutte (Thus do they all), 1790

Singspiel (German opera)

Die Entführung aus dem Serail (The Abduction from the Seraglio), 1782

Die Zauberflöte (The Magic Flute), 1791

Notice that most of those operas were composed in Italian even though they were intended for an Austrian audience whose language was German. Opera was still thought of as an Italian art form. Today, it doesn't matter what language the singers sing because modern opera houses have a translation in English lit up across the top of the stage or elsewhere. These are called "supertitles," because they are above, just as "subtitles" are shown below the screen in foreign movies. In Mozart's day, the audiences probably knew the opera plots before they saw the opera, and it is advisable for modern operagoers to read the plot in advance as well. It is usually provided in a program given to audience members when they enter the hall where the opera will be performed.

Operas are often based on plays, and, like plays, their action is divided into large sections called **acts.** Those acts are sometimes further subdivided into **scenes.** Usually, a performance will have an intermission between acts, but not between scenes. Scenes sometimes require different sets—a first scene might be in one room of a palace, and the second in another room, for example— but the staging is planned so that the changes take a minimal amount of time during which the audience must wait in their seats. Major set changes, if necessary at all, happen between acts. Operas in the classical period and later usually have two or three acts and one or two intermissions. *The Marriage of Figaro,* however, is particularly long in having four acts. Performances sometimes have three intermissions or just two, with the third and fourth acts performed without a break. Those decisions are made by the director. A full performance of *The Marriage of Figaro* with intermissions usually lasts well over three hours.

The Marriage of Figaro

The opera *Le Nozze di Figaro (The Marriage of Figaro)* is based upon a French play by Beaumarchais (real name, Pierre Augustin Caron, 1732–1799), translated into Italian and cast in the form of an opera libretto by Lorenzo da Ponte, a popular librettist at the time. On the surface, the plot is typically intricate and amusing, including a pair of lovers, intrigues between servants and masters, a case of discovered identity, and a few unlikely coincidences. The play on which the opera was rather closely based, however, was extremely controversial. It was first produced in 1782, just seven years before the beginning of the French Revolution. In many ways the play represented the antiaristocratic attitudes that erupted in the revolution, a fact which displeased French King Louis XVI, who would ultimately end up beheaded by his own people.

The play portrays Count Almaviva as both abusive to his servants and stupid enough to be fooled by them. The abuse is evident in his desire to take advantage of a "feudal right" (going back to the medieval period) to deflower any young bride on her wedding night. The stupidity is shown by the fact that Susanna and the countess are able to fool him into a very embarrassing situation in which he must ask his wife for forgiveness.

Louis XVI tried very hard to keep the play from being produced, banning one production after another just before its performance. Beaumarchais, however,

Chapter 14 Timeline

Classical Vocal Timeline

Mozart's *The Marriage of Figaro* is one of the most popular and frequently performed operas.

was able to get enough private readings performed that the play became well known despite the king's resistance. Public pressure on the king forced him to allow sixty-eight public performances, with the audiences applauding almost every line.

Napoleon, who ended up crowning himself the king of France after the French Revolution, said of the play, "If I had been a king, a man such as he [Beaumarchais] would have been locked up. . . . *The Marriage of Figaro* is already the revolution in action."

In the movie *Amadeus,* the Austrian emperor displays his anger at Mozart for having composed an opera on the play that he had banned out of support of the French monarchy. Mozart defends himself by saying that he took all of the politics out of the plot and made it into a love story, but anyone who sees the entire opera can tell that the political controversy was not removed.

The Characters

Tho Count Almaviva, A Spanish nobleman (baritone)

The Countess Almaviva, his wife (soprano)

Susanna, the countess' maid (soprano), promised in marriage to

Figaro, the count's servant (bass)

Cherubino, the count's page (female soprano singing the role of a young man)

Marcellina, housekeeper (soprano)

Bartolo, a doctor from Seville (bass)

Basilio, a music teacher (tenor)

Don Curzio, a lawyer (tenor)

Barbarina, a daughter of Antonio (soprano)

Antonio, the count's gardener and Susanna's uncle (bass)

Chorus of country people and peasants

Note: Cherubino is a young male page at the court, and the role is composed to be sung by a female soprano dressed in male clothing.

The Plot

The opera is set in Count Almaviva's country house near Seville. Figaro, a valet to Count Almaviva, is preparing to marry Susanna, the countess' chambermaid. Figaro has borrowed a large sum of money from Marcellina, the old castle housekeeper, promising to repay it by a certain date or marry her if he defaults. The count has designs on Susanna and tries to seduce her, but she tells Figaro and the countess, and together they scheme to frustrate the count's plans.

Because Susanna will not yield to him, the count decides to take Marcellina's side in the financial dispute and force Figaro to marry her. This plot is foiled by the discovery that Marcellina and her advocate, Dr. Bartolo, are actually Figaro's long-lost parents, from whom he was kidnapped as an infant.

Meanwhile, Susanna and the countess have been conniving; their trick involves a case of disguised identity. Susanna promises to meet the count in the garden that night, but it is the countess, dressed as Susanna, who actually keeps the appointment. Figaro learns of the meeting and thinks that Susanna is deceiving him. The count is caught red-handed by his wife, confesses his attempted infidelity, and begs forgiveness, which she laughingly grants. It all ends happily when Figaro marries Susanna and Marcellina and Dr. Bartolo decide to marry as well.

The aria "No more will you" is sung by Figaro at the end of Act I. The count's page, Cherubino, has discovered women and has been falling in love with every female at the palace, including the countess. The count has now told him that he must join the military. In this aria Figaro sings to him about how his life will now change. Figaro's aria is quoted in another of Mozart's operas, *Don Giovanni,* at the beginning of Act II, Scene 5, when Don Giovanni is seated at his dinner table and some of his "favorite music" plays.

Listening Guide

"Non più andrai" ("No more will you") from *Le Nozze di Figaro* *(The Marriage of Figaro)* WOLFGANG AMADEUS MOZART

CD 1
Tracks 37–42

Year: 1786

Meter: Quadruple

Form: ABACA-Coda

Tempo: Vivace (Fast and lively)

Instrumentation: Full orchestra

Voices: Bass-baritone voice

Language: Italian

Duration: 3:36

Action: Opera staging and action varies with the director, but in some traditional versions of the opera, Figaro has Cherubino dress in his military uniform during the aria, handing him his saber or musket and drawing a mustache on him.

	Timing	Italian text	English translation	Form
37	0:00	Non più andrai, farfallone amoroso, notte e giorno d'intorno girando; delle belle turbando il riposo, Narcisetto, Adoncino d'amor.	No more will you, amorous butterfly, flit around the castle night and day, upsetting all the pretty girls, love's little Narcissus and Adonis.	A
38	0:26	Non più avrai questi bei pennacchini, quell' cappello leggiero e galante, quella chioma, quell'aria brillante, quell' vermiglio, donnesco color.	No more will you have those fine plumes, that soft and stylish hat, those fine locks, that striking air, those rosy, girl-like cheeks.	B
39	0:56	*(Repeat of the music and lyrics of the A section)*		A

continued

	Timing	Italian text	English translation	Form
40	1:19	Tra guerrieri proffer Bacco!	Among warriors swearing by Bacchus!	C
		gran mustacchi, stretto sacco,	great mustachios, holding your pack,	
		schioppo in spalla, sciabla al fianco,	a gun on your shoulder, a saber hanging	
		collo dritto, muso franco,	at your right, musket ready	
		o un gran casco, un gran turbante,	or some great cask or a turban,	
		molto onor, poco contante,	winning honors, but caring little,	
		ed invece del fandango,	and in place of the fandango	
		una marcia per il fango.	a march through the mud.	
		Per montagne, per valloni,	Over mountains, over valleys,	
		colle nevi e i sollioni.	through the snow and the burning sun.	
		Al concerto di tromboni,	To the music of trumpets,	
		di bombarde, di cannoni,	of shells and cannons,	
		che le palle in tutti tuoni	with balls sounding thunder,	
		all'orecchio fan fischiar.	making your ears ring.	
41	2:24	*(Repeat of the music and lyrics of the A section)*		A
42	2:46	Cherubino alla vittoria,	Cherubino, on to victory,	Coda
		alla gloria militar.	on to victory in war!	

The following is a duet sung by the count and Susanna after Susanna has told him that she will meet him in the garden that evening. Then see "Hearing the Difference: Purcell's 'When I am laid in Earth' and Mozart's 'Non più andrai' ('No more will you')."

Listening Guide

"Crudel! Perchè finora?" ("Cruel one, why until now?") from *Le Nozze di Figaro (The Marriage of Figaro)* WOLFGANG AMADEUS MOZART

CD 3
Track 30

Tempo: Andante

Meter: Duple

Form: **Through-composed** (newly composed throughout, no repeated sections)

Instrumentation: Full orchestra

Voices: Duet for baritone (Count Almaviva) and soprano (Susanna) voices

Language: Italian

Duration: 2:42

Special feature: There are many repetitions and insertions of "sì" (yes) or "no" during the duet. At times the parts overlap or lines are sung by both singers together. Susanna's final line about lying is in parentheses because it is directed to the audience, because it is not she, but the countess, who really plans to meet the count in the garden. The count is not to know of the scheme yet.

Italian text	English translation
Conte: Crudel! Perchè finora farmi languir così?	**Count:** Heartless! Why until now did you leave me to languish?
Susanna: Signor, la donna ognora tempo ha di dir di sì.	**Susanna:** Sir, every lady has her time to say yes.
Conte: Dunque in giardin verrai?	**Count:** Then you'll come to the garden?
Susanna: Se piace a vio verrò.	**Susanna:** If it pleases you, I'll come.
Conte: E non mi mancherai?	**Count:** And you won't fail me?
Susanna: No, non vi mancherò.	**Susanna:** No, I won't fail you.
Conte: Mi sento dal contento Pieno di gioia il cor.	**Count:** My contented heart Now feels full of joy.
Susanna: (Scusatemi se mento, voi che intendete amor.)	**Susanna:** (Forgive me if I'm lying, all you who understand love's ways.)

30

HEARING THE DIFFERENCE
Purcell's "When I am laid in Earth" and Mozart's "Non più andrai" ("No more will you")

In comparing these two arias, we are comparing some characteristics of the baroque and classical periods. In the baroque, operas were generally based on Greek or Roman legends or historical stories. Purcell's "When I am laid in Earth" is from his opera *Dido and Aeneas,* from Virgil's *Aeneid* (19 BCE). Dido sings the aria just before throwing herself on a fire to die because Aeneas is leaving her to go to Italy and establish the city of Rome, which he has been destined to do. Baroque music tends to have a stress on the bass line, which is very much present in the accompaniment to Dido's aria. The form of the aria is binary, which is also a commonly used form in the baroque period. Mozart's "Non più andrai" ("No more will you"), on the other hand, is classical in its placement in an aristocratic household of the classical period, its accompaniment by a full orchestra, its lively character, and its more complicated formal structure.

	When I am laid in Earth	Non più andrai (No more will you)
Historical period	Baroque	Classical
Tempo	Slow	Fast, lively
Meter	Triple	Quadruple
Form	Binary (AABB)	ABACA-Coda
Voice	One female singer	One male singer
Accompaniment	Four bowed stringed instruments	Full orchestra
Language	English	Italian
Mood	Very somber and sung by a character who has lost her lover and is about to commit suicide	Jovial and teasing, sung by Figaro to a young page who has just been told that he must enter the military and who is very fearful about what that will mean to him

Summary

Although the main area of concentration for most classical composers was instrumental music, the age did produce lasting achievements in vocal music as well. Haydn's *Nelson Mass* well represents the classical treatment of the Mass. Considered a masterpiece, this work is a favorite in contemporary choral repertoires.

The greatest composer of opera in the classical era was Mozart. His first comic opera, *The Marriage of Figaro,* stands out among opera buffa for its realistic characters, amusing libretto, delightful solo and ensemble music, and skillful use of orchestral devices to enhance the characterization. Despite its entertainment value, *The Marriage of Figaro* was quite controversial when it was composed. It was based on a French play of the same name that made fun of a count who was trying to take advantage of his wife's maid. The maid, Susanna, and her fiancé, Figaro, collaborated with the countess to fool the count. For a play to show a member of the aristocracy in such an unflattering light did not sit well with King Louis XVI, because the king was aware of the antiaristocratic attitudes that were building in France. Those sentiments exploded in the French Revolution of 1789, in which Louis XVI was beheaded.

New People and Concepts

act	opera seria	through-composed form
opera buffa	scene	

Finale

Listen again to "Non più andrai" ("No more will you") from Mozart's opera *Le Nozze di Figaro (The Marriage of Figaro)* and compare your impressions now with your notes from your first listening. Do you hear more now than you did before? You should now be able to answer the following questions:

▮ What is the meter?

▮ What is the gender of the singer?

▮ What instruments are used to play the accompaniment?

▮ What is the language of the text?

▮ What is the mood of the aria and how does it fit into the story of the opera?

15 | The Music of Beethoven

You can't possibly hear the last movement of Beethoven's Seventh and go slow.
—PIANIST AND COMPOSER OSCAR LEVANT TO THE POLICE OFFICER WHO STOPPED HIM FOR SPEEDING WHEN HE HAD BEEN LISTENING TO THE LAST (FAST) MOVEMENT OF BEETHOVEN'S SEVENTH SYMPHONY

Listening Introduction

Listen to the example of music that represents this chapter, Symphony no. 5 in C Minor, first movement, by Beethoven, and make notes about what you hear. Give some attention to the following:

▌ Can you detect the meter?

▌ Can you hear a theme from the beginning that returns later in the movement?

▌ Can you hear any repeated sections?

▌ Can you hear any themes that contrast with the first theme?

▌ What would you guess the tempo to be?

Keep these notes to compare with your impressions about the music after you study the information in this chapter.

Ludwig van Beethoven

Probably no single composer has influenced the course of musical events more than **Ludwig van Beethoven** (1770–1827). His evolving style had a profound effect on the musicians of his time, and the music he left to the world has continued to influence musicians and to have great public appeal. His greatest contribution was that he carried forward the tradition of Mozart and Haydn, building on the structures they had developed and elevating them to new heights of power and expressiveness.

In comparison to the productivity of Mozart and Haydn, Beethoven's works seem surprisingly few. This was partly due to his method of composing. Mozart never lacked musical inspiration, and ideas flowed from his pen with miraculous ease; Haydn also kept to a regular schedule of composition, providing whatever music his patron wanted in time for the performance. Beethoven, however, had to struggle. Ideas did not come easily, and he filled innumerable pages with slowly evolving sketches. Even his finished compositions were continually rewritten and revised. Another reason for his limited production was his attitude toward composition. Above all, he regarded music as art, and he generally took on only those commissions that he personally wished to fulfill.

If Beethoven's works took longer to write than was usual at the time, they were also more substantial, in both content and length. His works include nine symphonies; nine concert overtures; five piano concertos; one violin concerto; sixteen string quartets; ten sonatas for violin and piano; five sonatas for cello and piano; thirty-two sonatas for solo piano; twenty-one sets of variations for piano;

one opera, *Fidelio;* one oratorio, *Christus am Ölberg* (Christ on the Mount of Olives); *Choral Fantasia* for piano, chorus, and orchestra; and two Masses.

Most musical scholars divide Beethoven's career into three periods: the first extending to about 1802, the second to 1814, and the last ending with his death in 1827. The first period was a time of assimilation of the classical tradition of Mozart and Haydn and includes his string quartets composed before 1800, the First Symphony (1799), and his first three piano sonatas.

The second period was perhaps the happiest of Beethoven's life, and certainly the most productive. During this period he wrote masterpiece after masterpiece: seven more symphonies; the *Rasoumovsky* string quartets of 1806; his opera, *Fidelio;* and two very important and popular piano sonatas, titled the "Waldstein" and the "Appassionata" (both 1804).

Beethoven's last creative period, a time of great personal troubles including his deafness, was less productive, but in many ways it was the most important of the three. This period culminated in his monumental Ninth Symphony (1823), the equally immense *Missa solemnis* (completed in 1824), and his late string quartets and piano sonatas. In these works he developed many of the musical ideas that influenced the style period to follow him, the Romantic Era.

Ludwig van Beethoven was born in the Rhineland city of Bonn, Germany. His father, a singer in the Electoral Court chapel, hoped to make his boy into a child prodigy like Mozart. Though never fulfilling his father's hope, young Beethoven did learn piano and violin quickly. He received instruction from several musicians at the court, and by the age of twelve was substituting at the chapel organ. In 1784 he was appointed to a permanent position as assistant organist and had become known for his virtuoso improvisations at the piano. While Beethoven was gaining recognition for his musical talents, personal problems arose. His mother died in 1787, his father's alcoholism grew worse, and Beethoven's home life became increasingly unbearable.

Composer Ludwig van Beethoven

The year 1790 marked a turning point in the young composer's career. Haydn heard Beethoven play when he passed through Bonn on his way to London. Impressed with Beethoven's talent, Haydn urged the Elector Max Friedrich, for whom Beethoven worked, to send him to Vienna for further study. Two years later, at the age of twenty-two, Beethoven moved to Vienna, where he remained the rest of his life. At first he studied composition with Haydn; but, unsatisfied with the older man's methods, he turned to other composers for instruction. Though he was a frequent performer at musical evenings held by prominent Viennese nobility, Beethoven did not play in public until 1795, when he performed one of his early piano concertos.

Unlike Mozart, Beethoven always retained his popularity with both the general public and the aristocracy of Vienna. Unlike Haydn, he never had to endure the rigors of the eighteenth-century system of musical patronage. Though he may have yearned at times for the prestige and security of a court position, he remained proudly and fiercely independent throughout his life. During most of his career he was able to count on annual stipends from a small circle of aristocratic friends and admirers. He seemed to enjoy moving about in the upper echelons of Viennese society, once remarking that "it is good to mingle with aristocrats, but one must know how to impress them."

Beethoven was one of the first composers to demand and obtain an equal footing with this aristocracy solely on the basis of his genius. It was his fortune to come upon the world in a time of rapidly changing values and increasing social mobility. The emerging middle-class audience and the growth of public concerts provided ample opportunities for performance of his music. Rising demand for his works enabled him to live off the sale of his music to publishers.

Chapter 15 Timeline

Beethoven Style Periods

During the first years of the nineteenth century, when Beethoven seemed to be approaching the height of his career, he became aware that he was growing deaf. He became deeply depressed when he realized that his career as a performer would end. In a moving letter to his two brothers, written from the small town of Heiligenstadt outside Vienna and intended to be read after his death, Beethoven confessed:

> My misfortune pains me doubly, in as much as it leads to my being misjudged. For me there can be no relaxation in human society, no refined conversation, no mutual confidences; I must live quite alone and may creep into society only as often as sheer necessity demands; I must live like an outcast. If I appear in company I am overcome by a burning anxiety, a fear that I am running the risk of letting people notice my condition. . . . Such experiences almost made me despair, and I was on the point of putting an end to my life—the only thing that held me back was my art. For indeed it seemed to me impossible to leave this world before I had produced all the works that I felt the urge to compose, and thus I have dragged on this miserable existence.

After his affliction became painfully obvious, Beethoven gave up conducting and playing in public. His principal means of communication became a notebook in which his few visitors were invited to write their remarks. As he withdrew into his art, his works became more complex, more abstract, and more incomprehensible to his fellow musicians. He never married, and when total deafness set in after 1820, he became almost a recluse. Beethoven died in 1827 at the age of fifty-seven.

In many ways Beethoven was a real romantic. Part of the reason he never married was that he fell in love with women who either were already married or were of such a high economic class that their fathers would not have allowed them to marry a working composer, regardless of his fame. In many ways Beethoven's only opera, *Fidelio,* is based on a character that Beethoven considered to be the perfect wife. It is about a woman who risks her life and everything she has to save her husband, who has been wrongly imprisoned. The 1994 movie *Immortal Beloved* portrayed Beethoven as a man who had lusted after many women and written a letter to the "immortal beloved," which was found among his things after he died. Such a letter was really written and found, but many other details about the movie are incorrect. Beethoven was probably not as insane as the movie suggests, and it is unlikely that he had the real-life affairs the movie uses to attract modern audiences. At the risk of giving away the mystery-like plot, the woman the movie represents as the "immortal beloved" is very unlikely to have been Beethoven's lover.

In general, Beethoven's works tend to be longer than those of Haydn or Mozart. He lengthened the development section of movements in sonata form and added further development to his codas. He added more instruments to the orchestra, giving it a more powerful and dramatic sound than the orchestras for which Mozart or Haydn wrote. He also changed the ways some of the instruments were used, writing independent timpani parts, for example. He added more players to the string section, giving it a fuller sound, and used two trumpets as a standard part of the orchestra. A comparison of the orchestra Mozart used for his Fortieth Symphony with that of Beethoven in his Fifth Symphony follows:

Mozart's Fortieth Symphony	Beethoven's Fifth Symphony
—	one piccolo (fourth movement)
one flute	two flutes
two oboes	two oboes
two clarinets	two clarinets
two bassoons	two bassoons
—	one contrabassoon (fourth movement)
two horns	two horns
—	two trumpets
—	three trombones (fourth movement)
—	timpani
first violins	first violins
second violins	second violins
violas	violas
cellos	cellos
double bass	double bass

Working with this expanded orchestra, Beethoven made important contributions to the craft of **orchestration**—writing and arranging music for orchestra to achieve the most effective overall combination. In this area he greatly influenced composers of the romantic era, for whom orchestration became a major component of musical composition.

Beethoven's Fifth Symphony, which he began in 1804, was first performed in Vienna in December 1808. It is probably the most popular of Beethoven's symphonies, not only for its famous opening but also for its unity. Until this symphony, separate movements in multiple-movement works had no themes in common. With his Fifth Symphony, Beethoven introduced the idea of a common thread that can be heard in all four movements, an idea that was expanded and often used in the romantic period.

The famous theme that opens Beethoven's Fifth Symphony is a rhythmic motive (a short melodic or rhythmic idea): three short notes, followed by one long one. That rhythm pattern is stated in the first theme of the first movement. It returns in the second theme of the second movement, and again in the scherzo (faster than a minuet) theme of the third movement. It reappears as a quote from the third movement during the development section of the fourth movement. This unification of a symphony with a musical idea that appears in each movement is referred to as **cyclic form** and is something that nineteenth-century composers used very often.

To this point we have heard individual movements of classical works based on the sonata form, the minuet and trio form, and the sonata rondo form. Another popular form that was often used for second movements of multimovement works and also for independent compositions was the **theme and variations form.** As the name suggests, a movement or piece in this form begins with the presentation of a theme, or main melody. That statement is then followed by a series of varied versions of the same theme. Letters are not usually used to describe the theme and variations form, but if they were, the form would be A1A2A3A4A5 and so on, perhaps ending with a coda.

Listening Guide

Symphony no. 5 in C Minor, first movement LUDWIG VAN BEETHOVEN

CD 1
Tracks 43–48

Year: 1808

Tempo: **Allegro con brio** (fast, with vigor and spirit)

Meter: Duple

Form: Sonata

Instrumentation: Two flutes, two oboes, two clarinets, two bassoons, two French horns, two trumpets, timpani, first violins, second violins, violas, cellos, double basses

Duration: 6:51

Special feature: The rhythm of the opening motive, three short notes and one long one, is an organizational feature that is used in all four movements of the symphony. That motive is called the "basic motive" in the listening guides. Remember, there is no piano as an instrument in the orchestra. "Piano" means soft.

	Timing		**Instrumentation**
	Exposition		
43	0:00	Theme 1	Basic motive stated twice, forte (loud)
	0:06		Piano (soft), motive sounds throughout strings; crescendo, three forte, separated chords, long-held note by violins on last chord.
	0:17	Bridge	Motive, fortissimo (very loud); piano, motive builds theme in strings; instruments gradually enter, crescendo, pitch rises; two separate chords, fortissimo
	Bridge		
44	0:41	Theme 2	Horn call, basic motive with extension, fortissimo
	0:44		**Legato** theme in violins, then clarinet, then flute; basic motive in low strings; fragment of theme in strings, other instruments gradually enter, crescendo
	1:02	Closing	Loud chord, strings in strong descending passage, repeated
	1:11		Basic motive descends in winds answered by strings; repeated; two separate statements of motive
	(Exposition is repeated)		
	Development		
45	2:40		Basic motive in horns, strings, fortissimo; motive developed among instruments, piano, slight crescendo, return to piano for further development
	3:00		Strings and winds toss motive back and forth, crescendo to strings hammering on repeated note
	3:15		"Horn call" from theme 2 developed, with answer from low strings; reduced to two-note fragment echoed between winds and strings; reduced to one-note echo, suspense builds through diminuendo to pianissimo
	3:45		Horn call erupts in full orchestra; one-note echo resumes; basic motive repeated fortissimo, directly into:
	Recapitulation		
46	3:57	Theme 1	Trumpets and timpani added for two statements of basic motive
	4:04		Motive through strings with countermelody in oboe, piano; three separated chords, oboe cadenza concludes countermelody on last chord
	4:26		Motive, piano, build theme in strings; instruments gradually enter, crescendo, pitch rises; two separate chords, fortissimo
47	4:46	Theme 2	Horn call played by bassoon, basic motive with extension, fortissimo

continued

	Timing		Instrumentation
	4:49		Legato theme traded between violins and flute, basic motive in low strings; fragment of theme divided between strings and flute, crescendo in strings as other instruments gradually enter
48	5:11	Coda	Loud chord, strings in strong descending passage, repeated
	5:21		Basic motive descends in woodwinds answered by strings; repeated
	5:25	Second development	Separate statements of motive extended fortissimo to hammer on repeated note, basic motive piano, repeated note forte, motive piano
	5:43		Horn call from theme 2 in cellos and violas, new countertheme in violins; repeated; countertheme vigorously developed, full orchestra
	5:57		Fragment of countertheme tossed between winds and strings; repeated note leads directly into:
	6:29	Second coda	Basic motive stated twice, fortissimo
	6:36		Piano, basic motive in strings; fortissimo, full orchestra states basic motive three times with final chords

Beethoven particularly liked composing and improvising variations on themes. For the second movement of his Fifth Symphony, he has composed two themes, both of which are varied through the movement. Notice that the second theme contains the "short-short-short-long" rhythmic motive that was the primary theme of the first movement of the same symphony.

Listening Guide

Symphony no. 5, second movement LUDWIG VAN BEETHOVEN

CD 3
Tracks 31–33

Tempo: **Andante con moto** (walking pace with a sense of motion)

Meter: Triple

Form: Theme and variations with two themes

Instrumentation: Two flutes, two oboes, two clarinets, two bassoons, two French horns, two trumpets, timpani, first violins, second violins, violas, cellos, double basses

Duration: 9:16

Special feature: The B theme includes the "basic rhythm" of three short notes and one long one, unifying it with the first movement.

	Timing		Instrumentation
31	0:00	Theme A	Lyrical melody, low strings, piano; theme continues with violins and flute
32	0:50	Theme B	Clarinets, piano; violins, piano; full orchestra, fortissimo
	1:11		Trumpets, fortissimo; violins, pianissimo
	1:51	Variation A1	Lyrical melody of theme A, embellished with faster melody
	2:37	Variation B1	Theme B with active accompaniment; soft long-held chords; cadence
	3:39	Variation A2	Theme A embellished with an even faster melody than in Variation 1
	4:13		Theme played by low strings, ends rising to a high note
	4:38	Middle section	Strings repeat chords; clarinet, bassoon, and then flute play theme A;
	5:25		brass fanfare based on theme B; timpani rolls, strings, then staccato woodwinds and crescendo in strings leads into:
	6:49	Variation A3	Theme A played by full orchestra, fortissimo
33	7:32	Coda	Tempo faster, soft bassoon responded to by oboe; strings crescendo
	7:47		Beginning tempo returns; flute and strings play part of theme A
	8:27		Clarinets vary theme A; beginning of theme B in strings builds to fortissimo cadence

Beethoven's Fifth Symphony has two more movements. The third movement is a scherzo and trio, which is structured like the minuet and trio we heard earlier but flows a bit faster. Actually, the word *scherzo* means "joke," and the joke was that one could not dance a minuet to a scherzo even though the scherzo is also in triple meter. A scherzo is not only faster than a minuet, but it also has more of a stress on the first beat of each three-beat measure and less accent on the second and third beats. A minuet is danced to all three beats.

The fourth movement of Beethoven's Fifth Symphony is connected directly to the third, with no pause between the movements. There is a transitional section in which the triple meter of the scherzo is no longer played and the quadruple meter of the fourth movement has yet to begin. The fourth movement is in sonata form and the first theme is very triumphant. Beethoven helped create this triumphant effect by adding the piccolo, contrabassoon, and three trombones.

The Classical Piano

In the classical period, the harpsichord of the baroque gave way to the new **pianoforte** (or simply **piano**) as the preferred keyboard instrument. The harpsichord is a keyboard instrument that plucks the instrument's strings, giving it a very crisp tone quality. But there is no way for the player to control dynamic changes on the harpsichord other than to play fewer or more notes at one time, more notes creating more sound than one or two. No matter how hard or gently the player pushes the keys down, the exact same sound comes out of the instrument. That sound was fine when used for baroque music that often had terraced dynamics, not requiring a lot of crescendos or diminuendos in a single phrase, but classical style required dynamic versatility.

Pianos are different from harpsichords in that their sound is produced by hammers that hit the strings to make them vibrate. The hammers can hit lightly or hard, depending on the force the player uses on the keyboard, and the instrument will sound soft or loud accordingly. The piano's ability to play using contrasting dynamic levels gave it its name. Originally, the instruments were called *pianoforte* (soft/loud) or *fortepiano* (loud/soft). In later years, the name was shortened to piano, or simply "soft."

Early experiments in piano building were being made at the end of the baroque period, but makers had many problems controlling the bounce of the hammers after they hit the strings. Many experimental instruments were made through the 1750s and 1760s. A piano with improved hammer action was invented in England in 1777, and that was followed by better instruments made in Germany and Austria. Mozart, Haydn, and Beethoven all saw the musical advantages of the piano and composed works that made good use of the piano's dynamic range and ability to sustain sounds for a longer period of time than was possible on the old harpsichord. By the late classical period the piano was very popular as a solo instrument, a chamber music participant, and a solo concerto instrument.

A Piano Sonata by Beethoven

Beethoven's Piano Sonata op. 57 was given the name *Appassionata* by a publisher, not by Beethoven himself. It was completed in 1805 and dedicated to the

The fortepiano emerged during the classical period as the keyboard instrument of choice for composers like Beethoven.

Countess of Brunswick. The sonata has three movements with a short presto (very fast) conclusion. We will hear the first movement. The motive of three short notes followed by a long one that we heard as the recurring motive in Beethoven's Fifth Symphony is also featured in this movement. In the following listening guide it is called a "four-note motive."

Listening Guide

Piano Sonata op. 57 (Appassionata), first movement LUDWIG VAN BEETHOVEN

CD 4
Tracks 1–6

Year: 1805

Tempo: **Allegro assai** (rather fast)

Meter: Quadruple

Form: Sonata

Instrumentation: Solo piano

Duration: 9:58

	Timing		What to listen for
	Exposition		
1	0:00	Theme 1	Ominous theme, pianissimo; repeated; four-note motive in bass; sudden loud "cadenza," long chord
	0:45		Ominous theme developed; alternating soft and loud fragments
	1:03	Bridge	Repeated-note accompaniment, fragments leap high and low; diminuendo
2	1:25	Theme 2	Sweet, flowing theme, piano; suddenly breaks off, trills, long descending scale
	2:02	Closing	Robust, powerful theme, forte; brilliant passage work descends, diminuendo, to held note
	Development		
3	2:36		Ominous theme fragmented, developed, sudden changes of register, dramatic interruptions
	3:42		Repeated-note accompaniment and leaping fragments from bridge, extended development, crescendo
	4:14		Sudden piano, flowing second theme developed at length, shifting harmonies, gradual crescendo
	4:42		Sudden loud arpeggios rise higher in pitch, then fall lower; insistent repetition of four-note motive
	Recapitulation		
4	5:07	Theme 1	Ominous theme pianissimo, repeated-note accompaniment; four-note motive, sudden loud cadenza, long chord
	5:46		Ominous theme developed; alternating soft and loud fragments
	6:15	Bridge	Repeated-note accompaniment, fragments leap high and low; diminuendo
5	6:38	Theme 2	Sweet, flowing theme, piano; suddenly breaks off, trills, long descending scale
6	7:12	Coda	Robust, powerful theme, forte; brilliant passage work descends, diminuendo, smoothly into:
	7:46	Second development	Ominous first theme increasingly fragmented, pianissimo
	7:59		Flowing second theme developed, gradual crescendo
	8:14		Loud arpeggios erupt moving gradually higher; brilliant arpeggios sweep up and down the keyboard; four-note motive
	9:10	Second coda	Four-note motive fortissimo, faster tempo; ominous theme developed; fragments echo violently high and low; opening of ominous theme, piano, descends to quiet conclusion

Summary

Ludwig van Beethoven expanded nearly every aspect of classical composition. His works are longer and larger in scale than those of his contemporaries and predecessors. Beethoven's compositions place great emphasis on developmental procedures and use such effects as dynamics to reach new heights of expressiveness. Beethoven often used a lively scherzo rather than a minuet in third movements of multi-movement works. He also used a single theme or motive in more than one movement to unify longer works. He used this idea in his Fifth Symphony when the rhythm of three short notes, followed by a long note, was featured in all four movements.

Improvements in instruments and instrumental techniques directly influence Beethoven's compositions. He increased the size of the orchestra from that used by Mozart and Haydn. He was a virtuoso pianist, and his piano works fully exploited the new brilliance and power that the newer pianos of his time were capable of achieving.

New People and Concepts

allegro assai	**legato**	**pianoforte**
allegro con brio	**Ludwig van Beethoven**	**theme and variations form**
andante con moto	**orchestration**	
cyclic form	**piano**	

Finale

Listen again to Symphony no. 5, first movement, by Beethoven, and compare your impressions now with your notes from your first listening. Do you hear more now than you did before? You should now be able to answer the following questions:

▮ What is the meter?

▮ When do you hear the first theme return later in the movement?

▮ When does the exposition repeat?

▮ When does the second theme appear and then repeat?

▮ What is the tempo?

Characteristics of Classical Music

Texture	Largely homophonic, but flexible, with shifts to polyphony
Tonality	Major-minor system with frequent modulations to related keys; heavy dependence on tonic-dominant relationship
Rhythm	Variety of rhythmic patterns within a work
Melody	Composed of short, balanced phrases; melodic phrases often contrasted with each other
Mood	Expression of variety of moods within a work and sudden changes of mood
Dynamics	Gradual dynamic changes
Large works	Sonata, symphony, concerto, string quartet, Mass, oratorio, opera
Musical instruments	Piano and violin favored for solo concerto; makeup of orchestra becomes standardized; development of orchestra favors growth of symphonic works
Formal structures	Sonata principle (multimovement structure for long pieces); single-movement sonata form; rondo; minuet and trio; scherzo and trio; theme and variations; cadenza and double exposition used in concertos
Symphonic style	Follows four-movement plan, with first movement in sonata form; each movement self-contained; clarity and balance are major stylistic features

The Fall of an Avalanche in the Grisons by J. M. W. Turner (1775–1851). This painting displays nature as an uncontrollable power, a subject of great interest to artists in the Romantic era.

The word *romantic* as it is applied to the arts in the 1800s means much more than our common use of the term, which conjures up visions of lovers dining with candles on the table or strolling on the beach. Nineteenth-century romanticism describes a school of thought that encapsulated much of the philosophy, literature, and visual arts of an era that rejected the Enlightenment's "reasoned" view of the world. Instead, Romantics were drawn to "the exception to the rule." They were excited by the turbulence that followed the French Revolution. They were fascinated by the power of the individual, especially the man or woman of feeling who dwelt in a private world of emotions and solitary dreams, and the hero, who represented the grandest possibilities of the individual. They searched for the exotic, the mysterious, and the unfamiliar. They were adventurers drawn to experience that affected their senses and stimulated their passions.

The Romantics were preoccupied with nature. In the past, landscapes had been painted only as backgrounds for portraits or other subjects. Nineteenth-century artists made scenes of meadows, trees, clouds, lakes, and mountains the primary subjects of much of their work. At times they showed the power nature could have over mankind through storms, fires, or other uncontrollable natural occurrences. The English painter J. M. W.

Prelude | Music of the Romantic Era

Turner (1775–1851) painted many such scenes.

Writers sought inspiration in nature and found in its changes metaphors for their own moods and emotions. For some Romantics, such as the poet Wordsworth (1770–1850), nature was elevated into a religion. Rejecting absolutely the Age of Reason, William Wordsworth wrote:

> One impulse from a vernal wood
> May teach you more of man,
> Of moral evil and of good,
> Than all the sages can.
> Sweet is the lore which Nature
>   brings;
> Our middling intellect
> Misshapes the beauteous forms
>   of things:
> We murder to dissect.

The French Revolution and the political turbulence that followed it discredited the Enlightenment ideal of the supremacy of reason. After Napoleon's armies brought much of Europe under French control, he was finally defeated and had to resign as Emperor of France in 1815. European leaders then began to regroup their people under new governments. The growing middle class of citizens in some of the major areas of power pressured for representative governments. By the end of the century, France, Germany, and Italy were all organized as countries with elected parliaments.

As countries unified, there was a great sense of nationalism that can be seen in many of the arts of the era. Composers expressed their pride in their countries in a variety of ways. For example, Chopin displayed his love for his native Poland by using the rhythms of Polish dances as the basis of solo piano works. Smetana composed orchestral works about the beauty of his homeland of Bohemia. He and many other composers wrote operas about their countries' histories or that told stories that were favorite folk tales of their countries' people.

Other major changes took place during the 1800s. The populations of most areas of Europe grew dramatically. Part of the reason was improvements in medicine and in food supply. The first vaccine was invented in 1798, for smallpox, a disease that had ravaged eighteenth-century Europe. Cholera deaths decreased after the 1850s when it was learned that the disease was spread by the drinking of polluted water. The discovery that minerals could be added to land in the form of fertilizer increased and improved food production.

The Industrial Revolution had begun during the 1700s, but its effects were most universally felt in the 1800s. Some of the most important inventions at the beginning of the Industrial Revolution were the spinning jenny (1767), which spun sixteen threads of cotton during the time a spinning wheel could spin only one, and the cotton gin (1793), which made the removing of seeds from the fibers needed for cloth easier and faster. A simple type of steam engine had been used to drain mines for years, and in the 1780s improvements were invented to make it efficient enough to power entire factories. In the early 1700s, the primary source of power was running water. Machines that needed power had to be built near rivers. Once the steam engine was put into regular use, large factories could be built anywhere. The factories hired workers to each do one particular task, which allowed the work to be done in much less time than ever before. Cities developed around factories, and more products than ever before were produced and sold at ever lower prices.

Throughout the romantic era, towns grew, interregional trade quickened, fortunes were made, and the middle class enjoyed a certain amount of economic power. By 1825, the steam engine was used to power trains to carry both freight and passengers. The sewing machine was invented in the 1850s, bringing down the cost of clothing. The telephone, phonograph, and electric light bulb followed in the 1870s. All of these inventions made the world more comfortable for the growing middle class.

The downside of the Industrial Revolution was that people were often forced to work extremely long hours, and poor and lower middle-class children were added to the workforce. The novels of Charles

The Third-Class Carriage by Honoré Daumier
(**1808–1879**). This painting displays sympathy for the
overworked poor who are crowded into the rail car.

The Stone Breakers by Gustave Courbet (1819–1877). One
of these workers looks too young and the other looks too
old to be doing this heavy work. Like novels by Charles
Dickens, this painting is a portrayal of the burdens placed
on the poor during the romantic era.

Dickens (1812–1870) depicted the mistreatment of children and the abuse of the poor that was part of this era. Artists portrayed the situation, too. The painting, *The Third-Class Carriage* (c. 1862) by Honoré Daumier sympathetically depicts poor people crowded into a rail car, not really paying any attention to one another. Gustave Courbet's *The Stone Breakers* (1849) shows two men breaking stones to build a road, but the one on the left looks far too young and the one on the right looks too old to be doing such heavy work.

In the literature of the romantic era one can see a great interest in the exotic, the mysterious, and even the occult. Edgar Allan Poe (1809–1849) told any number of terrifying tales in his short stories and poems; Emily Brontë's *Wuthering Heights* (1847) was about a brooding and tormented man who unfairly controlled those around him. Emily Brontë's sister Charlotte wrote the novel *Jane Eyre* (1847), in which one of the main characters secretly keeps his insane wife hidden away from the world. Artworks such as *The Sleep of Reason Produces Monsters* by Francisco Goya (1746–1828) reflect similar preoccupations.

In music, we will hear part of Hector Berlioz's *Symphonie fantastique* (1830), which depicts a young musician who dreams that he has killed his beloved and must die for the crime only to then find himself at a witches' Sabbath attended by fearful

The Sleep of Reason Produces Monsters, by Francisco Goya (1746–1828). Romantics were interested in throwing aside reason and concentrating on dreams and mysterious powers, as can be seen here.

monsters, all awaiting his burial. One of Schubert's best loved songs, "Erlkönig" ("King of the Elves"), tells the story of a father riding through a storm on horseback carrying his son in his arms. The boy sees and is tempted by the Elf King and cries out to the father. Legend has it that if the Elf King touches the child, he will die. The father does not believe the child, ignores his cries, and the child dies. The idea that innocent children know more than adults

who have been corrupted by the world is very Romantic.

In this era of a growing middle class, public concert halls were built to allow the average person to hear music outside of church. That brought about the beginning of the "superstar" performer. Musical virtuosos such as violinist Niccolò Paganini (1782–1840) would do almost anything to thrill his large audiences. He sometimes cut partway through a string on his violin before the concert so that it would break while he was playing and he could amaze the audience by finishing the piece on the three remaining strings. At times, he would play on a single string, dramatically moving his fingers up and down the string instead of shifting over to another. The rumor spread that Paganini had sold his soul to the devil in order to play as well as he did.

Women composers and instrumentalists also had more opportunities to have careers that brought them international fame than had been possible in the past. Female composers and instrumentalists of the past were usually connected to a particular royal court and were able to perform for court patrons and guests, but they were not necessarily free to tour all over Europe independently. Clara Schumann (1819–1896) spent much of her life on stage and was still performing on concert tours into her seventies.

Despite the new opportunities for women in some professions, female writers found that they could have more success getting works published and sold if they used men's names. Emily Brontë first published her books under the name Ellis Bell. Chopin's long-time mistress, Amandine-Aurore-Lucile Dudevant, published novels under the name George Sand. Liszt's mistress, Marie d'Agoult, published under the name Daniel Stern.

The romantic era includes, for the most part, the entire nineteenth century. Various inventions that led to the Industrial Revolution in the late 1700s and many Romantic attitudes resulted from the reaction to the French Revolution that began in 1789. By 1800, the romantic era was well on its way to becoming one of the most dramatic eras in the history of the arts. Some aspects of romanticism continued on into the twentieth century, but in many other ways, composers late in the century began to reject traditional harmony and move toward the new sounds and attitudes of the next era. Certainly, the romantic period saw more people than ever before being able to live fuller lives and have more control over their lives than ever before in European history. Music of the era reflected on individual emotions and experiences, and much of that music is still being enjoyed today.

16 | Romantic Songs

No one understands another's grief, no one understands another's joy. . . . My music is the product of my talent and my misery. And that which I have written in my greatest distress is what the world seems to like best.

—COMPOSER FRANZ SCHUBERT

Listening Introduction

Listen to the example of music that represents this chapter, "Erlkönig" ("King of the Elves") by Schubert, and make notes about what you hear. Give some attention to the following:

▌ Can you detect the meter?

▌ Can you tell what instrument is used to play the accompaniment?

▌ Can you tell the language of the text?

▌ Does the piece have a general mood that might give you an idea about the meaning of the text?

▌ Can you hear any melody that repeats from one verse of the poem to another?

Keep these notes to compare with your impressions about the song after you study the information in this chapter.

The Salon

The Industrial Revolution helped to create a very large middle class, including an upper middle class who were not born to wealth but were able to afford a good life. These people could afford pianos for their homes, and it became common for families to invite guests in for intimate concerts at which the children or other members of the household would perform. The concert might be followed by the serving of dessert and tea or coffee, as well as polite conversation. Upper-middle-class people sometimes contracted musicians to perform for their guests at catered gatherings.

Upper-class people, including the aristocracy, held "salons" in their homes. These informal literary or musical gatherings were not unlike the kind of entertainment put on by aristocratic patrons such as the Esterházy family for whom Haydn worked for so many years, though on a much smaller scale. The painting *Liszt at the Piano* by Josef Danhauser shows a salon scene in which many famous people of the time are gathered to hear the great pianist Franz Liszt play, including novelists Alexandre Dumas, Victor Hugo, George Sand (Amandine-Aurore-Lucile Dudevant), and Daniel Stern (Marie d'Agoult), along with opera composer Gioacchino Rossini and violinist Niccolò Paganini.

***Liszt at the Piano* by Josef Danhauser (1805–1845).** Liszt is seated at the piano with his mistress, Marie d'Agoult (who wrote novels under the name Daniel Stern), on the floor to his right. The woman seated behind Liszt is George Sand. Writer Alexandre Dumas is seated on the far left, next to George Sand. The three men standing behind Sand (left to right) are writer Victor Hugo, violinist Niccolò Paganini, and composer Gioacchino Rossini.

Art Song

Many songs with piano accompaniment, as well as solo piano works, were composed for performance in salons in elegant homes such as that portrayed in the painting *Liszt at the Piano*. The **art song** is a musical setting of a poem for solo voice and piano. In Germany and Austria the words *lied* and *lieder* (plural) became the standard terms for this type of song.

In the mid-1700s, the *lied* had been a simple song with keyboard accompaniment. The musical setting used strophic form, that is, the same melody repeated for every stanza (or strophe) of the poem. The text was treated syllabically (one note for each syllable), and the accompaniment served merely to support the singing voice.

Toward the end of the 1700s, the **ballad,** a narrative poem set to music, became popular in Germany. The ballad was long, emphasized dramatic situations, and alternated in structure between narration and dialogue. These characteristics required greater musical resources than the strophic form. Ballads were in through-composed form; that is, each section of the text had music that was different from the music preceding and following.

Both the strophic and through-composed forms were used in the lieder of the 1800s. A variant of the strophic form, called **modified strophic,** was also used. In it, some verses of the poem were sung to the same melody, and others were not. The composer chose the form that would best suit the poem. If the poem's verses all fit the same melody and also had similar moods, the strophic form was perfect. If some verses repeated but others changed in mood or number of words so that they needed to be sung to a new melody, then modified-strophic form was used. If, on the other hand, the poem told a story that changed in mood or character, then the composer would most likely use the through-composed form to vary the mood and melody. The earliest, and in many respects the most important, lieder composer was **Franz Schubert** (1797–1828).

Franz Schubert

Composer Franz Schubert

Chapter 16
WebQuest

Romantic Songs

In many ways, the circumstances of Franz Schubert's life were the very essence of the Romantic's view of an artist's condition. During his brief and troubled lifetime, Schubert lived in poverty and never gained the recognition his talent deserved. He was born in a suburb northwest of Vienna, the fourth surviving son of an industrious and pious schoolmaster. His formal musical training, never very systematic, began with violin lessons from his father and piano instruction from an older brother.

In 1808, at the age of eleven, Schubert obtained a place in the choir of the Imperial Court Chapel and was thereby privileged to attend the City Seminary, one of Vienna's most prestigious boarding schools. In addition to his regular studies and music lessons, he became a violinist in the school orchestra, later assuming the duties of conductor on various occasions. The numerous works he composed during these years at the seminary include songs, overtures, religious works, part of a Singspiele (light opera), and six string quartets. His first symphony was written in 1813, the year he left the seminary, and his first Mass was successfully performed in 1814.

After leaving the seminary, Schubert returned home to live, first attending a training college for primary school teachers and then teaching at his father's school. The regimen of the classroom did not suit his temperament, and in 1816 he resolved to earn his living by taking music students, selling his compositions, and writing for the theater. In 1817, he moved to Vienna.

During the early 1820s, two of Schubert's Singspiele were produced with moderate success, and a number of songs and piano works were published. These successes were offset by his continuing inability to obtain a salaried position. In 1822, a serious illness necessitated a stay in the hospital and a prolonged period of recuperation. The following year, *Rosamunde,* a play with his incidental music, failed dismally, closing after only two performances. It was his last work for the theater.

Despite his ill health and poverty, Schubert was an extremely prolific composer. Between 1811 and 1828 he composed about one thousand works. They include nine symphonies, fifty chamber works and piano sonatas, a large number of short piano pieces, several operas and operettas, six Masses and about twenty-five other religious works, nearly one hundred choral compositions, and more than six hundred songs.

The last four years of Schubert's life were a continual struggle. Though his music, particularly the songs, continued to draw high praise from fellow musicians, including Beethoven, it was not until 1828 that a public concert of his works was given. He was unable to live on the pitifully small income from his music publications, but he continued to compose at a feverish pace. In the fall of 1828, Schubert died at the age of thirty-one. His last wish, to be buried near Beethoven, was granted, and on his tombstone was written: "The art of music here entombed a rich possession but even far fairer hopes."

Schubert is best remembered for his abundant body of songs. The song we are going to listen to is one of his most famous, "Erlkönig" ("King of the Elves"). The poem on which it is based is a ballad by Goethe. The story maintains the legend that the King of the Elves represents death and that anyone who is touched by the Elf King will die.

Illustration of the title page of the score of Schubert's "Erlkönig."

Listening Guide

"Erlkönig" ("King of the Elves") FRANZ SCHUBERT

CD 1
Track 49

Year: 1815

Tempo: *Schnell* (fast)

Meter: Quadruple

Form: Through-composed

Instrumentation: Solo voice and piano

Language: German

Duration: 4:05

Special feature: The text calls for the singer to take the roles of a narrator, father, son, and the Elf King. Notice how the range of notes changes, with the father singing lower notes than the son, and how the Elf King sounds lighter in tone quality.

German text	English translation
49 NARRATOR	
Wer reitet so spät durch Nacht und Wind?	Who rides so late through the night and the wind?
Es ist der Vater mit seinem Kind;	It is the father with his child;
Er hat den Knaben wohl in dem Arm,	he holds the boy in his arm, grasps him securely,
Er fasst ihn sicher, er hält ihn warm.	keeps him warm.
FATHER	
"Mein Sohn, was birgst du so bang dein Gesicht?"	"My son, why do you hide your face so anxiously?"
SON	
"Siehst, Vater, du den Erlkönig nicht?	"Father, do you not see the Elf King?
Den Erlenkönig mit Kron' und Schweif?"	The Elf King with his crown and train?"
FATHER	
"Mein Sohn, es ist ein Nebelstreif."	"My son, it is only a streak of mist."
ELF KING	
"Du liebes Kind, komm, geh' mit mir!	"Darling child, come away with me!
Gar schöne Spiele spiel' ich mit dir;	I will play fine games with you;
Manch' bunte Blumen sind an dem Strand,	Many gay flowers grow by the shore,
Meine Mutter hat manch' gülden Gewand."	my mother has many golden robes."
SON	
"Mein Vater, mein Vater, und hörest du nicht,	"Father, father, do you not hear
Was Erlenkönig mir leise verspricht?"	what the Elf King softly promises me?"
FATHER	
"Sei ruhig, bleibe ruhig, mein Kind:	"Be calm, dear child, be calm—
In dürren Blättern säuselt der Wind."	the wind is rustling in the dry leaves."
ELF KING	
"Willst, feiner Knabe, du mit mir gehn?	"You beautiful boy, will you come with me?
Meine Töchter sollen dich warten schön;	My daughters will wait upon you.
Meine Töchter führen den nächtlichen Reihn'	My daughters will lead the nightly round,
Und wiegen und tanzen und singen dich ein."	they will rock you, dance to you, sing you to sleep."

continued

German text	English translation
SON	
"Mein Vater, mein Vater, und siehst du nicht dort Erlkönigs Töchter am düstern Ort?"	"Father, father, do you not see the Elf King's daughters there, in that dark place?"
FATHER	
"Mein Sohn, mein Sohn, ich seh' es genau: Es scheinen die alten Weiden so grau."	"My son, my son, I see it clearly: it is the grey gleam of the old willow-trees."
ELF KING	
"Ich liebe dich, mich reizt deine schöne Gestalt; Und bist du nicht willig so brauch' ich Gewalt."	"I love you, your beauty allures me; and if you do not come willingly, I shall use force."
SON	
"Mein Vater, mein Vater, jetzt fasst er mich an! "Erlkönig hat mir ein Leids gethan!"—	"Father, father, now he is seizing me! The Elf King has hurt me!"—
NARRATOR	
Dem Vater grauset's, er reitet geschwind, Er hält in den Armen das ächzende Kind, Erreicht den Hof mit Müh' und Not; In seinen Armen das Kind—	Fear grips the father, he rides swiftly, holding the moaning child in his arms; with effort and toil he reaches the house— the child in his arms—
war tot.	was dead.

Schubert portrays the characters and sets them off from each other by a number of devices, particularly by manipulating the piano accompaniment. Whenever the Elf King enters, for example, the dynamic level drops to pianissimo, the accompaniment changes, and the vocal line becomes smooth and alluring. Schubert reflects the son's mounting terror by repeating the same melody at successively higher pitch levels each time he cries out to his father. The last verse demonstrates Schubert's sense of drama and his technique of manipulating the song's elements to heighten the emotional impact. The piano is silent as the narrator sings "the child in his arms," a single chord sounds, increasing the feeling of suspense, and the narrator concludes "was dead." "Hearing the Difference: Mozart's 'Non più andrai' and Schubert's 'Erlkönig'" compares these two works.

Schubert wrote two **song cycles** (a series of art songs that tell a story or are otherwise related to one another), *Die schöne Müllerin* (*The Maid of the Mill*, 1823) and *Die Winterreise* (*Winter Journey*, 1827).

Robert and Clara Schumann

Another Romantic composer who is well remembered today for his songs and song cycles is **Robert Schumann** (1810–1856). Robert Schumann was born in Zwickau, a town in central Germany, in 1810. His father was a writer, publisher, and bookseller, and young Robert took great interest in literature, as well

Composers Robert and Clara Schumann

HEARING THE DIFFERENCE
Mozart's "Non più andrai" and Schubert's "Erlkönig"

These two works are quite different from one another in that Mozart's is an aria from an opera accompanied by a full orchestra and Schubert's is an art song accompanied by piano. The two are not compared here for those obvious differences, but rather for the very classical formal structure of one and the very romantic structure and content of the other.

	Non più andrai	Erlkönig
Historical period	Classical	Romantic
Tempo	Vivace (fast and lively)	Fast
Meter	Quadruple	Quadruple
Performers	Bass/baritone singer accompanied by full orchestra	Mezzo soprano singer accompanied by piano
Language	Italian	German
Form	ABACA-Coda, a symmetrically balanced form often used in the classical period	Through-composed, to have the melody that is sung continually change to suit the ongoing story
Mood	Very jovial and teasing. The aria is sung to a young man who has just been told that he must enter the military.	Very intense. A fearful child is tempted by the Elf King and the father tries to calm him. The ending is very sad, as the listener learns that the child has died. The sense of mystery, and even the presence of the Elf King spirit, are subjects that some Romantics particularly enjoyed.

as in music. He had studied music as a child but began his university education majoring in law. He gave up the study of law to concentrate on music and, in 1830, began taking lessons from a well-known piano teacher in Leipzig, Friedrich Wieck.

Wieck had many students, but his primary concentration was on his extremely talented daughter, Clara, who was eleven years old when she first met Robert Schumann. By that age, **Clara Wieck** had performed many times in Leipzig, and within the next two years she gave concerts across Europe to Paris and back to Germany. She had composed many small pieces for the piano and undertook her largest composition, a Concerto for Piano and Orchestra in A Minor, op. 7, in 1836. Clara had not studied orchestration, but Robert Schumann had. The two had become friends, and Clara asked Robert to help her in writing the orchestral parts. He did that, and Clara premiered the work in November of 1835 with Felix Mendelssohn conducting the Gewandhaus orchestra in Leipzig. She joined Mendelssohn and another pianist in the performance of a concerto for three keyboard instruments by J. S. Bach on that same concert program. In the next few years, Clara continued to perform her concerto in concerts all over Germany and Austria. The work was published in 1837. It was performed by other pianists throughout the 1800s.

Successful as her concerto showed her to be as a composer, Clara Wieck's primary concentration was on performing. By 1832, Robert had lost his ability to perform as a pianist because of a problem he had with his hands. Modern historians are not certain, but he is thought to have damaged them by practicing too much or by overusing a device intended to strengthen his hands. Whatever the case, Robert turned his concentration to composition, and Clara became the first great interpreter of his music.

Robert also turned his attentions back to writing and, in 1834, cofounded and edited a successful music journal, the *Neue Zeitschrift für Musik (New Journal of Music),* which is still being published in Germany today.

Robert and Clara's friendship developed into love and a desire to marry. Clara's father did everything he could to prevent their marriage because he thought it would interfere with her career in music. After Clara turned twenty-one, her father could no longer prevent it, and she married Robert in 1840. That year became known as "the year of the song" for Robert because he composed so many songs about love. The song we will listen to is from his 1840 song cycle, *Dichterliebe (Poet's Love).* The songs in *Dichterliebe* all relate to love and love relationships. The cycle opens with a short, strophic song, "Im wunderschönen Monat Mai" ("In the wonderfully lovely month of May"). The entire cycle comprises sixteen songs.

Listening Guide

"Im wunderschönen Monat Mai" ("In the wonderfully lovely month of May") from *Dichterliebe (A Poet's Love)* ROBERT SCHUMANN

CD 4
Tracks 7–8

Year: 1840

Tempo: *Langsam, zart* (slow)

Meter: Duple

Form: Strophic

Instrumentation: Solo voice (baritone, in this recording) and piano

Language: German

Timing: 1:24

Special feature: The pianist and singer on this recording use a lot of **rubato,** or "robbed time," which means that they slow down and speed up the tempo to make the musical phrases more expressive. The final chord does not sound completely final because it is intended to lead into the next song in the cycle.

	Timing	German text	English translation	Form
7	0:00	Im wunderschönen Monat Mai, Als alle Knospen sprangen, Da ist in meinem Herzen Die Liebe aufgegangen.	In the wonderfully lovely month of May, when all buds were burgeoning, then in my heart did love arise.	A
8	0:44	Im wunderschönen Monat Mai, Als alle Vögel sangen, Da hab' ich ihr gestanden Mein Sehnen und Verlangen.	In the wonderful month of May, when all birds sang, then I told her of my desire and longing.	A

Robert and Clara Schumann had eight children, but her career as a performer did not end. Robert was very supportive and often hired people to watch the children so that he could accompany Clara on her many concert tours. Robert continued to compose orchestral works, string quartets, a variety of chamber works with piano, and solo piano works.

Robert Schumann had been experiencing bouts of depression in his twenties. By 1845 these bouts became much more severe and more frequent. In 1850, he took a position as music director of the municipal orchestra in Düsseldorf, Germany. He was not good at the administrative duties that were required by the job, and he resigned from the position in 1853. His mental condition worsened, and he tried to commit suicide in 1854. Clara was forced to put him into an asylum because she could no longer care for him herself. He died two years later at age forty-six.

Clara's concert career continued to be very successful, with tours that included many parts of Europe and took her as far as Russia. She became the principal teacher of the piano division of the Hoch Conservatory of Music in Frankfurt, Germany, in 1878. She died in 1896 at the age of seventy-six.

Summary

The Industrial Revolution created a large middle and upper-middle class of people who could afford to have pianos in their homes and could afford piano and singing lessons. It became very popular for such people to invite friends in to hear small-scale concerts performed by family members or by hired musicians. Many songs with piano accompaniment, as well as solo piano pieces, were composed for such settings.

Franz Schubert and Robert and Clara Schumann composed many art songs for performance in intimate settings. Of those three composers, Schubert and Robert Schumann focused most directly on composing. Clara Schumann composed music but made her primary career that of a performer. She was among the first women to tour internationally.

New People and Concepts

art song	**Franz Schubert**	**Robert Schumann**
ballad	**modified-strophic form**	**rubato**
Clara Wieck Schumann	**Singspiele**	**song cycle**

Finale

Listen again to "Erlkönig" and compare your impressions now with your notes from your first listening. Do you hear more now than you did before? You should now be able to answer the following questions:

▌ What is the meter?

▌ What instrument is used to play the accompaniment?

▌ What is the language of the text?

▌ What is the mood of the song and how does the music fit the text?

▌ Does the form in which the verses are each sung to different melodies work well for this song?

17 | **Romantic Piano Music**

*Bach is like an astronomer who, with the help
of ciphers, finds the most wonderful stars. . . .
Beethoven embraced the universe with the power
of his spirit. . . . I do not climb so high. A long
time ago, I decided that my universe will be the
soul and heart of man.*

—COMPOSER FRÉDÉRIC CHOPIN (1810–1849)

Listening Introduction

Listen to the example of music that represents this chapter, Ballade no. 1 in
G Minor, by Chopin, and make notes about what you hear. Give some attention
to the following:

▌ Can you detect the meter?

▌ Can you tell what instrument is playing?

▌ Can you hear sections of the music that repeat?

▌ Can you hear sections of the music that contrast with the beginning?

▌ What are the general moods of the piece?

Keep these notes to compare with your impressions about the music after you
study the information in this chapter.

Piano builders of the late classical period worked hard to improve the tone quality and dynamic range of the instruments they produced. By 1800, both high and
low notes had been added. Felt hammers replaced the old leather ones, allowing
for more depth to the tone. Cast iron frames were made to increase the volume of
sound.

Although such improvements gave concert pianos more and better sound,
the standard size and shape of the piano took up too much room to fit into the
parlors of middle-class homes. By the 1840s, piano designers had developed the
upright piano with the strings in a box that could fit against a wall instead of
being parallel to the floor. Upright pianos were manufactured on a very large
scale, and it became as important for a socially conscious middle-class family to
own a piano and for the children to learn to play it as it is for some to have a computer with video games today.

With so many people learning to play the piano, the demand for new music
and teachers increased dramatically. Music publication became a more lucrative
business than ever before. The general music literacy brought about by having so
many people learn to play an instrument also increased the public's interest in attending live concerts.

Chopin and Liszt

Two Romantic pianist-composers who stand out for their many compositions
still in the repertoire of performing pianists today are **Franz Liszt** (1811–1886)
and **Frédéric Chopin** (1810–1849). The two had personalities that were quite

The Pleyel piano factory in Paris, where upright pianos were manufactured for nineteenth-century homes.

opposite to one another. Liszt loved performing to large audiences, and he dramatized his playing by turning the piano sideways so that the listeners could see his hands. He also memorized his music so that it seemed to flow out of him and not just appear as an interpretation of music notation in front of him. Both the position of the piano and the practice of memorization have become common practice today.

Chopin, though also a fine pianist, did not enjoy large-scale performing as Liszt did. He did perform in public, but not any more often than he had to to maintain his reputation as a composer and teacher. Rather than the large-scale public concerts that Liszt and other performers such as Clara Schumann often played, Chopin preferred to play in the more intimate salon settings.

Liszt was Hungarian and moved to Paris in 1827, where he remained until 1848, when he moved to Germany to take a job as music director at the court of Weimar. Chopin was born in Poland, moved to Paris in 1831, and remained there until his death in 1849. Liszt and Chopin knew one another and shared many of the same friends and acquaintances. The painting *Liszt at the Piano* on page 153 shows Liszt in a salon with, among others, George Sand, who was, at the time, Chopin's mistress. It was Chopin's association with Sand that helped to introduce him to the intellectual elite of Paris. The other female in the painting, Marie d'Agoult, was, like Sand, a novelist who used a man's name—Daniel Stern. She was Liszt's mistress during the late 1830s and the mother of Liszt's three children, one of whom, daughter Cosima, later married composer Richard Wagner. Liszt and d'Agoult could not have married even if they had wanted to because she had left, but not divorced, her husband.

Franz Liszt was involved with music beyond his work as a pianist and teacher. After his move to Weimar, he worked with orchestras as a composer and conductor. He wrote symphonies and piano concertos and developed a new orchestral form that became very popular in the Romantic period—the **symphonic poem,** also sometimes called a **tone poem.** The symphonic, or tone, poem is a single-movement work for orchestra that is composed to tell a story or to go along with the events or moods in a particular poem. Liszt wrote twelve of these, the best known of which is *Les Préludes.*

Liszt's piano music includes variations on well-known symphonic works, brilliant showpieces, and technical studies. The *Transcendental Études,* the *Hungarian Rhapsodies,* and *Liebestraum (Love Dream),* along with the Sonata in B Minor, were important contributions to the literature for solo piano. His works

Composer Frédéric Chopin

Chapter 17
WebQuest

Romantic Piano
Music

for piano and orchestra include two concertos, *Hungarian Fantasia* and *Totentanz (Dance of Death),* the later of which is a large-scale paraphrase of the medieval funeral chant, the *Dies Irae.*

In his contributions to piano repertoire, Liszt created a grand and dramatic style that exploited the orchestral possibilities of the instrument and demanded enormous technical skill on the part of the performer.

In 1861, Liszt left his position at Weimar and moved to Rome to pursue religious training. He studied under church leaders and, in 1865, was given the honorary title of abbé. He composed religious music during that time. His compositions for the church included psalm settings, Masses, a requiem, oratorios, and other works for chorus and orchestra. Liszt died in 1886 at the age of seventy-four.

Unlike Liszt, Chopin limited himself to composing for the piano. He was born near Warsaw, Poland. His mother was Polish. His father was French and had come to Poland to teach the French language to Polish nobility. The young Frédéric showed great talent for the piano and gave his first public concert at the age of seven. By the age of fifteen, he had already published some compositions, and by nineteen, he had achieved eminence in both composition and performance. He traveled widely throughout Europe and was received enthusiastically wherever he played. So cordial was the reception at Chopin's first concert in Paris in 1831 that he decided to make that city his home. He expressed his Polish nationalism by composing a number of **polonaises** and **mazurkas** that were based on the rhythms of Polish dances of the same names.

Most of Chopin's music is for solo piano. He did write two piano concertos, a few chamber works for piano and other instruments, and some songs based on Polish poems with piano accompaniment. The **ballade** we will listen to is one of Chopin's larger solo piano works. Its form is similar to that of the classical rondo in that its first theme (A) returns with contrasting themes between. However, in addition to using three returning themes, Chopin—in a way that is decidedly Romantic—deliberately obscured the form by interspersing beautiful and lengthy episodes, transitions, and a coda between the statements of themes. The emphasis on these transitions stresses the apparently free-flowing and evolving character of the work.

In this chapter we have emphasized Liszt and Chopin, both of whom were performing pianists. Robert Schumann, whom we discussed in Chapter 16 as a composer of Romantic songs, also contributed much to the piano repertoire of the period. Almost all of his most popular and greatest works for piano date from his early years as a composer. They range from miniature **character pieces** (pieces portraying a single mood, emotion, or idea) whose titles establish them as wholly romantic—"Papillons" ("Butterflies"), "Carnaval," "Kinderscenen" ("Scenes from Childhood")—to large, classically oriented works such as the three piano sonatas, the Fantasy in C Minor, the **Symphonic Études** (study pieces), and the Piano Concerto in A Minor. Schumann considered the *Fantasiestücke (Fantasy Pieces)* to be among his best works for piano.

Listening Guide

Ballade no. 1 in G Minor FRÉDÉRIC CHOPIN

CD 1
Tracks 50–54

Year: 1831

Form: Irregular alternating form: ABCABBCA

Tempo: Largo; moderato; presto con fuoco (very slow; moderate; very fast with fire)

Meter: Triple

Instrumentation: Solo piano

Duration: 8:12

Special feature: The music moves dramatically from soft, gentle themes to very loud, intense passages. The player uses a lot of rubato, causing the triple meter to be less obvious in some sections than it is in the waltz-like "A" sections.

	Timing	Form	What to listen for
50	0:00	Introduction	Thoughtful monophonic melody; soft chords
51	0:32	A	Quiet, waltz-like theme; ends with cadenza-like rapid notes
	1:51	Transition	More rapid notes, quickly becomes agitated, loud; extended development; "horn calls" in left hand; intensity decreases; "horn calls" alone
52	2:40	B	Tender, lyrical melody, pianissimo
53	3:12	C	Faster rhythms in melody, with triplets, alternates with left-hand arpeggios
	3:45	A	Waltz-like theme, pianissimo, repeated note (pedal point) in bass; gradual crescendo into:
	4:12	B	Tender melody now passionate, fortissimo; ends with upward-surging scales, then downward-falling arpeggio
	4:41	Episode	Faster; begins pianissimo, gradual crescendo, fast passage work; extensively developed; pounding left-hand chords, fast notes build to high pitch, rapid downward scale
	5:26	B	Tender melody again passionate, fortissimo
	5:48	C	Triplet melody, accompanied by left-hand arpeggios; slowing, diminuendo
	6:18	A	Waltz-like theme, pianissimo, repeated note (pedal point) in bass; intensity builds to short descending scale
54	6:51	Coda	Suddenly faster, passage work leaping from high to low, extended development, mounting tension; cadenza-like scales up, down, up again
	7:35		Quiet chords; loud fragment, rapid scale up; quiet chords; loud fragment; extreme high and low pitches approach each other, join in descending chromatic scale; closing cadence

HEARING THE DIFFERENCE

Bach's "Little Fugue in G Minor" and Chopin's Ballade no. 1 in G Minor

In comparing these two keyboard compositions, we are taking notice of over one hundred years of stylistic change. The timbres of the organ and the piano are, of course, quite different from one another, but beyond that we will concentrate on comparing the form, texture, and general styles of the two pieces. Bach's work well represents the steadiness and structure that was typical in the baroque period, and Chopin's displays the irregularity and moodiness that was common in the romantic era.

	Little Fugue in G Minor	Ballade no. 1 in G Minor
Tempo	No tempo is indicated in the music, but it is played at a moderate pace. The beat is quite steady.	Varies from quite slow, to a moderate pace, and then fast with fire. The pianist appropriately uses a lot of rubato, causing further fluctuations in the tempo.
Meter	Quadruple	Triple
Texture	Polyphonic	Mostly homophonic
Form	That of a fugue, with statements of the subject being played in all four voices in the exposition and then being brought back in from time to time throughout the work	Irregular, with three themes that are presented and return
Instrumentation	Organ: The different sets of pipes on the organ allow for much variety of tone quality and a greater range of pitches than are available on the piano.	Piano: The pianist makes good use of the piano's dynamic range, but the tone cannot be varied as much as is possible on the organ.
Mood	The piece picks up energy from the first statement of the subject and never loses that sense of motion until the final cadence.	The piece is somewhat moody as it slows to partial pauses and then picks up with a new mood and pace.

Clara Schumann also composed a number of works for solo piano, including extended works such as multimovement sonatas. She also wrote chamber works with piano and a large number of songs for voice and piano. As mentioned earlier, however, she concentrated on performing more than on composing. In a world before recording equipment was invented, those performances, as well as those of Chopin and Liszt, unfortunately, have been lost to history.

Summary

By the early 1800s, the piano had taken over as a very popular musical instrument to be played by both professional performers and many middle-class people in their own homes. The upright piano was invented to fit into peoples' homes, and the prices of those instruments were low enough that they were easily affordable for families that wanted them. Pianos had been greatly improved to allow for more dynamic range. More notes were added, expanding the keyboard to the eighty-eight keys still in use today. With more people learning to play the piano, more composers and teachers were needed.

Chopin and Liszt stood out as virtuoso performers who also composed for and taught piano. Chopin preferred to play in intimate, salon settings, whereas Liszt enjoyed entertaining large audiences. Along with Robert and Clara Schumann, they added much to the piano repertoire still being performed today.

New People and Concepts

ballade (instrumental)	**Franz Liszt**	**polonaise**
character pieces	**Frédéric Chopin**	**symphonic poem**
études	**mazurka**	**tone poem**

Finale

Listen again to Ballade no. 1 in G Minor, by Chopin, and compare your impressions now with your notes from your first listening. Do you hear more now than you did before? You should now be able to answer the following questions:

▌ What is the meter?

▌ What instrument is playing?

▌ Where do you hear sections of the music that repeat?

▌ Where do you hear sections of the music that contrast with the beginning?

▌ What are the general moods of the piece?

18 | Program Music

*After silence, that which comes nearest to expressing
the inexpressible is music.*
—WRITER ALDOUS HUXLEY (1894–1963)

Listening Introduction

Listen to the example of music that represents this chapter, *Symphonie
fantastique,* fifth movement, "Dream of a Witches' Sabbath," by Berlioz, and
make notes about what you hear. Give some attention to the following:

▮ Can you detect the meter?

▮ Can you guess at the tempo?

▮ Can you hear any melodies or sections of music that repeat?

▮ What is the general mood of the music?

▮ Does the mood fit the title?

Keep these notes to compare with your impressions about the music after you
study the information in this chapter.

The romantic era gave rise to the establishment of a fascinating genre of music
that has become known as program music. We heard one program piece in the
baroque period, Vivaldi's *The Four Seasons,* in which the music portrayed sounds
of birds, a stream, and a storm to represent those images in a poem. This imagery
through music was unusual in the baroque period, during which most instrumental music was what we call absolute. Absolute music is composed for the
appreciation of the musical sound, and does not attempt to tell a story or depict
a scene in nature. Program music was somewhat rare until the romantic period.
Romantic program music depicts or portrays an extramusical phenomenon such
as a dramatic incident, a poetic image, a visual object, or some element in nature.
Romantic composers planned everything about the music, including its form,
around the program, which the listener should know in advance of listening to
the music. Usually, the program is told in a CD insert for a recording or in the
program provided at a live concert. Many Romantic composers wrote program
music, and one that stands out early in the period was the French composer
Hector Berlioz (1803–1869).

Hector Berlioz

Hector Berlioz grew up in a small town near Grenoble, France. He was expected
to follow his father's profession and was sent to medical school in Paris. However,
by his own inclinations he was drawn to the opera and the music library. When
he appeared in class, he would annoy his fellow students by humming at the

dissecting table. Finally, to the fury of his father, he quit the study of medicine to become a composer.

At twenty-three, Berlioz began what he called "the great drama of my life." At a performance of *Hamlet,* he was overwhelmed, both by "the lightning-flash" of Shakespeare's genius and "the dramatic genius" of Harriet Smithson, who played Ophelia. Berlioz tried to meet the actress, but his wild letters convinced her that he was a lunatic.

In 1830, on his fifth attempt, Berlioz won the Prix de Rome, a composition prize offered at the Paris Conservatory. In that year he also wrote the *Symphonie fantastique,* the outpouring of his passion for Smithson. When the composition was performed in Paris two years later, Harriet Smithson was in the audience. Having been told that the music was about her, she felt (according to Berlioz) "as if the room reeled." They were married a year later. The marriage was not particularly happy, although they stayed together for nine years and had one son. Berlioz continued to support his wife until her death in 1854.

Composer Hector Berlioz

Although he had become successful, Berlioz had difficulty getting his works performed. His music soon ceased to appeal to most of "the frivolous and fickle public." Both to support his family and to promote an understanding of the kind of music he advocated, Berlioz wrote musical criticism. He also wrote a fascinating prose autobiography. In it he emerges as a romantic hero, falling in love, scheming murder, talking politics, and passionately composing. He conducted performances of his own works throughout most of Europe, but in Paris he was overlooked for various honors and conducting posts. However, he was recognized as a gifted orchestrator, and his book *Treatise on Instrumentation and Orchestration* (1843) sold well for years and was translated into several languages. It is still in print today. Berlioz became the librarian of the Paris Conservatory in 1852. He died at the age of sixty-five.

Symphonie Fantastique

Berlioz's *Symphonie fantastique,* subtitled "An Episode in the Life of an Artist," is a **program symphony** in five movements. It is based on a story supplied by Berlioz out of his personal experience meeting and falling in love with Harriet Smithson.

Program of the Symphony

This prelude to the story of the symphony is not part of the music but is usually included in program and liner notes. A young musician of morbidly sensitive temperament and fiery imagination poisons himself with opium in a fit of lovesick despair. The dose of the narcotic, too weak to kill him, plunges him into a deep slumber accompanied by the strangest visions, during which his sensations, his emotions, and his memories are transformed in his sick mind into musical thoughts and images. The loved one herself has become a melody to him, an *idée fixe* ("fixed idea") that he encounters and hears everywhere. The use of a melody that appears in each movement unifies Berlioz's composition in much the same way that the rhythmic motive of Beethoven's Fifth Symphony unifies that work.

Part I. Reveries, Passions   He recalls the soul sickness, passion, and depression that he experienced before he first met his beloved. The *idée fixe* plays, representing their first meeting. It is followed by a grand expression of the passion that she inspired in him. The movement ends with tenderness and religious consolation.

Part II. A Ball   At a dance in the midst of a brilliant party, he encounters the loved one, again represented by the *idée fixe* melody.

Part III. Scene in the Country   One summer evening in the country, he hears two shepherds piping melodies to one another across the fields. This pastoral duet combines with the quiet rustling of the trees, gently brushed by the wind, and his newly entertained hopes to be able to give his heart an unaccustomed calm and his ideas a more cheerful color. But she appears (the *idée fixe*) again, and he feels a tightening in his heart and the fear that she might be deceiving him. One of the shepherds takes up his simple tune again, but the other no longer answers. The movement ends as the sun sets to the distant sounds of thunder. The mood is lonely and quiet.

Part IV. March to the Scaffold   He dreams that he has killed his beloved. He is condemned to death and led to the scaffold. The procession moves forward to the sounds of a march that is at times somber, fierce, and solemn. The muffled sound of heavy steps gives way, without transition, to a noisy clamor. At the end, the *idée fixe* returns for a moment, like a last thought of love interrupted by the fatal blow. Brilliant fanfares follow the public execution.

Part V. Dream of a Witches' Sabbath   He sees himself at the Sabbath, amid a frightening troop of ghosts, sorcerers, and monsters of every kind. They have all come together for his funeral. His beloved appears again, but the *idée fixe* has changed. It sounds mean and trivial. It represents his beloved coming to join the Sabbath. Bells toll for him as a dead man, and a melody from a medieval chant that represented judgment day, the **Dies Irae** ("day of wrath"), is played.

The five movements are linked together by the use of one melody that represents the hero's image of his beloved. This melody, the *idée fixe,* appears in each movement of the symphony in various transformations—in the second movement, it is a waltz tune; in the fourth, it appears fleetingly just before the fall of the executioner's blade; and in the fifth movement, it becomes a grotesque witches' dance. The technique of using one theme that changes throughout a composition is called **thematic transformation,** and it was used by many later Romantic composers to unify their works.

Throughout the work, Berlioz uses the orchestra to portray a wide range of images and emotional states. The orchestra in our recording is not quite as large as the one Berlioz wanted, which would have had at least fifteen first violins, at

A detail of *Witches' Sabbath* by Francisco Goya (1746–1828). A scene like this one is musically expressed in Berlioz's *Symphonie Fantastique.*

least fifteen second violins, ten violas, eleven cellos, and nine double basses. That large an orchestra is seldom assembled, even for Berlioz's masterwork. The tuba was not invented until 1835 in Germany, so Berlioz's orchestra would have had the low brass parts played on ophicleides and/or serpents, neither of which is in common use today.

This fifth movement of Berlioz's *Symphonie fantastique* tells only part of the story of the symphony, but it is often performed without the other movements. It helps to know the entire story to appreciate it. "Hearing the Difference: Beethoven's Symphony no. 5, first movement, and Berlioz's *Symphonie fantastique*, fifth movement," compares a piece of absolute music with a program symphony.

Listening Guide

Symphonie fantastique, fifth movement, "Dream of a Witches' Sabbath" HECTOR BERLIOZ

CD 2
Tracks 1–3

Year: 1830

Tempo: Larghetto-allegro (Larghetto is less slow than Largo)

Meter: Sextuple

Form: No major sections repeat.

Instrumentation: Two flutes, two oboes, two clarinets, four bassoons, four French horns, two trumpets, two cornets, three trombones, two tubas, timpani, bass drum, snare drum, cymbals, three sets of bells, first violins, second violins, violas, cellos, double basses

Duration: 9:57

Special feature: The *idée fixe* is transformed into a grotesque, mocking little melody.

	Timing	What to listen for
1	0:00	Larghetto—soft, muted strings create a mysterious atmosphere and basses repeat an ascending motive. Muted horns and high woodwinds enter, playing playful but ominous lines that fall to lower notes as if dead, rumbling timpani accompany.
2	1:33	Allegro—A high clarinet plays a grotesque, mocking form of the *idée fixe*. The strings bring forth a strong response. The *idée fixe* repeats and bassoons enter with a countermelody. Intensity builds, then subsides.
	3:00	Bells toll for the dead.
3	3:24	The Dies Irae (day of wrath) melody played first by tubas and bassoons, then repeated faster, played by horns and trombones. The melody continues to repeat in different instrumental groups.
	5:12	Witches' Dance—A melody played by low strings is imitated by three other groups of instruments in fuguelike counterpoint.
	7:02	The Dies Irae returns in string basses. Tension builds.
	8:08	The Dies Irae is played again, this time by high brass.
	8:38	The strings play their strings with the wood of the bows, creating an eerie sound as the woodwinds play a dance melody. Crescendo with repeat of the Dies Irae, strong cadence.

HEARING THE DIFFERENCE

Beethoven's Symphony no. 5, first movement, and Berlioz's *Symphonie fantastique,* fifth movement

As we mentioned earlier, both of the symphonies from which these movements come have a single musical idea to unify them—Beethoven's Symphony no. 5 has the "short, short, short, long" motive that is present in all four movements; Berlioz's *Symphonie fantastique* has a melody called the *idée fixe* that is present in all five movements. This is a similarity worth noting, but the differences are of more importance here. Our primary interest in comparing these two particular movements is that one comes from the classical period and is designed to demonstrate repeating and contrasting themes (absolute music), while the other, from the romantic period, is designed to tell a story. There are other differences that are also typical of the two periods from which the works come, including the size of the orchestra, and we will outline those in the comparison.

	Symphony no. 5, first movement	*Symphonie fantastique,* **fifth movement**
Historical period	Classical	Romantic
Tempo	Allegro con brio (fast, fiery)	Larghetto introduction, then allegro
Meter	Duple	Sextuple
Form	Sonata form (Exposition, Development, Recapitulation, Coda)	Nonsectional form with repeating melodies holding it together
Instrumentation	A somewhat expanded classical orchestra with trumpets and timpani beyond what Haydn or Mozart usually used	A greatly expanded orchestra, including two more bassoons and French horns, plus two cornets, three trombones, two tubas, and many more percussion instruments than Beethoven used. There are also more strings, with divided parts, giving the string section a much fuller and thicker sound.
Subject matter	This is from an "absolute symphony"—in other words, it focuses on two main themes.	This is a movement from a program symphony. It tells the part of the story in which the hero has been executed for killing his beloved and their ghosts are now present at a Witches' Sabbath. The *idée fixe,* which represents the beloved, has become a grotesque melody. Bells toll for the dead. Death is also represented by the Dies Irae.

Other Program Music

Most Romantic composers who composed for orchestra also wrote program music. The desire to use music to tell life stories, real or imagined, was irresistible in the era. Some other programmatic works by Berlioz included the "dramatic

THE LIVE EXPERIENCE
The Importance of the Program in Program Music

Does it really matter whether you know the program or not when you listen to a piece of program music? If you listened to the fifth movement of *Symphonie fantastique* and answered the questions in the Listening Introduction for this chapter, you might have said something about the mood of the piece, comparing it to the title, "Dream of a Witches' Sabbath." That title alone might well have told you that there was a story, or at least a mood, behind the work. Do you now think that knowing the whole story about the composer's love for a woman who had rejected him and his dream of having killed her and then been executed for her murder is necessary to really appreciate the fifth movement? Perhaps not. Perhaps the dynamic sounds of the orchestra and the changing intensity and moods are enough. On the other hand, did you find that having read the story behind the symphony helped you to appreciate the music more? Having learned that the people involved were already dead, that the chimes represented bells tolling for the dead, and that the Dies Irae melody is from an old chant that has always

represented death might well have given you a deeper sense of the eeriness of the music.

If you had heard Berlioz's music for the first time by turning on the car radio, and you had not heard any announcements about the work, including the title, would you be able to guess that it was program music? If you listened carefully, you might have heard that the music had many mood changes and did not seem to follow a clear repeating and contrasting form. That alone might indicate that it followed some type of story.

An even harder question is, If you were to listen to this or another piece of program music having been told that it follows a story, but you were not told what the story was, do you think you could guess any of the story just by listening? It might be fun to find a recording of another piece of program music and then come up with your own story. However, you will probably get the most out of a piece of program music if you know the program ahead of time, either by reading the "program" when you attend a concert, or by reading the insert that usually comes with a CD.

symphony" *Romeo and Juliet* (1839); the *King Lear* Overture (1831); the *Waverley* and *Rob Roy* overtures (c. 1827 and 1831), both of which are based on novels of Sir Walter Scott; and the symphony *Harold in Italy* (1834), based on the poem by Byron.

The pianist Franz Liszt developed the symphonic poem, or tone poem. For his symphonic poems, Liszt ignored the tradition of having symphonic works organized into several movements. He also avoided the idea that sonata form provided necessary balance for a first movement of a symphonic composition. He often unified his works by using a single theme or melody that he continuously transformed as the piece progressed. This technique is much like that used by Berlioz with the *idée fixe*. Liszt's *Les Préludes* (1853) is a single-movement work that follows the events and emotions in a poem called *Méditations poétiques* by Alphonse de Lamartine. Liszt wrote it to be played by a large orchestra that included a harp and several percussion instruments besides timpani. The manner in which the orchestra is used is also typically Romantic. The winds are often used as solo instruments; the horn, a favorite Romantic instrument, is particularly prominent; fluctuations in tempo and dynamics occur frequently, something that would not have happened in the classical period.

Liszt composed twelve symphonic poems. For some he drew on Greek myths such as *Orpheus* (1853) and *Prometheus* (1850). Another of his symphonic poems that is often performed today is *Hamlet* (1858), based on Shakespeare's play. His two symphonies tell the stories of other literary works. *Faust* (1854–1857) is from a play of that name by Johann Wolfgang von Goethe (1749–1832), and *Dante* (1855–1856) was composed in three movements to fit the structure of *The Divine Comedy* (c. 1307) by Dante (1265–1321).

Chapter 18
WebQuest

Program Music

Another important composer of program music was **Richard Strauss** (1864–1949). Although Strauss's life extended nearly halfway through the twentieth century, the bulk of his tone poems were written in the nineteenth century. Some of his works, such as *Also sprach Zarathustra* (*Thus Spake Zarathustra*, 1896, used in the 1968 movie *2001: A Space Odyssey*), have general, philosophical programs, whereas the comic *Till Eulenspiegels lustige Streiche* (*Till Eulenspiegel's Merry Pranks*, 1895) and *Don Quixote* (1897) have more specific programs.

Summary

Romantic composers who chose to abandon the classical forms found new ways of unifying their larger instrumental works. A favorite method was to compose the music to fit a nonmusical idea, frequently a story. Such music is known as program music.

The more radical Romantic composers, such as Hector Berlioz, composed major works that were very dramatic and were often inspired by literary texts. His *Symphonie fantastique* was based on his own life. It derives its unity from the *idée fixe,* a melodic idea appearing in various transformations throughout the five-movement symphony.

Franz Liszt and Richard Strauss also composed many programmatic works for orchestra that are still often performed today. The idea of having a theme change or transform as the piece is played was also employed by other Romantic composers.

New People and Concepts

Dies Irae	*idée fixe*	**Richard Strauss**
Hector Berlioz	**program symphony**	**thematic transformation**

Finale

Listen again to *Symphonie fantastique,* fifth movement, by Berlioz, and compare your impressions now with your notes from your first listening. Do you hear more now than you did before? You should now be able to answer the following questions:

▌ What is the meter?

▌ What is the tempo?

▌ Where do melodies or sections of music repeat?

▌ What is the general mood of the music?

▌ In what ways does the mood fit the title?

19 | Nationalism in the Romantic Era

The history of Western music has had much to do with the progressively making explicit of what nature leaves implicit.

—NOVELIST AND COMPOSER ANTHONY BURGESS (1917–1993)

Listening Introduction

Listen to the example of music that represents this chapter, "The Moldau" by Smetana, and make notes about what you hear. Give some attention to the following:

❚ Can you guess at the tempo?

❚ Can you detect the meter?

❚ Do you hear a melody that repeats later in the work?

❚ The Moldau is a river. Can you hear anything that sounds like water?

❚ The mood changes throughout the work. Can you guess at a meaning behind any of the sections?

Keep these notes to compare with your impressions about the music after you study the information in this chapter.

During the later part of the romantic era, nationalism became an important force in music. *Nationalism* in this context refers to any musical expression that is intended to emphasize the unique character and interests of a particular nation. There had been some stylistic differences in the music of different nations in past eras. Certainly, J. S. Bach's music was composed in a very Germanic style, whereas opera was generally thought of as an Italian art form into the classical period. For the most part, however, the classical style of Mozart, Haydn, and Beethoven was international and cosmopolitan.

During the romantic era, however, self-conscious and even aggressive nationalistic feeling flared up in both literature and music. Common musical expressions of nationalism ranged from the use of historical or other national subjects to the quoting of folk melodies and/or rhythms in new works.

Russia had been isolated from the influence of Western European culture until the reign of Peter the Great (1672–1725). Peter forced Western customs and ideas on his people to the point of eliminating many of their own traditions. Italian opera became particularly popular at the Imperial Court. Most of the musicians were brought in from the West, and performances were available only for the upper classes. In the nineteenth century, a new sense of national pride began to grow, demanding that there be something "Russian" about the music played in Russia. One of the early Romantics to do this was Mikhail Glinka (1804–1857)

Chapter 19
WebQuest

Nationalism in
the Romantic
Era

who composed the opera *A Life for the Tsar* (1836). The work was full of Russian folk melodies and expressed a proud Russian spirit.

Later in the century, a group of five Russian composers shared the feeling that musical influences from the West should be completely abandoned. They referred to themselves as "the Five." Of these composers, the most significant were Alexander Borodin (1833–1887), who is best known for his opera *Prince Igor;* Nikolai Rimsky-Korsakov (1844–1908), well remembered for his orchestral tone poem *Sheherazade;* and Modest Musorgsky (1839–1881), who wrote *Pictures at an Exhibition* for solo piano and the opera *Boris Godunov.*

The distinctive nature of Russian folk music and Slavic culture made the nationalist movement in Russia very obvious. But Russia was not the only country in which nationalistic forces influenced the musical scene. Ralph Vaughan Williams and Edward Elgar in England, Jean Sibelius in Finland, Edvard Grieg in Norway, Manuel de Falla of Spain, and Ottorino Respighi in Italy each reflected in some way the particular nationalistic flavor of their native countries.

The forces of nationalism also influenced musical developments in Bohemia, an area that is now part of the Czech Republic. Bohemia had been an Austrian colony for centuries and thus had always been in touch with the mainstream of European music. Many fine musicians were produced in this region, but until the romantic era, no distinctively Czech national style had developed. Even when a nationalist movement did arise, no extreme effort was made to avoid Western influence.

Bedřich Smetana

Regarded as the founder of the Czech national school, **Bedřich Smetana** (1824–1884) was a composer dedicated to merging the spirit of Bohemian folk music with the innovations of the European musical pioneers of his day. A gifted pianist from childhood, Smetana performed the works of the classical masters. His traditional orientation was supplanted, however, when on a visit to Prague, he had the opportunity to hear Liszt and Berlioz. Smetana came to share with these men not only a fascination with progressive musical ideas but also a spirit of nationalism to which his dream of a Bohemia free from Austrian rule responded.

Composer Bedřich
Smetana

The spirit of Czech nationalism was widespread in Austrian-ruled Bohemia, and rising unrest culminated in the revolution of 1848. The uprising was a failure and left in its wake a long period of repression that Smetana eventually found unbearable. In 1856, he traveled to Sweden, where he worked as a teacher and conductor. He returned to his homeland after six years, this time finding a new and dynamic liberalism in the air. Shortly after his return, a Czech national theater for opera, drama, and ballet was established, and Smetana began work on an opera in the Czech language.

Over the next twenty years, the composer produced ten operas, eight of them on patriotic themes. *The Bartered Bride* (1866), which told of a village romance and recounted the comic antics of local Bohemian peasants, was instrumental in establishing his reputation.

In 1874, Smetana suddenly became deaf. But, like Beethoven before him, he continued to compose until close to the end of his life. He died at the age of sixty.

Aside from his operas, Smetana is best known for his famous cycle of symphonic poems, *Má Vlast* (*My Country,* 1879). The six works in this cycle celebrate his country's legendary past, its splendid rivers and hillsides, and great moments in Bohemian history. One of the finest of the six is called "Vltava" ("The Moldau"). It traces musically the course of the river Moldau from its sources through central Bohemia to Prague and on to join another river, the Elbe.

Listening Guide

"The Moldau" BEDŘICH SMETANA

CD 2
Tracks 4–11

Year: 1874

Tempo: Allegro commodo non agitato (fast, but unhurried and not agitated). The tempo varies according to the program.

Meter: Mostly duple; the Moldau theme is sextuple

Form: Through-composed to fit the program, with one returning theme that represents the river

Instrumentation: One piccolo, two flutes, two oboes, two clarinets, two bassoons, four French horns, two trumpets, three trombones, one tuba, timpani, bass drum, triangle, cymbals, harp, first violins, second violins, violas, cellos, double basses

Duration: 11:32

	Timing		What to listen for
4	0:00	**Two Springs, Sources of the River**	Flutes portray a cold spring bubbling up; harp and **pizzicato** (plucked) strings accompany
	0:24		Clarinets enter to portray a warm spring; two springs remain separate, then blend together to form a single stream
5	0:58	**The Moldau**	A triangle note; flowing accompaniment suggests movement of water
	0:59		The Moldau theme

continued

	Timing		What to listen for
6	2:44	**Forest Hunt**	Hunting horns suddenly heard from the forests along the river, as flowing accompaniment continues; louder trumpet calls increase excitement; calls and accompaniment die away
7	3:39	**Peasant Wedding**	Music in the style of a Czech folk dance portrays a peasant wedding celebration on the banks of the river; dies away to single notes in bass
8	5:03	**Moonlight, Dance of Water Sprites**	Woodwinds hold long notes like beams of moonlight; serene melody high in violins; quietly undulating woodwind accompaniment, occasional harp arpeggios portray the calm of the river in the moonlight
	6:54		Distant brass fanfares, pianissimo, recall the ruins of ancient castles reflected in the water and bygone days of chivalry; timpani roll and crescendo in woodwinds lead to:
	7:44	**The Moldau**	Return of the Moldau theme, flowing accompaniment
9	8:37	**St. John Rapids**	Sudden brass calls, fortissimo, cymbal roll signal the white water turbulence of the St. John Rapids; sudden drop to pianissimo, then upward rushing crescendo
	9:45	**The Moldau**	The Moldau theme, the river flows majestically through the great city of Prague
10	10:13	**Vysihrad Castle**	Brasses peal forth the theme of Vysihrad Castle, home of great heroes of Bohemia's past
11	11:03	**Coda**	Fragment of the Moldau theme sweeps up and down through the strings, gradually softening and slowing as the river flows into the distance; two closing chords, forte

"The Moldau" is not nationalistic only because it portrays the beauty of the famous Bohemian river; it is also nationalistic in the particular events Smetana chose to put into the work. The portrayal of a hunt represented a land of plenty that provided for its people, and the wedding represented the beginning of a family and all of the related values.

It is interesting to notice how beautifully Smetana gave sound to moonlight. His long-held notes in the woodwinds can easily be heard as beams of light coming from the moon, and yet moonlight itself is without sound. Modern movie composers like to steal ideas from programmatic composers of the romantic era because the Romantics did such a wonderful job of giving sound to the soundless things such as moonlight.

Summary

Nationalism refers to any musical expression that is intended to emphasize the unique character and interests of a particular nation. Common musical expressions of nationalism range from the use of historical or other types of national subjects for operas and symphonic poems to the occasional quoting of folk melodies and/or rhythms in new works.

Early in the nineteenth century, Russia began to produce nationalistic music. Mikhail Glinka drew from his country's vast supply of folk music and liturgical chant to write the opera *A Life for the Tsar,* first performed in 1836. A group of Glinka's successors formed a nationalistic school known as "the Five." The outstanding members of this group were Alexander Borodin, Nikolai Rimsky-Korsakov, and Modest Musorgsky.

The forces of nationalism were also felt in other European countries. In particular, a national style developed in Bohemia through the efforts of Bedřich Smetana. Nationalistic influences were also felt in Spain, Italy, Finland, the Scandinavian countries, and England.

New People and Concepts

Bedřich Smetana   **pizzicato**

Finale

Listen again to "The Moldau" by Smetana and compare your impressions now with your notes from your first listening. Do you hear more now than you did before? You should now be able to answer the following questions:

▮   What is the tempo?

▮   What is the meter?

▮   When do you hear the Moldau theme repeating in the work?

▮   When do you hear the hunt?

▮   When do you hear the wedding?

▮   When do you "hear" moonlight?

▮   When do you hear the St. John Rapids?

▮   When can you tell that the great city of Prague has been reached?

20 | The Concert Overture

Music is a code that opens a door to a world everybody interprets differently because our aesthetic and sensory values are different and each generation has to discover its own.

—CELLIST YO-YO-MA (BORN IN 1955)

Listening Introduction

Listen to the example of music that represents this chapter, the *Romeo and Juliet* overture, by Tchaikovsky, and make notes about what you hear. Give some attention to the following:

▌ Can you guess at the tempo?

▌ Can you detect the meter?

▌ This is a rather long composition. Listen carefully to the first nine minutes, and then see if you hear any repetition of those melodies later in the work. Do any repeat?

▌ What kind of contrasts do you hear between or among the themes (melodies) that are played during the nine-minute exposition?

▌ If you know the story of Romeo and Juliet, can you connect the sounds of the main themes to people or events in the story?

Keep these notes to compare with your impressions about the music after you study the information in this chapter.

Prior to the nineteenth century, the overture had been an instrumental piece that functioned as an introduction to a longer musical work (such as an opera or oratorio) or, in some instances, as **incidental music** to a play. Although this type of overture continued to be written during the nineteenth century, the romantic period gave rise to a new type of overture, one that was not an introduction to something else. The **concert overture** was a one-movement, self-contained musical work intended for performance in the concert hall.

Some concert overtures were written for specific festive occasions. Beethoven's "Consecration of the House" is one such work. Others, such as Mendelssohn's "Hebrides Overture," attempted to evoke some aspect of nature. And still others, including Brahms's "Tragic Overture," expressed a generalized mood or human condition.

Many concert overtures have programmatic and descriptive elements and in some respects resemble the symphonic poem. But unlike the symphonic poem, the concert overture retains the strong musical organization embodied in sonata form. In this respect, the concert overture is much like the first movement of a symphony, except that it is complete in itself.

Chapter 20
WebQuest

The Concert
Overture

Peter Ilyich Tchaikovsky

One of the most popular concert overtures written during the romantic era, *Romeo and Juliet*, was composed by the Russian **Peter Ilyich Tchaikovsky** (1840–1893). During the romantic period there were two schools of musical thought in Russia. The nationalists, such as Glinka and his successors, "the Five," attempted to create a music that was totally Russian in character and style. Other composers, such as Tchaikovsky, were more cosmopolitan and looked to Western European traditions for their inspiration while still incorporating Russian elements into their music. Tchaikovsky was the first Russian composer to gain an international reputation.

Composer Peter Ilyich Tchaikovsky

Tchaikovsky was born in Votkinsk, in a remote province of Russia. He received his earliest musical training from a French governess. When he was ten, his family moved to St. Petersburg. Upon graduating from school at the age of nineteen, he became a government clerk but soon decided to give that up to pursue a musical career. He was accepted into the newly established St. Petersburg Conservatory, where he began serious composition under Anton Rubinstein (1829–1894), the institution's founder and an eminent pianist and composer.

Tchaikovsky graduated in 1865, winning a gold medal for a cantata based not on a Russian subject but, significantly, on a German one—Schiller's *Hymn to Joy*. The following year he became a professor of harmony at the Moscow Conservatory, a position he was to hold for twelve years. His early works, which included overtures, string quartets, and a programmatic symphony, demonstrated little of the individual style that marked his later achievements. He widened his experience, however, through frequent trips abroad.

In 1876, Tchaikovsky acquired the support of an unusual benefactress, Nadezhda von Meck, a widow who had inherited an immense fortune. Impressed by his music and informed that the composer was in financial need, she commissioned several works at large fees. She arranged to pay him a fixed annuity so that he could devote himself completely to composition. Their relationship, lasting thirteen years, was carried on entirely by letter. They agreed never to meet, and except for several accidental encounters in public places, the bargain was kept.

In 1877, Tchaikovsky married Antonina Milyukova, a conservatory student who threatened suicide if he would not marry her. The marriage was a disastrous failure, for Tchaikovsky's sympathy for the girl quickly turned to revulsion, in part because of his homosexuality. After he himself made an attempt at suicide by plunging into the Moscow River, a legal separation was arranged. With the financial help of von Meck, he embarked on a trip to Italy, Paris, and Vienna.

Despite an increasing tendency toward depression, Tchaikovsky remained a highly productive composer. His Fourth and Fifth Symphonies (1877 and 1888) and the ballets *Swan Lake* (1876) and *The Sleeping Beauty* (1889) were soon performed all over Europe. By the 1880s he had reached the height of his career. Suddenly, for reasons that have never been fully explained, Mme. von Meck withdrew her support and friendship. Though her action was a severe blow to his pride, Tchaikovsky was by then able to afford the financial loss, and his capacity for work remained undiminished. During 1891 and 1892, he undertook several concert tours in America, Poland, and Germany. He went to St. Petersburg in 1893 to conduct the premiere of his Sixth Symphony, the *Pathétique*. He died just nine days after that performance.

Much mystery has surrounded Tchaikovsky's death. It was initially reported that he had fallen victim to a cholera epidemic that had been raging in the city, but it was later thought by some that he might have committed suicide by taking arsenic. The truth will probably never be known. He was fifty-three years old.

Romeo and Juliet Overture

Many of Tchaikovsky's works are often performed today. His last three symphonies, his operas, his first piano concerto, his violin concerto, and particularly his ballets *Swan Lake, The Sleeping Beauty,* and *The Nutcracker* are among the most popular works in the concert repertoire today. His concert overture *Romeo and Juliet,* sometimes referred to as a **fantasy overture,** was a relatively early work, composed in 1870 (revised in 1881). It is based on Shakespeare's play of the same title, although it was not intended to be performed with the play. Its themes are based on characters and events in the play, making it necessary to know the play to fully appreciate the music.

The primary characters and events represented in the overture are:

Romeo Montague—a young man who falls in love with the daughter of a family that is hated by his family

Juliet Capulet—loved by Romeo and falls in love with him

Friar Laurence—who secretly performs the marriage of Romeo and Juliet

Romeo is banished from the town because he killed Juliet's cousin in a street fight. Unaware of the marriage between Romeo and Juliet, Juliet's family plans for her to marry someone else. To escape her family and attempt to be united with Romeo, Juliet obtains a sleeping potion from Friar Laurence that makes her seem to be dead. The Friar then sends a messenger to find Romeo to tell him that she is not dead and that Romeo should meet her at her family's tomb when she wakes up from the potion. That message never reaches Romeo, but the news of Juliet's death does. He finds her body at the tomb, thinks she is dead, takes poison, and dies. She then wakes up to find Romeo dead and stabs herself to death.

The point was made earlier that Tchaikovsky's overture was not intended to be played during a performance of the play, although a movie version of the play made in 1968 used Tchaikovsky's themes in the score. The overture represents the essence of the play in some interesting ways, however. The foreboding music at the beginning sets the mood for a tragedy; the feud theme almost sounds like swords clashing in a street fight; and the love theme is beautiful and gentle. Tchaikovsky's coda is brilliant in that the feud and love themes compete with one another, then the feud theme takes over, to be followed by a funeral march. It was the feud that broke up the lovers and caused their deaths.

Tchaikovsky used Shakespeare's most famous drama as the basis for the concert overture *Romeo and Juliet.*

Listening Guide

Romeo and Juliet Overture PETER ILYICH TCHAIKOVSKY

CD 4
Tracks 9–15

Year: 1870

Tempo: Slow introduction, faster with some variation later

Meter: Quadruple

Form: Sonata with an introduction

Instrumentation: Two flutes (piccolo), two oboes, two clarinets, one English horn, two bassoons, four horns, two trumpets, three trombones, one tuba, timpani, cymbals, bass drum, harp, first violins, second violins, violas, cellos, double basses

Duration: 18:53

Special feature: Notice how well the themes fit the characters or emotions in the play: The Friar Laurence theme is serious and sounds like it might be played in a church, the feud theme sounds like a street fight, and the love theme is beautiful and gentle.

	Timing		What to listen for
	Introduction		
9	0:00	*Friar Laurence*	Hymnlike, homophonic theme softly in clarinets and bassoons
	0:31		Foreboding fragments begin in low strings, build gradually to winds with harp
	1:54		Strings pizzicato, Friar Laurence theme more agitated in woodwinds
	2:24		Foreboding music returns, then with harp arpeggios
	3:44		Timpani roll introduces intense, threatening motives climaxing in loud, fast passage
	4:15		Timpani, threatening motives: woodwind-string echoes build directly to:
	Exposition		
10	4:59	*Theme 1: Feud*	Agitated feud theme in orchestra; strings rush up and down; agitated feud theme; rising three-note motive tossed between strings and winds
	5:22		Fragments of feud theme and rushing strings combined, developed with three-note motive; full orchestra with cymbal crashes in loud chords and rushing strings build to climax
	6:01		Feud theme explodes in full orchestra; transition with rushing strings; feud theme builds to close
	6:22	*Bridge*	Energy released in woodwind development of three-note motive; low strings take over
11	7:06	*Theme 2: Love*	Flowing love theme in English horn and muted violas, pulsating horns accompany
	7:22		Harp arpeggio introduces muted strings with tender love music
	8:03		Flutes and oboes surge upward to love theme with countertheme in French horn creating a love duet; greatly extended with lush orchestration
	9:05	*Closing*	Harp chords and soft tones in strings and winds subside to restful close
	Development		
12	10:08		Fragments of feud theme; fast scales in strings accompany Friar Laurence theme intoned softly in horn; theme extended and developed
	11:22		Three-note motive interrupts in cellos and basses, with fragments of feud theme; downward rushing strings added and build to climax
	11:38		Cymbal crash, full orchestra develops feud theme fragment; Friar Laurence theme combined forte in trumpet; rushing strings with loud chords in orchestra lead directly into:

continued

Timing		What to listen for
Recapitulation		
13 12:12	*Theme 1*	Agitated feud theme in full orchestra with cymbal crashes; strings rush downward
14 12:35	*Theme 2*	Tender love music in oboes and clarinets; intensity grows as other winds enrich the sound; strings rise intensely upward into:
13:13		Love theme soars in strings and flute with countertheme in horn and throbbing woodwind accompaniment; grows to full, rich orchestration
14:18		Love theme fragment in cellos answered by flute; extended with fragments and horns answered by flute and oboe; strings begin love theme but it dissolves
15 14:55	*Coda*	Fragments of feud and love themes vie with each other in full orchestra; feud theme emphatically takes over, then combines with Friar Laurence theme in brass; extended development as feud music takes over; furious activity decreases to ominous timpani roll
16:12		Drumbeat continues as in a funeral march; fragments of love theme sound brokenly in strings, drumbeat ceases as woodwinds answer with a variation of tender love music; rising harp arpeggios signal union of the lovers, strings yearningly sing fragment of love theme
18:31		Drum roll crescendo to strong final chords, recalling the feud theme

Summary

The romantic era gave rise to a new type of overture, one that did not introduce a longer work but was instead a self-contained work in one movement, intended for performance in the concert hall. The concert overture, exemplified by Tchaikovsky's "Romeo and Juliet," often had programmatic elements but retained the sonata form of organization.

New People and Concepts

concert overture

fantasy overture

incidental music

Peter Ilyich Tchaikovsky

Finale

Listen again to the *Romeo and Juliet* overture by Tchaikovsky and compare your impressions now with your notes from your first listening. Do you hear more now than you did before? You should now be able to answer the following questions:

▌ What is the tempo and what happens to it during the mood changes in the work?

▌ What is the meter?

▌ Do any themes from the beginning repeat later?

▌ What kind of contrasts do you hear among the three main themes?

▌ How do those themes fit the story of Romeo and Juliet?

21 | The Romantic Concerto

As a child I was impelled to the violin, it seemed to respond to a desire for self expression. The violin . . . is part nearly of the body, vibrates with it . . . the tone is something which you make alone, it is flexible, it is something intimate . . . it is something mysterious.

—VIOLINIST AND CONDUCTOR SIR YEHUDI MENUHIN (1916–1999)

Listening Introduction

Listen to the example of music that represents this chapter, Violin Concerto in E Minor, first movement, by Mendelssohn, and make notes about what you hear. Give some attention to the following:

▍ Can you guess at the tempo?

▍ Can you detect the meter?

▍ Can you hear any themes that return?

▍ Can you hear times when the violin soloist is featured?

▍ What is the general mood of the music?

▍ Does the piece seem to be absolute music or program music?

Keep these notes to compare with your impressions about the music after you study the information in this chapter.

As we have already pointed out, Romantic audiences were dazzled by exhibitions of virtuosity. All through the romantic era there was a steady growth of virtuoso technique, particularly on the piano and the violin. The trend was begun by Beethoven, whose works were very advanced for their time. It was spurred on in 1820 by the arrival on the European concert stage of Niccolò Paganini (1782–1840); this phenomenal Italian violinist astounded and enchanted all who heard him by the incredible speed and brilliance of his playing.

The concerto for solo instrument and orchestra, with the improvised quality of its cadenza (an unaccompanied or solo section) lent itself especially well to displays of technical skill. The master composers of the period include Robert Schumann, Johannes Brahms, Felix Mendelssohn, and Peter Ilyich Tchaikovsky, all of whom wrote outstanding concertos with very memorable solo parts.

Felix Mendelssohn and Fanny Mendelssohn Hensel

Chapter 21
Video

Mendelssohn

Unlike most of the great composers of his generation, **Felix Mendelssohn** (1809–1847) not only achieved artistic success but also lived a life of relative ease and financial security. Born into a wealthy and cultured Jewish family—his

Composer Felix Mendelssohn

father was a banker, and his grandfather, Moses Mendelssohn, was a distinguished philosopher—he and his brother and two sisters were brought up as Christians. The remarkable musical abilities of Felix and his elder sister Fanny were quickly recognized by their mother Leah, who began teaching the children piano when they were quite young. After the family moved to Berlin in 1812, Felix and Fanny's formal musical training was entrusted to Carl Zelter, an eminent composer and teacher.

The Mendelssohn home was a meeting place for musicians and poets. Leah Mendelssohn organized concerts of chamber music for the enjoyment of their guests. Felix and Fanny's earliest compositions were performed at these musicales.

By 1821, Felix had composed trios, quartets, sonatas, and operettas. His debut as a concert pianist had been made even earlier—at the age of nine—and he mastered both violin and viola while still in his teens. The first striking demonstration of Felix's genius as a composer was the overture to Shakespeare's *A Midsummer Night's Dream,* composed in 1826, when he was seventeen. Three years later, he made his mark as a conductor when he revived J. S. Bach's *St. Matthew Passion.* This performance of the *Passion,* a great triumph for Mendelssohn, was the first since Bach's death almost eighty years earlier and began a wide-scale revival of Bach's music.

Mendelssohn's long-standing appreciation of Bach's music shows up in his several collections of preludes and fugues for piano. The bulk of his piano music, however, consisted of short character pieces in a highly Romantic vein. Although he composed many religious works, he is best remembered for two oratorios, *St. Paul* (1836) and *Elijah* (1846). In them, Mendelssohn incorporated elements of Bach's Passion style and Handel's oratorio form. They are generally considered the most successful nineteenth-century works of their kind.

Early in the 1830s, Mendelssohn traveled extensively throughout Europe. He conducted his concert overture "Fingal's Cave" ("The Hebrides") in London and met Hector Berlioz in Italy. Returning to Berlin in 1833, Mendelssohn decided to seek a permanent post as a music academy director. He was turned down—due to local politics—but in the same year he was asked to become town musical director and conductor at Düsseldorf. Two years later, he accepted an offer to become conductor of the famous Gewandhaus Orchestra in Leipzig. During the time he conducted the orchestra, he hired Clara Schumann to play more than twenty concerts with them.

In 1837, Mendelssohn married Cécile Jeanrenaud, the daughter of a French Protestant clergyman. In 1841, they moved to Berlin, where, at the request of Kaiser Friedrich Wilhelm IV, Mendelssohn took charge of the music division of the newly established Academy of Arts. The position did not require close supervision, and he was able to develop his plans for a conservatory at Leipzig. In 1843, the conservatory opened with a distinguished faculty that included both Robert and Clara Schumann. Several years later, Mendelssohn moved his family back to Leipzig.

Though his health began to deteriorate, Mendelssohn continued to immerse himself in his work. The unexpected death of Fanny, to whom he was deeply attached, was a major shock. Falling into a severe depression he died of a stroke in Leipzig at the age of thirty-eight.

Fanny Mendelssohn Hensel's (1804–1847) musical life was not as public or all-encompassing as was Felix's. Their father, Abraham Mendelssohn, did not want her to perform in public. Felix agreed with their father, although he was supportive of Fanny as a composer. He did not think that her name should appear on published music, so he put some of her songs in a collection of his. This sounds to us as if he was taking advantage of her, but the general feeling of the time was that a woman of her relatively high social and economic class should not write music for sale or perform for the general public.

In 1829, Fanny married Wilhelm Hensel, who was a more liberal-minded court painter. He encouraged her to play the piano, write music, and perform when she could. After her father's death, she was able to publish some of her works. She performed Felix's Piano Concerto no. 1 in 1838, and she continued to compose on a regular basis. Fanny continued the tradition of planning and playing in concerts at the Mendelssohn home. She performed in public occasionally as a pianist and directed and composed music for a local choral group. Most of her compositions are songs, but she also composed solo piano music, chamber works, a cantata, an oratorio, and a collection of choral works. She died in 1847, at the age of forty-one, apparently from a stroke.

Fanny Mendelssohn Hensel

Mendelssohn's Concerto

One of Mendelssohn's greatest concertos is the Violin Concerto in E Minor (opus 64, 1844). Mendelssohn composed the concerto for his good friend Ferdinand David. The two had met when Mendelssohn was sixteen and David fifteen. Both were child prodigies and were already highly respected performers at that time. Mendelssohn appointed David to be concertmaster of his Gewandhaus Orchestra in 1836. In 1838, Mendelssohn told David that he was planning to compose a concerto for him and that he already had such a clear idea of what he wanted it to sound like that the opening melody "sticks in my head, the beginning of which will not leave me in peace." The concerto was not completed until 1844. The first performance was such a success that the work continued to be popular, receiving many other performances during the rest of Mendelssohn's life, and it remains one of the most popular violin concertos to this day.

The concerto retains the fast-slow-fast movement structure of the classical concerto but has a solo bassoon hold a note between the first and second movements to connect them. Classical concertos, such as the Mozart Piano

Chapter 21 WebQuest

The Romantic Concerto

Concerto we listened to earlier, usually had the orchestra introduce the themes before the soloist played at all. For this concerto, Mendelssohn featured the soloist by having him or her introduce the first theme before it was played by the orchestra. Mendelssohn also wrote the cadenza, as did most Romantic composers. The Mendelssohn concerto is scored for solo violin and a fairly small orchestra.

Listening Guide

Violin Concerto in E Minor, first movement, FELIX MENDELSSOHN

Year: 1844

Tempo: Allegro molto appassionato (fast and quite passionate)

Meter: Duple

Form: Double-exposition sonata

Instrumentation: Two flutes, two oboes, two clarinets, two bassoons, two French horns, two trombones, timpani, solo violin, first violins, second violins, violas, cellos, double basses

Duration: 13:41

Note: Timings will vary by recording.

Timing		What to listen for
Exposition		
0:00	Theme 1 (soloist)	After a very short introduction, the violin soloist plays theme 1 with orchestral accompaniment; orchestral chords
1:05	Theme 1 (orchestra)	Orchestra plays first theme then goes into a transition while the soloist plays an extension of the theme with orchestra accompaniment
3:06	Theme 2	Woodwinds play second theme, violin soloist plays and extends the theme
4:27		Soloist returns to theme 1, played with brilliant display of virtuoso technique; stressing runs up to very high notes accompanied by pizzicato strings; orchestra plays fortissimo chords
Development		
5:47		Fragments of both themes played by orchestra and soloist with dynamic contrasts
7:34	**Cadenza**	Soloist plays alone using arpeggios, trills, **quadruple stops** (all four strings played together), and other virtuoso techniques ending on extremely high notes
Recapitulation		
9:12	Theme 1	Orchestra plays theme; soloist plays brilliant passage that includes parts of the theme
10:10	Theme 2	Woodwinds play theme; soloist joins in and extends the theme
11:31		Fragments of theme 1 return in the orchestra; soloist accompanied by pizzicato strings; orchestra plays chords; intensity builds
12:26	**Coda**	Soloist plays transitional passage alone; tempo gets faster, building intensity to end

HEARING THE DIFFERENCE

Vivaldi's "Spring," first movement, from *The Four Seasons,* and Mendelssohn's Violin Concerto in E Minor, first movement

Earlier, we compared Vivaldi's "Spring" with Mozart's Symphony no. 40 and found that the presence of the harpsichord with a string orchestra in "Spring" was a sound very typical of the baroque period, while the full orchestra with woodwind and brass instruments in the symphony were typical of the classical orchestral sound. Those two works are also quite different from one another in that "Spring" is a violin concerto while the symphony does not feature any particular solo instrument. Here, we are comparing two violin concertos, but, again, each comes from a different historical period and consequently has different characteristics. In addition to the presence of the harpsichord, one of the most noticeable baroque characteristics in "Spring" is the rhythmic regularity and sense of motion from start to finish. The many tempo fluctuations in Mendelssohn's concerto help to create a sense of drama and passion that are very characteristic of the romantic period. Other differences are outlined below.

	"Spring" from *The Four Seasons*	**Violin Concerto, first movement**
Historical period	Baroque	Romantic
Tempo	Allegro	Allegro molto appassionato (fast and quite passionate)
Meter	Quadruple	Duple
Form	Ritornello; the piece is structured around and unified by the regular returns of the ritornello theme	Double-exposition sonata form, which means that it begins with an exposition that allows both the soloist and the orchestra to introduce two themes. That is followed by a development of those themes, and then a recapitulation of them.
Instrumentation	The string orchestra includes a harpsichord on the chordal continuo part. The crisp timbre of the harpsichord is a very baroque sound.	There is no harpsichord in the orchestra, and the orchestra includes woodwinds, brass, and timpani in addition to strings.
Solo styles	The solo violinist stands out above the orchestra at times, but also occasionally exchanges solo parts with members of the orchestra. There is no cadenza to feature the soloist alone.	The solo violinist is featured from the beginning to the end of the concerto. The solo part is often very high, soaring above the orchestra. It is also often very fast and technical, compared to the orchestral parts. The cadenza allows the soloist to be heard without the orchestra.
Story behind	Program music. Themes have been composed to fit the bird song, stream, and storm sections of the poem, "Spring."	Absolute music, composed to allow two themes to be repeated and developed.

Summary

The interest of Romantic audiences in virtuosity encouraged composers to write concertos containing very intricate solo parts. Most concertos were still composed in three movements, fast-slow-fast, as they had been since the baroque period, and they continue to use the classical tradition of a double-exposition sonata form as the basic structure of the first movement. Some composers, such as Felix Mendelssohn, allowed their soloists to be featured by having them introduce the first theme before the orchestra had a chance to play it. Romantic composers usually composed their own cadenzas instead of allowing performers to improvise them as was the practice in the classical period.

New People and Concepts

Fanny Mendelssohn Hensel   **Felix Mendelssohn**   **quadruple stops**

Finale

Listen again to Violin Concerto in E Minor, first movement, by Mendelssohn, and compare your impressions now with your notes from your first listening. Do you hear more now than you did before? You should now be able to answer the following questions:

▊ What is the tempo?

▊ What is the meter?

▊ When does the first theme return?

▊ When do you hear the cadenza?

▊ What is the general mood of the music?

▊ Is the concerto absolute or program music?

22 | Romantic Choral Music

Without craftsmanship, inspiration is a mere reed shaken in the wind.

—COMPOSER JOHANNES BRAHMS (1833–1897)

Listening Introduction

Listen to the example of music that represents this chapter, Brahms's *Ein deutsches Requiem* (*A German Requiem*), op. 45, sixth movement, and make notes about what you hear. Give some attention to the following:

▐ How many separate and contrasting sections does the movement have?

▐ Can you guess at the tempo of each section?

▐ Can you detect the meter of each section?

▐ What type of voice sings the solo parts (soprano, alto, tenor, baritone, bass)?

▐ Can you tell the language of the text?

▐ What is the overall mood of each section?

Keep these notes to compare with your impressions about the music after you study the information in this chapter.

The choral literature of the nineteenth century presents a fascinating array of compositions, ranging from short, modest pieces for unaccompanied chorus to colossal works that use a very large chorus and orchestra. Choral festivals were popular during the romantic period and virtually every major composer made significant contributions to choral literature and the choral tradition.

The oratorio tradition established in the baroque period by Handel and continued through the classical era by Haydn received the attention of such composers as Franz Liszt (*Legend of St. Elizabeth*), Hector Berlioz (*Childhood of Christ*), and Felix Mendelssohn, whose oratorio *Elijah* became very popular and is still often performed today. In other instances a chorus was incorporated into symphonic works, such as Robert Schumann's *Scenes from Faust*, Franz Liszt's *A Faust Symphony*, and Hector Berlioz's *Romeo and Juliet*.

Also, the great religious texts of the Catholic Church, including the Mass, Requiem, Te Deum, and Stabat Mater, were set for soloists, chorus, and orchestra by a wide variety of composers, such as Anton Bruckner, Franz Schubert, Antonín Dvořák, and Gioacchino Rossini. Verdi's *Requiem*, in memory of the author Alessandro Manzoni, is a large and dramatic setting of the moving requiem text and the work is very familiar to modern-day concertgoers.

Composer Johannes Brahms

When we listened to Berlioz's *Symphonie fantastique,* we saw what an extremely large orchestra Berlioz had hoped to use for it. He thought "big" in other compositions, as well. In three great works, *The Damnation of Faust,* the *Requiem* (*Grande messe des morts*), and the ***Te Deum*** (*Praise to God*), Berlioz reached the epitome of the colossal Romantic choral style. The musical forces involved in these works are gigantic. The *Requiem* was written for 210 singers, a large orchestra, and four brass bands positioned in various locations around the concert hall to represent the summons to the Last Judgment. The *Te Deum* requires two choruses of 100 singers each, 6 children's voices, and an orchestra of 150 players.

Johannes Brahms

Johannes Brahms (1833–1897) composed some of the most enduring choral music of the romantic period. He wrote in diverse styles for a wide variety of choral combinations. Smaller works include a cappella choruses for various voice combinations, motets, canons, part songs, and psalm settings, many employing various types of instrumental accompaniment. One of the most popular of these works is the "Liebeslieder Walzer" ("Lovesong Waltzes") for **piano, four hands** (two players on one piano) and either a vocal quartet or a four-part chorus. Brahms composed several large works for chorus and orchestra, some with soloists. Among these are the cantata "Rinaldo," "Schicksalslied" ("Song of Destiny"), for chorus and orchestra, and "Triumphlied" ("Song of Triumph"). The most important of his large-scale choral compositions was one of his early works, *Ein deutsches Requiem* (*A German Requiem*). It was composed over a period of eleven years and was finished in 1868, when Brahms was thirty-five. It not only preceded much of his other choral writing but was written a full eight years before his first symphony.

Brahms was born and raised in Hamburg, Germany. He received his earliest musical training from his father, a double-bass player. The family was not wealthy, and at an early age Brahms had to contribute to the family income by playing the piano in local taverns. At the age of twenty, he met the famed Hungarian violinist Eduard Reményi and toured Germany as Reményi's accompanist. His first attempts at composition were heard by Joseph Joachim, the foremost violin virtuoso of the time, on one of his tours. Through Joachim, Brahms was introduced to Franz Liszt and Robert Schumann, who were greatly impressed by the young composer. Schumann, always eager to do what he could to advance the career of young, promising composers, wrote a laudatory article heralding Brahms as the coming genius of German music.

In his thirties, Brahms took several posts in various German towns, conducting and organizing choral groups and music societies. He spent much of his time in Vienna, finally settling there in 1868. His reputation as a composer grew to international proportions, and Cambridge University offered him the honorary degree of doctor of music. He declined, being reluctant to make a long journey that would require him to cross the English Channel, but in 1880 he accepted a similar honor from the University of Breslau, acknowledging it by writing the celebrated "Academic Festival Overture," which is based in large part on popular German student drinking songs.

Brahms was not a controversial figure, as so many of his contemporaries were, and he had no enemies. Yet in his dealings with others, his characteristic charm could give way to the most acerbic sarcasm. To one musician who was trying to maneuver Brahms into paying him a compliment, he said, "Yes, you have talent, but very little." But when the daughter of Johann Strauss (the "Waltz King" of Vienna) presented him with her fan so that he might autograph it, he wrote on it the first few measures of Strauss's "Blue Danube Waltz" and signed it, "Not, alas, by Johannes Brahms."

Brahms remained a bachelor all his life, living simply and composing methodically. He enjoyed the respect and admiration of his peers and inspired the noted conductor Hans von Bülow to coin the famous phrase, "the Three B's of Music": Bach, Beethoven, and Brahms. After Brahms's death his fame grew, as many societies were founded to publish and perform his works. In the concert repertoire, Brahms's symphonies occupy a place second only to that of his acknowledged master, Beethoven. Brahms died of cancer just one month before what would have been his sixty-fourth birthday.

Brahms's *Requiem*

Unlike the requiems of Mozart, Berlioz, Verdi, and later Fauré, Brahms's setting does not employ the traditional Latin text, which is actually a Mass for the dead. Rather, it is a setting of nonliturgical (not part of Catholic mass) German texts that Brahms selected from the Lutheran Bible. A comparison of the Brahms text with the Roman Catholic liturgy shows a marked difference in intention and feeling: The Latin text prays for the soul of the dead, whereas Brahms's text is designed to console the living.

Chapter 22
WebQuest

Romantic
Choral Music

The opening words of the two texts confirm this:

Roman Catholic Text	**Brahms Text**
Requiem aeternam dona eis Domine	Selig sind, die da Leid tragen, denn sie sollen getröstet werden
(Give them eternal rest, O Lord)	(Blessed are they that mourn, for they shall be comforted)

Brahms's entire composition conveys this pervasive feeling of consolation in both the text and the music.

Brahms's *Requiem* consists of seven movements and is scored for soprano and baritone soloists, chorus, and orchestra. The chorus and orchestra participate in all seven movements, although the orchestration varies somewhat from movement to movement. By comparison, the role of the soloists is minimal, with the baritone appearing in the third and sixth movements and the soprano appearing only in the fifth. Brahms builds a sense of overall unity into the piece, including themes from the first movement in the last movement.

In many respects, the sixth movement is the most dramatic of the entire work. It is characterized by extreme contrasts and driving climaxes, and its power is intensified by its position between the gentle fifth movement and the quiet, consoling seventh. The sixth movement consists of three large sections: the first two involve the solo baritone, whereas the third is an extended fugue for chorus and orchestra.

The final movement of the *Requiem* balances with the first. The first movement begins with "Blessed are they that mourn, for they shall be comforted" (Matthew 5:4), and the seventh and final movement ends with "Blessed are the dead which die in the Lord from henceforth; yea, saith the Spirit, that they may

Listening Guide

Ein deutsches Requiem (*A German Requiem*), op. 45, sixth movement JOHANNES BRAHMS

CD 4
Tracks 16–18

Year: 1868

Tempo: Section I, andante (a walking pace); Section II, vivace (lively); and Section III, allegro (fast)

Meter: Section I, quadruple; Section II, triple; and Section III, duple

Texture: Sections I and II, mostly homophonic with polyphonic sections; Section III, mostly polyphonic with homophonic ending

Form: Three major sections with the music following and emphasizing the text

Voices: SATB choir, baritone soloist, orchestra

Instrumentation: One piccolo, two flutes, two oboes, two clarinets, two bassoons, one contrabassoon, four French horns, two trumpets, three trombones, one tuba, timpani, first violins, second violins, violas, and cellos

Language: German

Duration: 10:36

Special feature: Sections of text are repeated, in some cases, several times.

Timing	German text	English translation	Notes
Section I (Andante, quadruple meter)			
Text source: Hebrews 13:14			
[16] 0:00	Denn wir haben hier keine bleibende Statt, sondern die Zukünftige suchen wir.	For here have we no continuing city, but we seek one to come.	Chorus and orchestra
Text source: 1 Corinthians 15:51–55			
1:06	Siehe, ich sage euch ein Geheimnis: Wir werden nicht alle entschlafen, wir werden aber alle verwandelt werden, und dasselbige plötzlich in einem Augenblick zu der Zeit der letzten Posaune.	Behold, I show you a mystery: we shall not all sleep, but we shall all be changed, in a moment, in the twinkling of an eye, at the last trump:	Baritone solo Chorus repeats Baritone & chorus accelerando and crescendo
Section II (Vivace, triple meter)			
[17] 2:51	Denn es wird die Posaune schallen, und die Toten werden auferstehen unverweslich, und wir werden verwandelt werden.	for the trumpet shall sound, and the dead shall be raised incorruptible, and we shall be changed.	Chorus
3:25	Dann wird erfüllet werden das Wort, das geschrieben steht:	Then shall be brought to pass the saying that is written:	Baritone
3:51	Der Tod ist verschlungen in den Sieg. Tod, wo ist dein Stachel! Hölle, wo ist dein Sieg!	death is swallowed up in victory. O death, where is thy sting? O grave, where is thy victory?	Chorus Fortissimo to cadence
Section III (Allegro, duple meter)			
Text source: Revelation 4:11			
[18] 5:31	Herr, du bist würdig zu nehmen Preis und Ehre und Kraft, denn du hast alle Dinge erschaffen, und durch deinen Willen haben sie das Wesen und sind geschaffen.	Thou art worthy, O Lord, to receive glory and honor and power: for thou hast created all things, and for thy pleasure they are and were created.	Choral fugue

rest from their labors; and their works do follow them" (Revelation 14:13). Perhaps more than any other, this work demonstrates Brahms's unique ability to combine classical design—its carefully balanced and contrasting elements—with the expressive qualities of the Romantic spirit.

"The Live Experience: Choirs and Choral Singing" describes how choral groups are formed and performed.

THE LIVE EXPERIENCE
Choirs and Choral Singing

Many people enjoy singing in a choir. A recent survey taken by the organization Chorus America indicated that over 50 percent of Americans sing or have sung in a choir. Choirs in many churches, schools, and community centers usually do not require an audition and are large enough that one does not have to have a wonderful solo voice to join in with others. Of course, some church, school, and professional choirs require an audition that people with some vocal experience can pass or that others can pass after taking some singing lessons or a voice class. Professional choirs may be as small as barbershop quartets (they exist for both men and women), or they may have more than one hundred singers and perform large-scale works on a regular basis. There are special interest choirs, for example, of gay men, cancer survivors, or people who work at a particular profession. Many communities and churches also have children's choirs.

Whatever the group, choral music is available from all periods in music history, and it covers just about all styles of music. Choirs sing Gregorian chants, Renaissance madrigals, and masterworks of the baroque, classical, and romantic periods. They also sing vocal jazz arrangements, popular songs, folk songs, and music from the non-Western world. As we will see in the twentieth century, modern composers draw on many styles of music and mix them with new compositional techniques to create beautiful and original choral works.

This youth choir gives an outdoor performance.

Summary

The lush sound of a large chorus was well suited to the Romantic style, and nearly every composer of the period wrote choral music in some form. Hector Berlioz frequently utilized a large chorus combined with an enormous orchestra in his works. Oratorios and settings of Catholic liturgical texts were written by such composers as Mendelssohn, Liszt, Berlioz, Schubert, Bruckner, and Verdi. Choruses also were used in programmatic symphonic works.

Some of the most enduring choral music of the romantic era was written by Johannes Brahms. The greatness of his most significant work, *Ein Deutsches Requiem* (*A German Requiem*), rests on its masterful and eloquent marriage of the music and texts. In contrast to the traditional Catholic funeral Mass, Brahms's *Requiem* uses texts from the Old and New Testaments that give a message of comfort and consolation to the bereaved mourners.

New People and Concepts

Johannes Brahms   **piano, four hands**   *Te Deum*

Finale

Listen again to Brahms's *Ein deutsches Requiem* (*A German Requiem*), op. 45, sixth movement, and compare your impressions now with your notes from your first listening. Do you hear more now than you did before? You should now be able to answer the following questions:

▌ How many separate and contrasting sections does the movement have?

▌ What is the tempo of each section?

▌ What is the meter of each section?

▌ What type of voice sings the solo parts?

▌ What is the language of the text?

▌ In what ways does the overall mood of each section support the meaning of the text?

How can one express the indefinable sensations that one experiences while writing an instrumental composition that has no definite subject? It is a purely lyrical process. It is a musical confession of the soul, which unburdens itself through sounds, just as a lyric poet expresses himself through poetry.... As the poet Heine said, "Where words leave off, music begins."
—COMPOSER PETER ILYICH TCHAIKOVSKY (1840–1893)

Listening Introduction

Listen to the example of music that represents this chapter, Dvořák's Symphony no. 9 in E Minor (From the New World), fourth movement, and make notes about what you hear. Give some attention to the following:

▮ Can you detect the tempo?

▮ Can you detect the meter?

▮ Can you hear any themes that return?

▮ There is a very marchlike theme near the beginning. Can you tell what instrumental family plays it first?

▮ Can you tell what instruments then play a contrasting second part of the marchlike theme?

▮ What solo instruments do you hear featured from time to time?

Keep these notes to compare with your impressions about the music after you study the information in this chapter.

Among Romantic composers, attitudes toward the classical forms developed by Haydn and Mozart and expanded by Beethoven varied considerably. As we have seen in earlier chapters, some of the more radical composers abandoned these traditions altogether, turning instead to other sources of inspiration and organization. For example, Berlioz's *Symphonie fantastique,* with five movements all organized around the tale of a drugged and dreaming lovesick man, broke most classical symphonic traditions. Some Romantic composers, however, continued to follow more classically oriented forms, usually also expanding the forms in some ways. In doing so, they utilized elements from both the classical and the romantic eras.

The Romantic Symphony

The Romantic symphony grew in the shadow of Beethoven's symphonic writing. Virtually all the early Romantic composers were affected by Beethoven's music, some by his use of the orchestra, others by the ways he expanded the forms, lengthening developments and adding development sections to codas.

The symphonies of Franz Schubert, whose song "The Erlkönig" we heard earlier, displayed a Romantic gift for lyric melody but were written in the traditional

195

classical forms. He composed nine symphonies in all. His famous Symphony no. 8 was written in 1822, when the composer was twenty-five years old, but he never chose to extend it beyond the original two movements. Nicknamed "The Unfinished," the work was not performed until 1865, forty-three years after Schubert's death. Today it is better known than any of his other symphonies.

If Schubert was the outstanding symphonist of the beginning of the romantic period, Johannes Brahms deserves that honor for the latter part of the century. Brahms occupies a unique place in the history of the romantic era. Although he was much admired by his contemporaries, he disagreed with the popular Romantic notion—championed by more radical composers such as Berlioz and Wagner—that literature, the visual arts, and philosophy should be united with music. In a period of experimentation and change, he looked back to Beethoven and the classical era, finding in traditional forms new and worthwhile ideas to express. His four symphonies rank with Beethoven's as masterworks of the symphonic repertoire.

Another late-romantic composer, **Antonín Dvořák** (1841–1904) composed nine symphonies based on classical forms. Like Bedřich Smetana, whose symphonic poem *The Moldau* we heard earlier, Dvořák was Bohemian. He was born in a small village near Prague and moved to that city at the age of sixteen to study music of the German classical tradition. The Prague public first became aware of Dvořák with the performance of his patriotic choral work *Hymnus* in 1873. This success prompted a grant from the Austrian ministry of fine arts, which supplied the composer with a small income. However, it was the patronage of Brahms, whom he met a year later, that thrust Dvořák into musical prominence. In 1877, Brahms persuaded a German music publisher to print the composer's *Moravian Duets* and *Slavonic Dances*. This allowed Dvořák to spend the 1880s touring Europe conducting his own works. He eventually obtained the position of professor of composition at the Prague Conservatory.

Dvořák's career ultimately brought him to America, where he served from 1892 to 1895 as artistic director of the National Conservatory of Music in New York. One of his students at the conservatory was Henry T. Burleigh, an African American composer and baritone who introduced him to African American spirituals. Dvořák was also introduced to the melodies of the American Indians. In these traditions, he believed, lay the basis of a new musical school capable of expressing the unique spirit of the American people. His own nationalistic fervor impelled him to urge his American students toward the creation of a national style that would draw on these musical resources.

Homesick for his native country, Dvořák spent only three years in the United States. In 1901, he was appointed to the directorship of the Prague Conservatory. His death in 1904 at the age of sixty-two was mourned throughout his beloved Bohemia.

Dvořák's versatility is reflected in his legacy of concertos for violin, cello, and piano; his fourteen string quartets; his four great oratorios; his five symphonic poems; his cantata; his four piano trios and two quintets; and his eleven operas and nine symphonies, among a multitude of other works.

Composer Antonín Dvořák

As we said earlier, Dvořák was very much interested in the music of African Americans and of American Indians. Indeed, these elements helped shape his "American style" and gave his symphony no. 9, subtitled "From the New World," much of its particular flavor. In a letter written while he was composing the symphony, he declared: "I should never have written the symphony like I have, if I hadn't seen America." However, the influence of American music was general rather than specific. Some of the melodies were not quoted from but suggested by Native or African American sources. The influences of Czech and American music are also evident in the folklike character and syncopated rhythms of portions of the work.

Listening Guide

Symphony no. 9 in E Minor (From the New World), fourth movement ANTONÍN DVOŘÁK

CD 4
Tracks 19–28

Year: 1893

Tempo: Allegro con fuoco (fast, with fire)

Meter: Quadruple

Form: Sonata

Instrumentation: One piccolo, two flutes, two oboes, two clarinets, two bassoons, four French horns, two trumpets, three trombones, timpani, first violins, second violins, violas, cellos, double basses

Duration: 11:44

	Timing		What to listen for
	Exposition		
19	0:00	Introduction	Two-note motive stated, expanded with faster rhythms, timpani roll
20	0:16	Theme 1	Emphatic, marchlike theme in brass, powerful chords from orchestra, repeated
	0:44		Strings state contrasting second phrase of theme
	0:59		First phrase returns in orchestra, brass chords
	1:17	Bridge	Jaunty **triplet** (three notes per beat) theme in violins, woodwinds, violins; energy dissipates, soft cymbal crash
21	2:02	Theme 2	Clarinet sings tender melody, comments from cellos with triplet motive from bridge; violins take over melody; drum roll leads to:
22	2:50	Theme 3	Czech village dance theme, first phrase closes with three-note motive moving down scale; repeated
	3:05		Second phrase closes with same three-note motive descending
	Development		
23	3:15		Three-note motive continues in low strings, vigorous new countermelody in violins; three-note motive shifts to winds, returns to low strings with countermelody; countermelody winds down to pianissimo
	3:46		Three-note motive in pizzicato strings, then woodwinds with high trills; horns suddenly intone opening theme, forte
	3:57		Three-note motive softly in woodwinds; opening motive forte in horns
	4:12		Opening motive in faster notes alternates with triplet motive from bridge
	4:50		Flutes softly sing "Goin' Home" (an African American spiritual-like theme from second movement), strings alternate in fragment from third movement

continued

Timing		What to listen for
5:21		Crescendo with faster rhythm; brass blares out "Goin' Home" fragment; these two ideas then repeated
5:38		Opening motive developed in simultaneous fast and slow rhythms, crescendo into forte statement of fragment from first movement; development of opening motive takes over with powerful chords, crescendo
Recapitulation		
24	6:07	Theme 1	Trombones proclaim marchlike theme; rhythmic motive developed as energy subsides
25	7:17	Theme 2	Tender melody in strings, answered by woodwinds with triplet melody; intensity grows, then fades
26	8:08	Theme 3	Village dance theme now in slower, reflective version
	8:26		Second phrase, closes into horn call softly recalling theme from first movement; three-note motive excitedly developed as transition
Coda		
27	9:11	Second development	Brass proclaims opening marchlike theme, strings respond with triplet theme from bridge
	9:29		Trombones triumphantly blast out theme from first movement; orchestra continues to develop opening motive with powerful chords; timpani figure and rushing strings lead to climactic chord; energy dissipates
	10:11		Clarinet in "Goin' Home" theme of second movement set against fragment from third movement
28	10:28	Second recapitulation and coda	Horn softly intones opening marchlike theme; orchestra restates theme forte
	10:47		Themes of first and fourth movements boldly stated simultaneously
	11:20		Triumphant cadence closes movement; long-held chord dies away

Although we did not listen to the first three movements of Dvořák's symphony, you might notice the many references to themes from these movements in the listening guide to the fourth movement. This technique of unifying long musical works with recurring themes is cyclical in much the same way in which Beethoven's rhythmic motive returns in each movement of his Fifth Symphony. Many Romantic composers used this technique in their longer works. The idea is much like the "thematic transformation" we discussed in Berlioz's *Symphonie fantastique* in which the *idée fixe* kept returning in each movement. The difference is that Berlioz changed, or "transformed," the theme for each of its returns, whereas Dvořák quoted the old themes much the way they had been played before.

Other Romantic Traditionalists

Anton Bruckner (1824–1896), an Austrian composer and organist, joined Brahms in the effort to use classical forms within an expanded framework. Bruckner was a simple and very religious man, deeply involved with Catholic beliefs. His three Masses are of sufficient caliber to rank Bruckner as the most important church composer of the late nineteenth century.

Bruckner's nine symphonies show his kinship to classical tradition in their formal design, but their exceptional length and weighty orchestration mark them as Romantic works. The German Romantic opera composer, Wagner, was one of Bruckner's idols. Bruckner influenced later composers of his native Vienna, particularly Mahler and Schoenberg.

The Austrian **Gustav Mahler** (1860–1911) was a conductor, as well as a symphonic composer. His nine completed symphonies are immense and complex and encompass a vast emotional range. Although the symphonies follow the classical outline and have separate movements, their style incorporates many elements from vocal music, including opera. His symphonies contain long, lyrical melodies; four of them have parts for voices, as well as instruments. Mahler's works span the spectrum of emotions, from ecstasy to despair. He tried to make each symphony a complete world in itself, with all types of themes and techniques. These large-scale works are unified by the use of recurring themes and motives.

The world Mahler created for his first symphony was one that charted experiences of the human soul. It begins with two movements that express springtime, full of flowers and joyous dancing. The mood changes in the third movement, which begins with a mock funeral march that was inspired by an engraving titled *The Huntsman's Funeral Procession.* The engraving was a popular children's image in which forest animals cry as they carry the casket of a hunter to his grave. The third movement also uses the melody of the children's song *Frère Jacques,* which Germans and Austrians called *Brüder Martin* (Brother Martin), as a primary theme. Mahler varied the melody slightly and set it in a minor mode, changing it from what was originally a cheerful song into a lament. A dance-like melody is played in the first contrasting section, followed by another section that introduces a slightly faster and lighter but lonely sounding melody. The funeral march and *Frère Jacques* melody return in the final section. The symphony's last movement is vigorous, dramatic, and then reflective as a deeply wounded soul moves toward paradise. We will listen to the third movement.

Chapter 24
WebQuest

The Romantic
Traditionalists

Listening Guide

Symphony no. 1 in D Major, third movement GUSTAV MAHLER

CD 2
Tracks 12–15

Year: 1888

Tempo: "Solemn, measured, not hurried"

Meter: Quadruple

Form: Sectional with a return of the first theme near the end, giving the movement a feeling
 of balance

Instrumentation: Four flutes, four oboes, four clarinets, four bassoons, seven French horns, five
 trumpets, four trombones, one tuba, percussion, first violins, second violins, violas, cellos,
 double basses, and harp

Duration: 10:01

Timing		What to listen for
12 0:00	Section One	Timpani establish a steady beat with two alternating notes, suggesting a funeral march
0:07		Minor version of *Frère Jacques* is played as a round. Double bass (solo) begins
0:27		Bassoon enters with round melody
0:47		Tuba enters with round melody
1:01		Oboe adds a contrasting melody above the round and drum beat (volume somewhat louder)
1:15		Flute enters with round melody

continued

	Timing		What to listen for
	1:34		Oboe repeats contrasting melody (gradual decrease of volume)
	2:00		Round concludes, long held chord *(piano)* leads into next section
13	2:07	Section Two	A dance-like melody is played by soft oboes joined by trumpets accompanied by pizzicato strings. High clarinets, bass drum, and cymbals are added playing slightly faster and louder
	2:54		The dance-like melody is repeated by strings and woodwinds with a contrasting melody by trumpets
	3:37		A varied version of the dance-like melody returns a bit slower. The funeral march beat continues and then finishes with the end of the *Frère Jacques* melody *(diminuendo)* and then sustained notes.
14	5:00	Section Three	A slightly faster and lighter, but somewhat lonely sounding melody is played by muted strings, then joined by flute, two violins, clarinet and horns, and finally oboe. That melody gets slower and softer.
	6:45		Flutes play a slower concluding melody
15	6:57	Section Four	Faster timpani beat and *Frère Jacques* march returns and are joined by contrasting melody from section one played by high clarinet and then taken over by flute and strings
	7:33		Trumpets enter march
	7:59		Dance-like melody from section two is played by clarinets, cymbals, and drums
	8:21		Clarinets play suddenly faster and louder, then the tempo retards with descending fragments of melody bringing a sense of quiet conclusion
	9:24		Low bassoon plays the contrasting melody from section one, decrescendo, gong

Mahler composed eight other symphonies and had not yet finished a tenth one when he died at age 50. He is also well remembered for his songs and song cycles; the *Kindertotenlieder (Songs on the Death of Children),* composed in 1902, and *Das Lied von der Erde (The Song of the Earth)* from 1908 are particularly outstanding. Themes from his songs are often echoed in his symphonic works, including the one we just listened to. Mahler's first symphony used melodies from *Lieder eines fahrenden Gesellen* (Songs of a Wayfarer), composed in 1884, in both the first and third movements. The echo in the third movement is the "lonely sounding" melody in section three (see Listening Guide).

Summary

Although many composers of the romantic era broke away from classical forms and traditions to base their works on stories or other extramusical ideas, others stayed closer to the classical traditions established by Haydn, Mozart, and Beethoven. Of the various different types of works composed during the romantic period, symphonies tended to be the most traditional. Composers who adhered the most closely to traditional forms include Franz Schubert, Johannes Brahms, Antonín Dvořák, Anton Bruckner, and Gustav Mahler.

Using Dvořák's Symphony no. 9 ("From the New World") as an example, we saw that the fourth movement was composed in a fairly standard structuring of sonata form, except that Dvořák had three main themes when two were more common in the classical period. He also extended the coda to include a second development section followed by a second recapitulation and coda. Like we have heard before in Beethoven's Fifth Symphony and in Berlioz's *Symphonie fantastique,* Dvořák unified the entire symphony by having themes from earlier movements return in the fourth movement.

The formal structure of the third movement of Mahler's first symphony, with its march-like beginning and ending sections and two lighter contrasting sections between them, is based on the classical forms of the Minuet and Trio and the Scherzo and Trio. Both forms, commonly used for third movements of classical symphonies, were structured ABA, with the minuet or scherzo as the "A" sections and the trio as the "B." If you see Mahler's march sections as "A" and the contrasting sections as "B" and "C" trios, then Mahler's third movement is an expansion of the classical form from ABA to ABCA. Of course, minuets and scherzos are in triple meter and the march is in quadruple, but the structure is still an expansion of the classical one. Many romantic composers were similarly influenced by classical traditions, but felt the need to expand them.

New People and Concepts

Anton Bruckner   **Gustav Mahler**   **triplet**

Antonín Dvořák

Finale

Listen again to Dvořák's Symphony no. 9 in E Minor (From the New World), fourth movement, and compare your impressions now with your notes from your first listening. Do you hear more now than you did before? You should now be able to answer the following questions:

▌ What is the tempo?

▌ What is the meter?

▌ How many themes from the exposition return in the recapitulation?

▌ Can you tell what instrumental family plays it first?

▌ What instruments play the marchlike theme near the beginning, and what instruments play the contrasting second part of the marchlike theme?

▌ What solo instruments do you hear featured from time to time?

24 | Romantic Opera in France and Italy

Nothing primes inspiration more than necessity, whether it be the presence of a copyist waiting for your work, or the prodding of an impresario tearing his hair. In my time, all the impresarios of Italy were bald at 30.

—COMPOSER GIOACCHINO ROSSINI (1792–1868)

Listening Introduction

Listen to the example of music that represents this chapter, "Sì, mi chiamano Mimì" ("Yes, they call me Mimì") from *La Bohème,* Act 1, by Puccini and make notes about what you hear. Give some attention to the following:

▌ Can you guess at the tempo?

▌ Can you detect the meter?

▌ Can you tell the voice type (soprano, alto, tenor, baritone, or bass) of the singer?

▌ Can you tell the language of the text?

▌ Does the piece have a general mood that allows you to guess the meaning of the text?

Keep these notes to compare with your impressions about the aria after you study the information in this chapter.

French Opera

Opera was one of the most important musical genres of the romantic period. During the first half of the era, Paris was the operatic capital of Europe. Beginning about 1820, with the rise of a large and influential middle class, a new type of opera developed. Called **grand opera,** it concentrated on the spectacular elements of the production: crowd scenes, ballets, choruses, and elaborate scenery. The integrity of the drama and the music was often sacrificed for these special effects. Giacomo Meyerbeer (1791–1864), a German composer who had studied and worked extensively in Italy before going to France, introduced grand opera to Paris with such operas as *Les Huguenots* (1836) and *Le Prophète* (1849). One of the longest grand operas of the early romantic period was *Guillaume Tell* (*William Tell,* 1829) by an Italian, Gioacchino Rossini. The overture to *William Tell,* which includes the famous "Lone Ranger" theme, remains popular today.

Although grand opera received the lion's share of Parisian attention, the less pretentious *opéra comique* (comic opera) continued to be popular. The distinguishing feature of *opera comique* was its use of spoken dialogue rather than sung recitative. Both the music and the plot tended to be simpler than in grand opera. Despite the word "comic," many operas in this form had serious plots. Bizet's

Carmen, for example, has some light and entertaining moments, but the main character ends up being stabbed to death by her former lover.

Later in the nineteenth century, a new form developed as a compromise between the overwhelming spectacle of grand opera and the lightness of *opéra comique.* Called **lyric opera,** it evolved from the more serious type of *opéra comique.* Using plots taken from Romantic drama or fantasy, these works relied primarily on the beauty of their melodies. One of the finest lyric operas of the period, Charles Gounod's *Faust* (1859), was first performed with spoken dialogue, but Gounod decided to replace the dialogue with recitative, moving the opera into the "lyric" category for performances in 1860 and after. The opera was based on the first part of Goethe's famous play, *Faust,* in which the lead character sells his soul to the devil in return for youth and romance. As one might assume, the romance ends with tragedy and the deaths of Faust, his infant son, and his lover Marguerite, although Marguerite manages to avoid hell by calling for Divine mercy and then ascending to heaven.

Toward the latter part of the century, a new literary movement, **naturalism,** developed in France. Naturalist writers rebelled against the Romantic tendency toward escapism and artificially poetic language. They sought to depict life as it was, objectively and truthfully. Often they portrayed characters from the lower classes whose lives were controlled by their own passions.

Georges Bizet (1838–1875) introduced naturalism to opera in his *opéra comique* masterpiece *Carmen* (1875). Whereas grand operas often portrayed historical and mythological figures, with the performers using stylized gestures to express their feelings, Bizet's main character was a gypsy girl whose fiery temper and passionate nature were dramatized realistically. The language she used was crass and realistic for her character type. Bizet's brilliant and very memorable melodies and colorful Spanish rhythms effectively complemented the characterization and dramatic action.

Italian Opera

By the nineteenth century, opera was virtually the only important musical form being cultivated in Italy. The classical distinctions between *opera seria* and *opera buffa* were still maintained, although both were influenced by French grand opera, and the orchestra began to play a more important and colorful role.

One of the most outstanding Italian opera composers of the early part of the nineteenth century was Gioacchino Rossini (1792–1868). His sense of melody and effective staging made him an instant success. *Opera buffa* seemed to be a natural outlet for his talents, and *Il Barbiere di Siviglia* (*The Barber of Seville,* 1816) ranks with Mozart's *The Marriage of Figaro* (1786) as a supreme example of Italian comic opera. The two operas are based on plays by Beaumarchais and include many of the same characters. Rossini's retelling of the Cinderella fairy tale in *La Cenerentola* (1817) further strengthened his popularity and success as a composer of comic operas.

In his operas and oratorios, Rossini sought to cultivate the aria to its highest possible level. Its function was to delight audiences with melodious and spontaneous music. This **bel canto** style, which emphasized beauty and purity of tone and an agile vocal technique, was also exemplified in the work of two of Rossini's contemporaries. Gaetano Donizetti (1797–1848) composed some seventy operas, including *The Elixir of Love* (1832), *Lucia di Lammermoor* (1835), *The Daughter of the Regiment* (1840), and *Don Pasquale* (1843). Vincenzo Bellini's (1801–1835) lyric and expressive style is particularly evident in *Norma* (1831). All of the operas just mentioned are often performed today.

Composer Giuseppe Verdi

Giuseppe Verdi

There is no one better represented in the repertoire of today's opera companies than **Giuseppe Verdi** (1813–1901). Verdi was born of a poor family in a little hamlet in Bussetto, Italy. He began his musical training as the apprentice of the local church organist. His hard work and talent were rewarded with a stipend contributed by his town to enable the continuation of his studies at the Milan Conservatory. He was subsequently turned down by the examiners, but through the financial aid of a friend, he continued his studies by means of private lessons.

Verdi's first opera, *Oberto* (1839), written when he was twenty-six, was an instant success. To this musical triumph he added another with the presentation of his third opera, *Nabucco*, in 1842, based on a plot taken from the Old Testament of the Bible, Daniel 4:29–33. It was this work that brought him not only musical recognition but also national fame. The story dealt with the plight of the Jews in Babylon, but the parallel with the Milanese crusade for freedom from Austrian rule was so striking that Verdi was exalted as a patriot and champion of the Italian cause. His name soon became linked with the cry for independence, and his evident sympathies, as they were reflected in his works, brought him under police suspicion.

After producing a number of successful works, Verdi settled on a country estate in 1849. There he continued to pursue his political activities and produced, in succession, three of his best-known works: *Rigoletto* (1851), *Il Trovatore* (1853), and *La Traviata* (1853). These productions are regarded as the culmination of his first creative period.

Years of intensive musical productivity followed, during which such memorable works as *Un Ballo in Maschera* (*The Masked Ball,* 1859) and *Don Carlos* (1867) were created. In 1871, Verdi's masterpiece of spectacular grand opera, *Aida,* was written. With its pageantry, grand crowd scenes, and tragic but beautiful ending, this work is regarded as the height of his second creative phase.

Following this triumph, Verdi produced no operatic work for sixteen years. Then, in 1887, *Otello,* based on the Shakespeare play *Othello,* was performed in Milan. It is regarded by many critics as the pinnacle of Italian tragic opera. Verdi's last opera, *Falstaff,* also based on a Shakespearian character, was written in 1893 when the composer was nearly eighty and is one of the finest in the comic opera style. Verdi was eighty-seven years old when he died.

Verdi's style is frequently contrasted with that of his German contemporary Richard Wagner, whose music we will study in the next chapter. Although each of these composers brought Romantic opera to its height in his native country, they used quite different approaches. Wagner's plots usually involved larger-than-life, mythological characters whose activities were meant to symbolize underlying philosophical issues. Verdi's plots more often favored real people cast in dramatic, action-filled situations and are notable for their spontaneity and sure sense of effective drama.

Verdi and Wagner disagreed on the relative importance of the singers and the orchestra. Wagner used orchestration to convey his philosophical ideas, sometimes overshadowing the singers, whose role was to move the surface action along. By contrast, Verdi's operas are dominated by the singing voice. Melody is the vehicle for expressing a vast range of emotions, and singers are rarely forced to compete with the orchestral background.

Giacomo Puccini

Toward the end of the nineteenth century, a movement toward naturalism and realism also took place in Italian literature. Called **verismo** (realism), it quickly penetrated Italian opera. Bizet's *Carmen* served as a model for the three Italian composers who led the movement: **Giacomo Puccini** (1858–1924), Ruggiero Leoncavallo (1857–1919), and Pietro Mascagni (1863–1945). Leoncavallo is remembered for *I Pagliacci* (*The Players,* 1892) and Mascagni for *Cavalleria Rusticana* (*Rustic Chivalry,* 1890). Puccini, the most successful of the verismo composers, effectively united grand opera and realism.

Composer Giacomo Puccini

Puccini was descended from a line of musicians that stretched back over five generations. During most of his childhood, Puccini showed only a modest talent for music; nevertheless, his mother insisted that he continue his studies, and by the age of sixteen he was composing in earnest—chiefly organ music for church services.

In 1880, Puccini obtained a scholarship to enter the Milan Conservatory. Once graduated from the Conservatory, he entered an opera competition with *Le Villi* (1884), a work based on a Slavonic legend. He failed to win the contest, but the opera was produced in Milan on May 31, 1884. The success of the premiere persuaded the well-known publisher Giulio Ricordi to commission a second opera by Puccini. Largely because of a poor libretto, *Edgar* (1884–1888) was not a success; however, Ricordi continued to support the composer, and both men worked over the book for the next work, *Manon Lescaut,* based on the 1731 novel by Abbé Prévost. Its premiere on February 1, 1893, was an immense triumph.

Although *Manon Lescaut* made Puccini famous in Italy, it was his next opera, *La Bohème* (*Bohemian Life,* 1893–1896), that brought him worldwide fame. Ironically, Puccini's only serious failure was his favorite opera, *Madame Butterfly* (1904). Despite the hisses and catcalls at the premiere, however, the work became quite popular outside Italy and continues to be popular today. The main story of the modern musical *Miss Saigon* (1989) moves the story of *Madame Butterfly* from early twentieth-century Japan to Vietnam in 1975 to 1978 when U.S. troops were leaving the country.

Puccini's next opera, *La Fanciulla del West* (*The Girl of the Golden West,* 1910), was based on a play by David Belasco, as was *Madame Butterfly.* The premiere of *The Girl of the Golden West* at the Metropolitan Opera in New York was one of the most glittering events of 1910, with Arturo Toscanini conducting and the famous tenor Enrico Caruso singing the lead male role.

During World War I, Puccini remained in Italy, working quietly on more operas. His last work, *Turandot,* was left incomplete at his death. In 1923 he began suffering from what turned out to be throat cancer, and the following year he died of a heart attack. He was sixty-five years old. The task of finishing the final scenes of *Turandot* was entrusted to Franco Alfano, a distinguished younger composer. The opera was produced under Arturo Toscanini at La Scala, Milan, on April 25, 1926. In the early twenty-first century another Italian composer, Luciano Berio (1925–2003), undertook to remove Alfano's ending and compose a new one that he thought was more in line with Puccini's original plan. The new ending has met with mixed reviews.

Shown here is a scene from a production of Puccini's opera *La Bohème*.

Puccini's operas reflect his realistic bent and his fascination with exotic settings. *Madame Butterfly,* for example, is set in Japan, and *Turandot* in China. The opera that brought him international acclaim, *La Bohème,* combines rich and sensuous Romantic melodies with realistic details of plot and characterization.

La Bohème

The opera begins on Christmas Eve in the Latin Quarter of Paris (the artists' district on the Left Bank) in the 1830s. Rodolfo (a struggling young poet) and his friend Marcello (a painter) are freezing in their garret (a room located just under the roof of a building) studio on Christmas Eve. Suddenly a friend enters with money, groceries, and firewood, and insists they all go out to celebrate. Rodolfo stays to finish an article he is writing but is interrupted by a knock at the door. The caller is Mimi, a neighbor, whose candle has blown out. She asks for a light, and he invites her in. She is ill and faints. When she feels strong enough to leave, they discover that her key has fallen. As they search for it on the floor, their hands meet, and they give up the search to wait for more light from the moon. Rodolfo tells Mimi about his life and hopes. She describes her life as a maker of artificial flowers and talks about her longing for spring and sunshine. Rodolfo declares his love, and Mimi responds passionately. As the act ends, they leave to join his friends at the café.

The next act opens with a holiday crowd in the streets near the café. Marcello sees his old flame, Musetta, with a wealthy old codger in tow. She tries to attract Marcello's attention, embarrassing her escort and amusing the spectators. Finally she sings a provocative waltz and, having sent her escort off on a fool's errand, leaps into Marcello's eager arms.

Act Three is set some months later. Rodolfo's jealousy has caused Mimi to leave him. She seeks out Marcello to ask his help and tells him of Rodolfo's unbearable behavior; Rodolfo arrives, and Mimi hides. He starts to complain to Marcello of Mimi's flirting but admits that he is actually in despair over her failing health. When Mimi's coughing reveals her presence, Rodolfo begs her to stay with him until spring, and she agrees.

Act Four is set back in the garret shared by Rodolfo and Marcello the following fall. Rodolfo and Marcello are there. Fellow artist friends arrive for dinner, and a hilarious evening begins. Musetta interrupts their gaiety, announcing that Mimi has collapsed on the stairs. They carry her in; all except Rodolfo leave to pawn their treasures to buy medical supplies for Mimi. Rodolfo and Mimi recall their first meeting. Their friends return and Mimi drifts off to sleep. She dies, and Rodolfo embraces her while the others weep.

Notice how different this plot is from Mozart's *The Marriage of Figaro.* Mozart's opera was about French aristocrats and their dealings with servants. Classical opera plots often dealt with aristocratic lifestyles or the old Greek or Roman plots that were most common in the baroque era. With *La Bohème,* we have an opera about starving artists and a sweet and innocent woman who is dying of tuberculosis, a common cause of death in the nineteenth century. The reality of the verismo movement and its connection to the large, Romantic, middle class is clear. This is a story that most human beings can relate to and identify with on every level.

The aria that is discussed here is from Act One, when Rodolfo touches Mimi's hand for the first time and then tells her about himself.

Chapter 24
Timeline

Romantic
Opera in France
and Italy

Listening Guide

"Che gelida manina" ("What a frozen little hand") from *La Bohème,* Act 1 GIACOMO PUCCINI

CD 3
Track 34

Year: 1896

Tempo: Slow, varies with text

Meter: Mostly duple and sung with much rubato to fit the text

Form: Some short repeating phrases, but not structured

Performers: Tenor and orchestra

Language: Italian

Duration: 4:24

Italian text	**English translation**
Che gelida manina, se la lasci riscaldar. Cercar che giova? Al buio non si trova. Ma per fortuna, è una notte di luna, . . . e qui la luna l'abbiamo vicina.	What a frozen little hand, would you let me warm it? What's the good of searching? We won't find it in the dark. But by luck it is a moonlit night, and we'll have the moon near us here.
Aspetti, signorina, le dirò con due parole chi son, chi son, e che faccio, come vivo. Vuole? Chi son? Chi son? Sono un poeta. Che cosa faccio?	Wait, Miss, and I'll tell you in a couple of words who I am—who I am, and what I do, how I live. Would you like that? Who am I? Who am I? I'm a poet. What do I do?
Scrivo. E come vivo? Vivo. In povertà mia lieta scialo da gran signore rime ed inni d'amore. Per sogni e per chimere e per castelli in aria l'anima ho millionaria. Talor dal mio forziere ruban tutti I gioielli due ladri: gli occhi belli. V'entrar con voi pur ora, ed i miei sogni usati, ed i bei sogni miei tosto si dileguar! Ma il furto non m'accora poichè—poichè v'ha preso stanza la speranza! Or che mi conoscete, parlate voi, deh! Parlate! Che siete? Vi piaccia dir!	I write. And how do I live? I live. In my poverty I feast as gaily as a grand lord on rhymes and hymns of love. For dreams and fancies and castles in the air, I have a millionaire's soul. Now and then two thieves rob all the jewels from my strongbox: two beautiful eyes. They came in with you, just now, and my old dreams, my beautiful dreams, quickly dissolved. But the theft doesn't hurt me, since—since such sweet expectation has taken its stead. Now that you know me, come, you speak. Who are you? Please tell!

The 34 appears in a box to the left of the Italian text.

This next aria follows the one we just discussed. Mimi tells Rodolfo about herself.

Listening Guide

"Sì, mi chiamano Mimì" ("Yes, they call me Mimi") from *La Bohème,* Act 1 GIACOMO PUCCINI

CD 1
Track 55

Year: 1896

Tempo: Slow, but varies with the mood of the text

Meter: Mostly duple and sung with much rubato to fit the text

Form: Some short repeating phrases, but not structured

Performers: Soprano soloist with orchestra

Language: Italian

Duration: 4:33

Italian text	English translation
55 Sì. Mi chiamano Mimì, ma il mio nome è Lucia. La storia mia è breve. A tela o a seta ricamo in casa e fuori. Son tranquilla e lieta, ed è mio svago far gigli e rose. Mi piaccion quelle cose che han si dolce malia, che parlano d'amor, di primavere, che parlano di sogni e di chimere—quelle cose che han nome poesia. Lei m'intende?	Yes. They call me Mimi, but my name is Lucia. My story is brief. I embroider silk or linen at home and outside. I'm contented and happy, and it's my pleasure to make lilies and roses. I like those things that have sweet charm, that speak of love, of springtimes, that speak of dreams and fancies—those things that are called poetry. Do you understand me?
Mi chiamano Mimì, il perchè non so. Sola, mi fo il pranzo da me stessa. Non vado sempre a messa, ma prego assai il Signor. Vivo sola, soletta, là in una bianca cameretta; guardo sui tetti e in cielo, ma quando vien lo sgelo il primo sole è mio—il primo bacio dell'aprile è mio! Il primo sole è mio! Germoglia in un vaso una rosa. Foglia a foglia l'aspiro! Così gentil è il profumo d'un fior! Ma i fior ch'io faccio, ahimè, i fior ch'io faccio, ahimè, non hanno odore! Altro di me non le saprei narrare: sono la sua vicina che la vien fuori d'ora a importunare.	They call me Mimi, but I don't know why. All alone, I make dinner for myself. I don't always go to Mass, but I often pray to the Lord. I live alone, all by myself, in a little white room over there; I look on the roofs and into the sky, but when the thaw comes, the first sunshine is mine—the first kiss of April is mine! The first sunshine is mine! A rose opens in a vase. Leaf by leaf I sniff its fragrance. So lovely is the perfume of a flower. But the flowers that I make—alas! the flowers that I make—alas! have no odor. I wouldn't know anything else to tell you about myself—I'm your neighbor who comes at this odd hour to trouble you.

The musical *Rent* (1996) by Jonathan Larson is based on the story of *La Bohème. Rent* is set in New York instead of Paris, and Mimi has AIDS instead of tuberculosis. Rodolfo is renamed Roger and is an HIV-positive songwriter.

"Hearing the Difference: Mozart's 'Non più andrai' and Puccini's 'Si, mi chiamo Mimì'" compares these two arias.

HEARING THE DIFFERENCE
Mozart's "Non più andrai" and Puccini's "Sì, mi chiamano Mimì"

In comparing these two opera arias, we are comparing two different period styles. Mozart's aria is classical in its regular meter and tempo and clearly defined form. Puccini's romantic style is clear in the meter and tempo variations as well as the non-structured form. The stories of the operas from which these two arias come are also representative of their style periods. Mozart's *The Marriage of Figaro* is about happenings in the lives of people at a royal court of Mozart's time, but *La Bohème* is about four starving artists and a frail, dying woman one of them loves. Mozart's opera makes fun of a duke, while Puccini's displays great sympathy with the lives of the poor people who live for the love of their art.

	"Non più andrai" ("No more will you")	"Sì, mi chiamano Mimì" ("Yes, they call me Mimi")
Historical period	Classical	Romantic
Tempo	Fast and lively	Slow, varying with the text
Meter	Quadruple	Mostly duple
Form	ABACA-Coda	Some short repeating phrases, but not structured
Language	Italian	Italian
Text	Very classical, structured aria that jokingly tells a young man what military life will be like	Very romantic, dramatic aria that portrays a simple, sensitive, and beautiful person who has just met the man in whose arms she will die at the opera's end

Summary

Opera was one of the most important musical genres of the romantic period, because its combination of music and drama was greatly appealing to the large middle class, as well as to the aristocracy. In Paris grand opera was composed to be performed on a very large scale with crowd scenes, ballets, choruses, and elaborate scenery. *Opéra comique* was a lighter type of opera set on a smaller scale than grand opera. It also made use of spoken dialogue. Lyric opera developed as a more serious type of opera than *opéra comique,* but was still set on a smaller scale than grand opera. In France, the literary movement *naturalism* brought about an interest in having operas based on "natural" and realistic characters who were often poor.

Italian composers continued to write in the *opera seria* and *opera buffa* styles and developed the vocal style *bel canto* (beautiful singing). Of the many successful opera composers of the era whose works are still often performed today the two Italians, Giuseppe Verdi and Giacomo Puccini, lead the list, having continuously provided audiences with laughter, tears, and every emotion in between through their works. The modern-day musicals *Miss Saigon* and *Rent* are based on Puccini's operas *Madame Butterfly* and *La Bohème,* respectively.

New People and Concepts

bel canto	**grand opera**	*opera comique*
Giacomo Puccini	**lyric opera**	**verismo**
Giuseppe Verdi	**naturalism**	

Finale

Listen again to "Sì, mi chiamano Mimì" ("Yes, they call me Mimi") from *La Bohème,* Act 1, by Puccini and compare your impressions now with your notes from your first listening. Do you hear more now than you did before? You should now be able to answer the following questions:

▌ What is the tempo?

▌ What is the meter?

▌ What is the voice type of the singer?

▌ What is the language of the text?

▌ What is the mood of the aria and how does it fit into the story of the opera?

25 | Romantic German Opera

*I wish I could write librettos for the rest of my life.
It is the purest of human pleasures, a heavenly
hermaphroditism of being both writer and
musician. No wonder that selfish beast Wagner
kept it to himself.*

—WRITER SYLVIA TOWNSEND WARNER (1893–1978)

Listening Introduction

Listen to the example of music that represents this chapter, "Den der Bruder schuf, den schimmernden Reif" ("Now the shining ring my brother once made"), from *Siegfried,* by Wagner and make notes about what you hear. Give some attention to the following:

▌ Can you detect the tempo?

▌ Can you detect the meter?

▌ Can you tell the voice types (soprano, alto, tenor, baritone, or bass) of the singers?

▌ Can you tell the language of the text?

▌ Does the piece have a general mood that allows you to guess the meaning of the text?

Keep these notes to compare with your impressions about the aria after you study the information in this chapter.

Whereas the Italian verismo composers were influenced by the realist movement in literature, nineteenth-century German opera drew its inspiration from the passionate, heroic, and adventurous ideals of the romantic era. The first significant composer of German Romantic opera was Carl Maria von Weber (1786–1826). A nationalist and romanticist, he built his style on the legends and songs of the German people and on Romantic elements. His opera *Der Freischütz* (*The Freeshooter,* 1821) features supernatural elements such as magic bullets and a pact with the devil, a typically Romantic fascination.

German Romantic operas, such as *Der Freischütz,* tended to stress mood and setting. Nature was represented as a wild and mysterious force. Supernatural beings mixed freely with ordinary mortals. Human characters often symbolized good and evil, and the hero's victory meant salvation or redemption.

Richard Wagner

In the latter part of the nineteenth century, one of the most powerful personalities in the history of music emerged—**Richard Wagner** (1813–1883). In his works, German Romantic opera reached its highest point. Born in Leipzig,

Richard Wagner with Franz Liszt and Liszt's daughter, Cosima.

Wagner was the son of a clerk in the city police court who died when his son was only six months old. Richard's mother later married Ludwig Geyer, a gifted actor, playwright, and painter. It was rumored that Geyer was Wagner's real father, and Wagner himself considered this likely. Wagner was a precocious child who showed an early interest in literature, writing a tragedy in the style of Shakespeare at the age of fourteen.

In his formal musical training Wagner was among the least systematic of the great nineteenth-century composers. He began piano lessons at age twelve but never became a first-rate performer on any instrument. Lack of adequate technical preparation, however, did not prevent Wagner from making early attempts at composition. By 1832, several of his works—including two overtures and a symphony—had been performed publicly. The following year, at age twenty, he began his professional career, becoming chorus master for the Würzburg Theater. Other, similar jobs followed, and he began combining his interest in music with his interest in theater by composing operas.

He married an actress, Minna Planer, and began work on an opera based on a historical novel set in Rome during the middle 1300s. The opera was called *Rienzi, Last of the Tribunes,* and with it Wagner tried to outdo every French or Italian grand opera of the past. The story dealt with Rienzi's rise and fall as the ruler of Rome and had such a large cast performing marches, processions, and ballets that it could be played only in a very large theater. Wagner spent the years 1839 to 1842 in Paris, where he tried vainly to get the work performed. His financial situation became desperate—partly because of his increasingly spendthrift ways—and he even landed in a debtors' prison for a short time. Although there had been problems in their marriage, Minna stood by him through the difficulties of the time.

Rienzi was finally accepted, but not in Paris. It was in Dresden, Germany, that it was first performed in 1842. Wagner returned to Germany to supervise the production. The première performance was over six hours long, including several intermissions. It was eventually split to be shown in two evenings and received hundreds of performances in Germany over the course of the next sixty years.

The success of *Rienzi* and that of Wagner's next opera, *Der fliegende Holländer* (*The Flying Dutchman,* 1843), based on an old German legend about a Dutchman who was condemned to sail the seas until he could find a faithful woman, led to his appointment as music director at the Royal Opera House in Dresden. For the next six years, Wagner busied himself producing operas and writing two more himself: *Tannhäuser* (1842–1844), about a German singer from the medieval era, and *Lohengrin* (finished 1848), based on a Grimm brothers fairy tale. Wagner's active participation in the revolutionary uprising of 1848–1849 caused a warrant to be issued for his arrest and forced him to flee to Switzerland.

While in exile, he turned to literary activity and wrote a number of essays, the most influential of which were "Das Kunstwerk der Zukunft" ("The Art-Work of the Future," 1850) and "Oper und Drama" ("Opera and Drama," 1851). In these he laid the foundations for "**music drama,**" the term he used for his unique type of opera.

During his ten years in Switzerland, Wagner began putting his artistic theories into practice. By 1852 he had completed the poems of an epic cycle of four music dramas, entitled *Der Ring des Nibelungen (The Ring of the Nibelung),* based primarily on the struggle of characters from Scandinavian and Germanic legends—gods, humans, and various types of mythical beings—to gain possession of a powerful gold ring. It took Wagner seventeen years to complete the entire cycle. These works lay heavy demands on the performers, and because the individual dramas last from three to five hours each, the whole set requires four separate evenings for its performance.

In the intervening years, Wagner wrote two other works that remain perhaps his most popular and frequently performed: *Tristan und Isolde* (1856–1859) and *Die Meistersinger von Nürnberg* (*The Mastersingers of Nuremberg,* 1862–1867).

Although highly prolific, Wagner experienced great difficulty in arranging performances of his works. Most were formidable in scale, requiring theatrical and musical resources beyond the means of even the largest opera houses. As he approached the age of fifty, he became discouraged. His debts continued to pile up, and he separated from his wife and even contemplated suicide.

Then in 1864, his fortunes changed. The new king of Bavaria, Ludwig II, a devoted admirer of Wagner's music, invited him to Munich with the promise of financial and artistic support. At this time, Wagner fell in love with Cosima von Bülow, the daughter of the great pianist and composer Franz Liszt and wife of one of Wagner's close associates, Hans von Bülow. Cosima left her husband to be with Wagner, completely devoting herself to his career. They were finally married in 1870, and together with help from Ludwig II they raised enough money to build an opera house. Located in the small Bavarian town of Bayreuth, the *Festspielhaus* ("festival drama house"), as it was called, was constructed especially for Wagner's works. He liked to use such a large orchestra that, in regular opera houses with the orchestra pit in front of the stage, the orchestra sometimes covered the sound of the singers, who were behind it. The *Festspielhaus* was designed with most of the orchestra set under the stage so that the sound of the orchestra and that of the singers came out to the audience together. The *Festspielhaus* is still run by the Wagner family and is used for performances of his works.

Chapter 25
Timeline

Wagner Life and
Works

The *Festspielhaus* was the scene of the first complete performance of the *Ring* cycle, in 1876. One of the great artistic events of the century, this performance was the fulfillment of Wagner's lifelong dream. He completed one more work, *Parsifal* (1882), before illness forced him to travel to Italy in hope of regaining his health. He died of a heart attack, in Venice, in 1883 at the age of sixty-nine.

Wagner believed that a music drama should be a *Gesamtkunstwerk* (universal artwork), combining elements from all the arts. The most important element should be drama, with the music serving to reinforce the dramatic expression. This view was different from that held by many earlier opera composers, including Mozart, who believed that music was the most important element in opera because it is the music that creates the drama.

In Wagner's works the music is essentially continuous throughout each act, with one section moving smoothly into the next. In place of the traditional arias and recitatives, Wagner developed a musical line he called *Sprechsingen* (singing speech). This style combined the lyric quality of the aria and the speaking quality of the recitative and permitted a continuous musical flow that Wagner termed "endless melody."

To allow the music to support the drama as much as possible, Wagner used melodies or fragments of melodies to identify particular characters, objects, or ideas. These melodies are called **leitmotifs** (pronounced "light moteefs," means "leading melodies" or signature tunes). Berlioz used this technique in the *idée fixe* that represents the beloved in *Symphonie fantastique,* but Wagner attached leitmotifs to many characters, objects, or ideas in an opera, not just one. Indeed, some characters had several leitmotifs depending on their different moods or activities. Movie composers often use this very idea. In *Star Wars* (1977), for example, composer John Williams gave each main character his or her own melody, which becomes obvious to the listener during the movie. In fact, *Star Wars* has many connections with Wagner's *Der Ring des Nibelungen*. Another movie, *Excalibur* (1981), used not only the leitmotif idea but also the same melody that Wagner did in the *Ring* cycle to represent the sword Nothung.

A story with an even closer story line connection to Wagner's *Ring* cycle is J. R. R. Tolkien's (1892–1973) *The Lord of the Rings* trilogy. Both cycles are based on similar mythical themes of loss and recovery and a quest for magical power. In fact, Tolkien took his story from legends similar to those Wagner had used.

The first opera in Wagner's cycle is *Das Rheingold (The Gold of the Rhine)*. That music drama begins in the Rhine River, where a pile of magic gold is being guarded by the Rhine maidens. The gold is stolen and part of it is made into a ring by a hunchbacked dwarf of the race of the Nibelungs. The ring becomes the center of attention for much of the cycle of dramas because anyone who possesses it and renounces love will rule the world. Various characters steal or kill to get the ring as the dwarf tries to get it back.

The second music drama is *Die Walküre (The Valkyries)*. The Valkyries are the daughters of the father of the gods, Wotan. Their primary job is to ride their horses above battlegrounds and take fallen heroes to Valhalla, the home of the gods. Wotan has told one of the Valkyries, Brünnhilde, to intercede in a sword fight and Brünnhilde does so but tries to save the wrong person. Both men end up dead, and Brünnhilde is punished by losing her status as a goddess and by being put to sleep on a rock surrounded by fire. Only a hero will be able to wake her.

The third music drama is named for Wotan's heroic grandson, *Siegfried*. Siegfried's mother, Sieglinde, had died in childbirth and had asked a Nibelung, Mime, to raise her son. Like most other creatures in the cycle, Mime would like

Shown here is a scene from a production of Wagner's *Ring* cycle.

to gain control of the ring, which was made by and stolen from his brother. In the scene we will listen to, Siegfried is fixing the sword that was shattered when his father died as Mime plots to get the ring. The name of the sword is "Nothung."

Listening Guide

"Den der Bruder schuf, den schimmernden Reif" ("Now the shining ring my brother once made") from *Siegfried,* the conclusion to Act I RICHARD WAGNER

CD 3
Track 35

Year: 1857

Tempo: "Mässig bewegt" (moderato, allegretto)

Meter: Changes back and forth between sextuple and duple

Form: No repeating sections

Voices: Two tenors and orchestra

Instrumentation: Two piccolos, two flutes, three oboes, one English horn, three clarinets, one bass clarinet, three bassoons, eight French horns, one contrabass tuba, three trumpets, one bass trumpet, three tenor and bass trombones, one contrabass trombone, two pairs of kettledrums, one triangle, one pair of cymbals, one side drum, one glockenspiel, six harps, sixteen first violins, sixteen second violins, twelve violas, twelve cellos, eight double basses

Language: German

Duration: 2:40

Special feature: When he is not singing, Siegfried is hammering on the sword to get it back together. At the end of this section, he holds it up with great pride.

continued

Timing	German text	English translation

<table>
<tbody>
<tr><td>35</td><td>0:00</td><td colspan="2">Mime</td></tr>
</tbody>
</table>

35 | 0:00 | ***Mime*** |

0:03	Den der Bruder schuf, den schimmernden reif,	Now the shining ring my brother once made,
	in den er gezaubert zwingende Kraft,	wherein he worked a mighty spell,
	das helle Gold das zum Herrscher macht,	the glist'ning gold that o'er masters all,
	ihn hab' ich gewonnen, ich walte sein!	won is it by Mime, I hold it mine!
	Alberich selbst, der einst mich band,	Alberich, you who once were lord
	zur Zwergen frohne zwing' ich ihn nun;	shall now be forced to serve me as master;
	als Nibelungen Fürst fahr' ich darnieder,	as Nibelungen's prince down there I'll go,
	gehorchen soll mir alles Heer.	and all the hordes shall obey me.
	Der verachtete Zwerg, wie wird er geehrt!	To the dwarf so despised all living shall kneel!
	Zu dem Horte hin drängt sich Gott und Held.	To the hoard will throng gods and heroes all.
	Vor meinem Nicken neigt sich die Welt;	The world shall cower at my command;
	vor meinem Zorne zittert sie hin.	and all will tremble under my wrath!

Siegfried

| 0:48 | Nothung! Nothung! neidliches Schwert! | Nothung! Nothung! conquering sword! |
| | Jetzt haftest du wieder im Heft. | Now enclosed once more in your hilt. |

Mime

| 1:00 | Dann wahrlich müht sich Mime nicht mehr: | For truly Mime no more shall toil. |

Siegfried

| 1:04 | War'st du entzwei, ich zwang dich zuganz: | Severed in two, made one by my hand; |
| | kein Schlag soll nun dich mehr zerschlagen. | no stroke again your steel shall shatter. |

Mime

| 1:11 | Ihm schaffen and're den ew'gen Schatz. | For him shall others win endless wealth. |

Siegfried

1:14	Dem sterbenden Vater zersprang der Stahl;	The dying father once broke thy blade;
	der lebende Sohn schuf ihn neu:	the living son shaped it anew:
	nun lacht ihm sein heller Schein,	to him now its luster laughs,
	seine Schärfe schneidet ihm hart.	to him its sharpness cuts harsh.

Mime (Note: Mime begins singing at the end of Siegfried's last phrase and Siegfried begins his next phrase while Mime holds his last note.)

| 1:31 | Mime, der Kühne, Mime ist König, | Mime, the valiant, Mime is ruler, |
| | Fürst der Alben, Walter des All's! | prince of Nibelungs, lord of the world! |

Siegfried

1:37	Nothung! Nothung! neidliches Schwert!	Nothung! Nothung! conquering sword!
	Zum Leben weckt' ich dich wieder.	Again to life have I woke thee.
	Todt lagst du in Trümmern dort,	Dead did you lie in splinters here,
	jetzt leuchtest du trotzig und hehr.	now you shine defiant and fair.

Mime

| 2:00 | Hei! Mime, wie glückte dir das! | Hei! Mime, how lucky you are! |

Siegfried (Note: Again, each singer overlaps the other.)

| 2:03 | Zeige den Schächern nun deinen Schein! | Show to all miscreants now your sheen! |

Mime

| 2:06 | Wer hätte wohl das gedacht! | Who could believe this of you? |

Siegfried

2:07	Schlage den Falschen, fälle den Schelm!	Strike at the traitor, cut down the knave!
	Schau, Mime, du Schmied:	See, Mime, you smith:
	So schneidet Siegfrieds Schwert!	So cuts Siegfried's sword!

Productions of Operas

When you see an opera for the first time, you might think that what you see is exactly like other performances of the same opera, but that is not the case. Operatic productions of the same opera can vary greatly.

First, an opera will have been based on a libretto, or "the book," which is the text that is sung or occasionally spoken. The librettist has often taken the story from a play, a novel, a legend, a historical event, or his or her own imagination. A composer then took that libretto and wrote the music for the singers and the orchestra. (Wagner was unusual in that he both wrote the librettos and composed the music for his "music dramas," as he called his operas.) The libretto sometimes has a few instructions that indicate when a particular character should come out on stage or to whom they should sing an aria. It may also note items that are necessary to the action, such as a particular piece of furniture or some other prop.

But the libretto does not include directions for the design of the stage set, the look of the costumes, the lighting, or other visual aspects of the performance. The opera's "look," however, is important to its overall effect on the audience, and this is left up to the director of a particular production.

Of course, certain conventions are often followed. In Mozart's *The Marriage of Figaro,* for example, the set is usually a classical looking palace. On the other hand, other operas are not so focused on a single time and place, so a director can do any number of creative things with the set.

One of the best examples of this is Wagner's *Der Ring des Nibelungen (The Ring of the Nibelung),* which is set in an undated time and in a world full of humans, gods, and numerous fantastical creatures not unlike those found in *Star Wars* or Tolkien's *Lord of the Rings.* So where might a director set this world? Two recorded (and easily available) productions are worth examining in response to this question.

The 1976 production at Wagner's own opera house—the *Festspielhaus* in Bayreuth, Germany— was shockingly modern. It was performed in celebration of the *Festspielhaus*'s centennial, with

Pierre Boulez conducting. The costumes varied from eighteenth-century attire that included powdered wigs to twentieth-century formal wear. The Rhine River was represented by a modern looking water-processing plant, and the Rhine maidens were dressed like prostitutes. Overall, the production was modern and "Industrial" looking, yet it did not identify itself with any particular historical period. It was performed for four years at the *Festspielhaus,* where it was booed at its opening and received a 45-minute standing ovation at its final performance. It was recorded in 1980, televised, and is now available on videocassette and DVD.

Another production of the same set of operas, by New York's Metropolitan Opera Company, conducted by James Levine and recorded in 1990, is much more traditional in its sets and costuming. The overall look is that of some world out of the past with ugly dwarves and giants, beautiful Rhine maidens, and gods in gowns with breastplates. It was also televised and is now available on videocassette and DVD.

Which is the better production? Which one should a director choose to be influenced by when planning a new live production? There is no set answer to either question. The point here is that when you watch an opera, be it a live performance or a recording, you are experiencing several levels of creative work.

The singers themselves bring their own dimension to each new production of an opera. In general, if all of the singers are both good singers and good actors, you will enjoy the opera even if you dislike the sets and costumes. Singers are usually chosen based on their abilities; whether or not they look the part seldom matters. For example, in Wagner's second opera of the *Ring* cycle, *Die Walküre,* the two main characters, Siegmund and Sieglinde, are supposed to be genetically fraternal twins. Yet in the Metropolitan Opera's 1990 production of *Die Walküre,* those parts were sung by Caucasian-American tenor Gary Lakes and African-American soprano Jessye Norman. For opera lovers, the breach in realism was more than justified by the quality of their performances.

As the drama *Siegfried* continues on, Siegfried uses his sword to slay both the dragon and Mime. A bird leads him to Brünnhilde, who is asleep on her rock. He awakens her, and the two fall in love with each other. In his quest to find Brünnhilde, Siegfried is challenged by Wotan, and Siegfried's sword breaks Wotan's spear, causing Woton to lose his power.

The final music drama is *Die Götterdämmerung* (*The Twilight of the Gods*). In it, Siegfried is killed in an attempt to steal the ring, and Brünnhilde commits suicide by riding her horse into his funeral pyre. But before dying, Brünnhilde promises that the ring will be returned to the Rhine maidens, which it is. Brünnhilde's death, however, causes a flood and then a fire that destroys Valhalla and all of the gods and heroes in it. The ring, therefore, ends up exactly where it was at the beginning of the cycle, over fifteen hours earlier.

Brünnhilde and her sisters, the Valkyries, are usually dressed with breastplates and sometimes wear helmets with wings on the sides. When one sees cartoons that make fun of opera, it is often that image that is portrayed.

One subject that cannot be ignored in a discussion about Richard Wagner is the fact that he was anti-Semitic and was Hitler's favorite composer. In 1850, Wagner wrote an essay called "Jewishness in Music" in which he blamed Jewish musicians for commercializing music and stated that music by Jewish composers was not up to the quality of music by other Germans. He continued on that any popularity of their works was the result of a corrupting of the tastes of the general public. Wagner published the original essay under a pseudonym, but he added comments about the "yoke of the ruling Jewish society" to it and republished it under his own name in 1869. Some modern listeners have responded to this by saying that Wagner's music is so great that it transcends his personal flaws; others say that the music is destroyed for them because they can see Wagner's anti-Semitic views in his works. Much controversy arises whenever a conductor tries to put anything by Wagner on a concert program in Israel.

Summary

Romantic opera in Germany was strongly influenced by the romantic movement itself. The composer who first established a genuinely Germanic style was Carl Maria von Weber. The most important composer in German Romantic opera was Richard Wagner, who wrote "music dramas" that encompassed all the arts in a unified whole. To Wagner, the most important element was the drama, with the music serving the dramatic expression. Dramatic unity was enhanced by the use of leitmotifs, or melodic fragments associated with persons, objects, or ideas.

One of Wagner's greatest accomplishments was the composition of a cycle of four music dramas, *Der Ring des Nibelungen* (*The Ring of the Nibelung*). Not unlike J. R. R. Tolkien's trilogy *The Lord of the Rings,* which was also based on legends, the cycle tells of loss, recovery, and a quest for magical power.

New People and Concepts

leitmotif   **music drama**   **Richard Wagner**

Finale

Listen again to "Den der Bruder schuf, den schimmernden Reif" ("Now the shining ring my brother once made"), from *Siegfried,* by Wagner and compare your impressions now with your notes from your first listening. Do you hear more now than you did before? You should now be able to answer the following questions:

▌ What is the tempo?

▌ What is the meter?

▌ What are the voice types of the singers?

▌ What is the language of the text?

▌ What is the mood of the aria and how does it fit into the story of the opera?

Characteristics of Romantic Music

Texture	Variety of textures
Tonality	Major-minor system with less firm sense of tonal center
Rhythm	Frequent fluctuations in tempo; use of rubato
Pitch	Greatly expanded pitch range
Tone color	Fascination and experimentation with instrumental color
Melody	Lyrical, expressive, flowing; sometimes ornamented
Dynamics	Wide range of dynamics; frequent fluctuations in dynamic levels; dynamics used for dramatic effect
Small works	Art song (Lied); character pieces and miniatures for piano
Large works	Concerto, symphony, program symphony, symphonic poem (tone poem), opera, choral works, chamber works, concert overture
Musical instruments	Piano was a favorite instrument; large orchestra; unusual instrument groupings; emphasis on orchestration and color
Performance style	Steady growth of virtuoso technique
Formal innovations	Carefully constructed classical forms were freely manipulated and expanded; cyclical procedure; thematic transformation; development of programmatic and descriptive music as manifested in the program symphony and tone poem; verismo movement in opera; development of nationalism in music

The Starry Night, by
**Vincent van Gogh
(1853–1890).** As is typical
of the style called
expressionism, this painting
is as much about inner
feelings of conflict and
unrest as it is about stars in
a nighttime sky.

As we have seen with past eras, new periods often begin as reactions against the excesses of the previous ones. The classical period began with simple, direct, and well-balanced musical phrases in contrast with the great amount of activity and complexity of late baroque music, and the romantic period provided an emotional reaction against the intellectualism of the classical period. At the end of the romantic era, the extremes of emotion that were commonly portrayed in the arts of the mid-nineteenth century gave way to much experimentation in the new century. This happened in all the arts, usually with music following the visual arts.

Technological advances also affected the development of new styles. By the mid-nineteenth century, artists were able to buy oil paint in tubes instead of having to mix their own colors in their studios. That was a tremendous boon, because the use of easily transported premixed paints allowed artists to paint outdoors while they were viewing their subjects. In some cases, it allowed them to concentrate not only on the subject of their work but also on the sunlight illuminating it. Gradually, many of these artists, particularly in France, began applying their paint in small brush stokes or even just tiny flecks of pure colors to show

Prelude | The Early Twentieth Century

reflected light. Sometimes those brush strokes created blurred or distorted images, as in Claude Monet's *Impression: Sunrise,* on page 227, a look that lacked the detail common in earlier styles of painting. This style was widely criticized at first because its lack of detail caused it to look like a mere "impression" of a scene instead of being a realistic portrayal of it. Those criticisms gave the name *impressionism* to the style.

Music followed impressionistic art with compositions by Claude Debussy and others during the late nineteenth and early twentieth centuries. In this music we hear flowing rhythms that do not follow a steady beat and melodies that seem to come out of nowhere and then disappear without a strong conclusion. Those aspects of the music gave it a vagueness that is similar to what we see in the impressionistic style in the visual arts.

Ways of reflecting and preserving images had been experimented with since Leonardo da Vinci's scientific work of the sixteenth century. The first photograph was made in 1826, and by 1839 photographs could be printed on paper. With improvements in cameras and photographic techniques being made during the rest of the 1800s, it became less necessary for artists to realistically portray people or scenes. That gave artists more freedom to experiment in new, less "realistic" directions.

Another factor that helped bring about changes in artistic styles at the turn of the century in Europe was the growing awareness and influence of non-Western art and music. In Paris in 1889, the French celebrated the one hundredth anniversary of the French Revolution by inviting musicians, dancers, and other performers from all over the world to a World Exhibition. French artists and composers were able to see and hear dances, costumes, and music from such distant places as Asia, the Middle East, and Africa. The influence of those sights and sounds was expressed in art that included facsimiles of African masks, decorations from Asian costumes, and, in the case of music, non-Western instruments, particularly percussive ones.

We hear a proliferation of non-Western influences as composers begin to do away with the traditional major and minor scales and use new or non-Western scale structures. Traditional European music tends to use relatively repetitious rhythmic patterns, concentrating more on melody than on rhythm. Much non-Western music uses very complex rhythms, including several different rhythms played simultaneously.

Expressionism was a style that developed out of impressionism. Expressionism concentrated on the expression of the inner feelings of conflict and unrest. Expressionism began with Vincent van Gogh's

(1835–1890) late paintings, such as *The Starry Night* (1889). *The Scream* (1893), by Norway's Edvard Munch (1863–1944), is another famous example. After World War I, German artists developed their own type of expressionism, because it readily lent itself to the reflection of inner thoughts and torments felt by a people torn by war and social injustice. Later in the twentieth century, Arnold Schoenberg (1874–1951) composed musical counterparts to Germanic (German and Austrian) expressionism in art.

Abstract art also developed out of impressionism. Abstract art is art that is appreciated for its shapes, color, and/or texture but that does not represent any particular scene or being. An important leader in the development of abstract art was Russian-born artist Wassily Kandinsky (1866–1944), who left Russia to study art in Germany in 1896. After seeing an exhibit of paintings by Claude Monet in which he found it difficult to determine the subject, Kandinsky took the drastic step of completely abandoning representational painting. By 1903 he had come to be considered the founder of abstract art. Kandinsky's works, such as *Composition 238: Bright Circle,* were displayed all over Western Europe and influenced many other artists to develop their own nonrepresentational styles.

While Kandinsky was enjoying the praise of artists in Germany and

Le Coq d'Or (1908) was banned because the story made fun of autocrats. The opera is still missing from many lists of the composer's works. After the Bolshevik Revolution of 1917, artists and composers had hoped for more freedom, but government control of the arts became even tighter. The new Soviet government required artists to realistically portray workers doing manual labor, including scenes that indicated that Russia was advancing industrially. They also wanted works that showed their own communist leaders doing kind acts for their people. Works that did not do that were banned. In music, it was necessary that compositions be "understood" at first hearing. Some compositions were banned because they were too religious or because they used musical elements deemed unsuitable. Even triple meter was to be avoided because music should be "marchable," which requires duple or quadruple meters.

Composers such as Sergei Prokofiev (1891–1953) and Dmitri Shostakovich (1906–1975) managed to work within the Soviet system enough to create brilliant compositions that were allowed to be performed both in and out of Russia. Even they had problems with censorship, however. Shostakovich's opera *Lady Macbeth of Mtsensk* (1934) was praised when it was first performed. Unfortunately, Stalin himself went to see the opera in 1936 and thought it was "chaos instead of music." The work was

The Scream by Edvard Munch is another example of expressionism in art because of the way it displays a being so frozen with terror that the entire surrounding world seems to be screaming with him or her.

also in France, where he spent the last eleven years of his life, the Soviet government in Russia outlawed abstract art altogether. Early in the twentieth century the Russian government had refused to allow the performance of any artwork that was not supportive of the czar's regime. For example, composer Rimsky-Korsakov's opera

Without Title by Wassily Kandinsky is an example of abstract art because it does not represent any particular figure or view of the world. It is an abstraction of colors and shapes.

some of the faces but also because the women's figures are sectioned into planes of geometric shapes, a style that later became known as *cubism.* Music we will hear by Igor Stravinsky (1882–1971) also contains "primitive" elements, such as very complex rhythms influenced by non-Western music.

During World War I, expressionistic German artists such as Otto Dix (1891–1969) personally experienced the horrors of war while serving as soldiers. After the war they responded by exhibiting paintings that portrayed those horrors, calling their exhibition "No More War!" When Adolf Hitler came to power in 1933, he said that the works were too likely to influence the German people against fighting, and he had many of those paintings destroyed. *Trench Warfare* (1932) on page 245 is one of Dix's antiwar paintings that survived Hitler's fires. Dix survived as an artist in Germany only because he agreed to paint nothing other than landscapes until he was forced to fight again in World War II.

It is ironic that the Soviets and the Nazis were absolute enemies (except for a treaty in 1939 that did not last), and yet they both used the arts in similar ways to control and "educate" their people about advantages of life under their systems of government. Like the Soviets, the Nazis opposed modern art for more reasons than just its antiwar content. They wanted the world to see Germanic peoples as

eventually banned (although it has been revived in recent years).

In Western Europe, artists and composers were experimenting with new techniques and creating new styles one after another. The general term *modernism* refers to a number of these new styles. Pablo Picasso's (1881–1973) *Les Demoiselles d'Avignon* (1907) was viewed as "primitive," not only because of its use of African-type masks for

Les Demoiselles d'Avignon by Pablo Picasso is seen as "primitive" because of the use of African-type masks for some faces and also the sectional shapes of the figures.

straints of the Third Reich were fired from their teaching positions and not allowed to display their works in public. The government also destroyed many works that included personal expressions or that did not support and reflect Nazi attitudes.

In the freer environment of Switzerland, another movement in art came about as a reaction to World War I, called Dadaism. The statement behind most Dadaist works was that modern warfare had shown human life to be meaningless. Dada works were sometimes fashioned out of trash. A famous Dada sculpture by Marcel Duchamp (1887–1968) was a real urinal, placed in an art exhibit and called *Fountain* (1917).

Surrealism developed out of Dadaism and expressionism, and was inspired by Sigmund Freud's (1856–1939) early-twentieth-century studies of the unconscious or the dream state. Surrealistic works portrayed things from the real world but put them into forms that could not really exist, making them "beyond the real," or things that could only be dreamed—such as Salvador Dali's (1904–1989) *The Persistence of Memory* (1931).

Other new styles emerged as artists and composers attempted to go beyond classical and Romantic traditions and try new techniques and sounds. In some cases, however, artists and composers chose not to reject the past altogether but to base their works on older forms while still using newer ideas. One

perfect and proud, and so allowed only classic or sentimental portrayals of life. Wagner's operas and music dramas were favorites because Wagner used Germanic lore and legends and because he had the reputation of believing that the German race should remain "pure." In 1937, Nazi leaders took expressionistic and other works that they deemed corrupting out of muse-

ums and galleries and put 650 of them in a special exhibit they called "Degenerate Art." The exhibit toured throughout much of Germany and Austria, showing the works on walls covered by graffiti with signs that encouraged people to ridicule both the work and the artists who created it. Painters and art professors who refused to work within the subject and style con-

The Persistence of Memory by Salvador Dali is an example of surrealism in art because it portrays things from the real world in ways they could not really exist in that world. Surrealism means "beyond the real."

such style was called *neoclassicism* because new works were constructed using old (from any past era) types of images or, in the case of music, forms such as sonata or rondo. Before he worked with primitivism, Pablo Picasso spent some time painting figures that were suggestive of earlier styles, even those of ancient Greece. The composer Igor Stravinsky, whose works continued to change in style throughout his life, composed the oratorio *Oedipus Rex* (1927), based on the Greek tragedy of that same title.

In 1950 he composed music for another opera, *The Rake's Progress,* in which he used the singing styles of arias and recitatives much the way Mozart had. The opera was based so much on Mozart's style that Stravinsky even used harpsichord accompaniment for the recitatives.

In summary, the early twentieth century introduced many new sights and sounds to the arts. Some we might find beautiful and excitingly new, whereas others we might find disturbing. In the case

of expressionism, the music is often meant to be disturbing. The people who created in that style were not living happy and free lives. Their art and music reflected their discontent. Censorship by Soviet and Nazi governments controlled artists and composers in Russia and Germany, but many artists and composers who wanted to freely produce works that were not dictated by governments were able to leave and have very successful careers in other countries.

26 | Impressionism and Symbolism

Music is the arithmetic of sounds as optics is the geometry of light.

—COMPOSER CLAUDE DEBUSSY (1862–1918)

Listening Introduction

Listen to the example of music that represents this chapter, Prélude à "L'après-midi d'un faune" (Prelude to "The Afternoon of a Faun") and make notes about what you hear. Give some attention to the following:

▌ Can you guess at the tempo?

▌ Can you detect the meter?

▌ Can you identify any particular instruments in the orchestra?

▌ Do you hear any percussion instruments at all?

▌ What is the general mood of the piece?

▌ Does the piece sound like it might be programmatic or absolute?

Keep these notes to compare with your impressions about the music after you study the information in this chapter.

The musical culture of France was closely connected to the other arts, particularly painting and literature. One of the outstanding artistic movements of the turn of the century was **impressionism,** in which painters sought to capture the visual impression, rather than the literal reality, of a subject. Although their work and methods were at first ridiculed by the critics, the impressionists persisted in their exploration of the play of light and their use of patches and dabs of color to build up an image. They also continued their habit of working outdoors and utilizing bright afternoon light; mood and atmosphere and the richness of nature were among their major inspirations, as can be seen in Claude Monet's *Impression: Sunrise.* Meanwhile, poets were experimenting with rhythm, sound, and the clustering of images to suggest moods or emotions. This poetic style came to be known as **symbolism.**

Coming slightly later than the movements in art and literature, the impressionist movement in music was similarly characterized by experimentation and the rejection of past viewpoints. It, too, emphasized mood and atmosphere more than structure, and it, too, adopted nature as a frequent subject. Impressionist music is recognizable by its fragile and decorative beauty, its sensuous tone colors, its subdued atmosphere, its elegance and refinement, and its rhythmic fluidity. It cast off the more pompous, heavy, and serious quality of the Romantic German tradition. The influence of impressionism extended to England, Spain, Italy, and America, but France produced the most important composers: **Claude Debussy** (1862–1918) and Maurice Ravel.

Impression: Sunrise, **by Claude Monet.** The lack of detail in this painting makes it appear more like an impression of a scene than the scene as we might see it in real life. The colors and the reflection of light are as much the subject of the painting as are the water, boats, and sun.

Claude Debussy

Debussy was born in St. Germain-en-Laye, near Paris, and was educated at the Paris Conservatory, where he received traditional training in the cosmopolitan late-romantic style of composition. He absorbed it well enough to win the Prix de Rome at the age of twenty-two, but soon after he began to reject the Germanic tradition in general and Wagner's philosophy in particular.

Composer Claude Debussy

Debussy was put off by what he heard as the grand themes and ponderous quality of German Romantic music. For him the primary goal of music was to give pleasure, to appeal to the senses. An incisive critic, Debussy wrote articles on music that were published in the leading French journals. His reaction to Wagner's use of the leitmotif is characteristically witty and caustic: Wagnerian characters "never appear unless accompanied by their damnable leitmotiv, and there are even those who sing it! It's rather like those silly people who hand you their visiting cards and then lyrically recite key information they contain."

Opera was one of Debussy's lifelong interests, and his operatic style was very much a reaction against Wagner's influence. *Pelléas et Mélisande* (1902), which Debussy worked on during the 1890s, was taken from a symbolist play by Maurice Maeterlinck. It contains vague references and images of text that Debussy matched by restrained orchestral tone colors. Throughout the work, the voices dominate over a continuous orchestral background. The first performance

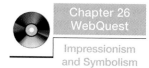

Chapter 26
WebQuest

Impressionism
and Symbolism

of the opera was met by mixed reactions. Some critics attacked it for its lack of form and melody, and others were enchanted by its subtle, elusive quality. Eventually, the opera caught on and established Debussy as the leader of the impressionist movement in music.

World War I and the devastating effects it had on France disturbed Debussy so profoundly that for a time he felt incapable of writing music. It was his sense of nationalism that impelled him to return to his art, and he began composing again with furious energy—an effort spurred on by the fact that he was slowly dying of cancer. His death came in March 1918, as Paris was being bombarded by German artillery. He was fifty-five years old.

Debussy was an accomplished pianist, and his piano compositions are among the most significant for his era. His early works were not impressionistic, but by 1903 he was well established in that style, with two collections of *Préludes* and two of *Images*.

His orchestral works are all impressionistic. We will listen to and discuss the first of those, Prélude à "L'après-midi d'un faune" (Prelude to "The Afternoon of a Faun"). This piece is programmatic but in a very general way. There is little attempt to tell a story or express specific feelings. Rather, it creates a "mood" or atmosphere to correspond with its program. The basis of the program is a poem by the symbolist writer Stéphane Mallarmé. Debussy described the prelude as a "very free illustration of Mallarmé's poem." In the poem, the faun (a sensual forest deity of pagan mythology, half man, half goat) awakens from sleep, his mind

Listening Guide

Prélude à "L'après-midi d'un faune" (Prelude to "The Afternoon of a Faun") CLAUDE DEBUSSY

CD 2
Tracks 16–20

Year: 1894

Tempo: Moderate tempo, changing throughout work

Meter: Irregular and unclear

Form: Modified ternary (AA'BA") with no literal repetition. Sections indicated as being repeated merely contain suggestions of the melodies of the earlier ones.

Instrumentation: Three flutes, two oboes, one English horn, two clarinets, two bassoons, four French horns, two harps, antique cymbals, first violins, second violins, violas, cellos, double basses

Note: The only brass instruments are the very mellow-sounding French horns, and the only percussion instruments are two "antique cymbals," which produce a very delicate sound.

Duration: 10:27

Special feature: It might be helpful to look at the painting *Impression: Sunrise* by Claude Monet again before listening to this piece. The painting has a different subject from the orchestral work, but you might notice that the lack of clear outlines in the painting and the lack of complete and resolved melodies display a similar mood. The painting was also created by brush strokes of pure colors that the viewer's eye must combine to see the subject. In Debussy's "Prélude," a single melody often begins played by one instrument, then by another and then another. The music moves from one tone color to another in much the same way that the painting moves from one brush stroke to another.

	Timing		What to listen for
16	0:00	A	Languid, sensuous flute melody floats down and up; horn calls and harp **glissandos;** sensuous melody again in flute with quiet tremolo (fast, repeated notes) in strings; crescendo in orchestra as intensity builds, then fades away
17	2:03	A'	Sensuous melody, flute, with added decoration, accompanied by occasional harp arpeggios
	3:20	Bridge	Splashes of instrumental color through the orchestra grow in volume and animation, suggest the faun's awakening senses, then subside; slow, dreamlike clarinet solo with delicate strings moves directly into:
18	5:10	B	Lyric, long-breathed melody in woodwinds with gently pulsing string accompaniment, crescendo; suddenly soft as lyric melody repeats in strings with harp arpeggios and pulsing woodwinds
	6:10	Bridge	Fragments from previous bridge in strings, then in various woodwind colors; solo violin longingly sings beginning of lyric melody
	7:10		Harp arpeggios accompany flute in anticipation of sensuous melody; woodwind fragments of melody and staccato chords interrupt; harp arpeggios accompany opening of sensuous melody in oboe; again soft interruptions
19	8:11	A"	Sensuous melody in flutes, with the delicate ring of antique cymbals and subdued tremolo in strings, yearning solo violin counterpoint; melody repeated in flute and cello, flute wanders drowsily off, melody completed by oboe
20	9:43	Coda	Harp and strings in floating, static notes, fragment of sensuous melody in horns, ringing antique cymbals, pizzicato in low strings

befuddled by wine. The faun recalls two nymphs he had seen earlier in the day. Did he carry them off to his lair or was it only a fantasy? "Is it a dream that I love?" he asks. But the afternoon is warm and the effort to remember too great, so once again he drifts off to sleep. Without following the events of the poem literally, Debussy evokes a musical impression of the poem.

The vague events in the poem on which Debussy's prelude is based makes it a very different work from programmatic works we heard in the romantic period, particularly those that told very specific stories. "Hearing the Difference: Smetana's 'The Moldau' and Debussy's Prélude à 'L'après-midi d'un faune'" examines some of these differences.

Maurice Ravel

Maurice Ravel (1875–1937) is often linked with Debussy as the other major figure who most fully realized the possibilities of musical impressionism. But Ravel's music, especially the compositions written in his later years, combines the sonorous impressionism of Debussy with a classical orientation toward form and balance.

Philosophically, Ravel had much in common with Debussy. Both composers agreed that music should serve an aesthetic purpose and that the creation of beautiful sound was the ultimate aim. They considered themselves rebels against German Romanticism and the Wagnerian school. They shared an attraction to the rhythms of Spanish dance music, as well as non-Western modes, scales, and instrumental tone colors.

Ravel created many compositions for the piano, as well as a number of songs for voice and chamber ensembles or voice and orchestra. He is best known for his orchestral works, however. His interest in Spanish dance rhythms can be heard in his most famous work, "Boléro" (1928), which employs a gradual uninterrupted crescendo and a repetitive single melody.

HEARING THE DIFFERENCE

Smetana's "The Moldau" and Debussy's Prélude à "L'après-midi d'un faune" (Prelude to "The Afternoon of a Faun")

Both of these works are single-movement, programmatic compositions for orchestra. The primary reason we are comparing them is that they each represent a different historical period. "The Moldau" is typically romantic: It tells a specific story and was composed to depict scenes in that story. The melody that represents the Moldau River comes back several times and is played all the way through each time. "Prélude à l'après-midi d'un faune," however, has the sense of subtle vagueness that we have seen in impressionistic paintings. Melodies seem to come from nowhere, and then slip back into the mellow sound of the large orchestra.

	The Moldau	**Prélude à "L'après-midi d'un faune"**
Historical period	Romantic	Early-twentieth-century impressionism
Tempo	Allegro, but varies to fit the story	Moderate, but changes throughout the work
Meter	Duple and sextuple	Irregular and unclear
Form	Through-composed with one returning theme that represents the river	AA′BA″ with each "A" section varied enough not to be heard as a real repetition, but as a suggestion of the earlier "A" section
Instrumentation	A large orchestra with effective use of percussion, especially when the rapids occur and the listener is to imagine the waves and boat hitting the rocks	A large orchestra that includes two harps, but no loud brass instruments, only the mellow sounding French horns; the only percussion instruments are two sets of tiny antique cymbals
Program	Specifically represents a hunt, a wedding dance, moonlight, water nymphs, rapids, an old castle, and the city of Prague, as well as a melody that represents the river	Has a program in that it follows the moods of a very vague symbolist poem, but no specific events or characters portrayed by the sound of the music

Summary

Around the beginning of the twentieth century, the musical culture of France was closely related to the other arts. Two of the dominant movements at the time were impressionism in painting and symbolism in literature, both of which influenced the development of impressionism in music. Impressionist music is characterized by its fragile beauty, sensuous tone colors, subdued atmosphere, and elegance. It cast off the more pompous, heavy, and serious quality of the German tradition. Claude Debussy is the composer primarily associated with musical impressionism. His use of free-flowing rhythms and light instrumental colors are characteristic of the style. Maurice Ravel, who is often linked with Debussy, incorporated many impressionistic devices into his music, but also displayed a classical orientation toward form and balance.

New People and Concepts

Claude Debussy   **impressionism**   **symbolism**

glissando   **Maurice Ravel**

Finale

Listen again to Prélude à "L'après-midi d'un faune" (Prelude to "The Afternoon of a Faun") and compare your impressions now with your notes from your first listening. Do you hear more now than you did before? You should now be able to answer the following questions:

❚ What is the tempo?

❚ What is the meter?

❚ Can you hear when the harps play?

❚ Do you hear when the antique cymbals play?

❚ What is the general mood of the piece?

❚ What is the program?

27 | Primitivism and Neoclassicism

I don't write modern music. I only write good music.
—COMPOSER IGOR STRAVINSKY (1882–1971)

Listening Introduction

Listen to the example of music in this chapter, *Le Sacre du printemps (The Rite of Spring),* introduction through "The Ritual of Abduction," by Stravinsky, and make notes about what you hear. Give some attention to the following:

▌ Can you detect the tempo?

▌ Can you detect the meter?

▌ Can you identify any particular instruments in the orchestra?

▌ What is the general mood of the piece?

▌ Does the piece sound like it might be either programmatic or absolute?

Keep these notes to compare with your impressions about the music after you study the information in this chapter.

Primitivism

The French World Exhibition of 1889 introduced visual images, music, and dance from many non-Western cultures to artists and composers in Paris. The artist Paul Gauguin (1848–1903) was so impressed with what he saw as an "honest exoticism" that, in 1891, he moved to the South Sea island of Tahiti. There, he painted many wonderful lush and colorful scenes of islanders enjoying a relaxed life in the tropics, such as *Mahana no Atua (Day of the Gods)* (1894).

This style came to be known as **primitivism.** The term *primitive* refers to more than the portrayal of technologically underdeveloped people. It also refers to flat shapes, lack of traditional sense of perspective, and colors so vivid that they are beyond what might look real. Without perspective, the figures in the background are not all that much smaller than those in the foreground. The viewer can tell they are in the background only because they are slightly smaller and higher on the canvas. Many artists, such as Gauguin and Henri Rousseau, whose works are also categorized as primitive, were self-taught and were interested in breaking away from traditional "realistic" styles while still representing live subjects. Much "folk art" is also considered primitive. Primitivist influences manifested themselves in Pablo Picasso's painting *Les Demoiselles d'Avignon (The Young Women of Avignon).*

Mahana no Atua (Day of the Gods), by Paul Gauguin, portrays the relaxed life of Tahitian natives.

Igor Stravinsky

Like Picasso in the visual arts, composer **Igor Stravinsky** (1882–1971) had a long, successful career that encompassed many different twentieth-century styles, including primitivism. Stravinsky, the third son of one of the most celebrated bass baritones in the Imperial Opera, was born in a small Russian town on the Gulf of Finland near St. Petersburg. He began piano lessons at the age of nine, but his parents, though encouraging his piano studies, regarded his musical activity as a sideline and decided that he should study law at the University of St. Petersburg, where he had the good fortune to make friends with the youngest son of Rimsky-Korsakov. He soon met the composer himself, at that time the leading figure in Russian music and one of the members of the "Five." By 1903, Stravinsky was studying orchestration with Rimsky-Korsakov. They became close friends, and the elder composer acted as best man at Stravinsky's wedding to a cousin in 1906.

Composer Igor Stravinsky

After completing his university studies in 1905, Stravinsky decided on a career as a composer. His earliest serious works were written under Rimsky-Korsakov's supervision. In 1909, he met Sergei Diaghilev, the impresario of the newly formed Ballet Russes, a Russian ballet company in Paris. Diaghilev commissioned the young composer to write music for the ballet based on an old Slavic legend. The work, entitled *L'oiseau de Feu (The Firebird),* had its premiere at the Paris Opera the following year. It was so successful that Stravinsky became a celebrity almost overnight.

Two more ballets quickly followed: *Petrouchka* (1910–1911) and *Le Sacre du printemps (The Rite of Spring)* (1912–1913). The first performance of *The Rite of Spring* sparked the most famous riot in music history (some of the reasons for the wild reaction are discussed later in this chapter). Despite that temporary setback, Stravinsky continued to compose music that was critically acclaimed. Until the outbreak of World War I, Stravinsky divided his time among Switzerland, Russia, and France. A member of the most distinguished musical and artistic circles of Europe, he came in close contact with Debussy, Ravel, the writer Jean Cocteau, and artist Pablo Picasso.

From the outbreak of World War I until 1919, Stravinsky lived in Switzerland. The difficulty in gathering together large groups of performers during this period of world war contributed to his evolving compositional style. He turned from huge orchestral works to compositions scored for instrumental ensembles of more modest size.

Stravinsky had given up his Russian citizenship at the time of the Russian Revolution of 1917. At the end of World War I, he returned to Paris, where he became a French citizen. Much of his time during the 1920s and 1930s was spent on tour through the principal cities of Europe and America. When World War II began, he moved again, this time to Hollywood, California. Deciding to remain in the United States permanently, he gave up his French citizenship to become a naturalized American in 1945.

Stravinsky continued to compose well into his late years, and he conducted concerts of his music all over the world into his eighties. He died in 1971 at the age of eighty-eight.

Stravinsky used rhythmically complex ideas from non-Western cultures and combined those with his knowledge of Russian folk music when he was commissioned to compose *The Rite of Spring* for the Ballet Russes de Monte Carlo. The ballet was subtitled *Pictures of Pagan Russia,* and it depicts the Russian peasants' pagan (pre-Christian) rites to convince the gods to end the winter and bring the earth back to life with spring. The rite culminates in the sacrifice of a young virgin, who dances herself to death while the tribal elders watch. Stravinsky's music incorporated the idea of "paganism" by stressing angular melodies and offbeat, "primitive" rhythms. Not only were the subject matter and the music unexpected by the audience, but the choreography by Vaslav Nijinsky was even more shocking. Nijinsky's wife danced in the first performance, and she described the dancers as follows:

> The men in *The Rite of Spring* are primitive. There is something almost bestial in their appearance. Their legs and feet are turned inwards, their fists clenched, their heads held down between hunched shoulders; their walk, on slightly bent knees, is heavy as they laboriously straggle up a winding trail, stamping in the rough, hilly terrain. The women are also primitive, but in their countenances one already perceives the awakening of an awareness of beauty. Still, their postures and movements are uncouth and clumsy, as they gather in clusters on the tops of small hillocks and come down together to meet in the middle of the stage and form a large crowd.

This was not the kind of dance that Parisian ballet audiences in 1913 expected to see. The audience was not only shocked, but very angry. There were boos and catcalls followed by actual fighting. The dancers could not even hear the music, and Nijinsky had to call out beats and cues to keep the performance going. Stravinsky was accused of "destroying music as art." He left before the performance was ended by the police. Actually, the very same music was well received when it was played without the dancing only a year later. By the 1920s the work was lauded as a great achievement. The music then got another boost of popularity in

1940, when the Walt Disney Company used part of it in the movie *Fantasia* to accompany visions of animated dinosaurs.

The Rite of Spring takes about thirty-five minutes to perform. It has two large parts, the first of which features a series of pagan rituals involving the adoration of the earth and the choosing of the maiden who is to die. The second part includes dances with the chosen one and the tribal ancestors, as well as the final sacrificial dance. We will listen to the introduction, the "Dances of the Young Girls," and "The Ritual of Abduction."

Listening Guide

Le Sacre du printemps (The Rite of Spring), Introduction through "The Ritual of Abduction" IGOR STRAVINSKY

CD 4
Tracks 29–31

Year: 1913

Tempo: Varies throughout the work

Meter: Irregular and changing

Form: Sectional, following the program

Instrumentation: Two piccolos, three flutes, one alto flute, four oboes, two English horns, four bassoons, two contrabassoons, eight French horns, five trumpets, one bass trumpet, three trombones, four tubas, a very large percussion section, first violins, second violins, violas, cellos, double basses

Duration: 8:16

Special feature: In order to fully appreciate the irregularity of the rhythms, it might help for you to try counting duple or triple metric patterns while you listen to the music and notice how unexpected the placement of the accented beats is.

Timing	What to listen for
Introduction	
0:00	Gentle, springlike melody in high bassoon; clarinet, high bassoon; new melody begins in English horn; bassoon; English horn completes its melody
1:55	Additional melodies polyphonically in woodwinds; trill in violin; woodwind polyphony continues at length
2:24	Oboe introduces fragment, high woodwinds only; clarinet squeals answer
2:37	Low chord in double basses supports woodwind polyphony of previous fragments
3:01	High bassoon alone in gentle opening theme; clarinet trill; back-and-forth motive in pizzicato violins, directly into:
"Auguries of Spring—Dances of the Young Girls"	
3:37	Pounding barbaric rhythm in strings, loud horn punctuations; back-and-forth motive, English horn; barbaric rhythm, flirtatious melody in muted trumpet, oboes
4:02	Back-and-forth motive, violent trumpet fanfares and woodwind shrieks
4:16	Barbaric rhythm; mocking melody in bassoons, echoed in trombone, bassoons, bassoons again, oboes, trombone, oboes
4:55	Violent interruption, drumbeats, long note in trombone
5:00	Shrieks down through winds, violin solo trill, back-and-forth motive in English horn, with interruptions

The track markers **29** and **30** appear to the left of the timings 0:00 and 3:37 respectively.

continued

Timing	What to listen for
5:17	Back-and-forth motive in strings, smooth melody in horn, answered by flute; flirtatious melody in oboes and trumpet; smooth melody in alto flute
5:52	Activity mounts; heavy melody in trumpets, added triangle and cymbals
6:12	Sudden piano, strings loud punctuations; smooth melody in piccolo, extended and developed, mounting whirling activity, full orchestra, crescendo

"The Ritual of Abduction"

6:57	Very fast, sustained brass chord, violent drumbeats, shrieking woodwinds, raucous trombones
7:11	Horn calls answered by woodwinds and strings; violent drumbeats, raucous trombones return; violent, polyphonic activity continues
7:32	Full orchestra suddenly comes together playing frantic rhythms
7:40	Suddenly reduced, softer, horn calls; loud, descending interruption
7:46	Fanfare-like brass, drum interruptions; whirling strings, violent interruptions; solitary trill in flute continues into the next section, "Roundelays of Spring"

La Toilette, by Pablo Picasso, is an example of neoclassical art in that the figures are reminiscent of ancient Greek vase painting.

In this chapter we have concentrated on the style of primitivism because that is the style of *The Rite of Spring*. However, rather like the artworks of Picasso, Stravinsky's music cannot be generally categorized as "primitive." His work includes a great variety of styles. With his ballet *Pulcinella* (1919), based on music by the eighteenth-century composer Giovanni Battista Pergolesi, and the *Octet for Wind Instruments* (1923) Stravinsky began working in a style called **neoclassicism.**

Neoclassicism

As we saw in the introduction to the medieval period, the term "classical" is used to describe the civilization of ancient Greece. In music, we call the late eighteenth century classical because of its concentration on symmetrically balanced forms reminiscent of ancient Greek art. When the term appears in the early twentieth century, this time called "neoclassical," it refers to art or to music that is based on the objectivity, balanced formal structure, and emotional restraint of the works of an earlier period, usually ancient Greece, the baroque, or classical.

Much of Stravinsky's music through about 1950 is neoclassical, including his chamber work for winds and strings, *The Dumbarton Oaks Concerto* (1938). The texture and rhythms of the concerto were very much influenced by Bach's *Brandenburg Concertos*. Other neoclassical works by Stravinsky include his opera-oratorio *Oedipus Rex* (1927), based on the Greek tragedy of the same title, and the opera *The Rake's Progress* (1950), titled after a series of engravings by the English artist William Hogarth. *The Rake's Progress* features Stravinsky's brilliant musical

language of varied rhythms and his colorful use of woodwinds, but it is also very much like Mozart's operas in many ways. Like Mozart, Stravinsky had the orchestra accompany emotional arias, and he had the harpsichord accompany recitative-styled dialogue. Romantic opera composers had done away with the harpsichord and had composed more melodic singing for sections of dialogue, so Stravinsky's style and instrumentation marked a return to the older classical style, making it neoclassical. Mozart's operatic style can again be heard at the end of *The Rake's Progress* when the lead singers come out on stage to sing the moral of the tale, "For idle hands / And hearts and minds / The Devil finds / A work to do." Mozart ended *Don Giovanni* by having the characters who remain after Don Giovanni's death stand and sing the opera's moral lesson: "This is the end of the evil-doer: His death is as bad as his life."

Summary

In this chapter we have discussed two styles of the early twentieth century, primitivism and neoclassicism. Composer Igor Stravinsky wrote in both styles. The development of primitivism was heavily influenced by non-Western art and music. In the case of Stravinsky's ballet *The Rite of Spring,* the subject was a pagan ritual in which a young maiden was sacrificed to encourage the gods to awaken the world with the new life of spring. The music is full of syncopated, jarring rhythms and angular themes.

The dance was even more shocking to the Parisian ballet audience in 1913 because the dancers were hunched over with clenched fists to look like a pagan tribe. The audience rioted at the first performance, but the music was eagerly accepted only one year later. Stravinsky's neoclassical works followed *The Rite of Spring.* They took various forms, but all were based in some way on forms or subjects from earlier periods.

New People and Concepts

neoclassicism   **primitivism**   **Igor Stravinsky**

Finale

Listen again to *Le Sacre du printemps (The Rite of Spring),* introduction through "The Ritual of Abduction," by Stravinsky, and compare your impressions now with your notes from your first listening. Do you hear more now than you did before? You should now be able to answer the following questions:

▍ What is the tempo?

▍ What is the meter?

▍ What instrument plays the introductory melody?

▍ What is the general mood of the piece?

▍ What is the program?

28 | Eastern European Nationalism

The sacredness of church music, the joyfulness and
soulfulness of folk songs are the two pivots around
which revolve true music. A nation creates music . . .
the composer only arranges it.
—COMPOSER BÉLA BARTÓK

Listening Introduction

Listen to the example of music that represents this chapter, *Music for Strings, Percussion, and Celesta,* third movement, by Bartók, and make notes about what you hear. Give some attention to the following:

▌ Can you detect the tempo?

▌ Can you detect the meter?

▌ Can you identify any particular instruments?

▌ Do you hear any sections that repeat?

▌ What is the general mood of the piece?

Keep these notes to compare with your impressions about the music after you study the information in this chapter.

As we discussed in earlier chapters, one aspect of nationalism is the expression of pride in one's country. We saw Chopin exhibit a sense of nationalism when he composed mazurkas and polonaises based on Polish dance rhythms. Smetana displayed similar pride in his country of Bohemia when he composed *The Moldau,* using it to describe the beauty of that Bohemian river. Many other composers have composed works based on national folklore or historical events, particularly operas. Mussorgsky's opera *Boris Godunov,* for example, took its libretto from a drama by Pushkin about a tsar in Russia's past. Composers have usually tried to look at what the people in the small villages of their country sang, danced, and cared about, the theory being that such people are not "tarnished" by having traveled to foreign places. They were villagers and farmers who took pride in their work and lifestyles.

Before recording machines were invented, it was difficult for people outside of these small villages to hear and appreciate the music played and sung by villagers, but by the early twentieth century it had become possible for recordings to be made. The earliest experiments in sound recording were conducted during the mid-nineteenth century, and in 1877 Thomas Edison (1847–1931) patented the first phonograph. It was a mechanical device that gathered sound in a horn and then transferred the sound waves onto a wax-covered cylinder. The same device could then play back the sounds that had been recorded. Flat discs soon replaced the cylinders. It was not until the 1920s that the devices were made to run on electricity. Though the quality of sound was primitive at best, the phonographs did at least reproduce a melody or rhythm pattern which allowed composers to record what they heard in villages and then play that music back for further study whenever they wanted. Hungarian composer **Béla Bartók** (1881–1945) was the first major composer to study folk music by making field recordings and using the ideas he gained in his compositions.

Béla Bartók

Bartók was the son of the director of a government agricultural school. His first piano lessons, begun at the age of five, were given by his mother. Following the death of his father in 1888, the family moved to Bratislava (now the capital of Slovakia), where Bartók began formal studies in music. In 1892, he made his first public appearance as a composer and pianist, playing one of his own works, and he formed a close friendship with Ernö Dohnányi, in later years one of Hungary's most noted pianists and composers.

In 1899, though admitted to the prestigious Vienna Conservatory, Bartók decided to follow Dohnányi to the Royal Academy of Music in Budapest. There he became strongly attracted to the music of Wagner and Richard Strauss. He also was caught up in the nationalistic movement in politics, literature, and the arts then sweeping through Hungary. His first major composition, an immense orchestral tone poem entitled *Kossuth* (1903), commemorated the nationalist leader of the unsuccessful revolution of 1848. Bartók became friends with Zoltán Kodály (1882–1967), the third member (with Dohnányi and Bartók himself) of the great trio of modern Hungarian composers.

Both Bartók and Kodály developed a strong interest in the problem of creating a national music and began collecting and analyzing Hungarian folk music. The earliest product of their research was a joint publication of arrangements, *Twenty Hungarian Folksongs* (1906). Bartók's interest in folk music began to have an immediate effect on his own work; folk-derived rhythms and melodic patterns appeared side by side with the most current devices in composition.

Following his graduation in 1902 from the Royal Academy, Bartók began a series of concert tours throughout major European cities that lasted for the next several years. During this period, he became increasingly influenced by the French Impressionistic music of Debussy and his contemporaries. Bartók's own effort at composition, however, did not seem to get off the ground during this period, and for a while he leaned toward a career as a concert pianist rather than a composer.

In 1907, Bartók accepted an appointment as a piano teacher at the Budapest Academy, a post that he held for nearly thirty years. In 1909, he married Márta Ziegler, one of his pupils, and settled into a routine of teaching, composing, and making extensive concert tours. He also continued his research and study of Hungarian folk music, which continued to influence his own compositions. In 1923, he was divorced and married another of his piano students, Ditta Pásztory. They often toured together, playing works for two pianos, and in 1927, they traveled to America for a series of solo recitals and appearances with various orchestras.

By the late 1930s, Nazi Germany had designs on Hungary, and the political turmoil brought on by the conflict convinced Bartók that he must leave Hungary. In 1940, he emigrated to the United States, where he was given an appointment at Columbia University. While in New York, however, he developed leukemia, and his health began declining seriously. He died in September 1945 at the age of sixty-four.

Béla Bartók's works include music for solo piano, chamber music for strings (often with piano), concertos, orchestral works of various types, and such vocal works as *Bluebeard's Castle* and *Cantata Profana*.

Throughout his life, Bartók studied the folk music of Eastern Europe. His studies influenced his style of writing melodies, which sometimes had a folklike character. He rarely used actual folk songs in his compositions, but he understood

Bartók visiting a Hungarian village in 1907 to record local folk songs on a recording machine that captured sound waves in the horn and engraved them on a wax-covered cylinder. The machine was hand-cranked and could play the songs back when Bartók reached his home studio. Bartók's music was much influenced by the folk traditions of such villages.

Composer Béla Bartók

how they were constructed and effectively imitated them. The diverse, irregular rhythms of Hungarian folk music also had a significant impact on his work. In individual passages of much of his music, the meter changes so often as to have the effect of a strongly complex rhythmic impulse.

Chapter 28
WebQuest

Eastern
European
Nationalism

In many ways Bartók's music can be categorized as neoclassical because he often used traditional compositional devices such as fugue and canon, as well as sonata form. In his *Music for Strings, Percussion, and Celesta* (1936), Bartók used an **arch form,** in which the beginning and ending of the piece are related, the second and second-to-last sections are related, the third and third-from-last are related, and the middle section stands alone, like the keystone on an archway. He also used another idea sometimes characteristic of some baroque religious music when he gave instructions for the two string ensembles to sit on opposite sides of the stage so that they might be heard in an antiphonal, or stereo, effect. The seating arrangement was:

	Double Bass I	Double Bass II	
Cello I	Timpani	Bass Drum	Cello II
Viola I	Side Drums	Cymbals	Viola II
Violin II	Celesta	Xylophone	Violin IV
Violin I	Piano	Harp	Violin III
	Conductor		

Note: A celesta is a small keyboard instrument in which the hammers strike tuned metal bars instead of strings, as a piano would.

"The Live Experience: Playing Percussion" gives insight into how percussionists work in a musical ensemble.

Listening Guide

Music for Strings, Percussion, and Celesta, **third movement** BÉLA BARTÓK

CD 4
Tracks 32–37

Year: 1936

Tempo: Adagio, but with variations of tempo

Meter: The meter is unclear in many sections, although it is mostly quadruple. The D section introduces quintuple meter with the "five-note bell-like motive," and the C/B section is, in part, in triple meter.

Form: Arch form (ABCDCBA)

Instrumentation: Two string quartets (or the piece could be played by two string orchestras) separated by piano, harp, celesta, and various percussion instruments

Duration: 7:26

Special feature: Notice the separation of the string sections in the two different speakers during the C/B section. The irregular metric patterns and rhythms were influenced by the asymmetrical rhythms found in much Hungarian folk music.

Timing		What to listen for
32 0:00	**A**	Repeated notes on xylophone increase and decrease rhythmically; timpani glissandos
0:29		Halting, fragmented theme in violas; theme is extended through imitation among strings, accompanied by timpani rolls and glissandos, and repeated xylophone notes; repeated notes in xylophone

Timing		What to listen for
2:16	**Transition**	Opening phrase of first-movement theme
33 2:26	**B**	Ghostly trills and glissandos in violins; eerie, sinuous theme in celesta and high solo violins
3:23	**Transition**	Repeated xylophone notes, timpani glissandos, fragments in piano; second phrase of first-movement theme
34 3:43	**C**	Glissandos in celesta, harp, and piano; wandering, chromatic theme softly in tremolo strings; gradual crescendo; glissandos stop as chromatic theme takes over, builds quickly to:
35 4:22	**D**	Cymbal crash, climactic dissonant chord, sudden drop to piano; five-note bell-like motive echoes through the instruments, slow and fast rhythms, played forward and backward, builds to great intensity, softens as celesta and pizzicato strings predominate
5:06	**Transition**	Third phrase of first-movement theme, bowed strings
36 5:15	**C/B**	Sinuous B theme very softly and expressively imitated between high strings on left and low strings on right, glissandos in celesta, harp, and piano, wandering C theme in high solo violins tremolo on right
6:21	**Transition**	Fourth phrase of first-movement theme, celesta and piano, pianissimo; loud, startling pizzicato chord
37 6:33	**A**	Fragments from halting A theme imitated among strings, timpani glissandos; repeated notes, xylophone, sustained close

THE LIVE EXPERIENCE
Playing Percussion

When you watch an orchestra, band, or other musical ensemble play, it is easy to see the string sections playing the same lines together because you can see their bows moving the same way at the same time. You can also see the woodwind and brass players playing solos or playing together with their sections. They are all sitting or standing at their instruments and playing them when needed or perhaps changing temporarily to a related instrument to play for a while—a flute player playing a passage on piccolo, for example. But the really interesting players to watch in most ensembles are the percussionists. In most orchestras, they stand in the back or at the side, and each player is responsible for any number of different instruments that seemingly have little relationship to one another. Professional percussionists do not specialize in a single instrument. Each percussionist has to be ready to pick up a set of four mallets and play full melodies or chords on the keyboard-like bars of a xylophone or a marimba. They then might have

to switch abruptly to a set of kettledrums. Next, the same player might have to grab two cymbals and crash them together at just the right time. The point is that there are many percussion instruments in orchestras and each has to be played with the proper sticks, mallets, or even the players' hands. In some cases, the instruments have to be tuned and retuned during the performance.

Instruments or other sound makers that are needed for a particular piece of music but that are not part of the standard ensemble will also end up in the percussion section. For example, a very modern piece that asks the musicians to start a motorcycle engine at a particular time or set off a siren or a tape player will often fall under the percussionist's domain.

Of course, all of this complexity occurs in music from the later romantic period through to the present. Most classical composers had only timpani for percussion, which were usually used to back up the trumpets.

Summary

Composers have often expressed nationalistic ideals in their music by basing their work on the melodies and dance rhythms of traditional folk music. Béla Bartók was the first major composer to do a detailed study of the folk music of his native Hungary by actually taking recording equipment to Hungarian villages. That allowed him to have the music to replay in his home studio. His compositions did not exactly quote folk melodies or rhythms, but his music was strongly influenced by them. In the work we heard, *Music for Strings, Percussion, and Celesta,* third movement, the irregular metric patterns and rhythms were influenced by the asymmetrical rhythms found in much Hungarian folk music.

Much of Bartók's music fits into both the categories of primitivism and neoclassicism because of his use of strong, "primitive" rhythms and reliance on formal structures from the baroque and classical periods.

New People and Concepts

arch form   Béla Bartók

Finale

Listen again to *Music for Strings, Percussion, and Celesta,* third movement, by Bartók, and compare your impressions now with your notes from your first listening. Do you hear more now than you did before? You should now be able to answer the following questions:

▮ What is the tempo?

▮ What is the meter?

▮ What instruments can you identify?

▮ When do sections repeat?

▮ What is the general mood of the piece?

29 | Germanic Expressionism and the Development of Serialism

I occasionally play works by contemporary composers for two reasons. First to discourage the composer from writing any more and secondly to remind myself how much I appreciate Beethoven.
—VIOLINIST JASCHA HEIFETZ (1901–1987),
EXPRESSING WHAT MANY ROMANTIC MUSICIANS
FEEL ABOUT SERIALISM

Listening Introduction

Listen to the example of music that represents this chapter, "A Survivor from Warsaw," by Schoenberg, and make notes about what you hear. Give some attention to the following:

▌ Can you detect the tempo?

▌ Can you detect the meter?

▌ Can you identify any particular instruments?

▌ Can you tell what voice types you hear?

▌ Can you tell the language of the text?

▌ Does the mood of the music seem to fit the meaning of the text?

Keep these notes to compare with your impressions about the music after you study the information in this chapter.

Expressionism in art generally represents the tormented feelings of people stuck in a world of pain and conflict. The artworks often used harsh colors and distorted images to achieve intense emotional effects. The subject matter of expressionism was modern humanity in its varied psychological states: isolated, irrational, rebellious, and tense. Expressionistic artists did not attempt to produce beautiful or realistic art, but only to penetrate and reveal inner feelings. Several early twentieth-century composers shared the goals of the artists.

In their efforts to create a new kind of tonality, it occurred to twentieth-century composers that they might be able to avoid the traditional concept of tonality completely. But the idea of the tonal center (a note such as the "key" note of the piece that, when played at the end of a phrase, can give the music a sense of finality) was so fundamental to musical organization that it could not simply be dropped. Rather, it had to be replaced by an organizing principle of equal strength. One of the most effective of the systems developed to replace traditional harmony and tonality was **serialism,** developed by the Austrian composer **Arnold Schoenberg** (1874–1951).

**Composer Arnold
Schoenberg**

Arnold Schoenberg

At the start of his career, Schoenberg was closely allied with late German romanticism, although he moved further from it than almost any of his contemporaries. With two of his students, **Alban Berg** (1885–1935) and **Anton Webern** (1883–1945), Schoenberg devised a way to reject tonality, creating a style that was **atonal.** His new system of musical organization involved arranging the twelve chromatic tones in a chosen (non-scale-like) order, called a **tone row** and then writing the music using different versions of that row one after another. The notes of the row could be used in sequence, forming a melody or theme, or simultaneously in groups to form chords. This system is called **twelve tone** or **dodecaphony** (a dodecagon has 12 sides). The repeated use of the twelve-tone row over and over created a type of "series" and is, therefore, called *serialism.* Twelve-tone music opened the door to new methods of composing and new ways of constructing harmonies.

Schoenberg was born into a Viennese middle-class family; although both of his parents loved music, neither provided much guidance in his early training. While in grammar school, he studied the violin and cello and was soon composing and playing in chamber ensembles. When Schoenberg was in his late teens, a friend who directed an amateur orchestral society, Alexander von Zemlinsky, first interested him in serious musical study. After working several years as a bank employee, Schoenberg decided in 1895 to embark on a musical career.

The two great influences on his early compositions were the giants of late-nineteenth-century German music: Brahms and Wagner. During the 1890s Schoenberg wrote several string quartets and piano works and a small number of songs. In 1901 he married his friend's sister, Mathilde von Zemlinsky. Shortly afterward, he was hired as a theater conductor in Berlin. There he became acquainted with composer Richard Strauss, who helped him obtain a teaching position and expressed great interest in his work. In 1903, Schoenberg returned to Vienna to teach musical composition. Composer Gustav Mahler became a supporter of his music, and, more important, Schoenberg took on as students two younger men, Alban Berg and Anton Webern. Both pupils would later adopt Schoenberg's twelve-tone methods and would develop them in their own individual ways; Webern would decisively influence the future course of music.

It was during the first decade of the twentieth century that Schoenberg began turning away from the late Romantic style of his earlier works and gradually developed his new twelve-tone method. Although his name spread among composers and performers, public acclaim eluded him. His famous song cycle *Pierrot Lunaire (Moonstruck Pierrot)* (1912) drew invectives from critics but praise from **avant-garde** (new and experimental) sympathizers. *Pierrot Lunaire* employed a half-sung, half-spoken vocal technique called ***Sprechstimme*** (literally, "speech voice").

Schoenberg's reputation was beginning to grow when his career was interrupted by World War I, in which he served with the Austrian army. Soon after, however, he was again active as a composer, a lecturer on theory, and a teacher. The

Trench Warfare, by Otto Dix, expressed some of the horrors of World War I. War shadowed the first half of the twentieth century, and had a strong impact on all the arts.

1920s marked a new direction. He went to Berlin in 1925 to teach composition at the State Academy of the Arts, taking with him his second wife, Gertrude Kolisch. (His first wife had died in 1923.)

In 1933, Schoenberg's career again took another direction. When the Nazi Party assumed power, Schoenberg, being Jewish, was dismissed from his post. He emigrated first to France, then to the United States. Although his reputation as a teacher and a "modernist" preceded him, he nevertheless had financial difficulty. After working in Boston and New York, he joined the faculty of the University of California at Los Angeles. He died in Los Angeles at the age of seventy-six.

Much of Schoenberg's music fits into the style of expressionism. "A Survivor from Warsaw" was composed by Schoenberg in 1946–1947 and was first performed in 1947. It is a short but dramatic cantata written for a male narrator, men's chorus, and an orchestra. Schoenberg compiled the text himself using as the basis reports of the atrocities of the Warsaw ghetto uprising. The piece is a twelve-tone work.

"A Survivor from Warsaw" is among Schoenberg's most personal, dramatic, and gripping works, inspired by bitter experience as a Jew living through the hellish nightmare that led up to World War II.

Other Serial Composers

Composer Alban Berg

Schoenberg's student Alban Berg adopted most of Schoenberg's twelve-tone system of composition but used it with a great deal of flexibility. His works allow for a sense of tonality and combine twelve-tone techniques with established formal procedures from earlier musical periods, including the suite, the march, and the rondo. Much of his music has a warmth and lyricism that stem from the Romantic

Listening Guide

"A Survivor from Warsaw" ARNOLD SCHOENBERG

CD 4
Tracks 38–39

Year: 1947

Tempo: Varies throughout the work

Meter: Quadruple, but not at all easy to follow

Form: No obvious repeated sections

Instrumentation: Two flutes (piccolos), two oboes, two clarinets, two bassoons, three trumpets, four French horns, three trombones, one tuba, a large percussion section (including xylophone, chimes, snare drum, bass drum, timpani, cymbals, triangle, tambourine, gong, and castanets), one harp, ten first violins, ten second violins, six violas, six cellos, six double basses

Voices: Male narrator and a men's chorus

Language: English, German, and Hebrew (The German and Hebrew texts are italicized.)

Duration: 7:04

Special feature: The brief orchestral introduction sets the mood for the text, which is told by a narrator who from time to time assumes the role of the German soldier who barks orders and hurls threats at the Jewish people. The final chorus represents the statement of faith that remained in the humiliated people.

Text

38 I cannot remember everything! I must have been unconscious most of the time; I remember only the grandiose moment when they all started to sing, as if prearranged, the old prayer they had neglected for so many years—the forgotten creed! But I have no recollection how I got underground to live in the sewers of Warsaw for so long a time. The day began as usual. Reveille when it still was dark. "Get out!" Whether you slept or whether your worries kept you awake the whole night: you had been separated from your children, from your wife, from your parents. You don't know what happened to them. . . . How could you sleep? The trumpets again. "Get out! The sergeant will be furious!" They came out; some very slowly, the old ones, the sick ones, some with nervous agility. They fear the sergeant. They hurry as much as they can. In vain! Much too much noise, much too much commotion! And not fast enough!

The Feldwebel shouts!

German	**English translation**
"Achtung! Still gestanden!	Attention! Stand still!
Na wird's mal, oder soll ich mit dem	How about it, or should I help you along with
Gewehrkolben nachhelfen? Na jut; wenn Ihr's	the butt of my rifle? Oh well, if you really
durchaus haben wollt!"	want to have it!

English

The sergeant and his subordinates hit everyone young or old, strong or sick, guilty or innocent. . . . It was painful to hear them groaning and moaning. I heard it though I had been hit very hard, so hard that I could not help falling down. We all on the ground who could not stand up were then beaten over the head. I must have been unconscious. The next thing I heard was a soldier saying, "They are all dead!" Whereupon the sergeant ordered them to do away with us. There I lay aside half conscious. It had become very still—fear and pain. Then I heard the sergeant shouting.

German	**English translation**
"Abzählen!"	Count off!

English

They started slowly, and irregularly: one, two, three, four

German	**English translation**
"Achtung."	Attention.

English

The sergeant shouted again:

German	**English translation**
"Rascher! Nochmals von vorn anfangen!	Faster! Once more, start from the beginning!
In einer Minute will ich wissen wieviele	In one minute I want to know how many I am
ich zur Gaskammer abliefere! Abzählen!"	going to send off to the gas chamber! Count off!

English

They began again, first slowly: one- two- three- four, became faster and faster; so fast that it finally sounded like a stampede of wild horses. Then, all of a sudden, in the middle of it, they began singing the *Shema Yisroel*.

Hebrew	**English translation**
39 *Shema Yisroel Adonoy elohenu Adonoy*	Hear, O Israel, the Lord our God, the Lord is one!
ehod. Veohavto es Adonoy eloheho	And thou shalt love the Lord thy God with all thy
behol levoveho uvehol nafsheho uvehol	heart, and with all thy soul, and with all thy
meodeho. Vehoyu haddevoreem hoelleh	might. And these words, which I command thee
asher onohee metsavveho hayyom al	this day, shall be in thy heart. And thou shalt
levoveho. Veshinnantom levoneho	teach them diligently unto thy children, and speak
vedibbarto bom beshivteho beveteho	of them when thou sittest in thy house, and when
uvelehteho baddereh uveshohbeho	thou goest on thy way, and when thou liest down, and
uvekumeho.	when thou risest up.

(Note: The Hebrew hymn is from Deuteronomy 6:4–9)

tendencies of earlier composers, like Mahler. In addition, such elements as his ability to sustain large forms and his use of large orchestras reflect the Romantic aspect of his style.

The opera *Wozzeck* (1917–1921) is considered by many to be Berg's greatest work. It was unquestionably influenced by the environment created in Europe by World War I. The central character is Wozzeck, a soldier who is belittled and abused by his superior, the captain, and used as a hired guinea pig in medical "experiments" by his doctor. He is betrayed by his mistress, Marie, and eventually driven to murder and suicide by a completely hostile society.

The vocal style of *Wozzeck* depends heavily on Schoenberg's *Sprechstimme* technique, which alternates with ordinary speech and conventional singing in an extremely expressive manner. The prevailing mood of the opera is one of cynicism, irony, helplessness, and depression. Few portrayals of life are as hopeless as that of *Wozzeck*.

Schoenberg's other important and influential student was Anton Webern. Whereas Berg came to represent a link to the past among the followers of Schoenberg, Webern's music represents a more radical denial of and departure from established compositional procedures and concepts. His mature works crystallize the serialist constructionist approach to musical composition inherent in the twelve-tone system as originally postulated by Schoenberg.

Composer Anton Webern

Chapter 29
WebQuest

The Development
of Serialism

Whereas Berg was writing in complex forms for large musical forces, Webern was striving for economy of material and extreme compactness of form. He felt strongly that each individual note in a composition was important in itself; he added nothing for "general effect." As a result of this preoccupation, most of his works are "miniatures." Webern's music is the epitome of clarity, economy of material, spareness of texture, and brevity.

It is not surprising, then, that Webern wrote very little music and that all of his works tend to be quite short, some individual pieces lasting less than a minute and some of the "longest" works not exceeding ten minutes. His complete output totals less than five hours of music.

During his lifetime, Webern suffered the same lack of public recognition as Schoenberg, but his music, like that of his teacher, became increasingly influential after World War II. In particular, in the 1970s and 1980s, many young composers, such as Pierre Boulez and Milton Babbitt, captivated by the lean character of his style and his isolation of the single note as an important musical event, adapted features of his music and expanded the techniques of serialism to suit their own purposes. The twelve-tone system initiated by Schoenberg and advanced by Berg and Webern became a powerful force in the world of music and still influences some composers today.

Summary

The development of the atonal style was led by Arnold Schoenberg, a Viennese composer. Schoenberg rejected the concept of tonality completely and devised the twelve-tone system of arranging the twelve notes of the chromatic scale in an order that could be used in a series. The general system is called *serialism*. Under the system, the notes of the tone row could be used in sequence, forming a melody or theme, or simultaneously in groups to form chords. "A Survivor from Warsaw" is a good example of the use of the twelve-tone method in a dramatic work for narrator, men's chorus, and orchestra.

Schoenberg has had a major influence on contemporary composition. Much of that influence has been transmitted through the music of his pupils and colleagues. Alban Berg and Anton Webern represent the further development of two divergent aspects of Schoenberg's style: Berg was more Romantic and produced the great opera *Wozzeck*. Webern's music was abstract.

New People and Concepts

Alban Berg	**avant-garde**	***Sprechstimme***
Anton Webern	**dodecaphony**	**tone row**
Arnold Schoenberg	**expressionism**	**twelve tone**
atonal	**serialism**	

Finale

Listen again to "A Survivor from Warsaw," by Schoenberg, and compare your impressions now with your notes from your first listening. Do you hear more now than you did before? You should now be able to answer the following questions:

▌ What is the tempo?

▌ What is the meter?

❚ What instruments can you identify?

❚ What voice types you hear?

❚ What are the languages of the text?

Does the mood of the music seem to fit the meaning of the text?

Characteristics of Twentieth-Century Music (to World War II)

Texture	Both homophonic and contrapuntal textures employed; variety of textures within a single composition
Tonality	Major-minor system retained by some composers, but methods of establishing tonal centers altered; other composers employed atonal systems, including serialism
Rhythm	Complex rhythms; rhythmic patterns used; frequent absence of well-defined beat; frequent changes of meter
Harmony	High dissonance levels; new methods of chord construction in addition to triadic harmony
Tone color	Instruments sometimes played in extreme registers; unusual instruments and instrument groupings
Melody	Melodies sometimes derived from very short motives; melodies often not easy to sing because of extreme range and melodic intervals
Dynamics	Dynamic extremes employed; rapid dynamic fluctuations
Ensembles	Wide variety in size of ensembles from very small to gigantic
New organizational procedures	Serialism (twelve-tone)
General stylistic trends	Impressionism, primitivism, neoclassicism, expressionism
Vocal style	Combination of ordinary speaking, conventional singing, and *Sprechstimme*

***Portrait of Paul Revere* by John S. Copley.** Paul Revere was an American patriot during the Revolutionary War who is famous for his 1775 midnight ride to warn the colonists that the British were coming. He is holding a silver pot because he was a silversmith by trade.

In the seventeenth century, Europeans colonized and settled parts of North America, including the eastern seaboard of what is now the United States. By 1700, more than a million colonists were scattered up and down the Atlantic coast, living mainly on farms, sometimes in villages, and occasionally in trading towns such as Boston, New York, and Charleston. The music performed in this "new world" was of European origin. English ballad operas (spoken dialogue and songs with simple melodies) were particularly popular. One example was John Gay's *The Beggar's Opera*.

American artworks and styles of clothing were much simpler than those in Europe. When France was leading the fashion world with highly decorative rococo styles, Americans were concentrating more on establishing their cities, negotiating or fighting with the Native Americans, or dealing with their British government. Compare the *Portrait of Paul Revere* by the American artist John S. Copley (1737–1815) with the décor of an eighteenth-century French interior on page 105 to see the differences in style. Remember the reference to the American "yankee" (New Englander) in the song "Yankee Doodle" who tried to adopt the French style by merely sticking a feather in his hat? (See the Prelude to the Classical Era.)

Prelude | American Innovations in the Arts

The American colonies did have a rich local tradition in the crafts, however. Even today, the names Paul Revere and Duncan Phyfe suggest excellence in silversmithing and furniture making, respectively. Many of the most talented painters in America, however, had to travel to London to make their reputations. John S. Copley moved to England in 1774, and Benjamin West (1738–1820), who painted *The Death of General Wolfe,* became president of the Royal Academy and court painter to George III.

As far as American music of the eighteenth century is concerned, Francis Hopkinson (1737–1791), whose signature is on the Declaration of Independence, and William Billings (1746–1800) were two of the first American-born composers to gain widespread reputations.

Benjamin Franklin played a number of musical instruments and invented one called the glass harmonica that was popular in America, as well as in Europe. The glass harmonica is based on the sound one can get by running a wet finger around the edge of a crystal glass. The ringing sound that results changes in pitch depending on the size of the glass. Franklin's instrument has a series of different sized bowls that are stacked on their sides with a bar through them to allow them to spin around in a tub of water. The player had merely to touch the rims of various different bowls to sustain a ringing tone. Even Mozart composed a quintet for the glass harmonica and wind instruments.

The first North American city to have an opera house was the culturally diverse city of New Orleans. French, Italian, and German operas were performed there on a regular basis in the late eighteenth century, but such grand events in foreign languages were not all that popular in other American cities. Some composers, however, found that they could use the operatic stories to entertain American audiences by making "Englished" versions of them. The composer would translate the opera into English, replace the recitatives with spoken dialogue, and shorten the arias into something closer to the popular songs from the English ballad operas. Not much of the original opera was left other than the story. Again, this was at a time when the full-scale operas were being performed all over Europe and enjoyed

The Death of General Wolfe **by Benjamin West.** General Wolfe was a British commander who died in a 1759 battle in Quebec, Canada. Wolfe was an important character in the novel *The Virginians* (1857–1859), by William Makepeace Thackeray, about two American brothers who fought on two different sides in the American Revolution.

***Fur Traders Descending the Missouri* by George C. Bingham.**
Portrayals of the newly explored American West became very
popular in the early nineteenth century.

by a growing middle, as well as
upper, class.

In art, purely American scenes
did not become fashionable until
the early nineteenth century. Then,
painters of the newly explored
American West found a large and
enthusiastic audience. George C.
Bingham (1811–1879) painted
scenes of Missouri flatboatmen,
river ports, and trappers.

American literature did share
some of the same interests in
individual freedom, appreciation of
the uncontrollability of nature, and
the sense of mystery that were
popular in the romantic era in

Europe. James Fenimore Cooper
(1789–1851), for example, had been
born into a wealthy land-owning
family, but he tossed away his family advantages by getting expelled
from Yale University and running off
to be a sailor and then a farmer.
Both experiences influenced his
novels. *The Pilot* made use of his
knowledge about the sea, and *The
Last of the Mohicans* made use of
his knowledge about and experiences with Native Americans. The
name of American short-story writer
Edgar Allan Poe (1809–1849) became synonymous with the words
"grotesque" and "mysterious" after

such stories as *Murders in the Rue
Morgue, The Pit and the Pendulum,*
and *The Tell-Tale Heart.*

One area in which American
writers took the lead in Romantic
thinking was in the development
of the philosophy of transcenden-
talism. Just as the European
Romantics rejected the scientific
rationalism of the Enlightenment,
American writers Ralph Waldo
Emerson (1803–1882) and Henry
David Thoreau (1817–1862) wrote
about the necessity for people to
reject tradition and authority and see
humans and the natural world as
divine. Thoreau built himself a cabin
at Walden Pond in Massachusetts
in order to experience a quiet life
without the material possessions
and pressures of the city. He told of
his experiences in his book *Walden;
or, Life in the Woods* (1854).

Stephen Foster was among the
successful popular songwriters of
the nineteenth century, but in the
field of serious concert music, most
American music was still based on
European models. The Bohemian
composer Dvořák tried to encourage American composers to make
use of African American and Native
American music in their compositions when he visited the United
States in the 1890s. Amy Beach
(1867–1944) was one of many
American composers to successfully follow his advice.

Taste for European opera eventually spread beyond New Orleans,
and opera companies and philharmonic societies were established in
large cities nationwide. Another

type of music was also gaining popularity, however, and that was music for concert or marching bands. U.S. Marine Band leader John Philip Sousa (1854–1932) composed many works for band that have become American classics. One of the most popular is *Stars and Stripes Forever* (1897).

By the late nineteenth century the Industrial Revolution was changing the American landscape and changing the lives of most Americans. Such improvements as a coast-to-coast rail system helped move the United States to a position of world dominance. Many American investors made large sums of money in the process.

By the beginning of the twentieth century the favored painter in the United States was John Singer Sargent (1856–1925), whose handsome portraits of the landed, powerful, and financially secure were eagerly sought and displayed in the best New York and Boston townhouses. Americans tended to have less interest in the works of such European avant-garde artists as Pablo Picasso or such composers as Arnold Schoenberg or Igor Stravinsky.

The music we have been talking about to this point was all written down in notation that we can read today, and, therefore, we have a fairly good idea of how it sounded. But another great American musical tradition, and one that would eventually gain a great deal of popularity in Europe and the rest of the world, was not written down. It is called

jazz. Early jazz was primarily an improvised music that was not formally composed using traditional notation. It developed out of the work songs and field hollers of African American slaves, which were further influenced by band music in New Orleans. The earliest jazz developed in that city and is called either *New Orleans jazz* or *Dixieland jazz.*

World War I (1914–1918) opened up many factory jobs in northern cities such as Kansas City, Chicago, and New York, and among the African Americans who moved from the South to those cities were jazz musicians. The instrumentation and style of jazz changed in the North, with bands getting much larger to appeal to large-scale Caucasian audiences who wanted to dance to the music. Swing jazz developed through the 1930s and continued to be very popular until the end of World War II. Swing experienced a popular revival in the 1990s.

Another style of music that was uniquely American and popular during the 1890s and after was called *ragtime.* Played on the banjo, piano, or by bands, ragtime is named for its "ragged" rhythms. Scott Joplin (1868–1917) was not the first to play the music, but he became the most famous ragtime pianist and composer. Joplin also composed operas, but he couldn't get the funding to produce them with full costuming, staging, and orchestra during his lifetime. *Treemonisha* (1911) was finally

Portrait of Lady Agnew by **John Singer Sargent.** Wealthy Americans wanted complimentary portraits of themselves and had little interest in the experimental European styles of painting.

produced in the 1970s, and Joplin's ragtime piano music experienced a revival of popularity after it was featured in the Academy Award–winning movie *The Sting* (1973).

As a result of the Great Depression that began with the fall of the stock market in 1929, the federal government commissioned murals and decorations for public buildings as part of its public works program. Painters such as Edward Hopper (1882–1967) portrayed commonplace aspects of American life. Other painters of the depression era were drawn to political subjects. Some, such as Thomas Hart Benton (1889–1975), idealized the worker as the

Early Sunday Morning by **Edward Hopper.** This painting portrays a plain and simple American street in the early morning during the Great Depression of the early 1930s.

very new and dissonant style. Ives would also, on occasion, have several rhythms going on at the same time, which was new for a music that developed out of the European traditions. Ives celebrated his American identity in his music by quoting American popular or patriotic melodies in his serious concert works.

In the field of popular music, American musicians combined African American blues and rhythm and blues with Caucasian American country styles to create rock-and-roll music during the late 1940s and early 1950s. Rock, as well as jazz, soon gained international popularity. Given that so many major performers in the fields of both jazz and rock music today are not Americans, it is easy for some to think of both styles as completely international. The fact is that, in their roots, jazz and rock music came into being as the result of the particular American mixture of transplanted Africans and transplanted Europeans.

backbone and real hero of the American people.

Jazz continued to develop new styles through the 1940s and beyond, and it also became an important influence on American classical composers such as George Gershwin (1898–1937), William Grant Still (1895–1978), and Aaron Copland (1900–1990).

America's first "modernist" composer was Charles Ives (1874–1954), whose music used tonality in new ways. Whereas Europeans such as Schoenberg were rejecting tonality completely, Ives wrote music with more than one tonality operating at the same time, as did Europeans like Stravinsky. This technique created a

30 | American Music before World War II

When I hear music I fear no danger, I am invulnerable, I see no foe, I am related to the earliest times and to the latest.

—WRITER HENRY DAVID THOREAU (1817–1862)

Listening Introduction

Listen to "When Jesus Wept," by Billings, and make notes about what you hear. Give some attention to the following:

▌ Can you detect the tempo?

▌ Can you detect the meter?

▌ Can you detect the texture?

▌ Can you tell the number and voice types of the singers?

▌ Can you tell the language of the text?

Keep these notes to compare with your impressions about each song after you study the information in this chapter.

The Seventeenth Century

Striking contrasts run through the history of music in the United States. Native Americans had their own musical instruments, traditional melodies, and dance rhythms, but those had little influence on the musical practices of the original European settlers. Similarly, African slaves had rich cultural and musical traditions, but their music did not have much affect on the music in the lives of the settlers. The music of the founding fathers and first citizens of the United States came from their European homelands.

Some Protestants thought music too distracting to use in their church services. Many of the Pilgrims, however, loved and practiced music, but they had little spare time for very much entertainment in their new land. They had come to the new world as religious dissenters, and their music was functional and used mostly for worship in church and at home. It consisted primarily of **psalms** and hymns, with tunes taken from older hymns or folk songs brought over from England and Holland.

The first extent book printed in the Colonies was a new rhymed translation of the psalms called the *Bay Psalm Book* (1640). It was published with musical notation in 1698. Because few of the Pilgrims could read music, a singing practice called **"lining out"** was developed, in which a leader, usually the preacher or deacon, would sing each phrase of the song alone and then pause for the congregation to repeat what he had just sung. That practice allowed everyone to participate in the musical aspect of the service. A system of notation was eventually developed to help untrained singers "read" music. It was called "shape note" notation because each note of the scale had a different shape.

The Eighteenth Century

Secular music began to flourish in the Colonies during the 1700s, particularly in such major cities as New York, Boston, Philadelphia, and Charleston. The people in these cities remained in close contact with the artistic life of Europe through shipping and trading contacts. As the cities prospered, a growing middle class acquired both the leisure and the money to support the arts.

Beginning in the 1730s, concerts and other musical events were organized and featured professional musicians with European training. These professionals worked both as performers and as "professors" of music. They taught music to gentleman amateurs who, in turn, supported the rapid growth of music in America. Their supporters included Thomas Jefferson, one of the outstanding music patrons of his day and an amateur violinist himself, and Benjamin Franklin, who served capably as performer, inventor of an instrument (the glass harmonica), and music critic. Another of the gentleman amateurs, Francis Hopkinson (1737–1791), wrote songs and claimed to be the "first native of the United States who has produced a musical composition."

Music by composer William Billings

By 1770, there was a group of American composers with enough in common to be considered a "school." The leader of this group was **William Billings** of Boston (1746–1800). Billings and his school of compatriots did not always follow traditional European styles and rules of composition. In fact, Billings was proud to assert that he was "not confined to any Rules for Composition by any that went before him." He went on to say that "Nature is the Best Dictator, for all the hard dry rules will not enable any Person to form an Air without Genius. Nature must inspire the thought." The result of this attitude was a distinctive style of music that some Europeans considered crude and inept but that had its own profound power and grace and had a lasting effect on the development of American music.

Billings, a tanner by trade, published a number of collections of his own compositions, among them *The New England Psalm Singer* (1770), engraved by Paul Revere; *Singing Masters Assistant* (1778); and *The Psalm Singers Amusement* (1781). These publications contained hymns, **anthems, rounds,** and **fuging tunes**—hymns or psalm tunes with brief polyphonic sections that have imitative entrances. The National Copyright Act of 1790 allowed composers to gain income from the publication and sale of their music.

One of Billings's most beautiful and popular compositions is the round (canon) "When Jesus Wept" from *The New England Psalm Tunes.* The song "When Jesus Wept," the anthem "Be Glad Then America," and the hymn tune "Chester," all by Billings, were used by the twentieth-century American composer William Schuman in his orchestral work *New England Triptych.*

Listening Guide

"When Jesus Wept" WILLIAM BILLINGS

CD 2
Track 21

Year: ca. 1776

Texture: Monophonic first and last phrases, polyphonic when new voices join in

Tempo: Moderato

Meter: Triple

Form: Round (single melody sung at different times, allowing four parts to be heard at once)

Voices: SATB

Language: English

Duration: 2:54

Special feature: The simple-sounding song becomes full-sounding and complex when all four
voices sing it polyphonically. The texture then thins out as each voice completes its second
time through and drops off. This allows the ending to return to the simplicity of the beginning.

	Timing	Text	Voices
21	0:00	When Jesus wept, the falling tear, In mercy flowed beyond all bound; When Jesus groaned, a trembling fear, Seized all the guilty world around.	All sing the complete text together one time
	0:34	When Jesus wept, the falling tear,	Sopranos (S) begin to sing alone
	0:42	In mercy flowed beyond all bound;	S continue, altos (A) sing the beginning
	0:50	When Jesus groaned, a trembling fear,	S and A continue, tenors (T) begin
	0:58	Seized all the guilty world around.	S, A, T continue, basses (B) begin
	1:07	When Jesus wept, the falling tear, In mercy flowed beyond all bound; When Jesus groaned, a trembling fear, Seized all the guilty world around.	Sopranos begin again and stop when they reach the end. All other voices do the same. The basses, who entered last, finish the last section of text alone.

The Nineteenth Century

The musical culture of nineteenth-century America was marked by two significant phenomena. The first was the division between what we now call "classical"
and "popular" music. Classical music was meant either for serious study and listening or for religious purposes, whereas popular music aimed only to entertain.
Earlier music had served both functions. For example, the eighteenth-century
fuging tunes were written for worship and enlightenment, but they also served as
enjoyable social entertainments.

The second phenomenon of nineteenth-century music was the imitation of
German music by American composers, a trend that became most evident after
the Civil War. By that time, the pattern of immigration to the United States had
changed, as more people came from the European mainland, particularly
Germany, and fewer from the United Kingdom. The Europeans brought to
America the ideas of the romantic movement, which was strongest in Germany.
Soon romanticism influenced every area of American musical life.

Popular music in the years preceding the Civil War included many extremely
sentimental songs written and published primarily for use by amateurs in their

own homes. The greatest songwriter of the period, **Stephen Foster** (1826–1864), did not follow in the European lieder tradition in which the songs took a great amount of skill and training to perform, but instead wrote for the amateur players and singers in parlors of America. Foster wrote his own texts, and his songs articulated the attitudes and thoughts of the average American in a way that no other writer had in the past.

Although his formal musical training was not extensive, Foster had an unmistakable gift for melody. Many of his songs are filled with nostalgic yearning, often for an unattainable love. Both the text and music of his best-known songs, such as "Jeanie with the Light Brown Hair," are gentle and tender. Foster also wrote many songs for the minstrel shows that were a popular form of entertainment, both before and after the Civil War. Dance tunes and songs using the dialects of African Americans were the basis of the shows, and Foster contributed many songs, including his well-known "Oh! Susanna" and "Camptown Races."

Listening Guide

"Jeanie with the Light Brown Hair" STEPHEN FOSTER

CD 5
Track 1

Year: 1854

Texture: Homophonic

Tempo: Moderato

Meter: Quadruple

Form: Strophic

Voices and instrumentation: Baritone voice accompanied by violin and piano

Language: English

Duration: 3:24

Special features: The piano accompanies the singer all the way through. The violin is added to that in a free-sounding **ad libitum** (additional, not essential to the basic accompaniment) style. The violin adds much interest to the performance. The violin and piano introduction, break, and ending are each four bars long (the same length as two lines of text).

Note: One full verse has been left out of this recording.

Timing	Text	What to listen for
0:00		Violin and piano introduction
0:17	I dream of Jeanie with the light brown hair, Born, like a zephyr, on the summer air;	Piano accompaniment without violin
0:33	I see her tripping where the bright streams play, Happy are the daisies that dance on her way.	Violin adds pizzicato chords
0:48	Many were the wild notes her merry voice would pour, Many were the blithe birds that warbled them o'er:	Violin adds an ad libitum line
1:06	Oh! I dream of Jeanie with the light brown hair, Floating, like a zephyr, on the soft summer air.	Rubato on "Oh!"
1:29		Violin and piano break
1:44	I long for Jeanie with the daydawn smile, Radiant in gladness, warm with winning guile;	Violin sustains double-stops (two or more notes produced simultaneously)

Timing	Text	What to listen for
2:00	I hear her melodies, like joys gone by, Sighing round my heart o'er the fond hopes that die:	Violin adds an ad libitum line
2:17	Sighing like the night wind and sobbing like the rain, Wailing for the lost one that comes not again:	Violin sustains double-stops
2:35	Oh! I sigh for Jeanie with the light brown hair, Floating, like a zephyr, on the soft summer air.	Sustained notes on violin
3:02		Violin and piano ending

Whereas Foster wrote in a vernacular style and drew from uniquely American experience, composers of sacred music centered their attention on European styles. The Civil War and Reconstruction years were marked by a growing taste for hymns adapted from the music of the great European composers, from Palestrina to Mendelssohn. Lowell Mason (1792–1872) composed and adapted many such hymns. His efforts also brought music education into the public school curriculum for the first time.

Much American music in the classical tradition included original compositions, arrangements of songs and dances, and sets of variations on well-known tunes written for the piano, the favorite instrument of the romantic era. American piano builders became some of the best in the world. One of the most colorful and talented figures in American music before the Civil War was a virtuoso pianist from New Orleans, **Louis Moreau Gottschalk** (1829–1869), who adopted many of the mannerisms of Liszt and was known in Europe as the "American Chopin." He composed numerous works for both piano and orchestra, many of which contained exaggerated sentimentality, and he also used such exotic musical materials as African Caribbean rhythms and Creole melodies. He had the piano imitate strummed chords to sound like a banjo in his piece *The Banjo,* and he quoted "The Star-Spangled Banner," "Yankee Doodle," and "Hail Columbia" in his solo piano piece *The Union.*

Most of the music performed by American orchestras was written by European composers, although the works of the American George Bristow (1825–1898) gained some attention. Bristow wrote six symphonies in a style similar to Mendelssohn's. The New York Philharmonic, of which he was a member, was founded in 1842. A typical orchestral program in this period carefully mixed "heavy" music (single movements of symphonies, rarely complete ones) with "lighter" music (marches and overtures).

After the Civil War

From the end of the Civil War to World War I, German Romantic music had its greatest influence. Symphony orchestras were formed in many of the major cities, and large concert halls were built, including Carnegie Hall in New York (1891). Conservatories were established, and music departments appeared in colleges and universities.

A group of Romantic composers emerged in Boston under John K. Paine (1839–1906), who became the first professor of music at Harvard. Other talented members of the Boston group were Horatio Parker (1863–1919) of Yale and George Chadwick (1854–1931). These men composed instrumental and choral music: symphonies, sonatas, chamber music, and oratorios. Stylistically, they were closely allied with the early German Romantics, such as Schubert, Mendelssohn, and Schumann.

Amy Beach (1867–1944) also lived in Boston and composed in the Romantic tradition. Her output included more than one hundred songs, short piano pieces, sacred and secular choral works, a piano quintet, and a symphony (1894). Her compositions for chorus and orchestra, *Three Browning Songs* (1900) and *The Canticle of the Sun* (1928), were among her most widely known works. Beach was recognized as a gifted pianist and composer in both the United States and Europe, which she toured from 1910 to 1914. Beginning in 1885, much of her music was published by Arthur P. Schmidt, an early champion of American female composers, including Beach, Margaret Ruthven Lang, Helen Hood, and Clara Kathleen Rogers.

Beach very much admired the work of the English poet Robert Browning (1812–1889). In 1900, she set three of his poems to music and dedicated the music to the Browning Society of Boston. The group of three songs begins with "The Year's at Spring," with its famous line "God's in His Heaven, all's right with the world!" and ends with an effective musical rendering of "I send my heart up to Thee." As a center piece, Beach chose the poem "Ah, Love, but a Day." She manipulated the text by repeating certain words and lines to facilitate the musical structure she designed to convey the overall quality of the poem. The piece consists of two larger sections. Each begins quietly, builds to a climax, then subsides. Between them is the brief refrain, on the words "Ah, Love, but a day, and the world has changed!"

Each successive setting of "Ah, Love" is heard as an increase of musical energy, growing toward a climax. The second "Ah, Love" is louder and higher than the first; the third is louder and longer; the fourth, the loudest, longest, and highest, is the climax of this progress and of the entire song. The craftsmanship exemplified in "Ah, Love, but a Day" made Beach a respected and popular composer during her lifetime.

Edward MacDowell (1860–1908) also came under the influence of German Romanticism but avoided the established instrumental forms in favor of program music. Having studied in Germany, he went on to achieve success there as a pianist, composer, and teacher. He wrote several tone poems for orchestra, an

Amy Beach with four other American female song writers in April 1924.
From left to right: Harriet Ware, Gena Branscombe, Mary Turner Salter, Ethel Glenn Hier, and Amy Beach.

Listening Guide

"Ah, Love, but a Day" AMY BEACH

CD 2
Tracks 22–24

Year: 1900

Texture: Homophonic

Tempo: Molto expessione (very expressive), which means that the
tempo changes to fit the expressiveness of the text

Meter: Quadruple

Form: Two sections with a refrain, or repeated line sung to the
same melody

Voice and instrumentation: Soprano with piano

Duration: 3:31

Language: English

Timing	Text	Dynamic and tempo changes
Part I		
22 0:00	1. Ah, Love, but a day,	
	And the world has changed!	*piano*
0:24	2. Ah, Love, but a day,	*mezzo forte*
	And the world has changed!	*decrescendo to piano*
0:43	The sun's away,	*crescendo, agitato* (agitated)
	And the bird estranged;	*crescendo*
	The wind has dropped,	*crescendo*
	And the sky's deranged;	*crescendo to forte*
0:56	Summer,	*forte*
	Summer has stopped,	*decrescendo and ritard*
	Summer has stopped.	*pianissimo, a tempo*
Refrain		
23 1:24	3. Ah, Love, but a day,	
	And the world has changed!	*decrescendo*
Part II		
24 1:52	Look in my eyes!	
	Wilt thou change too?	
2:07	Look in my eyes!	
	Wilt thou change too?	
2:22	Should I fear surprise?	*crescendo, agitato*
	Shall I find aught new	*crescendo*
	In the old and dear,	*accelerando*
	In the good and true,	*crescendo*
	With the changing year?	*crescendo*
2:40	4. Ah, Love,	*fortissimo, decrescendo*
	Look in my eyes.	*decrescendo, ritard*
	Look in my eyes,	
	Wilt thou change too?	*decrescendo, pianissimo, dying away*

often-performed piano concerto, many songs and choral pieces, and a number of small character pieces for piano.

Late in the century, a few American musicians began to react against the domination of German ideals and attitudes. Some American composers decided to make use of Native and African American themes—a challenge put forth by Bohemian composer Antonín Dvořák on his visit to America from 1892 to 1895. Arthur Farwell (1872–1952) was an American composer who accepted Dvořák's ideas and concentrated on using Native American themes in his works. Those who reacted against German influence also took interest in new musical ideas from France and Russia. Charles T. Griffes (1884–1920), whose creative talents were cut short by his premature death, showed the influence of Debussy, Ravel, and Stravinsky in his early works. An interest in Asian music influenced some of his last works.

Summary

Music in seventeenth-century America was primarily functional, used mostly for worship in church and at home. Secular music began to flourish in the eighteenth century, especially in the larger cities. Although a group of composers led by William Billings created their own American style, most American music continued to be based on European styles.

Nineteenth-century American music was marked by two significant phenomena: a division between "classical" and "popular" music and the imitation of German music by American composers. Although the songs of Stephen Foster and the instrumental works

of Louis Moreau Gottschalk incorporate many uniquely American elements, most composers continued to imitate Europeans. In the post–Civil War years, the Boston area produced several notable composers, including Amy Beach, whose style was much like that of the German Romantics. Late in the century, some composers reacted against the domination of German ideals and attitudes. Arthur Farwell used Native American themes in his music, and the works of Charles Griffes were influenced by French impressionists.

New People and Concepts

ad libitum	lining out	rounds
Amy Beach	Louis Moreau Gottschalk	Stephen Foster
anthems	psalms	William Billings
fuging tunes		

Finale

Listen again to "When Jesus Wept" by Billings and compare your impressions now with your notes from your first listening. You should now be able to answer the following questions:

❚ What is the tempo?

❚ What is the meter?

❚ What is the texture?

❚ How many vocal parts do you hear and what voice types sing them?

❚ What is the language of the text?

31 | Early Jazz Styles

Maybe our forefathers couldn't keep their language together when they were taken away from Africa, but this—the blues—was a language we invented to let people know we had something to say. And we've been saying it pretty strong ever since.
—GUITARIST/SINGER/SONGWRITER B. B. KING (BORN IN 1925)

Listening Introduction

Listen to the example of music that represents this chapter, "Lost Your Head Blues," and make notes about what you hear. Give some attention to the following:

▍ Can you detect the meter?

▍ Can you tell the gender of the singer?

▍ Can you tell what instruments are used to play the accompaniment?

▍ Can you understand the text?

▍ Does the piece have a general mood that supports the meaning of the text?

Keep these notes to compare with your impressions about the song after you study the information in this chapter.

Jazz is considered by many to be America's greatest contribution to music. Its impact on American society has been enormous, and its influence on world culture has been far reaching. Its message has been direct, vital, and immediate, enabling it to hurdle cultural, linguistic, and political barriers.

Origins of Jazz

The precise origins and early history of **jazz** cannot be chronicled because early jazz was neither notated nor recorded; it was **improvised** and existed only in performance. We know that the music was rooted in the American South, particularly in New Orleans, and that it was created by African Americans and influenced by some characteristics of both African and European music. Before going too deeply into just what elements of jazz are African and what are European, we need to discuss something about African music.

Africa is a very large continent with many diverse tribal groups and a variety of musical practices in different areas. To find the African roots of jazz, we have to pay attention to musical practices in the Western part of the continent, because that was the homeland of most Africans who were brought to the new world as slaves.

One general point about African music is that it involves everyone. The concept of people sitting quietly as part of a large audience and just listening to performers is not part of the traditional African experience. One can find concert halls there today only because they have been influenced by other cultures of the

Music is considered the rhythm of life by these African dancers.

modern world. Instead of listening passively, an African might dance or tap rhythms to accompany what someone else plays, music is commonly thought of as part of the rhythm of life.

For much of its history, the tribes of northwestern Africa had no written languages. In order to keep track of governmental and historical information, singers called **griots** (pronounced "grios") memorized and repeated songs that kept track of their people and history. Griots were highly respected in their societies, and what they sang was extremely important to their cultures.

In addition to the importance of lyrics, characteristics of African music include:

1. A practice known as **call and response,** in which a phrase sung by a leader is responded to by a group. (Note: This is different from the practice of "lining out" discussed in Chapter 30 because the response is not a repetition of the call.)
2. **Polyrhythms,** which are several distinctly different rhythm patterns being played at the same time.
3. Repetition of individual rhythmic patterns. This is essential when music is polyrhythmic because it allows the listeners to hear one rhythm as it repeats and then move attention to another as it also repeats itself. Without a lot of repetition, polyrhythmic music would sound chaotic.
4. Harmony, such as the chordal accompaniments common in European music, does not exist. Where harmony occurs, it exists mainly as a by-product of several melodies played or sung together.
5. A variety of scale patterns are used. Some are five-tone scales and some closer to the seven-tone scales found in European music.
6. A great variety of percussion instruments are used.

Our African listening example comes from Sierra Leone, in northwest Africa. It was recorded in a small village on Christmas Day in 1962. The villagers are entertaining the chairman of the Public Service Commission, who is visiting for the Christmas celebration. (Note: Both the Muslim and the Christian religions are practiced in Sierra Leone.) The male solo singer is probably a farmer from the village.

Listening Guide

"Village Celebration" THE MENDE TRIBE OF SIERRA LEONE

CD 5
Track 2

Year: 1962

Tempo: Moderate

Meter: Quadruple with polyrhythms playing against the
basic beat

Form: No structured repeating sections. Our example is only a
short section of a much longer celebration.

Instrumentation: One *segbure* (a rattle made from a gourd with
pebbles inside and netting sewn with beads around the outside;
the beads can be snapped against the gourd for a special
effect), one *sangbei* (a wooden drum about two feet high with
metal rings attached to rattle when the drum is played), and
a mouth organ (very soft in the background, probably
underrecorded)

Vocalists: The primary singer is a male leader. Responses are by
the villagers.

Duration: 6:20

Special features: The responses from the villagers often repeat the
same phrase, but occasionally the phrase is varied. The lead
vocals are improvised. The villagers are probably dancing along
with their singing responses.

We will hear many of these characteristics of African music in the jazz examples
we listen to.

Ragtime

Two styles of jazz-related American music that are based on African elements are
ragtime and the **blues.** Ragtime gets its name from melodies played in "ragged"
or syncopated rhythms. It is not polyrhythmic as African music often is, but the
syncopations come from the rhythms of Africa. An important European characteristic of ragtime is that it has a regular, sectional formal structure that could be
diagrammed with repeating and contrasting letters, just as we have outlined
form in the European examples earlier in this text.

Ragtime was popularized as the music used for cakewalk dances during the
1890s. It was played on banjos, fiddles (violins), the piano, or by bands. The piano
became the preferred instrument for many players, including **Scott Joplin**
(1868–1917), whose "rags" are still performed today. Other notable ragtime
pianist-composers of the 1890s include James Scott, Tom Turpin, and Joseph
Lamb. Ragtime music is not really jazz because it is notated and performed without improvisation. Jazz always involves improvisation. The blues is closer to jazz
in every respect and is often played by jazz musicians.

The Blues

Chapter 31
WebQuest

Early Jazz
Samples

As we said earlier, music was part of most life experiences in Africa. African slaves would often work to the rhythms of their songs. These **field hollers** and **work songs** formed the basis of the blues. The earliest type of blues is called "country blues" because it was performed in the rural South. In this type of blues, the singer often accompanies himself or herself on a guitar. The song text is usually very personal and full of feeling, although not always sad. It is sung in a rhythmically and structurally loose manner, allowing the singer to improvise new lines of text or more elaborate accompaniments.

By around 1900, the blues had developed into a highly structured style, with distinct forms for both the lyrics and the melodies. These forms reflect European musical traditions. African Americans had heard and sung structured songs of European origin with chordal accompaniments in churches, and they worked those types of structures into their own music.

The standard blues lyrical pattern consisted of two rhyming lines of poetry, with the first line repeated to create an "AAB" form, as in the following example:

> *Now listen baby, you so good and sweet,*
>
> *Now listen baby, you so good and sweet,*
>
> *I want to stay 'round you, if I have to beg in the street.*

The blues typically follows a twelve-bar harmonic progression with four bars for each of the three sections of text such as those above. Rhythmically, the blues is usually in quadruple meter, with each beat being subdivided unevenly (a flow of "long, short, long, short, long, short, long, short" pattern for each four beats). This flow creates a more "relaxed" feel than the evenly subdivided beats that are typically found in music of European traditions.

Blues singers often lower certain notes of the scale (the third, seventh, and, in complex jazz styles, the fifth) to give the melody a relaxed effect. These lowered notes are called **blue notes.** It is not certain whether blue notes were derived from African scale structures or became standard on their own in America. Blues singers also use other techniques that add to the relaxed flow of their music including sliding from one note to another.

The "Empress of the Blues" was **Bessie Smith** (1894–1937). Smith started her career singing the blues and jazz in minstrel shows, night clubs, and theaters. She sang and made records with a number of prominent jazz musicians throughout the 1920s and 1930s. In 1929 she appeared in the film *St. Louis Blues.* The musicians at the recording session said that Smith improvised "Lost Your Head Blues" in the studio because they needed one more song to make use of the time they had. By the time of her death in a 1936 auto accident, Bessie Smith had recorded close to 200 songs. "The Live Experience: Improvisation" discusses this quality of jazz and blues music.

Blues singer Bessie Smith

Listening Guide

"Lost Your Head Blues" BESSIE SMITH

CD 2
Tracks 25–29

Year: 1926

Meter: Quadruple with uneven beat subdivisions

Form: Five choruses of the twelve-bar blues

Voice and instrumentation: Bessie Smith with cornet (Joe Smith) and piano (Fletcher Henderson)

Language: English

Duration: 2:55

Special feature: African roots of the blues can be heard in many ways. The blue notes and sliding between notes come from the way African singers sang. Call and response is heard, although the responses are played on the cornet instead of being sung by a group. European influences are evident in the structure of the music and text, as well as in the chordal accompaniment played by the piano.

	Timing	Text	
25	0:00		Cornet and piano introduction
	0:11	I was with you baby when you didn't have a dime.	first chorus
		I was with you baby when you didn't have a dime.	
		Now since you got plenty money you have throw'd your good gal down.	
26	0:43	Once ain't for always, two ain't for twice.	second chorus
		Once ain't for always, two ain't for twice.	
		When you get a good gal you better treat her nice.	
27	1:15	When you were lonesome I tried to treat you kind.	third chorus
		When you were lonesome I tried to treat you kind.	
		But since you got money, it's done changed your mind.	
28	1:48	I'm gonna leave baby, ain't gonna say good-bye.	fourth chorus
		I'm gonna leave baby, ain't gonna say good-bye.	
		But I'll write you and tell you the reason why.	
29	2:19	Days are lonesome, nights are long.	fifth chorus
		Days are lonesome, nights are so long.	
		I'm a good old gal, but I've just been treated wrong.	

"Hearing the Difference: Beach's 'Ah, Love, but a Day' and Smith's 'Lost Your Head Blues'" compares these two American songs.

Jazz Styles

In the early 1900s, New Orleans was an active place. It was in the dance halls, gambling places, and brothels of the red-light district known as Storyville that **New Orleans jazz,** also called **Dixieland,** was born and nurtured. New Orleans jazz combos were usually made up of one or two cornets (or trumpets), one clarinet,

THE LIVE EXPERIENCE
Improvisation

Improvisation is an important part of jazz, particularly within small instrumental groups, although even big bands that play previously arranged music allow individual players to improvise solos from time to time. Jazz improvisation is a process of spontaneously inventing a new melody based either on an existing melody or on the chords to be played with the original melody. In its simplest form, improvisation can mean the addition of a few extra notes around the notes of a given melody or changes in the basic rhythms of that melody. In the most advanced form of improvisation, it may be possible to discern any suggestion of the original melody. In all cases the improvisation remains limited to the fundamental structure of that melody.

In traditional jazz, improvisation is not a "do your own thing" practice, but it does allow performers to put their own particular musical personality into their playing or singing. Still, the improviser must be aware of and sensitive to what the other musicians are playing so that the music makes sense as a whole.

The structure of the blues is so well established and understood by blues musicians that entire songs can be improvised, as Bessie Smith is reported to have done with "Lost Your Head Blues." Such free improvisation was possible because the pianist knew exactly what chords were needed when and the cornet player knew that it was his job to supply responses to Smith's vocal phrases.

and one trombone, which formed the **front line** (instruments responsible for playing the melodies); string bass, guitar or banjo, sometimes piano, and sometimes drums made up the **rhythm section** (responsible for the basic beat and accompaniment).

The most outstanding feature of New Orleans jazz was **collective improvisation.** Against a background supplied by the rhythm section, the front-line players improvised on well-known melodies. Usually the cornet played variations of the melody, while the clarinet improvised an upper melodic line and the trombone supplied yet another improvised melody below the cornet. All three instruments in the front line employed a lively, syncopated style against a steady beat maintained by the rhythm section.

A variety of factors, including the closing of the Storyville district in 1917, led to the migration of jazz musicians and their music to other parts of the country. In the Roaring Twenties, jazz spread over a wide geographic area, including Chicago, which became the scene of some important developments. Whereas the heart of the New Orleans style was collective improvisation, the focus of attention in the Chicago bands shifted to the *individual* soloist. By far the most important jazz soloist in the Chicago style was **Louis Armstrong** (1900–1971), a young cornetist from New Orleans.

Rhythmically, Armstrong's music was the embodiment of what came to be known as **swing.** His horn style—highly embellished, full of swoops, sudden dips, and darts—influenced the performing style of all later cornet and trumpet players and other instrumentalists as well. His brilliant **scat singing,** in which the singer sings nonsense syllables instead of words, has become a basic element of jazz vocal styles. Because the singer does not have to worry about a specific text,

HEARING THE DIFFERENCE
Beach's "Ah, Love, but a Day" and Smith's "Lost Your Head Blues"

These songs—both American and both written in the early twentieth century—are being compared here because of stylistic rather than historical differences. Amy Beach was an American composer trained in the classical European traditions. In this case, the song displays the influences of romantic *lieder* in that it uses many dynamic and tempo changes that fit the expressiveness of the very poetic and formal text. Blues singer Bessie Smith did not write the music to "Lost Your Head Blues" out on the page, she just sang as she was feeling it. She might even have made it up at the recording session. The text is casual, and very expressive of honest emotion.

	Ah, Love, but a Day	Lost Your Head Blues
Tempo	Molto espressivo	Not notated, but it could also be called molto espressivo
Meter	Quadruple with even beat subdivisions	Quadruple with uneven beat subdivisions
Lyrics	The lyrics are taken from a poem, with some lines being repeated, including a first phrase that returns as a refrain. The language is poetic and formal.	The lyrics are very casual and very much like speech that is communicative, but not formally planned out. The language includes "throwed," "ain't," and "gonna."
Form	Structured in two large sections with a refrain between them	Structured according to the tradition of the twelve-bar blues with the text following the AAB form for every twelve-bar chorus
Instrumentation	Soprano singer accompanied by piano	Deep-voiced mezzo soprano accompanied by piano with a cornet playing responses to vocal phrases
Dynamics	Dynamics are used very expressively to support the text in which the fear that her love might change is central.	The singer sounds relaxed about reporting the message that she has been badly treated and is planning to leave the man.

scat singing allows singers the same kind of improvisatory freedom instrumentalists have always enjoyed.

By the mid-1930s, with the national economy slowly recovering from the depression, larger ensembles began to make a comeback. Gradually, jazz moved out of the saloons and into ballrooms and dance halls. The "big band" sound, as it became known, soon reached an even larger audience via radio. During this period, New York became the cultural and communication center of America, replacing Chicago as the major jazz city. Thus began the swing era, which lasted roughly from 1935 to 1950.

Swing featured big bands of fifteen to seventeen players, with the old New Orleans front line of cornet, clarinet, and trombone increased to include sections of trumpets and trombones, along with woodwind sections of clarinets and

Jazz musician Louis Armstrong and his band

saxophones. The swing band rhythm sections included piano, string bass, sometimes guitar, and drums.

Sometimes the respect musicians and fans had for jazz band leaders caused them to call them by titles of European royalty—for example "Duke" Ellington, "King" Oliver, and "Count" Basie. **Duke Ellington** (Edward Kennedy Ellington, 1899–1974) was born into a middle-class African American family in Washington D.C. As a child, he studied both art and music; his piano studies included the popular ragtime music. Although an accomplished painter, he opted for a career in music and began to coordinate and lead bands for dances and social events, playing simple arrangements of popular tunes.

Jazz musician Duke Ellington

After relocating to New York in 1923, Ellington's band began to incorporate some of the new jazz styles that had started to become popular. In 1927, they started a five-year stint as the house band of Harlem's Cotton Club. During this time, Ellington's compositions and arrangements moved him and his band, which he began calling his "orchestra," into the forefront of the emerging big band style. Ellington's music from this era was featured in the 1984 movie *Cotton Club.*

"It Don't Mean a Thing, If It Ain't Got That Swing," was recorded in New York in 1932, just after Ellington's time at the Cotton Club and just before his orchestra began a long period of touring all over the United States and Europe as one of the most popular of the swing bands.

Listening Guide

"It Don't Mean a Thing, If It Ain't Got That Swing" DUKE ELLINGTON

CD 5
Track 3

Year: 1932

Meter: Quadruple

Form: AABA song form

Instrumentation: Voice (Ivie Anderson), three trumpets, two trombones, three saxophones, piano,
   banjo, bass, drums

Language: English

Duration: 3:10

Special feature: The sound of the trumpets is not as brilliant as usual because the players have
   put mutes in the bells of their instruments to cut down the sound.

	Timing	Text	What to listen for
3	0:00		Band introduction with scat vocals
	0:11		Improvised solo on muted trumpet with backing and responses by band.
	0:46	It don't mean a thing if it ain't got that swing.	Vocal with blue note on "ain't"
		It don't mean a thing all you've got to do is sing.	Same melody repeated
	1:03	It makes no difference if it's sweet or hot.	New melody (the **bridge**)
		Just keep that rhythm give it ev'rything you've got.	
	1:13	It don't mean a thing if it ain't got that swing.	Beginning melody returns
	1:22		Improvised saxophone solo
	2:41		Scat improvisation in vocal
	2:49	It don't mean a thing if it ain't got the swing.	Fadeout at end

By the time of his death in 1974, Ellington had heard himself described as one of the great American composers. His large body of work, from popular songs to jazz suites to simple arrangements of the twelve-bar blues, is still popular today.

Other African American swing band leaders included Fletcher Henderson, Count Basie (William Basie), and Cab Calloway. Caucasian musicians led swing bands as well. Among them were Benny Goodman, Harry James, Glenn Miller, Artie Shaw, Tommy Dorsey, and Woody Herman. The bands' swing styles varied depending on the tastes of the leaders, the skills of the star soloists, and the types of arrangements that were written for them. In general, swing music was very smooth and polished. The aim was to please the listening and dancing audience, which was an important part of life during World War II.

Summary

Perhaps the most significant American contribution to music is jazz, a musical language that grew out of the African American experience and musical traditions from Africa. Jazz was also influenced by formal structure and chordal accompaniments of European origin. Two styles of music that informed early jazz were ragtime and the blues. Ragtime is not technically jazz because it is formally composed and is performed without improvisation. Its "ragged" rhythms do, however, come from the same roots as jazz, and its energy has been an influence on jazz.

The blues developed a very structured twelve-bar form with lyrics that follow an "AAB" pattern of repetition and contrast. African elements in the blues include the use of blue notes, call and response, and uneven beat subdivisions.

Jazz bands first played in New Orleans. They played for all types of private and civic functions, including dances and entertainment in the red-light district of Storyville. New Orleans jazz bands used collective improvisation among the members of the front line, with accompaniment of a rhythm section.

When Storyville closed in 1917, jazz musicians moved to northern cities, including Chicago, where a new jazz style began featuring individual soloists over the collective improvisation of three or four players playing at the same time. As jazz developed further in New York, jazz bands grew bigger and began playing in a style known as swing. Swing bands played for dancers and at clubs such as the Cotton Club in Harlem. Duke Ellington led one of the most popular of the swing bands, which he called his orchestra.

New People and Concepts

Bessie Smith	field hollers	polyrhythms
blue notes	front line	ragtime
blues	griots	rhythm section
bridge	improvisation	scat singing
call and response	jazz	Scott Joplin
collective improvisation	Louis Armstrong	swing
Dixieland	New Orleans Jazz	work songs
Duke Ellington		

Finale

Listen again to "Lost Your Head Blues" and compare your impressions now with your notes from your first listening. Do you hear more now than you did before? You should now be able to answer the following questions:

▌ What is the meter?

▌ What is the gender of the singer?

▌ What instruments are used to play the accompaniment?

▌ What is the song about?

▌ What is the mood of the song and how does the music fit the text?

32 | Developments in Jazz in the Late Twentieth Century

This human thing in instrumental playing has to do with trying to get as much human warmth and feeling into my work as I can. I want to say more on my horn than I ever could in ordinary speech.
—JAZZ WOODWIND PLAYER ERIC DOLPHY
(1928–1964)

Listening Introduction

Listen to "Ko Ko" by Charlie Parker and make notes about what you hear. Give some attention to the following:

▮ Is the tempo slow, medium, or fast?

▮ Can you detect the meter?

▮ What instruments stand out by playing solos?

▮ What instruments play primarily as accompaniment to the soloists?

▮ Do you hear any repetition of melodies or sections of music?

Keep these notes to compare with your impressions about each piece of music after you study the information in this chapter.

Bebop

At the height of the swing era, an influential group of jazz musicians rebelled against the big band style and its commercialization. These young rebels began to organize small "combos" that offered more opportunity for individual expression. The result was **bebop,** or just "bop."

In special after-hours clubs young, adventuresome, experimental musicians such as guitarist Charlie Christian (1916–1942), pianist Thelonious Monk (1917–1982), and drummer Kenny Clarke (1914–1985) played music together to explore their personal potentials. These and other musicians, notably trumpeter **Dizzy Gillespie** (1917–1993) and saxophonist **Charlie "Bird" Parker** (1920–1955), would work all night with the swing bands in Manhattan nightclubs and ballrooms, then ride north to Minton's Play House in the early morning to participate in "jam sessions" in which they experimented with free-form solo work and improvisation. The new style they developed was given the name *bebop* (later shortened to *bop*). The bebop combo consisted of one to three soloists supported by a rhythm section of drums and bass and sometimes piano or guitar.

Bebop players sought to extend the role of the soloist in jazz. They used jagged, uneven phrases, wide melodic leaps, and a great deal of rhythmic variety to develop their new sound. Kenny Clarke introduced an extraordinary rhythmic innovation with his technique of "dropping bombs"—that is, placing unanticipated bass drum accents before or after the beat. Almost single-handedly, Clarke moved the focus of jazz drumming away from the objective of simply keeping time. Drummers began to work around an implicit, rather than a stated, beat, and

Bebop musicians (from left to right) Tommy Potter, John Coltrane, Dizzy Gillespie, and Charlie Parker.

whatever basic timekeeping was necessary usually fell to the bass player.

Bebop songs typically borrowed the chord changes from the popular songs of the day and added entirely new melodies to them. Whereas swing melodies were usually vocally conceived, bebop melodies were designed for instruments and were difficult to sing. Another bop innovation was the use of more complicated chords with much more chromaticism (notes outside the scale that are dissonant with the scale) than had been present in earlier jazz styles.

Among the early innovators of bebop, Charlie Parker had the greatest influence on those who followed. His playing brought together all of the important bop innovations—harmonic complexity, rhythmic inventiveness, technical virtuosity—and combined them with a brilliant melodic sensibility. The example we will listen to is "Ko Ko," recorded in 1945. Parker plays the alto saxophone. The other musicians on the recording are trumpeter Miles Davis, pianist and muted trumpeter Dizzy Gillespie, pianist Sadik Hakim, bassist Curly Russell, and drummer Max Roach. "Hearing the Difference: Smith's 'Lost Your Head Blues' and Parker's 'Ko Ko'" compares the blues song with the bebop piece.

Listening Guide

"Ko Ko" CHARLIE PARKER

CD 2
Track 30

Year: 1945

Tempo: Very fast—if you can pick out the bass player, he is playing one note per beat.

Meter: Quadruple

Form: Most solos are 8 bars long, and choruses are made up of 4 or 8 of those, to be 32 or 64 bars each. The beginning 32 bars are repeated at the end, giving the recording a sense of balance.

Instrumentation: Trumpet, muted trumpet, alto saxophone, piano, bass, and drums

Duration: 2:57

Special feature: This recording is very intense and energetic; it is intended for careful listening, not dancing. "Ko Ko" is based on the harmonic progression of the jazz tune "Cherokee."

	Timing	What to listen for
30	0:00	Trumpet and saxophone together (8 bars)
	0:07	Trumpet solo (8 bars)
	0:13	Saxophone solo (8 bars)
	0:19	Trumpet and saxophone together (8 bars)
	0:25	Extended saxophone solo in which Parker quotes from another jazz tune, "Cherokee" (64 bars)
	1:16	Another saxophone solo (64 bars)
	2:07	Drum solo
	2:29	First 32 bars repeated

HEARING THE DIFFERENCE
Smith's "Lost Your Head Blues" and Parker's "Ko Ko"

These two recordings would both fall under the general heading of jazz, but they represent two very different jazz styles. Bessie Smith was a classic blues singer and her style is gentle, but also extremely expressive of deep personal feelings. Charlie Parker, on the other hand, plays in the very intense and energetic instrumental jazz style called bebop.

	Lost Your Head Blues	Ko Ko
Tempo	Slow and in general somewhat relaxed	Very fast and energetic
Meter	Quadruple with uneven beat subdivisions	Quadruple with uneven beat subdivisions in the solo parts and no time for any subdivisions in the rhythm section (piano, bass, and drums) that play only on the beats
Form	Each chorus fits the twelve-bar blues form.	Chorus lengths vary from 8 to 32 or 64 bars with the 32-bar opening repeated at the end
Lyrics	Lyrics casual and clearly state the singer has been wronged and is leaving a man	No singer or lyrics
Instrumental style	The piano and cornet players both play to accompany and respond to the singer, but both avoid doing anything to compete with her singing. There is no effort to "show off" how fast or well the players can play their instruments.	Every player is caught up in the intense energy of the fast tempo, and each soloist plays to display his own skill rather than to merely accompany other musicians.

The flexibility of jazz and its ability to adapt to trends was evident in the period following World War II. At that time there was a revival of interest in Dixieland and Chicago styles, and a number of swing bands were able to survive and are still active today. Bebop continued as the mainstream of jazz development, evolving in the 1950s into a style known as hard bop. **Hard bop** took the basic feel of bebop and added a more prominent blues influence, simplifying harmonies and putting a greater emphasis on a straightforward, driving beat. Hard bop has continued as part of the "straight-ahead" style of today.

Cool Jazz

Trumpeter **Miles Davis,** who played on the recording "Ko Ko," grew tired of several characteristics of bebop. The format used in "Ko Ko," with front-line instruments playing together at the beginning and the end of the recording and a series

Trumpeter Miles Davis

of solos in between, had become old. He also felt that the competitive intensity of the solos was taking too much away from the music. In 1947, Davis and arranger Gil Evans (1912–1988) put together a group of nine musicians to experiment with a new style of bebop. Some of the basic characteristics of the new style were playing with a minimal amount of vibrato; concentrating on playing softer and lower, thus avoiding the loud, high solos common in bebop; and putting less emphasis on individual solos and more emphasis on an ensemble sound. The overall mood of this new music was subdued and introspective. At first, the group worked privately to establish the new style, but after Capitol Records released a few single records that impressed jazz critics, they put the group's recordings on the album *Birth of the Cool* (1949). The new style was called **cool jazz.**

The cool jazz sound was further developed by musicians who combined jazz with some characteristics of classical music. Two new groups, the Modern Jazz Quartet and the Dave Brubeck Quartet, began to structure their music by using rondo or fugue forms. They sometimes played actual classical compositions with a jazz flavor. Pianist Dave Brubeck had studied classical composition before making jazz his career, and he had his group experiment with odd meters such as five-beat bars, though the standard was four (quadruple meter). Composer Gunther Schuller called his own classically influenced jazz *third stream* music. His thinking was that the first stream of music was classical, the second jazz, and the combination of the two was, therefore, the third stream.

By the end of the 1950s, jazz musicians began to look for more ways to structure and create their music. Miles Davis was again at the forefront of a new movement when he recorded his *Kind of Blue* (1959) album, in which he had the musicians play using different scale structures (called modes) from the standard major or minor scales that had been the basis of jazz. This idea was then employed by several other musicians and led to the development of a new style, **free jazz.**

Free Jazz

Free Jazz (1960) was the name of a record by the Ornette Coleman Double Quartet. The album's title gave a name to the style it introduced. The album features a half hour of collective improvisation with no set organization. The music has many complex rhythms and abrasive dissonances. The impetus for this style stemmed primarily from the civil rights movement, with several African American jazz musicians seeking to reaffirm their African roots and abandon any "Europeanisms" in their music. The free jazz movement soon lost much of its momentum because the music was difficult for most jazz enthusiasts to listen to for very long.

By the late 1960s, rock music had gained enough popularity that it was a logical style to combine with jazz. Rock bands such as Electric Flag, Chicago, and Blood, Sweat, and Tears hired horn players to play jazz-styled front-line instruments, along with rock rhythm sections made up of electric guitar, electric bass guitar, and drums. Called "jazz rock," the music was popular for some years as a rock style and served to introduce many rock fans to elements of jazz.

Fusion

Another successful attempt to combine rock with jazz was by Miles Davis in the 1969 album *Bitches Brew*. The music was more jazz than rock, but because it did "fuse" elements of both styles, it came to be called **fusion.** The rock elements in fusion lie in the basic beat pattern, instruments, and a few other characteristics of rock that are not common in jazz. The beat pattern of fusion uses even beat subdivisions. Most jazz is played using uneven beat subdivisions, as is rock music that developed out of blues or other jazz-related music. Much rock music has roots in country traditions, however, and country is played with even beat subdivisions (a steady "one and two and three and four and" with the numbered beats and the "ands" taking equal amounts of time). Fusion played by Davis in the late sixties, and all fusion that developed as a result of his work, is played with even beat subdivisions. Rock instruments used in fusion are solid-body electric guitars, electric bass guitars, electric pianos, and other amplified instruments. Before fusion, jazz bands still used hollow-body electric guitars, large "stand-up" string basses, and acoustic pianos. Other rock characteristics in fusion include short "riff" (continuously repeating melody) patterns, often no longer than one bar. Before fusion, jazz riff patterns tended to be much longer.

"Miles Runs the Voodoo Down" is taken from the *Bitches Brew* album. The album was popular enough to have made number 35 on the *Billboard* pop charts in 1970.

Chapter 32
Timeline

Jazz After WWII

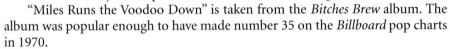

Listening Guide

"Miles Runs the Voodoo Down" (beginning) MILES DAVIS

Year: 1969

Texture: Thick with dense polyrhythms in the rhythm section

Tempo: Fairly slow, but it varies with the intensity of the music.

Meter: Quadruple with even beat subdivisions

Form: There are no repeated sections, but the electric bass plays a four-beat (one bar) riff pattern that repeats throughout the recording with some minimal changes on the repetitions.

Instrumentation: One trumpet, one soprano saxophone, one bass clarinet, electric guitar, two electric pianos, electric bass guitar, string bass, three set drummers, and other percussion instruments (some African)

Duration: We are discussing only the beginning three minutes of a fourteen-minute recording, but the musical characteristics we have discussed are established in that first three minutes.

Timing	What to listen for
0:00	Subtle opening played by the rhythm section with occasional notes by the bass clarinet.
0:34	Miles Davis begins his trumpet solo that includes clipped notes, long tones, slides up to and the bending of certain pitches, interspersed with silences.
3:00	Recording fades out.

Many of the musicians who played with Davis on *Bitches Brew* excelled in fusion and started their own groups. Saxophonist Wayne Shorter, who played soprano sax on "Miles Runs the Voodoo Down," and keyboardist Joseph Zawinul formed Weather Report, a group that brought collective improvisation to a new level with selections such as "Heavy Weather" and "Birdland." Guitarist John McLaughlin, who also played on "Miles Runs the Voodoo Down," fused jazz, rock, and Indian music in his recordings with the Mahavishnu Orchestra.

"Hearing the Difference: Parker's 'Ko Ko' and Davis's 'Miles Runs the Voodoo Down'" compares these two pieces.

HEARING THE DIFFERENCE
Parker's "Ko Ko" and Davis's "Miles Runs the Voodoo Down"

These two recordings represent two different jazz styles. Charlie Parker plays in the very intense and energetic instrumental jazz style called bebop, and Miles Davis, while having gotten his start in jazz as a bebop musician, has invented a later jazz style called fusion.

	Ko Ko	Miles Runs the Voodoo Down
Tempo	Very fast and energetic	Slow with an introspective mood
Meter	Quadruple with uneven beat subdivisions in the solo parts and no time for any subdivisions in the rhythm section (piano, bass, and drums) that play only on the beats	Quadruple with even beat subdivisions
Form	Chorus lengths vary from 8 to 32 or 64 bars with the 32-bar opening repeated at the end	Not structured and solos seem to be played freely for as long as the player chooses
Instrumentation	Acoustic trumpet, muted trumpet, alto saxophone, piano, bass, and drums	Much larger group, with several instrumentalists who play solos (although our discussion cuts off early and has only part of the first trumpet solo), and a very large rhythm section; both acoustic and electric instruments are used
Instrumental style	Every player is caught up in the intense energy of the fast tempo, and each soloist plays to display his own skill rather than to merely accompany other musicians.	The style is subdued in much the way cool jazz was played.
Length	The entire recording is less than three minutes long.	The entire recording is fourteen minutes long.

Summary

At the height of the swing era, a small group of musicians rebelled against the commercialism of the big bands and sought to expand the music they played. Their highly innovative experiments resulted in a small ensemble style called bebop, which brought the focus of jazz back to the soloist.

The 1950s and 1960s saw many experiments stemming from the bebop lead. Cool jazz, a reaction to the frenzied quality of bebop, brought a more detached emotional quality to jazz. Some musicians looked to classical music to further change their jazz styles, while others dropped all evidences of European classical music. By the late 1960s, some musicians added rock elements to create a music that came to be called fusion, a style often heard in jazz festivals all over the world even in the new century. Of all the styles to develop during that time, fusion was the most enduringly popular.

New People and Concepts

bebop	Dizzy Gillespie	hard bop
Charlie Parker	free jazz	Miles Davis
cool jazz	fusion	

Finale

Listen again to "Ko Ko" by Charlie Parker and compare your impressions now with your notes from your first listening. Do you hear more now than you did before? You should now be able to answer the following questions:

▌ Is the tempo slow, medium, or fast?

▌ What is the meter?

▌ What instruments stand out by playing solos?

▌ What instruments play the accompaniment (rhythm section)?

▌ Do you hear any repetition of melodies or sections of music?

33 | American Classical Music Influenced by Early Jazz

True music . . . must repeat the thought and inspirations of people and the time. My people are Americans. My time is today.
—COMPOSER GEORGE GERSHWIN (1898–1937)

Listening Introduction

Listen to *Afro-American Symphony,* first movement, by William Grant Still and make notes about what you hear. Give some attention to the following:

▌ Can you detect the tempo?

▌ Can you detect the meter?

▌ Can you identify any particular instruments when you hear them?

▌ Do you hear anything that seems it might be influenced by any jazz style of playing?

▌ Do you hear any repetition of melodies or sections of music?

Keep these notes to compare with your impressions about each piece of music after you study the information in this chapter.

By the early 1920s, jazz had spread from New Orleans to many parts of the country. The 1920s are sometimes called "The Jazz Age" for that reason. The jazz of this period was played by small groups composed of three or four front-line instruments and rhythm sections involving piano, bass, drums, and sometimes guitar and/or banjo. Collective improvisation was the front line, creating music that was lively, energetic, and complex. Another jazz-related music that had been popular since the late nineteenth century was ragtime. The "ragged" rhythms of ragtime bands remained popular into the 1920s.

As jazz was gaining popularity, many dance bands and orchestras were also playing rather sedate and rhythmically uninteresting pop-oriented commercial music in dance halls, night clubs, and ballrooms. This music was very easy to dance to, with none of the rhythmic or melodic complexity of jazz. These groups usually included violins and other string instruments, along with wind and rhythm instruments. Their style of dance music was sneeringly referred to, by jazz musicians, as "businessman's bounce."

As jazz became more popular, young people began to demand that it be played at their dances. Some of the dance halls or ballrooms were large enough to accommodate a thousand or more dancers, which meant that a smaller jazz group could not be heard, particularly before electronic amplification came into common use. Adding musicians to the jazz group would not work as long as the front-line instruments used collective improvisation, because from six to ten people all improvising a different melody at the same time would sound overly cluttered. The solution came with the development of the "big-band" swing style of jazz, in which the three or four instruments of the front line were replaced by sections of several trumpets, trombones, clarinets, and/or saxophones. The large "horn section" played with a rhythm section of piano, bass, and drums. Collective improvisation was no longer used, and arrangers wrote for the horn section in a block style, with most of the players keeping together and playing in similar rhythm patterns. They were still playing jazz in that they used ragged or syncopated rhythms and melodic lines with slides and blue notes, but the only improvisation was in individual solos. Fletcher Henderson was one of the first band leaders to organize a big band. His early band featured Louis Armstrong in the trumpet section.

George Gershwin

The swing jazz bands gained enough attention that some of the commercial dance orchestras began to move in their direction. Paul Whiteman was among the first to add jazz styles and rhythms to his orchestral dance arrangements. He commissioned **George Gershwin** (1898–1937) to write *Rhapsody in Blue* (1924) for his orchestra to play on one of its first U.S. tours. The idea of adding jazz influences to what was otherwise symphonic music was new enough that Whiteman called the program "An Experiment in Modern Music." *Rhapsody in Blue* is essentially a piano concerto, and the composer, George Gershwin, played the piano for the first performance.

The Piano Lesson (Homage to Mary Lou Williams) by Romare Bearden (1914–1988).

Composer George Gershwin

George Gershwin was born in New York, the son of Russian Jewish immigrants. Neither of his parents was a musician, but when a piano was purchased for the household, twelve-year-old George took to it immediately. By the time he was fifteen he had dropped out of school and begun working as a pianist for Jerome H. Remick & Co., a music publishing company. He also cut piano rolls to be used by player pianos, which were popular at the time. The process of "cutting" piano rolls involves playing music on a keyboard that puts a spot of ink on a long, moving roll of very strong paper each time a note is played. Someone else then cuts holes in the paper roll at the ink spots. When the roll is put into a player piano, the holes in the paper signal the mechanical player what notes to play when. Gershwin had cut more than one hundred piano rolls by the time he was twenty-eight.

Gershwin's background as a pianist had included the study of classical music, but most of his work experience was in popular genres. As a songwriter, he worked with his older brother Ira, who wrote lyrics. A number of their songs were published and featured in musicals. When Paul Whiteman hired Gershwin to write and play *Rhapsody in Blue*, most classical musicians and critics, even those in the commercial dance bands such as Whiteman's, thought of jazz as a very sloppy kind of music played by bad musicians. The way jazz musicians tended to slide from one note to another, to play "blue notes" that were out of tune with the traditional scale, and to play rhythms very freely went against classical traditions.

Jazz horn players also tended to vary the timbre of their instruments in very distinctive ways; for example, they would start to play a note while holding a mute in the bell and then gradually move the mute away. This created a "wa-wa" kind of sound that is very different from the classical horn style. Gershwin's goal was to compose a piece that was long enough to be included on a concert program and that used jazz rhythms and phrasing while being fully composed and having no places for players to improvise. His efforts were successful. Audiences and critics alike loved *Rhapsody in Blue,* and it gave Gershwin the title "the man who brought jazz into the concert hall." George Gershwin died when he was only thirty-eight years old, after surgery to remove a brain tumor.

Listening Guide

Rhapsody in Blue GEORGE GERSHWIN

CD 5
Tracks 4–9

Year: 1924, (this version for larger orchestra, 1942)

Tempo: Varies from section to section and varies within individual sections

Meter: Quadruple

Form: Irregular sectional form

Instrumentation: One clarinet (playing several sizes of clarinet, including bass), one soprano saxophone, one alto saxophone, one tenor saxophone, one baritone saxophone, two French horns, two trombones, one tuba, eight violins, double bass, timpani, banjo, celesta, and piano

Duration: 16:54

Special feature: The introductory glissando played by the clarinet sets the jazzy mood for the entire piece. No classical player would slide from note to note that way without having been influenced by jazz.

	Timing		What to listen for
4	0:00	**Introduction**	Clarinet trill, glissando to bluesy theme; reaches climax on high note, held; repeated-note theme, muted horns; clarinet trill, glissando
5	0:49	**A section**	Bluesy theme, muted trumpet; piano, five-note motive extended; bluesy theme, orchestra; five-note motive developed; pianistic display ends in upward scale.
	1:59		Bluesy theme and five-note motive alternate, ending in pianistic display
	3:21		Bluesy theme and five-note motive, faster tempo, orchestra
	3:56	**Bridge**	Short, exuberant melody ends in brief arpeggios in piano, directly into:
6	4:24	**B section**	Repeated-note theme (from introduction), clarinet, against sustained chords
	4:38		Assertive version of repeated-note theme, with motive from bluesy theme (A); sudden slowing at new idea in clarinet, muted trumpet, muted trombone; loud chords
7	5:28	**C section**	Exciting, jazzy theme, low instruments; developed at length, builds in tension
	6:24	**B section**	Piano enters on low note, rising passage to extended development of repeated-note theme; motion slows, meditative development of end of theme, pause
	8:25	**A/C sections**	Bluesy theme, piano, woodwinds with piano running notes; piano solo, trills and runs, arpeggio plunging downward
	9:31		Piano develops jazzy theme (C) at length, mounting excitement and brilliance; short cadenza with soft, rising conclusion; pause
8	11:25	**D section**	Warm, sensuous melody, orchestra, includes three-note "circular" motive; solo violin; orchestra, fuller instrumentation; transition, soft fragment of theme in bells

Timing		What to listen for
13:01		Piano, develops circular motive; sensuous melody with added flourishes from piano; fragments developed
9 14:03	**Piano cadenza**	Rapid-fire repeated notes; short pause, five-note motive (A); rapid-fire notes, upward glissando
14:57	**D section**	Orchestra returns with sensuous theme now in faster, exciting rhythm, piano figurations; builds to dissonant chord
15:30	**A section**	Agitated development of five-note motive; emphatic rising chords
15:54	**B section**	Exuberant statement of repeated-note theme
16:27	**A section**	Full orchestra, bluesy theme, Hollywood style; piano, five-note motive; climactic ending

By the early decades of the twentieth century, quite a few African American composers were writing music in the classical tradition. Certainly even Scott Joplin, who was best known for his ragtime piano pieces, also composed classically oriented concert works, including two operas, songs with piano accompaniment, and other works for piano solo. Other composers included Henry T. Burleigh (1866–1949), Florence B. Price (1888–1953), and William Dawson (1899–1990). Price was the first African American woman to write a symphonic work and have it performed by a major symphony orchestra, the Chicago Symphony Orchestra (1933). Although these composers were trained and wrote according to European traditions, they were also very much aware of the music in their own culture. Spiritual and minstrel melodies were influential on their works. Dawson, in particular, arranged many spirituals that are still performed today. Sometimes those melodies were quoted directly. The man who came to be known as the "Dean of Afro-American Composers" was **William Grant Still** (1895–1978).

William Grant Still

William Grant Still was born into a musical family in Woodville, Mississippi. His father was the town bandmaster. As a young man he intended to go to medical school but was drawn to music. He excelled in composition while a student at Oberlin College Conservatory, but his schooling was interrupted by his service in World War I. After graduation he moved to New York, where he continued to work as a composer while also playing oboe and other instruments in different performing groups.

Chapter 33 WebQuest

American Classical Music Influenced by Early Jazz

Throughout a long career, Still proved himself to be a versatile and resilient human being and musician. He played in theaters, orchestras, and dance bands; wrote arrangements for radio shows; composed for films (*Lost Horizon,* 1935; *Pennies from Heaven,* 1936; *Stormy Weather,* 1943) and television ("Gunsmoke" and "Perry Mason"); and wrote a large number and wide variety of concert works, among them operas, music for ballets, chamber music, and vocal and choral music, along with many art songs and symphonic works. Among his many awards are prizes from CBS television network, the New York World's Fair (1939), and the League of Composers. His opera *A Bayou Legend* (1941) was produced and broadcast on public television in 1981. Still died in 1978 at the age of eighty-three.

Still is perhaps best known for his first symphony, *Afro-American Symphony* (1930). It was the first symphonic work by an African American composer to be performed by a major symphony orchestra, the Rochester Philharmonic in 1931. In it, Still fully employed African American musical ingredients, including spirituals, blues, work songs, ragtime, and jazz, within a general style that is often described as neo-Romantic. He was also the first composer to introduce the tenor banjo into the ranks of a symphony orchestra. It is featured in the third movement.

Composer William
Grant Still

The *Afro-American Symphony* (which Still revised in 1969) is laid out in four movements and is scored for a large symphony orchestra. After the piece was finished, Still chose selected parts of poems by the African American poet Paul Laurence Dunbar (1872–1906) to reflect the spirit of each movement, giving the piece a kind of programmatic flavor. Dunbar was the son of a slave who became known for his writing in an African American dialect. The poem Still chose for the first movement of the symphony follows:

> *All my life long twell de night has pas'*
> *Let de wo'k come ez it will,*
> *So dat I fin' you, my honey, at las',*
> *Some whaih des ovah de hill.*

Listening Guide

Afro-American Symphony, **first movement** WILLIAM GRANT STILL

CD 5
Tracks 10–16

Year: 1930

Tempo: Moderato assai (very), but the tempo varies

Meter: Quadruple

Form: Sonata

Instrumentation: Three flutes (one with piccolo), two oboes, one English horn, two clarinets, one bass clarinet, two bassoons, four horns, three trumpets, three trombones, one tuba, first violins, second violins, violas, cellos, double basses, harp, and a large percussion section including vibraphone, celesta. (The tenor banjo is used only in the third movement.)

Duration: 7:20

Timing		What to listen for
Exposition		
[10] 0:00	**Introductory theme**	Slow, bluesy melody in English horn, begins monophonically; closes with accompaniment interjections
[11] 0:22	**Theme 1**	Muted trumpet states Theme 1 in three short phrases, syncopated responses between phrases
1:02		Clarinet repeats Theme 1, over rhythmic string accompaniment with "clicking" sound, syncopated woodwind responses between phrases
1:35	**Bridge**	Transitional fragments circle through woodwinds, ending with bassoon
1:47		Strings develop three-note pattern over long timpani roll, tempo accelerates; changes to two-note motive, tempo retards to cadence.
[12] 2:25	**Theme 2**	Tender, singing theme in oboe, accompanied by harp arpeggio, responses from woodwinds, muted brass, solo violin; second half of theme sung in violins; variant of first part of theme in flute to close
3:30		Cellos sing first half of theme; harp plays variant of second half of theme
[13] 4:04	**Development**	Two-note motive accelerates to allegro, rhythmic accompaniment pattern; violins alternate fragments of Theme 2 with other sections of orchestra
4:11		Violin fragments crescendo to full orchestra playing fragments of Theme 2, forte
4:57		Fragments move to English horn, softer dynamic; bass clarinet alternates with celesta as tempo slows
Recapitulation		
[14] 5:10	**Theme 2**	Tender, singing theme in shortened form, violins
5:39	**Bridge**	Slow transition in woodwinds, trill in low strings
[15] 5:50	**Theme 1**	Two-note motive against strong rhythm accompaniment in pizzicato strings; muted trumpets play first theme (three phrases) in "swing" rhythm, interjected responses from other sections of orchestra
6:36		Harp solo, slowing tempo provide transition
[16] 6:46	**Introductory theme**	Yearning strings introduce slow, bluesy theme, bass clarinet; quiet concluding chords

Although *Rhapsody in Blue* remains the most famous classical work that makes use of jazz stylings, at least from the Jazz Age of the 1920s, and *Afro-American Symphony* is a close second, there were other works that combined jazz and classical music, including Darius Milhaud's *La creation du monde* (1923) and Cole Porter's *Within the Quota* (1923). Gershwin himself continued to write jazz-influenced music, including his piano concerto of 1925 and his opera *Porgy and Bess* (1935). Meanwhile, some jazz band leaders moved in the direction of classical music. Duke Ellington's *Creole Rhapsody* (1931) and *Reminiscing in Tempo* (1935) are among the best known jazz-influenced classical pieces. Jazz was an important influence on Aaron Copland, whose music we will hear in the next chapter.

Summary

The widespread popularity of jazz in the Jazz Age of the 1920s caused many dance band leaders and even classically trained composers to put jazz stylings into their music. They did this in several ways:

They increased the size of jazz bands, making the front line a whole section of instruments that had to play arrangements instead of the old jazz style of collective improvisation. Collective improvisation involved each player improvising his own part, which would produce a cluttered sound if more than three players played at the same time. Larger bands marked the beginning of the swing style of jazz.

Commercial dance bands began to add jazz-styled solos to their arrangements. Jazz styling gave players more freedom with the rhythms they played, allowing them to slide between notes at times, to use mutes to give horns a "wa-wa" tone quality, and to play "blue" notes that sound out of tune by the standard scale. George Gershwin's *Rhapsody in Blue* is an example of this style.

African American composers added the spirituals and blues of their culture to their otherwise classical, even new-Romantic concert music. William Grant Still's *Afro-American Symphony* (1930) is one of the most famous works in this category.

Other classical composers also began to add jazz to their music, as we will see in the music of Aaron Copland in the next chapter.

New People and Concepts

George Gershwin   **William Grant Still**

Finale

Listen again to *Afro-American Symphony,* first movement, by William Grant Still and compare your impressions now with your notes from your first listening. Do you hear more now than you did before? You should now be able to answer the following questions:

▌ What is the tempo?

▌ What is the meter?

▌ Can you identify any particular instruments when you hear them?

▌ Do you hear anything that seems it might be influenced by any jazz style of playing?

▌ Where do melodies or sections of music repeat?

34 | American Nationalism

Listening Introduction

Listen to the example of music that represents this chapter, "Fanfare for the Common Man," and make notes about what you hear. Give some attention to the following:

▌ Can you guess at the tempo?

▌ Can you detect the meter?

▌ Can you tell what instruments are playing?

▌ Do you hear any melody that repeats?

▌ What is the general mood of the piece? Does that mood fit the title?

Keep these notes to compare with your impressions about the music after you study the information in this chapter.

During the first two decades of the twentieth century the German Romantic tradition continued to be influential on American composers. Eventually, however, French impressionism by such composers as Claude Debussy and Maurice Ravel, as well as the music of Stravinsky, made some inroads in American music.

Charles Ives

There were a few American musical pioneers, however, who began to experiment with new musical ideas of their own. One of those was **Charles Ives** (1874–1954). Not only did Ives use such advanced techniques as atonality, free dissonance, and extreme rhythmic complexity, but he also made effective use of home-grown musical and personal experience. Popular American songs and marches, hymn tunes, and quotations from famous European classics all made their way into his music. In a statement reflecting his open-minded approach, Ives said, "There can be nothing *'exclusive'* about a substantial art. It comes directly out of the heart of experience of life and thinking about life and living life."

Charles Ives was raised in the small town of Danbury, Connecticut, where his father was town bandleader, church organist, music teacher, and composer. His father had an unusual interest in musical experimentation and a fascination with unconventional sounds, which he transmitted to his son. This was undoubtedly one of the most important musical influences in Ives's life.

Composer Charles Ives

The young Ives studied music at Yale and then launched a successful career in life insurance. He deliberately chose to earn his living in an enterprise separate from his composing, on the theory that both efforts would be better for it, and he never regretted the decision. He composed furiously during evenings and weekends, storing his manuscripts in his barn. Ives's music was totally unknown until he published his *Concord Sonata,* a volume of songs, and a collection of essays in the early 1920s. His works were not readily accepted until after World War II, when they finally received significant recognition. They were then performed, published, and recorded. As his works became better known, Ives's influence increased, and successive generations of composers still draw inspiration from various aspects of his wide-ranging compositional techniques. The one hundredth anniversary of his birth was widely celebrated in 1974.

The musical isolation in which Ives worked led to the development of an unusual philosophy of music. Ives idealized the strength and simple virtue of ordinary people. He had little regard for technical skill, either in composition or in performance, but placed high value on the spirit and earnestness with which amateurs sang and played their popular hymns and songs. The freedom that Ives permitted himself in the choice of musical materials he also extended to performers of his works. Undismayed by an enthusiastic but inaccurate performance of his *Three Places in New England* (1903–1914), Ives remarked approvingly, "Just like a town meeting—every man for himself. Wonderful how it came out!"

Like much of his music, *Variations on "America"* displays an intriguing sense of humor. The piece was composed for organ in 1891, but it is best known today in the transcription for symphony orchestra made in 1963 by American composer William Schuman. That is the version we will listen to.

Listening Guide

Variations on "America" ("My Country 'tis of Thee") CHARLES IVES

CD 5
Tracks 17–24

Year: Composed for organ 1891, orchestral version 1963

Tempo: Each variation is different, with the second being the slowest and the fifth the fastest.

Meter: Triple with Variation 3 in sextuple meter

Form: Theme and variations

Instrumentation: Three flutes (two doubling on piccolo), two oboes, two clarinets, two bassoons, four horns, three trumpets, three trombones, one tuba, first violins, second violins, violas, cellos, string basses, timpani, three to four percussionists playing snare drum, bass drum, cymbals, triangle, castanets, tambourine, bells, xylophone

Duration: 7:07

	Timing		What to listen for
17	0:00	**Introduction**	
18	0:32	**Theme**	Presented as a varied and segmented version of "America." (Ives has every reason to believe that the audience already knows the theme.) Introduction returns, leading into:
	1:07		Muted trumpets and trombones play theme accompanied by strings playing on the "wood" of the bows (against the strings), creating an eerie sound. Bells make unexpected entrances at the end of each phrase of the tune.
19	1:49	**Variation 1**	Strings softly play the melody against rapid decorative material played by oboes, clarinets, bassoons, and xylophone, with trumpets and snare drum coming in with a finishing touch.
20	2:29	**Variation 2**	A somewhat simplified version of the first part of the theme is played by solo clarinet, doubled by solo horn, and accompanied by strings. The second part of the theme is played by muted solo trumpet accompanied by horns, trombones, and tuba (all muted), with the solo clarinet making a surprise entrance at the very end.
	3:12	**Interlude**	Flutes, oboes, clarinet, trumpets, and violins play the theme in F major, followed one measure later by horns, trumpet, and trombones playing the tune in D-flat major. This use of two different keys at the same time is called **polytonality.**
21	3:36	**Variation 3**	The theme is transformed into a lively dance played in sextuple meter. The theme is played by the oboe against a repeated jocular figure in the cello with string accompaniment. Solo flute plays a flippant phrase. Clarinet and second violin play the theme as the first violins add increased rhythmic activity. Glockenspiel adds to the flippant ending played by trumpet and extended by the piccolo.
22	4:33	**Variation 4**	Triple meter returns. Solo trombone and tuba play the first part of the theme, accompanied by strings, horns, and percussion. The second half of the theme is repeated by oboes, clarinets, and bassoons, while the flutes, piccolo, and trumpet enliven the background by adding short, clipped, decorative notes. The effect is grotesquely funny.
	5:16	**Interlude**	Brass instruments play a short interlude
23	5:31	**Variation 5**	High woodwinds play the theme with trumpet playing a countermelody. Strings then take up the theme, which is finished by the full orchestra.
24	6:27		Music from the introduction returns to lead to a coda, with full orchestra, fortissimo, ending the composition.

Remembering that Ives saw music as a representation of life, it is interesting to see ways in which he recreated live listening experiences in his music. *Three Places in New England,* for example, contains a famous musical representation of two marching bands playing in the same parade. Anyone who has seen a live parade that included bands might have experienced the effect in which one band has already passed the listener and the other is on its way toward him or her. If the bands are both still close enough to the listener, there is a point at which both can be heard at the same time. Usually, listeners "tune out" the band that has already passed and concentrate on listening to the approaching one. Ives, however, forced the awareness of actually hearing both bands at once. To do that he set up a mood of a Fourth of July parade in which both bands are clearly heard at the same time as if they were marching back to back or even passing one another. Each one is playing in a different rhythm and key, as if they cannot hear one another. The piece also contains bits of the melodies of his day, "Rally Round the Flag," "Yankee Doodle," and "The British Grenadiers."

American nationalism, at least in terms of the use of quotes of patriotic or popular American themes, is common in Ives's music. His piano sonata, *The*

Chapter 34
WebQuest

American
Nationalism

Concord Sonata, also credited several great American writers. The names of its four movements are "Emerson," "Hawthorne," "The Alcotts," and "Thoreau." Ralph Waldo Emerson and Henry David Thoreau were both nineteenth-century transcendentalist philosophers and writers who, among other things, emphasized the strength people can gain from communing with nature. Hawthorne is best known for his book *The Scarlet Letter,* and Louisa May Alcott for *Little Women.* The third movement, "The Alcotts," also credits Louisa May Alcott's father Bronson Alcott, who was also a writer and philosopher. Charles Ives died at the age of seventy-nine, having influenced many composers to follow him.

Aaron Copland

Another important American nationalist was **Aaron Copland** (1900–1990). Copland was born in Brooklyn, New York, the fifth child of Harris and Sarah Copland, both of Russian Jewish heritage. He was drawn to music at a very early age and first took piano lessons from his sister and then from a series of professional piano teachers. At age twenty he went to Paris to study at an American conservatory, where he met and studied composition with Nadia Boulanger, one of the most important composition teachers of the early twentieth century. While based in Paris, Copland also traveled to England, Belgium, Italy, and Germany. In those places he was able to meet and hear music by most of the major composers of the era. The thing that impressed him the most was the fact that music by French composers sounded French, music by German composers sounded German, and music by Russians sounded Russian. He decided that his goal was to write music that would sound American. He was familiar with Charles Ives's music, but he wanted to capture the American spirit in ways other than the quoting of popular melodies (although he also did that).

Composer Aaron Copland

When he returned to Brooklyn in 1924, he composed *Music for the Theater,* in which he included jazz rhythms and melodies with blue notes as sounds that were, at that time, exclusively American. At this point in his career, Copland began taking private composition students. He joined the League of Composers, founded music festivals, and started the Arrow Music Press, which specialized in the publication of contemporary music. His composition *Piano Variations* (1930) was widely acknowledged as a masterwork, but its use of dissonances and syncopated rhythms kept it from becoming popular with nonmusicians. Copland began to be dissatisfied with what he saw as the growing distance between the concertgoing public and the contemporary composer. "I felt that it was worth the effort to see if I couldn't say what I had to say in the simplest terms possible," Copland wrote. Increasingly thereafter, he drew on themes of regional America. Some of his best-known scores are three ballets: *Billy the Kid* (1938) and *Rodeo* (1942) are based on frontier stories and use melodies from actual cowboy songs, whereas *Appalachian Spring* (1944) depicts life in rural Pennsylvania and is among the most beautiful and enduring representatives of Americana in our musical heritage. The Shaker hymn "Simple Gifts" is the centerpiece of *Appalachian Spring.*

Copland also wrote film scores during this period, including scores for *Of Mice and Men* (1939), *Our Town* (1940), *The Red Pony* (1948), and *The Heiress* (1948). He won an Academy Award for his score to *The Heiress*. Other major awards he received included the Pulitzer Prize (1945), the New York Music Critics' Circle Award (1945), the Presidential Medal of Freedom (1964), and honorary degrees from Princeton University (1956), Oberlin College, and Harvard University. When Spike Lee was looking for music to put to his film *He Got Game* (1998), he chose music by Copland for the soundtrack, saying, "When I listen to Copland's music, I hear America, and basketball is America. It's like he wrote the score for this film."

Two compositions from 1942, "Fanfare for the Common Man" and "Lincoln Portrait," display Copland's American patriotism as well as any compositions can. Both works were inspired by the entry of the United States into World War II. "Fanfare for the Common Man" is a piece for brass and percussion instruments, as fanfares usually are. Fanfares have traditionally been works intended to introduce royal or state leaders. Copland's writing such a work dedicated to the "common man," or, one could say, the "average American citizen," displayed a very democratic attitude that includes respect for every citizen. "Lincoln Portrait" features an introduction composed of popular melodies from Lincoln's lifetime followed by a spoken text derived from President Lincoln's speeches and letters.

Listening Guide

"Fanfare for the Common Man" AARON COPLAND

CD 2
Track 31

Year: 1942

Tempo: "Very deliberately" (52 beats per minute)

Meter: Quadruple

Form: One main theme is repeated with some variation.

Instrumentation: Three trumpets, four horns, three trombones, one tuba, timpani, bass drum, and gong

Duration: 2:50

Special feature: Notice how the trumpets and horns are often used together as a single unit; the trombones and tuba are a separate unit; and the timpani, bass drum, and gong another unit. Those three units sometimes imitate or otherwise respond to one another, and sometimes they all play together.

Timing	What to listen for
31 0:00	Bass drum, timpani, and gong play together on a somber rhythm
0:20	Fanfare melody played by all three trumpets in **unison** (all playing the same notes at the same time)
0:46	French horns join the trumpets on the fanfare theme
1:16	The percussion unit repeats its introductory rhythm
1:24	Trombones and tuba begin the theme with imitative responses by the timpani; trumpets and horns join trumpets on the theme
2:00	Trombones and tuba begin the theme again, answered by the trumpets and horns. All play together with much force and power.
2:22	Trombones and trumpets play a slower and very deliberate version of the theme. The fanfare finishes with a loud crescendo accompanied by a drum roll.

Like Stravinsky and many other composers of the period, Copland turned to serial composition after 1950. His *Connotations for Orchestra* (1962) adapts the twelve-tone system to his special musical style. He did not use that technique for very long, having a lifelong concern for bridging the gap between the concertgoing public, which generally rejected serialism, and the modern composer. During the last several decades of his life, Copland spent much of his time conducting concerts of his own music all over the world. Copland died in 1990 at the age of ninety.

Summary

Early twentieth-century composers began to invent their own kinds of new music. Charles Ives was one of the most extraordinary and original composers that America produced in that era. His music contains elements drawn from a variety of American and European traditions. He used such advanced techniques as atonality, free dissonance, polytonality, and extreme rhythmic complexity, along with traditional procedures, in a fresh and free manner. At the same time, Ives included popular and patriotic American melodies in his music, giving it a tremendous appeal to listeners who might otherwise have been put off by its very contemporary compositional techniques. Ives's works have had a profound impact on later composers.

Another important American patriot whose music has affected many composers to follow him was Aaron Copland. Copland experimented with contemporary techniques such as free and syncopated rhythms and even serialism, but his basic belief was that the gap between contemporary composers and the general concertgoing audience needed to be filled. Much of his music does that by being quite listenable while still having a "contemporary feel." He expressed his nationalistic feelings by including jazz rhythms and melodies with blue notes into some works, by using cowboy and Shaker melodies in his ballet music, and by composing such works as "Fanfare for the Common Man" and "Lincoln Portrait" to help the war effort when the United States entered World War II in 1942. Copland also composed movie scores and received countless awards and honorary degrees from prestigious institutions. His music and his influence will live long beyond his lifetime.

New People and Concepts

Aaron Copland   polytonality   unison

Charles Ives

Finale

Listen again to "Fanfare for the Common Man" and compare your impressions now with your notes from your first listening. Do you hear more now than you did before? You should now be able to answer the following questions:

- What is the tempo?
- What is the meter?
- What instruments are playing?
- What is the form?
- What is the mood of the piece and how does it fit the title?

Composition is notation of distortion of what composers think they've heard before. Masterpieces are marvelous misquotations.
—COMPOSER/WRITER NED ROREM (BORN IN 1923)

Listening Introduction

Listen to the example of music that represents this chapter, "Poème électronique" by Edgard Varèse, and make notes about what you hear. Give some attention to the following:

▌ Is there any type of steady tempo?

▌ Can you detect any kind of meter?

▌ Can you tell what instruments are playing?

▌ Do you hear any repeated sounds?

▌ What is the general mood of the piece?

Keep these notes to compare with your impressions about the music after you study the information in this chapter.

Electronic Music

The development of advanced electronic technology in the 1950s and 1960s made possible radical changes in the way music could be composed and performed. Magnetic tape, synthesizers, and computers allowed the composer to control every aspect of music and made possible accurate rendition of the music without relying on live performers. The tape became both the music *and* its performance.

Musique Concrète

One kind of electronic music is ***musique concrète,*** French for "concrete music." Any kind of sound may be used in *musique concrète,* such as street noise, sounds from nature, human singing and speech, and usual or unusual sounds from traditional musical instruments, all of which can be manipulated and recombined on tape. After prerecording the chosen sounds, the composer can manipulate them in a variety of ways. They can be sped up, slowed down, edited, and combined with other sounds. The tape itself can be cut so that the order of the sounds is changed. By cutting the tape, the composer can cut out or reverse sections of it and then splice it back together in any order he or she chooses. After the sound alteration, cutting, and splicing are finished, the piece has been both composed and performed by the composer in a permanently accurate version.

293

Synthesizers and computers can create their own sounds by imitating acoustic musical instruments or other natural sounds, or by producing unique sounds that the composer can manipulate with few restrictions. With no performers to play the music too fast or too slow, or to make other mistakes, the composer has complete control. He or she does not even have to notate the music because it exists only as a recording that is unlikely to be produced in the same way a second time. Even when the composer chooses to imitate the sound of natural, acoustic instruments, electronics allow him or her much freedom to compose any note or combination of notes because the electronic instrument is not limited by the number of fingers on the musician's hands or technical difficulties of playing acoustic instruments. For example, certain notes or note combinations can be difficult to play on some musical instruments: A guitarist's or other string player's left hand cannot be both very high and very low on the fingerboard at the same time, and a pianist playing with hands spread far apart cannot also play a note in the middle of the keyboard. The **electronic** instrument can overcome these limitations, in addition to being able to play higher, lower, louder, and softer sounds than is possible on acoustic instruments. All of these considerations have prompted many movie or television composers to stop writing for live orchestras and produce their soundtracks on their computers.

This practice of radio, television, and movie scores being composed and recorded by synthesizers or computers has close to devastated musical communities in such places as New York and Hollywood. In those cities and other places that produce recorded music, many composers and musicians have for years depended on work in recording studios for their livelihood. Once electronic instruments advanced to the point of sounding almost live, it became possible for a studio to hire a single composer with a computer and sound equipment to produce a complete orchestral score. Of course, the sound is not really that of a live orchestra, but for a recorded movie score it does not have to be. In the 1990s, many musicians feared that the industry would completely dissolve. Though their fears have not been fully realized, the number of musicians making a good living doing such work has diminished greatly.

In most major cities in the United States, musicians who have been regularly hired to play live music to accompany a musical or other theatrical productions have also found themselves replaced by synthesizers. The result is not only that musicians are not getting work, but also that audiences are not hearing the same sound quality they did when the music was played live. "The Live Experience: Performance Situations for Electronic Music" discusses how this music may be used on stage.

Edgard Varèse

The piece of electronic music we are going to listen to is "Poème électronique" by **Edgard Varèse**. Varèse (1883–1965), one of the most innovative and influential composers of the twentieth century, was born in Paris but came to New York to live in 1915. He challenged traditional musical traditions by defining music as "organized sound." He meant *all* sound, including some sounds previously classified as nonmusical noises. Many of Varèse's compositions employ unusual combinations of instruments, which often play at the extremes of their abilities. The sound of the music sometimes tends to recall the noises of mechanized society. His *Ionisation* (1933) was written for percussion ensemble, employing a huge battery of standard orchestral percussion and exotic instruments as well.

THE LIVE EXPERIENCE
Performance Situations for Electronic Music

Since a piece of music that is produced electronically exists only as a recording, it is most often used in situations that do not require the listener to watch the musicians play. During the 1960s, electronic music was so new and exciting to audiences interested in the avant garde that it was not uncommon for a tape player to be brought out on stage and turned on for an audience to listen to. That made for some awkward situations, as members of the audience usually express their appreciation of the music with applause. If the composer was not present and there was no performer, who was the applause for? Perhaps if one did not enjoy the music, it was for the person who stopped the tape.

Some composers have written music to be played live over previously recorded electronic music. Performances of such music are obviously difficult to coordinate because of the unchanging steadiness of the recorded music. Usually, musicians and conductors flex tempos a bit in order to keep all performers together, but that is impossible with music that has been previously recorded. Other composers have written works in which the previously recorded music is interpolated into the live performance but does not necessarily coincide with the live playing. Tape recorders have also been used to record music as it is being played, then it is repeated later in the same live performance. Art rock bands such as Pink Floyd and King Crimson have made use of that technique in both their live and recorded performances.

Electronic music groups formed in the 1960s, and they often included performers who worked a variety of electronic instruments, tape players, and even sometimes radio receivers. Of course, if one includes a radio receiver, one cannot be concerned about exactly what will sound when, but that type of unpredictability was sometimes desired. The popularity of nonacoustic-sounding electronic music has fallen off in recent decades, but the use of electronic instruments to produce music in place of acoustic instruments is still very common, particularly in movie soundtracks.

Included was a "lion's-roar" (a primitive kind of friction drum that sounds like a roar) and three sirens.

Once he began to use electronically produced sounds, Varèse overcame the problem of combining them with live performances in his work *Déserts* (1954) by not having the live and recorded sections play together. "Poème électronique" (1958) is made up of both electronically produced sounds and *musique concrète*. It was recorded to be played from 425 speakers spread around the inside of an oddly shaped building featured at the Brussels World Fair in 1958. The building was designed by a Swiss architect named Le Corbusier. Visitors heard the music as they walked through the building viewing lights, images, and writing that were projected on the angled walls in a variety of shapes. The entire tape is eight minutes long, but there is no "real" beginning or ending because the tape was constantly repeated so that the piece was to begin for each listener when he or she entered the building and end when he or she exited the building.

The types of electronic sounds we heard in "Poème électronique" seemed very modern in 1958 and continued to be used to represent modern times in the

Chapter 35
Activity

Electronic vs.
Acoustic Music

Listening Guide

"Poème électronique" ("Electronic Poem") EDGARD VARÈSE

CD 2
Track 32

Year: 1958

Meter: None

Form: Some returning sounds, but no structured repeating or contrasting sections

Duration: 2:35

Instrumentation: Electronic generators, church bells, organs, human voices, and sirens

Special feature: The short section we will listen to does not include all of the sound makers listed in our instrumentation. The organs and human voices are clear, although distorted, later in the recording.

Timing	What to listen for
0:00	A large, low bell rings, chirping sounds, sirens, other electronic sounds, including fast tapping and sustained fuzzy tones
0:43	Dripping sounds, noises, short squawks
0:56	A pattern of three notes sliding from one to the other plays and then repeats two more times
1:10	Low, sustained sounds with rattling, then a siren
1:30	Short squawks and chirps, three-note group plays again, more squawks and chirps at different pitches
1:46	Squeaking sounds
2:03	A variety of percussion sounds, siren, tapping
2:35	Our recording fades

[32]

Le Corbusier Building at the Brussels World Fair, 1958.

early 1960s. One can still hear such sounds in reruns of the television show *The Twilight Zone,* particularly in those episodes that dealt with outer space or the future. Ironically, these sounds seem dated to us today.

Acoustic Music

Even given all of the advantages of electronically produced music, there has remained a strong attraction to live musical performances. Right alongside new technology, the late twentieth century has seen a continuing interest in live musicians playing to live audiences. Orchestras have not changed all that much from those of the romantic period, except that the percussion section has expanded and become more important. Sometimes the saxophone, guitar, or other popular instruments are included with a standard orchestra.

Ellen Taaffe Zwilich

Ellen Taaffe Zwilich (b. 1939) has become one of the most accomplished and recognized American composers in the second half of the twentieth century. She was born and raised in Miami, Florida, and studied piano and violin as a child. Composition always interested her, and she composed music for her high school band while she was a student playing in it. After high school she went to the Juilliard School in New York to study music and concentrate more on composition. In 1975, she was the first woman to receive the Doctor of Musical Arts degree from that prestigious institution. Her Symphony no. 1, *Three Movements for Orchestra* (1983) won the Pulitzer Prize in music. She was the first woman to be so honored. We will listen to the first movement of that symphony as an example of modern orchestral music.

Composer Ellen Taaffe Zwilich

Listening Guide

Symphony no. 1, first movement ELLEN TAAFFE ZWILICH

CD 5
Tracks 25–27

Year: 1983

Tempo: The introductory section is contemplative, the second allegro, and the coda again contemplative.

Meter: Mostly duple with some interpolations of triple meter

Form: Continuous development of motives (short themes) through three sections

Instrumentation: One piccolo, two flutes, one oboe, one English horn, one clarinet, one bass clarinet, one bassoon, one contrabassoon, four horns, two trumpets, two trombones, one tuba, piano, harp, first violins, second violins, violas, cellos, string basses, timpani, cymbals, tambourine, two bass drums, orchestral bells, vibraphone, tubular bells, snare drum, and suspended cymbals

Duration: 6:58

Timing	What to listen for
Introductory section	
0:00	Motto (germ motive stated three times) played piano (soft), continued with varied echo
0:28	Motto begins in winds, covered by energetic violin theme climbing to high pitch, continues into intensely yearning melody that falls abruptly
0:50	Motto in violins echoed in basses; horns state a melody beginning with repeated notes; violins take over and climb to high pitch; trumpets proclaim repeated-note melody (varied)

(box: 25 at left of 0:00 row)

continued

Timing	What to listen for
1:11	Motto in violins, high pitch, jumpy motive in flutes and piano, trumpet plays repeated notes; fast six-note idea tossed through orchestra in ascending, then descending pattern; repeated-note idea in bass instruments
1:31	Strings state motto against gradually ascending line, jumpy motive in flutes and piano
1:44	Trumpets open motto with dissonant chord, development of germ motive
2:00	Motto in flutes, dissonant chord held in horns, sustained descending line in strings overlap into:
2:04	Expansion of motto in brass recalls opening bars, now faster; interjections from woodwinds and strings
2:17	Brass continues, motto in trumpets, intensity builds; sudden pause
2:22	Brass begins motto, others join as tension builds further; emphatic descent to short break

Central section (allegro)

	Timing	What to listen for
26	2:32	Pizzicato strings accompany broad melody in horns, fast repeated notes also accompany; trumpet states broad melody; texture becomes fragmented
	2:57	Four-note scale fragment rises and falls, echoed through the orchestra, while suspended cymbal tapping continues repeated-note accompaniment; three-note upward thrust in trumpet, plus repeated notes, abrupt descent
	3:07	Powerful chords hammered, downward-tumbling scale appears; vigorous development of minor third in various instruments; repeated-note tapping on suspended cymbal
	3:22	Extended development of minor-third motives combined with downward-tumbling scale and repeated-note motive in snare drum; cymbal crash and snare drum statement alone twice, with pauses
	3:38	Minor thirds and downward scales continue; rising and falling four-note scale fragment and suspended cymbal take over; repeated-note accompaniment moves to bass drum, downward scales return with hammered chords
	4:02	Three-note upward thrust from basses, repeated bass drum notes; vigorous development of minor thirds in low strings; suspended cymbal returns; upward thrust in trombones continues into broad melody, repeated notes in brass and strings; hammered chords, downward scales, vigorous minor thirds in trombones, fragments into:
	4:34	Faster rhythms in strings, winds, and suspended cymbal; hammered chords crescendo to climax, upward thrust from trombones
	4:44	Single chime and sustained chord dissipate energy; double third motive repeated, linked with new two-note motive rocking back and forth; chord dies away, chime strikes three times.

Coda

	Timing	What to listen for
27	5:25	Chord dies away as two-note motive continues rocking movement; quiet chord in trombones
	5:45	Germ motive gently in oboe; motto (both ascending and descending) in bass instruments; warm, sustained melody in cellos
	6:19	Rocking motive alternates with quiet final statement of motto, peaceful close

HEARING THE DIFFERENCE
Mozart's Symphony no. 40, first movement and Zwilich's Symphony no. 1, first movement

Mozart's Symphony no. 40 follows the classical rules of repeating and contrasting themes in a balanced, sonata form; Zwilich's Symphony no. 1, composed almost two hundred years later, uses a much less structured form. Zwilich's work is structured in three sections and has a sense of balance in that the first and third sections express a contemplative mood, but most of the work represents a constant state of development of a germ motive. It is almost like Zwilich's work is all development, while development sections received some, but minimal, attention in the classical period. Zwilich also used a very large, modern orchestra with many more sound possibilities including bright brass instruments (Mozart used just two French horns), a good deal of percussion, and woodwinds that sound both higher and lower than those Mozart wrote for. In fact, many of the instruments Zwilich used were either not yet invented or not available to Mozart in his time. Both works are representative of the periods that produced them.

	Mozart's Symphony no. 40, first movement	Zwilich's Symphony no. 1, first movement
Style period	Classical (1788)	Twentieth century (1983)
Tempo	Allegro	The first and last sections are slow and contemplative, the center section is allegro
Meter	Duple	Mostly duple with some interpolations of triple meter
Form	Sonata (exposition of two themes, development, recapitulation of two themes, coda)	Three sections with continuous development of germ motives throughout
Instrumentation	Standard classical orchestra (one flute, pairs of oboes, clarinets, bassoons, horns, and strings)	Much larger orchestra that includes both higher and lower woodwind and brass instruments such as piccolo (very high flute), bass clarinet, contrabassoon, trumpets, trombones, and tuba. A full string section that includes a harp, and a large battery of percussion instruments

Summary

Electronic technology in the form of magnetic tape, synthesizers, and computers has had a powerful impact on music composition. *Musique concrète* utilizes naturally occurring sounds that are manipulated on magnetic tape. Synthesizers are used to create entirely new sounds and to accurately control aspects of a composition. Tapes and synthesizers are frequently used with each other, as well as with live performers, but it is more common for electronic music to be used for situations that would not normally feature a live performer, such as a movie soundtrack.

The orchestra continues to be popular for live concerts. Modern composers have expanded the size of the percussion section and sometimes use formal structures that were not developed in the classical period. They do, however, write music that is completely acoustic and that can stand side by side with new sounds in terms of audience appeal.

New People and Concepts

acoustic music	**electronic music**	*musique concrète*
Edgard Varèse	**Ellen Taaffe Zwilich**	

Finale

Listen again to "Poème électronique" and compare your impressions now with your notes from your first listening. Do you hear more now than you did before? You should now be able to answer the following questions:

❙ Is there a steady tempo?

❙ Is there any particular meter?

❙ What instruments are playing?

❙ Does it follow any standard form?

❙ What is the mood of the piece and what must it have sounded like in 1958?

36 | Musical Theater

Our attitudes control our lives. Attitudes are a secret power working 24 hours a day, for good or bad. It is of paramount importance that we know how to harness and control this great force.

—COMPOSER/PIANIST IRVING BERLIN (1888–1989)

Listening Introduction

Listen to the example of music that represents this chapter, "America" from *West Side Story,* and make notes about what you hear. Give some attention to the following:

▌ Can you detect the meter?

▌ Can you tell the number and gender of the singers?

▌ Can you hear Latin instruments being used to color the orchestra?

▌ Can you understand the text?

▌ Does the piece have a general mood that supports the meaning of the text?

Keep these notes to compare with your impressions about the music after you study the information in this chapter.

We have discussed opera as it began around 1600 in Italy, and we have described its development into different forms as its popularity spread all over Europe. One new turn English opera took at the end of the Baroque period was the development of **ballad opera.** Ballad operas were different from other operas in that they were usually based on popular stories or political satire, they featured spoken dialogue instead of sung recitative, and their songs were fitted to short, popular melodies, as opposed to the much longer and more dramatic arias of operas. The first popular ballad opera was *The Beggar's Opera* (1728) by John Gay. Ballad operas from England became popular in the American colonies long before Americans were ready to accept the formality of more serious operas.

Broadway Musicals

Many other types of popular entertainments, such as vaudeville shows, were popular in America in the nineteenth century, but American **"musicals"** developed most directly out of European operettas, such as Gilbert and Sullivan's *H.M.S. Pinafore* (1878), *The Pirates of Penzance* (1879), and *The Mikado* (1885). American musicals were so often written and produced on or near Broadway in New York that they came to be called "Broadway" musicals. Broadway musicals differed from European operettas in that they were usually based on everyday stories, the dialogue was spoken in everyday language, and the songs were musically important for their own sake. Such popular songs as "Over There," "I'm a Yankee Doodle Dandy," "Grand Old Flag," and "Give My Regards to Broadway" all came from musicals written between 1901 and 1912 by **George M. Cohan** (1878–1942). Cohan's

Composer George M. Cohan

life was the subject of the Academy Award–winning movie *Yankee Doodle Dandy* (1943), which popularized his songs once again for the World War II generation.

Most Broadway musicals of the 1920s and 1930s were based on the light "boy-meets-girl-and-they-fall-in-love" genre of stories. An important exception was *Show Boat* (1927), with music by Jerome Kern (1885–1945) and lyrics by Oscar Hammerstein II (1895–1960). *Show Boat* was based on a novel by Edna Ferber and described the lives of a family who ran a showboat on the Mississippi River in a more serious tone than was common in musicals of the time. It even included an interracial married couple, which was a very controversial subject when the musical was first performed. Many lastingly popular songs came from *Show Boat,* including "Ol' Man River," "Make Believe," and "Why Do I Love You?" With the success of *Show Boat,* musical writers and composers understood that audiences were ready to accept more serious themes as long as the songs were memorable.

Generally, musicals differ from operas in that they include very memorable and singable songs. Operas often include memorable arias, but performing them requires quite a bit of vocal training. Operas also tend to concentrate on the drama of their plots and may continue for a long time before offering a memorable melody. Musicals, on the other hand, use one song after another to help relate the story. The program for an opera includes a synopsis of the plot, while the program for a musical merely lists the songs in the order you will hear them; it is assumed that the audience can follow the plot as it is presented.

Of course, some musicals are also quite operatic. When George Gershwin's *Porgy and Bess* opened in 1935 it was called a "folk opera," and it is still performed by both opera companies and musical companies. *Porgy and Bess* is set in an African American community in South Carolina. The characters are poor and the plot involves a crippled man, Porgy, who commits murder to gain the woman he loves, Bess. While he is in prison, another man takes Bess off to New York, promising her a better life. When Porgy is freed from prison, he heads to New York to win Bess back. George Gershwin had been working with jazz melodies and rhythms in combination with classical music for some time. *Rhapsody in Blue* (1924) was one of his greatest accomplishments before *Porgy and Bess.* He again used jazz, as well as African American spirituals, in the opera, combining popular and classical styles of music. The song "Summertime," from *Porgy and Bess,* became a jazz standard.

By the middle of the 1940s, one musical after another had a run of over one thousand performances in New York before touring the country with great success. Some of the most memorable musicals from that era include *Oklahoma* (1943), *South Pacific* (1949), and *The Sound of Music* (1959). All three of those musicals were written by Richard Rodgers and Oscar Hammerstein, popularly known as **Rodgers and Hammerstein.**

Leonard Bernstein

Leonard Bernstein (1918–1990) composed the music for *West Side Story* (1957), which was based on the plot of Shakespeare's play *Romeo and Juliet.* Bernstein was as interested and successful in the world of serious concert music as he was in the world of popular musicals. Born in Massachusetts, he graduated from Harvard and worked as assistant conductor of the New York Philharmonic Orchestra. He became famous overnight when he filled in for a conductor who had fallen sick and led the orchestra through a concert that was broadcast nationwide. At age forty, Bernstein was the first American-born conductor to be hired as director of the New York Philharmonic. He composed many orchestral, choral, chamber, and operatic works, and gained fame for the much more pop-oriented musical *West Side Story.* The plot of *Romeo and Juliet* was discussed in Chapter 20 when we listened to Tchaikovsky's *Romeo and Juliet* overture. For the musical, the feuding

Composer Leonard Bernstein

Shown here are the Jets in a scene from *West Side Story.*

families were transformed into two New York street gangs, the Jets and the Sharks. Romeo's counterpart is Tony of the Jets, and Juliet's is Maria of the Sharks. Because the Sharks are Puerto Rican immigrants, Bernstein composed some wonderful jazzy, Latin-influenced music to set the atmosphere. We will listen to "America," which is full of complex and exciting rhythms. It is sung by the Sharks. Notice ways in which the lyrics refer to unfair treatment experienced by the Puerto Rican immigrants and the split between the boys of the Sharks, who dislike America, and the Shark girls, who are happy being in their new country.

Listening Guide

"America" from *West Side Story* LEONARD BERNSTEIN

CD 2
Tracks 33–36

Year: 1957

Tempo: Beginning, moderato; sextuple section, fast

Meter: Introduction: Duple with many triplet patterns inside the two beats;

    A sections: Alternating 6/8 and 3/4 measures. This can be counted within the sextuple beats by accenting **1** 2 3 **4** 5 6 followed by **1** 2 3 4 **5** 6.

    B sections: Sextuple

    Dance sections; use both 6/8 and 3/4 meters

Form: Introduction, introduction repeated with extension, ABABA-Dance–BA–Dance–B

Voices: Members of the Sharks: Bernardo (baritone), Indio (tenor), Anita (alto), Rosalia (soprano), girls, and boys

Instrumentation: Three flutes/piccolos, one bass clarinet, one bassoon, two French horns, three trumpets, two trombones, violins, cellos, contrabass, Spanish guitar, and percussion, including timpani, celesta, and the Latin sounds of claves (solid wood cylinders that hit one another), güiro (a notched hollow gourd that is scraped with a stick), and maracas (rattles made of a gourd or wood with seeds or other small items inside that rattle when the instrument is shaken)

Language: English

Duration: 4:52

Special feature: Occasional responses from the group add to the solo texts given here to create a party atmosphere.

	Timing		Text	Form
33	0:00	Instrumental introduction		
	0:09	**Bernardo:**	Puerto Rico, you lovely island, Island of tropical breezes. Always the pineapples growing Always the coffee blossoms blowing.	Introduction
	0:28	**Anita:**	Puerto Rico, my heart's devotion Let it sink back in the ocean Always the hurricanes blowing, Always the population growing, And the money owing, And the babies crying And the bullets flying. I like the island Manhattan! Smoke on your pipe and put that in!	Introduction repeats with extension
34	1:09	**Girls:**	I like to be in America! O.K. by me in America! Ev'rything free in America.	A (alternating sextuple patterns)
		Boys:	For a small fee in America!	
35	1:25	**Rosalia:**	Buying on credit is so nice	B (sextuple meter)
		Indio:	One look at us and they charge twice	
		Rosalia:	I'll have my own washing machine	
		Indio:	What will you have though to keep clean?	

Timing		Text	Form
1:37	**Girls:**	Skyscrapers bloom in America	**A**
	Rosalia:	Cadillacs zoom in America	
	Girls:	Industry boom in America	
	Boys:	Twelve in a room in America	
1:52	**Anita:**	Lots of new housing with more space	**B**
	Bernardo:	Lots of doors slamming in our face	
	Anita:	I'll get a terrace apartment	
	Bernardo:	Better get rid of your accent	
2:05	**Girls:**	Life can be bright in America	**A**
	Boys:	If you can fight in America	
	Girls:	Life is all right in America	
	Boys:	If you are white in America	
2:17		Dance music	Mixed sextuple and triple meters
3:00	**Anita:**	Here you are free and you have pride	**B**
	Bernardo:	Long as you stay on your own side	
	Anita:	Free to be anything you choose	
	Boys:	Free to wait tables and shine shoes	
3:13	**Bernardo:**	Everywhere grime in America	**A**
		Organized crime in America	
		Terrible time in America	
	Anita:	You forget I'm in America	
3:27		Dance music	Mixed sextuple and triple meters
4:10	**Bernardo:**	When I will go back to San Juan	**B**
	Anita:	I know what boat you can get on	
	Bernardo:	Ev'ryone there will give big cheers	
	Anita:	Ev'ryone there will have moved here	
		Instrumental closing	

The "36" marker appears to the left of the 2:17 row.

There is a set of lyrics to this song that is in more common use today than the version we have printed here. Those lyrics have removed references to the mistreatment of immigrants and simply have Anita and Rosalia singing back and forth about missing Puerto Rico and wanting to stay in New York. Some of the same text is used, but the overall effect makes less of a social statement. Other musicals by Leonard Bernstein include *On the Town* (1944), *Wonderful Town* (1953), and *Candide* (1956).

Later Musicals

The lyricist for *West Side Story* was **Stephen Sondheim.** He composed both the music and the lyrics for later musicals including *A Funny Thing Happened on the Way to the Forum* (1961), *A Little Night Music* (1972), and *Sweeney Todd* (1979). Sondheim's musicals are seldom big commercial successes because he tends to avoid the types of songs that are easy to sing out of context. The one exception is "Send in the Clowns" from *A Little Night Music,* which became popular in its own right.

The widespread popularity of rock music during the 1960s brought about a number of rock-based or influenced musicals, including *Hair* (1967), which told the story of "hippy" rock fans who were societal dropouts. The cast was completely nude by the end of Act One. The British rock band the Who performed *Tommy* (1969) as a musical, calling it a "rock opera." Film and then fully scored

Chapter 36
Timeline

American
Musical Theater

THE LIVE EXPERIENCE
Musicals Compared with Operas

Even the most operatic musicals maintain some basic differences from operas. The singing in musicals is usually amplified by the use of microphones worn by the singers, often attached to their foreheads. Amplifying the voices allows them to be heard in a large hall without the use of operatic "bel canto" singing techniques. The amplification also allows for the use of lighter, more pop-styled singing, in which singers scoop up to high notes or slide from one note to another. That is not to say that singers in musicals do not occasionally project their voices, only that the vocal style is strengthened by the amplification.

Generally, the songs in musicals are much less demanding in terms of vocal training, strength, and range required to sing them than are arias in operas. In fact, it is very common for the same singers to sing their roles in musicals six to eight times a week, whereas opera singers are rarely able to sing two nights in a row because of the great demands made on their voices.

Songs from musicals often become popular on their own, and that is one of the greatest strengths of the musical. The complexity and virtuosity of opera is part of what keeps it from reaching as many people as do musicals.

Dialogue is usually spoken in musicals, whereas in operas the dialogue is usually sung. The style used for the sung dialogue, called recitative, follows the inflections of the voice and is less dramatic than the singing in operatic arias.

Musicals also tend to use much smaller orchestras than do operas. Some musical productions have cut their budgets even further, using prerecorded music to accompany singing and dancing. Opera audiences would not tolerate prerecorded music because the orchestral parts are so integral to opera.

Professionally produced musicals often equal opera in their elaborate staging, costuming, and dancing. Plots of musicals can have just as much depth and drama as operas, and they can be just as funny and generally entertaining. On the other hand, the stories of musicals are usually much easier to understand through the songs than are opera plots, which are often so complicated that the synopsis must be studied in advance for the listener to completely understand what is going on.

---

musical versions of *Tommy* have been popular in later years. *Jesus Christ Superstar* (1971) and *Grease* (1972) also contained rock influences.

Jesus Christ Superstar, by the English composer **Andrew Lloyd Webber** (b. 1948), brought a more operatic style to musicals by having the dialogue sung instead of spoken. Lloyd Webber's father was the director of the London College of Music, and Andrew grew up listening to classical music of all kinds, including opera. Lloyd Webber met Tim Rice when he was in college, and the two began to write songs together. The first major project they completed was *Joseph and the Amazing Technicolor Dreamcoat* (1968), more of a staged cantata than a real musical. *Jesus Christ Superstar* (1971) was their second and much more ambitious "rock opera."

Some of Lloyd Webber's other musicals include *Evita* (1978) and *Cats* (1981). *Phantom of the Opera* (1986) is his most operatic in its elaborate staging and passionate story about a disfigured man, Eric. Eric lives under the Paris Opera House and tries to win the love of a young soprano by impressing her with his musical ability and by training her to be a star. Lloyd Webber has also composed music for movies and television. He was knighted by the Queen of England and was later given an honorary life peerage, making him Lord Andrew Lloyd Webber.

The Frenchman Claude-Michel Schonberg added *Les Misérables* (1987) and *Miss Saigon* (1988) to the repertoire of "Broadway" musicals. *Miss Saigon* is based on the plot of Puccini's opera *Madame Butterfly* (1904). The opera's story of an American serviceman stationed in Japan and his mistreatment of a Japanese lover has been updated to Vietnam in 1975, with an American serviceman who leaves a Vietnamese woman and takes their child, knowing that the woman will die as a result.

As we discussed in Chapter 24, the opera *La bohéme* (*Bohemian Life,* 1896) served as the model for the musical *Rent* (1996) with a similar updating of the story. "The Live Experience: Musicals Compared with Operas" discusses some of the differences between these forms.

Summary

Musicals developed out of several earlier theatrical styles. The English ballad operas were first composed in the middle 1700s and became popular in the American colonies. They were different from operas in that they used spoken dialogue instead of recitative and had short popular songs instead of the more elaborate arias of opera. Vaudeville shows and operettas by Gilbert and Sullivan also contributed to the development of the Broadway musical.

At the beginning of the twentieth century, George M. Cohan composed musicals that used everyday language and plots to relate to "real life" in America, giving him the name "Yankee Doodle Dandy." The success of Kern and Hammerstein's musical *Showboat* allowed other musical writers and composers to use more serious plots than they had previously thought audiences wanted. Gershwin's *Porgy and Bess* also featured a serious plot, and it added African American and jazz music to the genre.

Rodgers and Hammerstein wrote many very popular musicals in the 1940s, and Leonard Bernstein followed with several in the 1950s. Among Bernstein's successes was *West Side Story,* which set Shakespeare's tale of *Romeo and Juliet* in modern-day New York and added Latin instruments and rhythms to the American musical's repertoire.

Rock music influenced a number of musicals in the 1960s. One of those, *Jesus Christ Superstar* by Andrew Lloyd Webber, used sung dialogue, making Lloyd Webber's musicals more operatic than earlier musicals. Singing styles between musicals and operas differ in a number of ways, particularly in that the songs in musicals are more easily singable and often become popular on their own. Professional productions of both operas and musicals enhance the drama with elaborate sets and costumes.

New People and Concepts

Andrew Lloyd Webber

ballad opera

George M. Cohan

Leonard Bernstein

musicals

Rodgers and Hammerstein

Stephen Sondheim

Finale

Listen again to "America" and compare your impressions now with your notes from your first listening. Do you hear more now than you did before? You should now be able to answer the following questions:

- What is the meter?
- What is the gender of the singers?
- What instruments in the orchestra add to the Latin style of the music?
- What is the song about?
- What is the mood of the song and how does it fit into the story of the musical?

37 | Rock Music

I was the originator, I was the emancipator, I was the architect of rock 'n' roll. . . . When I made rock 'n' roll I got tired of the old people's music of that time. I did it because that's what I wanted to hear. I was tired of the slow music.
—ROCK SINGER/SONGWRITER/PIANIST LITTLE RICHARD (BORN IN 1932)

Listening Introduction

Listen to Little Richard's recording of "Tutti Frutti" and take notes about what you hear. Give some attention to the following:

▌ How would you describe the tempo?

▌ Can you detect the meter?

▌ What is the song about?

▌ Can you tell what instruments accompany the singing?

▌ Do you hear any repeated melodies or lyrics?

Keep these notes to compare with your impressions about the music after you study the information in this chapter.

Roots and Early Rock Performers

Rock music was born in the late 1940s and early 1950s out of a combination of blues, **rhythm and blues,** gospel, and country music. The styles of early rock music were varied. Some blues or rhythm-and-blues recordings that were particularly upbeat (fast) and energetic are now considered to be early rock. "Tutti Frutti," for example, follows the twelve-bar form of the blues, but the energy level created by the instruments and Little Richard's no-holds-barred vocal style make it as much rock and roll as blues. As Little Richard said in the quote that opens this chapter, "I was tired of the slow music."

Country music became part of early rock and roll when country musicians **covered** (rerecorded) blues songs. When those musicians tried to play the blues, their experience in playing country music changed the basic sound of the music. In comparison with blues musicians, country musicians tended to have a less relaxed approach to the rhythmic flow of the music; they often used slides to get from one note to another, and they used more repetition of short melodic patterns than improvisation in their instrumentals. An early example of this can be heard in the early-to-middle 1950s recordings by Bill Haley. Haley had a Western swing band called the Saddlemen in 1951. They covered "Rocket 88," a blues song that had been previously released by Jackie Brenston singing with Ike Turner's band. Haley's teenage audiences responded so well to it that Haley decided to change his image. He renamed the band the Comets, and they continued to record blues songs in their blues/country mixed style. Their cover of the blues song "Shake, Rattle and Roll" hit the top ten in 1954, assuring Haley that he was on the road to success. When Bill Haley and the Comets' recording of "Rock Around the Clock" was used in the opening credits of the teen movie *The Blackboard Jungle* (1954), it catapulted to number one on the Billboard charts, and rock music suddenly gained national attention. Haley's career continued with less success, but many other performers took up where he left off.

By 1955, Chuck Berry, an African American blues musician whose style included some characteristics of country music, recorded "Maybelline," an old country song originally called "Ida Red" to which he had written new lyrics. Its top-ten chart rating boosted Berry's career to rock and roll stardom, a status he still enjoys today. Berry's songs tended to be full of a lively spirit that reminded fans that rock and roll music was a great change from the past. "Roll Over Beethoven" is a good example of his claim that rock music had surpassed the importance of "old" music by such composers as Beethoven and Tchaikovsky. Berry became known as the "Father of Rock Guitar" because his guitar style was copied by so many later rock musicians to follow him.

Musician Chuck Berry

There was much racism in the 1950s, and although such African Americans as Little Richard and Chuck Berry sold enough records to have hits on the pop charts, there was a much bigger market for Caucasian musicians. Elvis Presley, whose good looks afforded him much of the same appeal as the popular actor James Dean, topped the charts nation-wide. Elvis Presley's recording career began in 1954, when he signed with a very small record company, Sun Records, in Memphis, Tennessee. Presley's early recordings at Sun popularized a style called rockabilly that combined "hillbilly" country music with blues influences. **Rockabilly** records were popular in the South, but the company owner and producer, Sam Phillips, did not have the money or connections to promote Presley's career nationally. RCA bought Presley's contract in 1956, and the manager they hired booked him on every television variety show in the country. Presley was a very strong and appealing performer, but for some TV producers Presley's way of shaking his hips when he sang was too suggestive. The Ed Sullivan show, for example, would only film Presley above the waist. His singing, stage presence, and engaging personality made him an overnight star. He began his long and successful movie career in 1956, and from then on he became known as the "King of Rock and Roll."

The Presley craze opened the floodgates for rock music and musicians. A number of other rockabilly musicians became popular, among them Jerry Lee Lewis, Carl Perkins, Buddy Holly, Roy Orbison, and Eddie Cochran. Other African Americans with blues and rhythm-and-blues backgrounds also gained national attention, including pianist/singer Fats Domino.

Elvis Presley

To many Americans, early rock music was a bit threatening and they still preferred to hear white pop-oriented singers. The pop singer Pat Boone made a cover recording of Little Richard's song "Tutti Frutti" that was a bigger hit than the original. Boone changed the lyrics, however, to remove the suggestion that he "rocks" with Suzy because such sexual references were not appropriate for Boone's clean-cut image. Of course, Little Richard received the writer's royalties for Boone's recording, so he didn't really mind. When asked what he thought about Boone's recording, Little Richard said he knew that kids had Pat's record to show their mamas, but they had his hidden in their bedroom drawers.

1960s Rock Music

There were a lot of things about 1950s rock music that people in the record industry did not like. For one thing, rock musicians tended to write their own songs, which cut the incomes for songwriters who traditionally wrote for pop singers. Rock music was also so clearly rooted in African American styles that some people, particularly in the South, did not want their young people to hear it. As Asa Carter of the North Alabama White Citizen's Council said in 1956, "Rock and roll is a means of pulling down the white man to the level of the Negro. It is part of a plot to undermine the morals of the youth of our nation." Other Americans disliked the sexiness of some rock singers and their songs and thought that the music would ruin young people's morals. The record industry eventually won out and was able to promote a very pop style of music that they tried to sell as rock. Pat Boone's "Tutti Frutti," for example, had none of the sexy energy that Little Richard's did. Part of the reason the record industry was able to win out was that many rock artists of the 1950s stopped performing at the end of that decade or the beginning of the next. Buddy Holly, the Big Bopper, and Ritchie Valens died in a plane crash; Elvis was drafted into the army; Jerry Lee Lewis's career was boycotted when his illegal marriage to his young cousin was reported; Eddie Cochran died in a car crash that also badly injured Gene Vincent; Little Richard quit singing rock and entered a Bible college; Carl Perkins was injured in a car crash; and Chuck Berry was imprisoned for two years for a violation of the Mann Act, which stated that it was illegal to take an underage female across state lines for immoral purposes.

Sometimes the day of Buddy Holly's plane crash is called "the day the music died." The reason is not just the loss of Holly, Valens, and the Big Bopper; it is also that pop singers such as Frankie Avalon and Fabian took their places on the continuation of the tour, and the fans did not seem to notice the movement from more aggressive and rhythmic 1950s rock to a smoother and more polite pop style. Pop styles were marketed so heavily that many "rock" recordings of the late 1950s and early 1960s had orchestral string sections and other instruments not associated with rock of the mid-1950s.

Many of the songs in this pop style, sometimes referred to as "teen idol" music, had lyrics such as "(Today I Met) The Boy I'm Gonna Marry" that were meant to appeal to very young teens. College-age teens wanted more to think about when they listened to music and many became fans of folk music. The civil rights movement began during the 1950s and continued on through the 1960s. The primary goals of the movement were to achieve greater equality for non-white Americans, particularly African Americans, who were not yet allowed to vote freely in parts of the South. The Vietnam War began and escalated during the 1960s, and so many young American men were drafted and died as a result that it was of great concern to young people. Folk music has traditionally taken a stand against war and against racism. Folk singer Bob Dylan became the spokesperson for the middle 1960s generation. Dylan put out his first album in 1962, but it was too folk-styled to become a hit on the pop charts. His popularity as a rock musician started in 1965, when he began to record with amplified rock instruments and drums, something pure folk musicians avoided. Dylan sang songs against war and was supportive of the civil rights movement. Other **folk-rock** groups such as the Byrds, the Mamas and the Papas, and Simon and Garfunkel followed.

Folk singer Bob Dylan

The British Invasion of 1964 also provided an alternative to teen-idol pop music in that the British bands had based their styles on American 1950s rock. The British bands' popularity, in effect, brought that more aggressive and less pop-oriented sound back to American audiences. The first two bands to "invade and conquer" the U.S. pop charts were the Beatles and the Rolling Stones. Members of both bands later became highly original writers in their own right, but they started their careers by copying the recordings and styles of Buddy Holly, in the case of the Beatles, and American blues and rhythm-and-blues musicians, in the case of the Stones. The Beatles named themselves after Holly's group, which was called the Crickets. "Rolling stone" was a slang term for a "man on the move, ready to satisfy every woman he meets" often used in songs by blues man Muddy Waters. At the time, this term evoked the image the Rolling Stones wanted. In general, British bands were so popular in America that American bands tried to pretend they were British. The Sir Douglas Quintet chose their name to attract fans of the British bands, but when they were interviewed by the press, the fact that they were from Texas became pretty obvious.

Soul music was another alternative for people who had no interest in early 1960s pop. Soul music developed out of black gospel music, and it shared many musical characteristics with gospel, such as the use of a solo singer backed by a group of two to four singers. Both gospel and soul solo singers tend to add what are called *melismas* (several notes sung to a single syllable of text) to decorate their vocal style. The primary difference between gospel and soul is that gospel music is religious while soul is secular. In fact, many of the most popular soul singers, such as Sam Cooke, James Brown, and Aretha Franklin, were all professional gospel singers before recording soul. Soul styles developed all over the United States, with major styles centered in Chicago, Memphis, Philadelphia, and Detroit, home of the Motown style. The singer, songwriter, and dynamic performer who came to be called the "Godfather of Soul" was James Brown. Brown was not only a great soul singer, but he also single-handedly invented **funk,** a style

Guitarist Jimi Hendrix

derived from the polyrhythms of African music, with his recording of "Out of Sight" in 1964. Brown also did much to cool tensions within the civil rights movement after the assassination of Dr. Martin Luther King with his recording and performances of "Say It Loud—I'm Black and I'm Proud" (1968). His message, not unlike that of Dr. King himself, was one of pride for African Americans and a peaceful movement toward equal rights and opportunities.

One of the most influential guitarists in rock history, Jimi Hendrix, enjoyed a short career between 1966 and 1970. Hendrix was playing in an American blues band when Chas Chandler of the British group the Animals heard him. Chandler invited him to come to England, where blues-based rock music had a bigger following than it did in the United States. Hendrix accepted the invitation and subsequently formed the Jimi Hendrix Experience with English musicians Noel Redding and Mitch Mitchell. He was a big success in England before he was introduced to American audiences at the Monterey Pop Festival in 1967. He is famous for having "sacrificed" his guitar in flames in that show, but that was not the standard for Hendrix. He generally showed great respect for his instrument. From Monterey until his death in 1970 he worked with a variety of groups in the United States and the United Kingdom. He is best remembered for the highly controlled sound effects he could get out of the guitar and for his electrifying stage presence. One of his most famous performances was the "Star Spangled Banner" at the Woodstock Festival in 1969. He turned the U.S. national anthem into an aural antiwar statement by using some of the sound effects he was famous for to make his guitar sound as if bombs were dropping between parts of the melody.

The Diversity of Rock of the 1970s

From its beginnings rock music has existed in a variety of styles, but during the 1970s it spread out even further when rock bands added characteristics of other kinds of music to their sound. The Byrds and the Eagles added the sounds of

Chapter 37
Timeline

Rock Music

the banjo and the mandolin to create a style called **country rock.** In the South, **Southern rock** was created by the Allman Brothers Band and others who played an aggressive form of the blues along with country influences. Jazz horn sections were added to rock bands such as Blood, Sweat and Tears to create the style **jazz rock.** Amplified rock instruments were added to jazz by Miles Davis to develop the jazz style called fusion. Moody Blues and other bands added whole orchestras or sections of instruments from orchestras to create the style **art rock.** Blues revival bands developed more powerful styles of **hard rock** and **heavy metal,** and elaborate stage theatrics became central to **glitter rock.** All of these diverse styles began in the late 1960s and grew to huge proportions during the 1970s.

Punk rock began during the middle 1960s in Detroit and New York, but it pretty much stayed in the northeastern United States until bands such as the New York Dolls and the Ramones went to England and sparked the punk movement there. Aggressive and angry punk bands stayed small and reached a whole audience of young people who did not care at all for grand arena performances by art, glitter, or heavy metal bands. Punk moved to the American west coast when the British band the Sex Pistols toured there in 1978. Punk had a big following throughout the 1970s, and post-punk styles continued to develop throughout the 1980s and 1990s.

The 1980s and Beyond

The hip-hop culture developed when Jamaican reggae disc jockeys such as DJ Kool Herc began playing music to encourage break dancing on street corners in New York's South Bronx. Others imitated his patter talk over the music. The style that resulted was **rap.** Much rap was and is very positive. Early rapper Afrika Bambaataa formed what he called the Zulu Nation and encouraged people of all races to join. Members participated in neighborhood cleanup projects, food drives, mentor programs, and talent shows. It was not until rap was taken up by street gangs in Los Angeles that the very angry and aggressive style called **gangsta rap** gave the patter-spoken vocals a negative reputation.

Much about the marketing of rock music and its many related styles changed dramatically when cable television became available nationwide and **MTV** was broadcast coast to coast. Suddenly a performer's ability to dance was as important as singing or playing musical instruments. People in the entertainment industry came to realize that images sold music much more easily than radio. Racism still being a factor in the entertainment industry, early MTV did not show many African American performers, but once Michael Jackson started making videos, his career was unstoppable. He was just too good to be ignored, and he eventually came to be called the King of Pop. Prince and Madonna were other dancer/singers whose careers were greatly aided by their videos on MTV. Of course, eventually other cable/satellite stations were added to show rock videos, and MTV itself added game shows and other types of entertainment to their programming, but the importance of MTV in the 1980s is without a doubt revolutionary to rock music of the era.

Also during the 1980s, music that was on the pop charts in England became popular in the United States as **alternative rock,** so named because it offered an alternative to the dance-oriented pop rock that MTV played most often. Bands such as the Smiths and the Cure gained alternative reputations in the United States. Other alternatives to pop rock were post-punk styles that developed in many parts of the United States. Some of those post-punk styles

Singer Madonna

were aggressively antidrug, including Ian MacKaye's band Minor Threat. In the 1990s MacKaye formed the popular band Fugazi, who led the movement to reduce CD and concert ticket prices. The Seattle band Pearl Jam was also part of that movement. It sued Ticketmaster because of the prices it charged for tickets. The suit was unsuccessful, but the effort was lauded by fans. Other bands from the Seattle area became known as **grunge rock** bands, including Soundgarden and Nirvana.

Another angry post-punk style was called **industrial rock.** Most industrial rock music used sound effects created by machines of all kinds, in addition to more traditional instruments, such as amplified guitars using feedback and fuzz-tone. Some bands played guitars with buzz saws or other nonmusical devices. Industrial vocals are often distorted to sound nonhuman. Trent Reznor's Nine-Inch Nails added a bit of melody to what was otherwise a mostly tortured and alienated sound. Depressing lyrics, but with less aggressive instrumentation, continued to be popular among young people during the 1990s with the music of the British band Radiohead.

Electronic dance music called **techno** featured hypnotic repetitions of synthesized music, along with an intense, throbbing beat. The music became associated with the rave culture that added the drug Ecstasy to their dance parties. Because the drug was illegal, rave dances tended to be held on private properties that were fairly well hidden from the general public.

As much as rock music has changed over the years since its inception in the early 1950s, most rock styles of the past have continued on through the changes. There are few young people today who have not heard of Elvis Presley, the Beatles, or any number of other performers who have not performed their original styles in decades. Rock music is not all that old. Some of its originators, such as Chuck Berry and Little Richard, are still around and performing in the 2000s. Paul McCartney, Mick Jagger, and Elton John have all been knighted by the Queen of England and have the official titles "Sir" before their names. All continue to perform the music that made them famous.

Summary

Rock music developed during the late 1940s and early 1950s as a combination of blues, rhythm and blues, gospel, and country music. Rockabilly combined "rock" and "hillbilly" country music with the blues to create an energetic and popular 1950s style. A more pop-oriented style was widely marketed as rock music during the early 1960s, but the British Invasion bands knocked it off the American charts and brought back music that was closer to 1950s rock styles. Soul music remained popular throughout the 1960s, both before and after the British Invasion. By the 1970s, rock diversified into a great variety of styles that combined rock music with instruments or other influences of such styles of music as jazz, art (or classical), and country music.

Punk was an angry and aggressive style that remained largely in the northeastern cities of Detroit and New York until it hit Britain. British bands popularized punk all over the United States. A variety of post-punk styles have continued to pop up in many U.S. cities, along with other depressed or angry music such as industrial rock. MTV popularized music and dance videos that, at first, countered more angry music. Rap grew in popularity through the 1980s and 1990s, going from simple patter talk to accompany break dancing to an entire new vocal style that is at times quite positive and at other times angry and negative.

Rock music continues to be played by some of its earliest stars, as well as by new musicians creating their own sounds every day. The music has changed from one performer or time period to another, but it still remains a viable and popular kind of music that exists in many varied styles.

New People and Concepts

alternative rock	glitter rock	punk rock
art rock	grunge rock	rap
British Invasion	hard rock	rhythm and blues
country rock	heavy metal	rockabilly
cover recording	industrial rock	soul music
folk-rock	jazz rock	Southern rock
funk	MTV	techno
gangsta rap		

Finale

Listen again to Little Richard's recording of "Tutti Frutti" and compare your impressions now with your notes from your first listening. Do you hear more now than you did before? You should now be able to answer the following questions:

▌ What is the tempo?

▌ What is the meter?

▌ What is the song about?

▌ What instruments are accompanying the singing?

▌ Where do melodies or lyrics repeat?

Characteristics of Music in America

Texture	Monophonic melodies composed to be sung as polyphonic "fuging" tunes; homophonic songs with simple piano accompaniment; works with a variety of textures in the European tradition; complex textures in bebop jazz
Tonality	Major-minor system retained; modes used in some jazz or jazz-influenced works; atonality in some electronic works
Rhythm	Standard meters following European traditions; "swing" beat (uneven beat subdivisions) in jazz and blues-based rock; "free" rhythms in free jazz and much electronic music
Harmony	Traditional European harmonies in song accompaniments; chord extensions common in advanced jazz styles
Tone color	Some jazz instruments use mutes to create "wah-wah" timbres; guitars amplified for use in jazz and rock; rock music uses solid-body electric guitars, electric bass guitars, and electric pianos to create a loud and full sound from few instruments; electronic sounds manipulated on tape add to the tone color of electronic and other works; singers' voices are amplified in musicals
Musical instruments	In addition to the widespread use of amplified instruments, electronic instruments become capable of both producing unnatural sounds and imitating acoustic sounds
Form	Twelve-bar blues form used in the blues, some jazz styles, and blues-based rock; "free" forms in free jazz and electronic music; traditional forms also used

38 | Film Music

*. . . in film composing, you're not in full control of it
the way you are in concert music—so the risk of
compromise, or dilution of idea or structure, is
great. In film, it's the director's vision, even of the
music, which prevails, whereas in concert
composing, it's your own vision.*

—COMPOSER/FILM COMPOSER JOHN CORIGLIANO
(BORN IN 1938)

Listening Introduction

Listen to the "Main Theme" from *Star Wars,* and make notes about what you
hear. Give some attention to the following:

▌ Can you determine the tempo? Does the tempo vary at all?

▌ Can you detect the meter? Does it change?

▌ Can you tell what instruments are playing?

▌ Can you hear any melody or melodies that return after they are first played?

▌ What is the general mood, and does it change?

Keep these notes to compare with your impressions of the music after you
have read this chapter.

By the early twenty-first century, film music had evolved into its own independent genre. In the 1980s, when cable television and VCRs first became available,
movie executives worried that these new technologies would replace movie theaters. Of course, their worries were misplaced. People still wanted to experience
visual effects on a big screen, and they wanted to hear the high-quality sound that
only theaters could provide. Film companies found that they could create independent "profit centers" by releasing films first in theaters and then on VCR,
DVD, cable, and satellite. Soundtracks created yet another source of revenue, and
for this reason studios began spending a good deal of money to produce music of
the highest possible quality. The movie soundtrack became popular as its own
genre, and by the 1990s it was not uncommon to see a movie soundtrack on CD
advertised at the end of a film.

The Earliest Film Music

Films offered an entirely new type of entertainment to a few select audiences during the middle to late 1890s. These early films were silent, and the projectors in
use at the time were very noisy. Theaters solved this problem by having live music

during the film. This practice began in Paris in 1895, when a solo pianist played light popular tunes throughout a screening. There was no effort to connect the music to the action or moods in the film. The following year in London, a harmonium (a type of reed organ) was used to accompany the showing of a film. By April of 1896, some London theaters were using small orchestras to accompany their films.

In 1908, *Le Film d'Art* company in Paris decided to have music composed specifically for its film *L'Assassinat du Duc de Guise*. The company hired a well-known and respected French composer, **Camille Saint-Saëns** (1835–1921), to compose the score. Saint-Saëns had previously composed incidental music for a ballet and for a number of plays, and he was anxious to attempt a film score. The film company was happy with the result, and Saint-Saëns made further use of his score by rewriting it as his concert work Opus 128 for Strings, Piano, and Harmonium. Live musicians played the score during screenings of the film, and the idea of having music designed to fit the film was generally thought to be a good one. However, there was a problem with this approach in that it not only required the film producers to pay a composer but it also required each movie theater to rent a particular score and to hire the musicians necessary to play it. This added expense prevented theaters and movie companies from making the film-specific score a regular practice.

In 1909, the Edison film company offered a solution by creating lists of well-known classical works that would fit different moods and dramatic situations. Other publishers produced similar lists. By 1912, an American named Max Winkler was not only suggesting certain music but also designing what he called music **cue sheets.** The cue sheet told the musicians exactly when to start and stop playing the suggested music in order to make sure that it matched the action of the film. He used classical works for his suggestions, fully recognizing that he was taking them out of their intended context: "In desperation we turned to crime. We began to dismember the great masters. We began to murder the works of Beethoven, Mozart, Grieg, J. S. Bach, Verdi, Bizet, Tchaikovsky, and Wagner—everything that wasn't protected by copyright from our pilfering."

Early Sound Films

In 1926, the Warner Brothers Studio produced the **Vitaphone** system, an invention that allowed music recorded on phonograph records to be played simultaneously with the film. The first film to use the system was *Don Juan*. The following year, *The Jazz Singer* (1927) used the Vitaphone to include both the first spoken dialogue and the first song in a movie. The dialogue and singing were synchronized with the actors' mouth movements. The vaudeville entertainer Al Jolson starred in the film, and the score added to his popularity by showcasing his singing. Many future films would use the Vitaphone in this way.

By the early 1930s, films had become very popular with the general public, with some 80 million Americans going to the movies as often as once a week. Because movies offered an inexpensive and much needed escape from the problems of the time, the film industry was one of the few businesses to succeed during the Great Depression. American movie studios produced as many as 500 films a year, and there was much incentive to improve the movie experience.

One of the first movie composers was **Max Steiner** (1888–1971). Steiner was born into a musical family in Vienna. His godfather was composer Richard Strauss, and he studied conducting with composer/conductor Gustav Mahler, whose first symphony was discussed in Chapter 23. Steiner learned to play

Entertainer Al Jolson in the film *The Jazz Singer*

instruments of several types, including string, brass, and keyboards. While he was still a teenager he worked as a conductor in Vienna and then in Britain. He took an opportunity to move to New York at the beginning of World War I, where he composed and conducted music for theatrical productions. In 1929 he moved to Hollywood, where he worked on a number of films. His first major achievement in film music was the score for *King Kong* (1933), made by the RKO Studio. The film was made under a tight budget, and Steiner was instructed to put together a score from tracks that had already been recorded for earlier films. Of course, this was the studio's first film about a giant ape threatening the population of an American city. Steiner's response to the suggestion that he use existing music was "For God's sake . . . what am I gonna use—music from *Little Women*?" The company gave in, and Steiner composed a score that helped make the movie a tremendous success. Income from the film actually saved the RKO Studio from having to close its doors.

Six years later, Steiner was given a chance to make his mark on the movie industry by composing a full three hours and forty-five minutes of music for *Gone with the Wind* (1939). The theme known as "Tara's Theme," which represented the Southern plantation, became one of the most memorable movie themes ever composed. Steiner wrote many other film scores during the 1940s, including the forever popular *Casablanca* (1942). (Although he did not write "As Time Goes By"—he took that from a musical called *Everybody's Welcome,* then on Broadway—the rest of the score was his, and it added much to the romantic tension of the movie.)

World War II had taken such a toll on many parts of Europe that moviemakers there could hardly keep up with the advancements being made in Hollywood. Europeans continued to produce movies, but the great film masterpieces were coming from the Hollywood

Scene from the film *King Kong*

studios. That is not to say that people in California were unaffected by the war. Money was tighter than it had been, and the very large and lush orchestras were reduced to smaller ensembles. One of the great movie classics from the early 1940s was Orson Welles's *Citizen Kane* (1941). American composer **Bernard Herrmann** (1911–1975) added to the dark character of the movie by using more dissonance than had been common in past movie scores. His work on *Citizen Kane* was so effective that horror filmmaker Alfred Hitchcock chose him to compose scores for his films *The Man Who Knew Too Much* (1934—the 1956 remake also used Herrmann's music), *The Trouble With Harry* (1955), *The Wrong Man* (1956), *Vertigo* (1958), *North by Northwest* (1959), *Psycho* (1960), and *Marnie* (1964).

American composer Aaron Copland was already well known for his classical compositions (see Chapter 34) when he began writing for the movies in 1939. Copland won an Academy Award for his movie score for *The Heiress* (1948). In one scene, the main character, Catherine, has her bags packed and is sitting with her aunt waiting for her fiancé to pick her up. A carriage is heard, and Catherine says goodbye to her aunt and runs outside with her bags. The carriage, however, just passes her by, and she slinks back into the house feeling depressed and disillusioned. When the movie was first screened in previews, audiences laughed at Catherine's having been rejected. That was not the response the director wanted, so he asked Copland to write music that would give the viewers a sense of the tragedy of the situation. Copland composed dissonant music for muted brass instruments, and both the scene and the movie were saved. As Copland said later, "I am sure that the audience had no idea that music was playing." Such is the effect music can have on movie audiences.

Later Film Scoring Practices

Many movies, from the silent era to the present, have used existing music as part or all of their soundtracks. One very famous example is *2001: A Space Odyssey* (1968), directed by Stanley Kubrick. The movie portrays the silence of space by devoting no more than forty minutes of its entire running time to dialogue. The first word is not spoken until almost a half hour into the film. The lengthy score is made up of carefully chosen compositions, including the tone poem *Thus Spake Zarathustra* by Richard Strauss; *The Blue Danube Waltz* by Johann Strauss; *Atmospheres, Lux Aeterna*, and *Requiem for Soprano, Mezzo-Soprano, Two Mixed Choirs and Orchestra,* by György Ligeti; and *Gayane Ballet Suite* by Aram Khatchaturian. The movie was nominated for five Academy Awards and won in the "Best Visual Effects" category. In many ways the music did more than the story line to give the effects the support they needed to make *2001: A Space Odyssey* one of the most popular science fiction films of all time.

It was another science fiction movie, *Star Wars* (1977), that successfully combined brilliant visual effects with the almost constant dramatic support of a large symphony orchestra: the music plays for 88 of the 121 minutes of the movie. Actually, the director of *Star Wars*, George Lucas, had originally intended to use previously composed music in much the same way that Kubrick had for *2001: A Space Odyssey*, but he decided to have composer **John Williams** (born in 1932) write the score, including some of the music that Lucas had chosen. Williams had had tremendous success with various television scores and with the movie *Jaws* (1975). The works Williams incorporated

Scene from the film
Star Wars

into the *Star Wars* score included music by film composers Eric Korngold and Alessandro Cicognini and music by classical composers Gustav Holst, Pyotr Ilyich Tchaikovsky, Sir Edward William Elgar, and Carl Orff. The famous "heroic theme" at the opening to *Star Wars* was a quote from the score to *The Sea Hawk* (1940) by Eric Korngold.

The "Main Theme" from *Star Wars* opens the movie and functions much like an opera overture in that it sets the mood for *Star Wars* by quoting themes that will be heard again throughout the movie. Like Richard Wagner (see Chapter 25), Williams assigns each character his or her own theme. *Star Wars* begins with a fanfare and a theme that represents the movie's hero, Luke Skywalker. (Because the same theme was used in the later *Star Wars* films to represent a larger heroism, we will call it the "heroic theme"; however, it was specific to Luke in the original movie.) The heroic theme is followed by music that foretells the impending battle between the Empire and the Rebel Alliance, and then Princess Leia is introduced by her theme. Apart from Leia's gentle introduction, the opening music projects the heroic nature of the film and foreshadows the conflicts to come.

The oversized orchestra used for the soundtrack of *Star Wars* was very expensive. Musicians who played on the film score not only received money for

Listening Guide

The "Main Theme" from *Star Wars* JOHN WILLIAMS

Year: 1977

Tempo: Moderate, but slows near the end

Meter: Mostly quadruple, but the battle music is triple

Instrumentation: Three flutes (including piccolo), three oboes (including English horn), three clarinets (including bass clarinet), two bassoons, six French horns, five trumpets, three trombones, one tuba, percussion, first violins, second violins, violas, cellos, double basses, and harp

Duration: approximately 5:52

Timing	What to listen for
(The exact timings will vary depending on the recording used.)	
0:00	Fanfare
0:09	Heroic theme played by brass and percussion then continued by the orchestra
1:18	Light and soft transition
1:36	Strings build intensity
2:03	Battle music (triple meter), then syncopated punctuations obscure meter
2:22	Heroic theme returns in quadruple meter
3:19	Princess Leia's *leitmotif* is played by cellos and basses
4:07	Heroic theme in high brass
4:39	Fanfare-like statements in brass with a background of swirling strings
5:02	Strings slow tempo and intensity drops
5:17	March music taken from "The Coronation March" by Elgar, music builds to a dramatic finale

their time in the recording studio but also received continuing residual payments after the film was released for rental, sale, or televised showings and other royalties for soundtrack sales. These payments had been negotiated between movie companies and musicians' unions, and, as a result of such negotiations, the 1970s saw many Hollywood musicians make a very good income by playing for film and television soundtracks. However, there was a new sound maker on the horizon: the synthesizer.

Robert Moog unveiled his synthesizer in 1964, and it became widely popular through Walter Carlos's album *Switched-On Bach* (1968). By 1970, rock bands and musicians such as Pink Floyd, Kraftwerk, Tangerine Dream, Mike Oldfield, Rick Wakeman (keyboardist for Yes), Jimmy Page (guitarist for Led Zeppelin), and Keith Emerson (keyboardist for Emerson, Lake, and Palmer) were using it on a regular basis. Throughout the 1970s, the Moog synthesizer continued to be improved, and soon other synthesizers and computerized sound makers were developed, including the Jupiter-8, Prophet-5, and the Synclavier II. These instruments could produce sounds that imitated those of orchestral instruments and could generate sound effects ideal for film scores. What did this mean for Hollywood film studios? It meant that a single composer with a synthesizer could produce an entire soundtrack and consequently save the studio a great deal of money on residuals and royalties. This practice, along with the practice of having movie scores recorded in countries that did not come under Hollywood musicians' union agreements, greatly reduced the number of musicians enjoying successful careers in Hollywood. Of course, something similar happened in the 1920s when the first sound films did away with the need for pianists and orchestras in movie theaters.

It did not take long for synthesizer-produced music to gain acceptance among movie fans. The first synthesizer movie score to win an Academy Award was *Midnight Express* (1978), with music by Italian-Swiss producer Giorgio Moroder. (Moroder was also famous for having invented the disco sound called *eurodisco* through his synthesized productions of hits by Donna Summer, including "Love to Love You Baby" and "Hot Stuff.") In 1981, another synthesized score, this time for *Chariots of Fire,* won an Academy Award for Greek composer/producer Vangelis.

Despite their popularity, synthesized scores are not all we have today. In many cases, film scores have been composed for live orchestras by some of the most successful classical composers of our time. Two of those composers include **John Corigliano** (born in 1938) and **Philip Glass** (whose music we will study in Chapter 40). Corigliano is well known for his concert works, including his opera *The Ghosts of Versailles,* produced by the Metropolitan Opera Company of New York in 1991. His film scores include *Altered States* (1980), for which he received an Academy Award nomination, *Revolution* (1985), which won an award from the British Film Institute, and *The Red Violin* (1999), which won an Academy Award for Best Original Score. Like Saint-Saëns before him, Corigliano used musical themes he had composed for the movie *The Red Violin* for his concert work, *The Red Violin: Chaconne for Violin and Orchestra.*

As we discuss in Chapter 40, Philip Glass's first film score to gain widespread public attention was *Koyaanisqatsi* (1983). The film is a collage of images of nature that accumulatively demonstrate the negative effects mankind has had on the world. Although Philip Glass has often composed for live orchestras, he used a synthesizer to produce sound effects for *Koyaanisqatsi.* For a later project that ultimately grew into two semi-horror movies, *Candyman* (1992) and its sequel *Farewell to the Flesh* (1995), Glass made effective use of gothic-influenced organ music. His next film project, *Kundun* (1997), was set in Tibet and related the early life of the Dalai Lama. Glass's later film scores include *The Hours* (2002) and *Undertow* (2004).

One of the most highly respected names in film music today is **James Horner** (born in 1953). Horner received a Ph.D. in music composition and theory from UCLA and gained experience in film scoring at the American Film Institute. His first commercial film was *Wolfen* (1981). It was followed by *Aliens* (1986), for which he was nominated for an Academy Award. He has also been nominated for *Field of Dreams* (1989), *Braveheart* and *Apollo 13* (both 1995), and *A Beautiful Mind* (2001); in 1997 he won the award for *Titanic* (1997). His other film scores are too numerous to list here. Horner effectively uses both recordings made by live musicians and synthesizer-produced sounds in his film scores. He describes his process as follows: "I'm a throwback. I know all about the machines. . . . When I work with synths, I don't want what you think of . . . as synthetic sounds. I want very organic sounds that I can manipulate. The orchestral stuff, I write at a desk and orchestrate, and then send it off to the copyist. The synth stuff, I play ideas to myself on the piano, and notate ideas, but most of it happens by coloring in, like painting, at the actual recording session, because I play everything myself on a MIDI keyboard."

Summary

The relationship between music and film has changed a great deal in the last hundred and twenty years. In the silent era, live music was played as much to drown out the sound of the projector as to add to the film experience. Today, film extravaganzas filled with visual effects of all kinds are accompanied by music as good as any other composed in the twenty-first century. The progress from silent films to those with sound took over thirty years, and even then the music was minimal.

By the mid-1920s, the Vitaphone system allowed previously recorded music and dialogue to be played along with films. Soon original scores were being composed and recorded, adding much to the impact of the movie experience. By the late 1930s, the art of film scoring had developed to include the sound of full orchestras recorded to play simultaneously with the film. Tighter wartime budgets reduced the size of those orchestras, but composers adjusted their writing accordingly.

During the late 1960s and through the 1970s, science fiction movies such as *2001: A Space Odyssey* and *Star Wars* expanded the visual effects to represent their space-age themes, and the music used to support those, whether borrowed from previously composed classical scores or newly composed, further popularized the effects music can have on a film.

Synthesizers began to be used to produce film scores during the 1970s, and since then film composers have used them, used live orchestras, or combined the two for many very successful and popular soundtracks. Many of the major classical composers today write for films, and many composers who concentrate on film music write at the same level of quality as do composers of other art music of our time.

New People and Concepts

Bernard Herrmann	James Horner	Max Steiner
Camille Saint-Saëns	John Corigliano	Philip Glass
cue sheet	John Williams	Vitaphone

Finale

Listen again to the "Main Theme" from *Star Wars* and compare your impressions now with your notes from your first listening. Do you hear more now than you did before? You should now be able to answer the following questions:

▌ What is the tempo and when does it change?

▌ What is the meter and when does it change?

▌ What instruments are playing?

▌ What melodies return after they are first played?

▌ What is the general mood, and when and why does it change?

George Harrison with Ravi Shankar

Our first prelude on the twentieth century made the point that a World Exposition in Paris in 1889 introduced European artists and musicians to music, costumes, and dances from Asia, the Middle East, and Africa. By the time Debussy composed his "Prelude to the Afternoon of a Faun" in 1894, the sense of rhythmic freedom heard in some world music had become part of Debussy's style and added much to the beauty and interest of the work. Influences of music from outside of Europe continued to affect European and American composers through the twentieth century.

By the 1970s, the United States had been involved in two world wars and a series of smaller wars in such places as Vietnam, Cambodia, and Korea. Later in the century, Iraq was added to the list. The American service men and women who served in those wars returned to the United States with experience and understanding of those "foreign" cultures. Through contact with veterans, as well as through reports in the media, Americans learned about the people and cultures of those places.

Improvements in transportation, particularly the development and widespread use of jet planes, allowed average Americans and Europeans to travel to regions all over the globe. Included among those travelers were musicians who not only visited and experienced music from distant places but also took advantage of opportunities to study music during their visits. One of the most famous examples occurred in 1965 when the

Prelude | New Ideas and Styles Developed out of Twentieth-Century Internationalism

Beatles' guitarist George Harrison became interested in the Indian religion of Hinduism. He bought an Indian sitar and played it on Beatles' recordings such as "Norwegian Wood" and "Within You Without You." In 1968, Harrison and other members of the Beatles, the Beach Boys, and other musicians took a trip to India to study the Hindu religion and its related meditation and music.

Harrison studied the sitar with Indian virtuoso Ravi Shankar, and the two became close friends. The Beatles' popularity gave Shankar fame outside of India, allowing him to be featured in such important rock events as the 1967 Monterey Music Festival in San Francisco. Shankar was a serious and talented classical musician in India, something quite different from the many rock musicians who also played at Monterey. Shankar also played at the famous Woodstock Festival in 1969. Harrison's friendship with Ravi Shankar and his relationship with Indian culture continued on throughout his career. In 1971 Harrison organized a charity concert called the "Concert for Bangladesh" to raise money to feed starving people in Bangladesh.

By the 1980s, many other popular musicians were listening to music from all over the world and adding performers from such distant places as Africa to their recordings. American folk-rock musician Paul Simon added the South African vocal group Ladysmith Black Mambazo to his Grammy award–winning *Graceland* album in 1986. He then went on to produce two albums of Ladysmith Black Mambazo's music for world-wide sale. Through Simon's work, many music fans heard the gentle vocal style of Ladysmith Black Mambazo for the first time, and this ended up influencing the styles of many male vocal groups the world over. Simon went on to record *The Rhythm of the Saints* (1990), with musicians from West Africa and Brazil, further popularizing world music and rhythms.

British singer/songwriter Peter Gabriel added Senegalese singer/percussionist Youssou N'Dour to his *So* album in 1986, helping to popularize N'Dour's West African vocal style. N'Dour has continued to be popular with rock fans through his work for Amnesty International. Gabriel and N'Dour have often performed at Amnesty International fund-raising events and concerts, sharing bills with Bruce Springsteen, Sting, and Tracy Chapman.

Still in the area of rock music, Talking Heads' former singer David Byrne moved in the direction of world music after he began his solo career. He included African polyrhythms to his *My Life in the Bush of Ghosts* (1981) album and added musicians from Brazil, Cuba, and Asia to his *Rei Momo* (1989) album and tour. He also has a record label, called Luaka Bop, which produces music from all over the world, though primarily from Latin America. Former Led Zeppelin members Robert Plant and Jimmy Page included Egyptian musicians and instruments on their *No Quarter* (1994) album, and Tracy Chapman sometimes plays the Australian aboriginal wind instrument the didjeridoo in her performances.

The trend toward world music has also manifested itself in classical music. Since the beginning of the twentieth century, classical composers have continually been looking for new sounds and ideas in a series of efforts to move music beyond the traditions of the nineteenth century. Schoenberg's development of the twelve-tone compositional technique was very much a part of that urge to be new and different. The Kronos Quartet, a string quartet from San Francisco, has concentrated on broadening the string quartet repertoire beyond its traditional European base. The quartet has commissioned works from many contemporary composers and has reached out to composers in a variety of non-Western cultures. It played works by African composers on its *Pieces of Africa* (1992) album; works influenced by music from Portugal, Hungary, Turkey, Romania, Lebanon, Iran, and India on its *Caravan* (2000) album; and Latin music on its Grammy award–winning *Nuevo* (2002). On other albums the Kronos Quartet has recorded works by a great variety of modern composers whose music is also rooted in world music, including Terry Riley, John Cage, Steve Reich, Philip Glass, and George Crumb.

When discussing music from another culture, one must consider whether the music is *ethnic, folk,* or *traditional*. Although these terms might at first glance seem synonymous, they are not. *Ethnic* music usually refers to the music of groups of people who have shared a common cultural history over many generations. *Traditional* music is sometimes considered "classical" or "sophisticated" because it follows more or less rigorous principles of content, style, and performance. Traditional music is usually performed by artists who have refined the music through continued use or disciplined training. *Folk* music is the music of everyday life—work songs, children's songs, lullabies, love songs, and ballad-story songs sung and played by ordinary people. In contrast to traditional music, folk music has no formal or ceremonial content.

The music we have spent most of our time exploring in this text— the concert music of Western Europe and the United States—is based on a tradition of written notation in which the artistic expression of individual composers is carefully preserved. The musical heritages of many world cultures, by contrast, are usually transmitted orally. Young musicians learn by carefully listening to, observing, and imitating elder musicians. Although music composition is treated with seriousness and reverence, in many cultures the name of an individual composer is not attached to the piece. In some ancient cultures, music was linked with supernatural beings and mythical gods and was considered a reflection of universal order and spiritual purity.

Musical instruments also affect the character and sound of music. In general, modern historians have classified world instruments as *aerophones* (wind instruments), *chordophones* (string instruments), *idiophones* (solid instruments that are beaten, such as gourds) and *membranophones* (drums). When one compares these classifications of instruments with those used in a standard European orchestra—*string, woodwind, brass,* and *percussion*—a major difference is obvious. Wind instruments are classified as both *woodwind* and *brass* in the European tradition, whereas they all fit into the single category of *aerophones* in world music. European percussion instruments are classified as a single group, even though there are both pitched and nonpitched members of that group. Percussion instruments are so very plentiful in much world music that they are given two categories, *idiophones* and *membranophones*.

The music in this last set of chapters represents the interaction and communication among people from many different cultural backgrounds. Anyone who has traveled to a variety of distant places knows that Western music has greatly affected other cultures. Certainly rock, jazz, and other music popular in the United States and Europe have almost universal acceptance. Interest in the popular music recorded in the United States and Europe extends to musicians from non-Western countries who play their own versions of rock, jazz, or other popular music. One can walk the streets of Tokyo, Japan, on a Sunday afternoon and hear a fabulous jazz group that sounds straight out of New Orleans or Chicago, only to get closer and see that the musicians are all Japanese. Whether people from various parts of the world play each other's music or add influences of it to their own, the European/American traditions that have been the subject of this text to this point have been, and continue to be, greatly enriched by such cross-culturalization.

As composer George Crumb wrote in his essay "Music: Does it have a future?"

Numerous recordings of non-Western music are readily available, and live performances by touring groups can be heard even in our smaller cities. Such influences would, of course, be felt on different levels: only a few Western composers would have a sophisticated technical knowledge of the Indian Raga, for example; but, in general, the sounds, textures, and gestures of this music would be well known. This awareness of music in its largest sense—as a world-wide phenomenon—will inevitably have enormous consequences for the music of the future.

Influences from Indonesia and China

When you learn something from people, or from a culture, you accept it as a gift, and it is your lifelong commitment to preserve it and build on it.

—CELLIST YO-YO MA (BORN IN 1955)

It is better to make a piece of music than perform one, better to perform one than to listen to one, better to listen to one than to misuse it as a means of distraction, entertainment, or acquisition of "culture."

—COMPOSER JOHN CAGE (1912–1992)

Listening Introduction

Listen to the example of music that represents this chapter, Sonata V by John Cage, and make notes about what you hear. Give some attention to the following:

▌ Can you tell what the tempo might be?

▌ Can you detect the meter?

▌ Can you tell what instrument(s) is/are playing?

▌ Do you hear any sounds that you have not heard before?

▌ What is the general mood of the piece?

Keep these notes to compare with your impressions about the music after you study the information in this chapter.

So many cultures make up Asia that it is impossible to discuss the music of all of them in a book such as this one. We have chosen music from two, Indonesia and China, to show some of the influences their music had on two important and influential American composers of the twentieth century, Henry Cowell and John Cage.

Indonesian Gamelan Music

Chapter 39 Activity

World Instruments

Indonesia is in Southeast Asia, just north of Australia, southeast of India and southwest of the Philippine Islands. A **gamelan** is the Indonesian term for a musical ensemble. The instruments in gamelan groups can vary, but **idiophones** (solid instruments that are hit with some kind of mallet) made of metal are often the most prevalent. Xylophones with metal bars are sometimes called **metallophones,** although they still fall into the general category of idiophones. A gamelan will typically have sets of knobbed and hanging gongs of various sizes, in addition to metal xylophones. **Membranophones** (drums), both plucked and bowed **chordophones** (string instruments), and **aerophones** (wind instruments) can also be part of the gamelan. Singers are sometimes included. The musical example we will listen to is played by a *degung* gamelan from Sunda in the western part of Java.

Listening Guide

"Kang Mandor" UJANG SURYANA

CD 5
Tracks 28–30

Tempo: Moderate

Meter: Duple with polyrhythms

Form: ABABABAB

Instruments: *Bonang* (a set of knobbed gongs), *saron barung* (xylophone with metal bars),
   suling (end-blown flute), *kĕmpur* (hanging gongs), *kĕndang batangan,* and *kĕndang génding*
   (double-headed drums)

Duration: 5:43

	Timing		What to listen for
28	0:00		Introduction by gamelan
29	0:06	**A**	Main theme played by the *saron barung,* accompanied by the gamelan; theme repeats
30	0:34	**B**	*Saron barung* plays accompaniment pattern, *suling* plays melody
	1:47	**A**	Main theme music repeats
	2:14	**B**	*Suling* melody part repeats
	3:24	**A**	Main theme music repeats
	3:50	**B**	*Suling* melody part repeats
	4:58	**A**	Main theme music repeats
	5:23	**B**	*Suling* melody part repeats, fade out ending

Gamelan group

Henry Cowell

An American composer who became an important figure in gamelan music was **Henry Cowell** (1897–1965). Cowell was born and raised just outside of San Francisco. His Irish father taught him to love music from Ireland, but he also exposed him to Appalachian, Chinese, Japanese, and Tahitian music, all of which were part of his musical experience by the time he began composing. In 1914 Cowell attended the University of California at Berkeley, where he was able to study with Charles Seeger (the father of the famous folk banjo player and singer, Pete Seeger), who was well known for his work in musicology, including **ethnomusicology** (the study of non-Western and folk music). By the late 1920s Cowell had moved to New York and was teaching courses in world music by invitation. He won a Guggenheim Foundation grant to study in Berlin, where he studied gamelan music with Raden Mas Jodjhana of Java.

In writing music for dancers, Cowell began to think that music should not dominate dance but that dancers should, instead, have freedom with the music they were dancing to. He suggested that segments of his music be played in any order the dancers chose, an idea that ran counter to the European concept of composers being in complete control of the organization of their work. We will

Composer Henry Cowell

see this idea lead to other, later composers, such as Cowell's student John Cage, giving much more freedom to performers than ever before. By the 1960s and 1970s this freedom was taken to the extreme at which composers actually wrote into a musical score that performers could play or sing the music at any time they chose or even play or sing anything they wanted to for a given amount of time. The use of such randomness creates what is called **aleatory, indeterminacy,** or **chance music.**

Cowell's compositions reflect many characteristics of the international music he had studied throughout his life. Cowell is best known for a very percussive technique of smashing down a large group of adjacent notes on the piano to create a dense and dissonant sound. Although that sound is not exactly like the sound of a gamelan, the percussive influences are certainly there. He called this sound a **tone cluster.** His early piano works, including *Advertisement* (1914) and *Tiger* (1928), popularized the tone cluster. It is said that the Hungarian composer Béla Bartók wrote to Cowell asking permission to use this "invention" of his American colleague in one of his own works.

An accomplished pianist, Cowell did much experimentation to coax new sounds out of the piano. In *Aeolian Harp* (1923), he asked the player to use one hand to silently depress keys so that the strings for those keys would be free to ring. The player then had to reach over the keyboard with the other hand and strum the strings. The light strumming created a quiet and quite beautiful sound that had not been heard on the piano before. The sound was reminiscent of a real Aeolian harp, which is a sound box with strings that are set to vibrate when wind blows across the box. Aeolian harps were popular in nineteenth-century Ireland. Cowell's Irish heritage also manifested itself in his piece *The Banshee* (1925), in which the player must strum and even scrape the piano's strings while an assistant holds down the damper pedal so that the strings are all free to ring. In Irish mythology, banshees are ghosts that scream to announce an impending death. Some of the scraping on the strings in Cowell's piece sounds like such screams.

Cowell also wrote music for instruments other than piano. His *Persian Set* (1957) for orchestra was composed after he returned from long visits to Iran, India, and Japan. The music of Iran was of particular interest to him because he had not heard it before. About *Persian Set* he wrote, "This is a simple record of musical contagion, written at the end of a three-month stay in Iran, during which I listened for several hours nearly every day to the traditional classical music and folk music of the country. . . . Of course I made no attempt to shed my years of Western symphonic experience; nor have I used actual Iranian melodies or rhythms, nor have I imitated them exactly. Instead I have tried to develop some of the kinds of musical behavior that the two cultures have in common." We will hear music by other twentieth-century composers who have been influenced by non-Western music without making any attempt to imitate it.

Music from China

Chinese music and culture have also had important influences on twentieth-century European and American art music. From its beginnings, Chinese music was conceived of as a system that would reflect the order of the universe. Musicians and philosophers in ancient China believed in the existence of one true "foundation tone" upon which the whole edifice of musical composition should be built. The foundation tone, or *huang chung,* was thought to have social, cosmological, and mystical significance. For many centuries, the disappearance of a dynasty was attributed to its inability to find the true *huang chung.* Several methods were used to discover the elusive tone. One method prescribed the correct height of the pipe that would produce the true *huang chung.* It would be equal to ninety average-sized grains of millet laid end to end. From this tone the Chinese musical system derived twelve tones, or *lu.* The tones were comparable to the twelve months of the year, so that each month had its own tone.

Because each tone was invested with mystical significance, Chinese music developed as a system in which the perfect performance of individual tones was regarded as the highest art. The philosopher Confucius (ca. 551–479 B.C.E.) played a stone slab on which only one note could be produced. Yet he is said to have played it with such a full heart that its sound was captivating.

The sophistication needed to enjoy subtle colorations and inflections on only one tone was, of course, not a universal gift among the ancient Chinese. Popular discontent with "scholarly music" led to the development of more accessible forms that could be enjoyed by everyone.

Ancient Chinese orchestras were immense in size and diverse in instrumentation. The orchestra of the Temple of the Ancestors at Beijing included more than 150 players. Some musicologists have come to believe that the Chinese used a variety of instrumental timbres to give the music a very dense texture. The existence of this variety of instruments also encouraged programmatic styles, in which the instruments were used to create realistic sound effects, such as animal cries or roaring gales. Henry Cowell tried to emulate those effects in a number of his piano pieces.

Our Chinese listening example is played by a much smaller group, which allows each instrument to be heard fairly clearly. The instruments are an *erhu,* a bowed string instrument with two steel strings, a *pi-p'a,* a plucked string instrument with a mandolin-like tone, and a *hsaio,* a flutelike instrument with a somewhat nasal tone quality. The melody comes from the T'ang Dynasty (the seventh to the tenth centuries C.E.). There was no music notation during that era, but melodies were written down with words representing each note and other signs indicating the length of time each note was to be held.

As is common in much Chinese music, the scale used is **pentatonic** (based on the notes D, E, G, A, C, and D). The texture is **heterophonic,** which means that the music is based on a single melody being played at any one time, with the instrumentalists adding their own variations to the melody as they play it.

Chapter 39
Video

Chinese
Instruments

Chinese musical instruments, including an *erhu,* a *pi-p'a,* and a *hsaio*

Listening Guide

"Moonlight on the Ching Yang River" YO SU-NAN OF THE T'ANG DYNASTY

CD 5
Track 31

Tempo: Moderate with fluctuations

Meter: Duple

Texture: Heterophonic

Form: Melodies repeat and are varied, but not in any regular pattern

Instruments: *Erhu* (bowed fiddle), *pi-p'a* (plucked string instrument), and *hsaio*
(a flutelike instrument)

Duration: 5:57

Composer John Cage

John Cage

A student of Henry Cowell's, **John Cage** (1912–1992), used many of Cowell's innovative ideas. Like Cowell, Cage was also very much influenced by non-Western music, particularly that from China.

John Cage was born in Los Angeles. In 1930 he left college to travel in Europe for eighteen months. Composition was part of his concentration, but he was also looking for new ideas about visual images that connected with music. He said, "In Sevilla on a street corner I noticed the multiplicity of simultaneous visual and audible events all going together in one's experience and producing enjoyment. It was the beginning for me of theater and circus."

When he returned to California he applied to study with Arnold Schoenberg, the famous Austrian composer who had developed the twelve-tone system of composition. When the two discussed the cost of lessons, Schoenberg made it clear that he wanted much more than money from Cage. Schoenberg required that Cage promise to devote his entire life to music. Cage agreed to the bargain. The lessons were free. Cage also studied with Henry Cowell, who encouraged him to experiment with what the piano could do.

Cage was hired to provide music for a dance production in 1940. There was no room for instruments other than the piano that was already on the stage, but Cage wanted to come up with something full and percussive to fit the African character of the dance. He replicated that full and percussive sound by placing bolts, screws, bamboo, and pieces of weather stripping on and between the piano's strings so that they would rattle and make other sounds when he played the keyboard. The result was so successful that he continued to write for such a **prepared piano** much of the rest of his life. The music to his prepared piano works had a drawing of the strings showing where all the objects were to be placed to obtain the sounds the piece required. Cage even composed a concerto for prepared piano and orchestra.

In the mid-1940s Cage discovered Zen Buddhism, an Asian belief system that emphasizes meditation as the means to reach an enlightened state. He also studied with an Indian singer and tabla player, further interesting him in the sounds of Asia. His *Sonatas and Interludes for Prepared Piano* (1946–1948) is a set of sixteen sonatas which are broken up with other pieces, called interludes. Percussive sounds that come from the piano's extensive "preparation" show clear Asian, including gamelan, influences. We will listen to Sonata V of the work.

Listening Guide

Sonata V from *Sonatas and Interludes* JOHN CAGE

CD 2
Tracks 37–38

Year: 1948

Tempo: 92 beats per minute

Meter: Duple

Form: Binary

Duration: 1:48

Special feature: Notice how effective it is when the repetitive accompaniment figures stop and
then resume. The upper melody also changes from being fairly active to holding longer notes
and then picks up the activity again. The percussive sound of the "preparation" materials on
the piano's strings gives the sonata an almost gamelan-like timbre.

	Timing		What to listen for
37	0:00	A	Ten and three-quarters bars of an active upper melody, then eight and one-quarter bars in which the melody changes from one long-held note to another
	0:23	A	Repeat of section
38	0:46	B	Nine bars of long-held notes in the upper melody followed by eight and one-quarter bars of a new active melody that uses grace notes (fast ornamental notes) in a few places, then a three-quarter-bar rest and sustained notes. One extra beat is added in the last bar.
	1:17	B	Repeat of section

In addition to studying Zen Buddhism, Cage became interested in other aspects of Chinese culture, including the *I Ching* (Book of Changes), an ancient text
that is meant to provide guidance for its reader. The reader determines what parts
of the text he or she should read by throwing coins or yarrow stalks. The idea of
making choices in what should be read by such a random method interested
Cage. His composition *Music of Changes* (1951) used the tossing of coins to determine the order in which the sections of music should be performed.

In 1952 Cage went into an "anechoic" or isolation chamber at Harvard University. The experience of being completely cut off from sounds of the world
around him provided him not with silence but with the sounds of his own body.
As he described it, he heard "the unintended operation of my nervous system and
the circulation of my blood." His most famous composition, 4′33″, resulted from
that experience. The piece instructs the performer to walk on stage and sit at the
piano. The performer then holds his or her hands over the keys as if to play but
never touches a key. When four minutes and thirty-three seconds have elapsed,
the performer bows and leaves the stage. The "music" results from members of
the audience moving in their seats and whatever other sounds occur during the
period of silence. It has been suggested by many historians that the choice of exactly that amount of time was done randomly, but it is also possible that it was
chosen because it represents a different kind of silence. Four minutes and thirty-
three seconds is equal to 273 seconds. Scientists use the Kelvin scale to measure
temperatures, and zero on that scale is equal to negative 273 on the Celsius scale.
The temperature at zero or negative 273 is the coldest possible temperature, one

HEARING THE DIFFERENCE
Chopin's Ballade no. 1 in G Minor and Cage's Sonata V from *Sonatas and Interludes*

In comparing these two piano compositions, we are comparing works from two different periods, the romantic era and the twentieth century. The romantic work by Chopin has continually changing expressions of emotions from tender and passionate to very intense. Cage's work has a much more intellectual affect on the listener in that it concerns itself primarily with the timbre of the piano. The pianos on which the two works are played are different because Cage's piece requires that the instrument be prepared in advance. The many materials that have been placed on the strings give the notes and chords a variety of tone qualities that produce a percussive effect. The two compositions are representative of their eras in that the passion of the nineteenth century is evident in Chopin's piece and the intellectualism of the twentieth century is evident in Cage's piece.

	Ballade no. 1 in G Minor	**Sonata V**
Style period	Romantic	Twentieth century
Tempo	Varies greatly, from a very slow beginning to a fast and fiery conclusion	Very steady, broken only by occasional rests between sections
Meter	Triple	Duple
Form	Irregular and alternating ABCABBCA	Binary (AABB)
Themes	Many varied melodies (themes) contrast with one another: some waltz-like, others tender and passionate, others tense and energetic	Melodic patterns either fairly repetitious or made of long-held notes
Instruments	Sound is that of a piano played in the traditional manner, making full value of the instrument's dynamic capabilities	Sound resembles that of a gamelan group more than a solo piano; metal bolts and screws that sit on the strings rattle to give the piano a percussive sound, pieces of rubber on the strings deaden the sound of some notes

at which there can be no motion and therefore no life. The silence of the piece relates to this lack at motion, as well as to the music of one's surroundings.

In later years Cage composed theatrical works and used electronics mixed with live sounds. The idea of randomness continued to interest him in that it made performances of his works "happenings" that would never be repeated in exactly the same way.

A map of the heavens supplied the note heads for Cage's *Atlas Eclipticalis* (1961–1962). This work consisted of eighty-six instrumental parts "to be played in whole or part, any duration, in any ensemble, chamber or orchestral." The effect is as if a traveler with no particular place to go wanders the earth. John Cage is perhaps the best-known composer of chance music, but the idea became popular enough that many other composers used it as well.

Summary

Indonesian gamelan music is generally very percussive because many of the instruments in the gamelan are idiophones, such as sets of bronze bowls, gongs, and xylophones with metal bars (metallophones). Gamelans can also include membranophones, chordophones, aerophones, and singing, but the metal percussion instruments create the primary sound. Piano works by both Cowell and Cage have made use of percussive effects, including plucking or scraping the strings of the piano and placing items such as screws, bolts, or bamboo on the piano's strings to change the instrument's tone when they rattle as the piano is played. The two composers might not have ever come upon their musical ideas had they not studied Indonesian music and applied what they had heard of that music to their own work.

John Cage was also interested in China because of his studies in Zen Buddhism and his interest in the Chinese Book of Changes, the *I Ching*. To gain guidance from the *I Ching,* one must randomly throw coins or yarrow sticks, which gave Cage the idea of having random decisions made by performers when his music was played. The music thus changes with every performance. Several terms are used to describe such music: aleatory, indeterminacy, and chance music.

New People and Concepts

aerophones	**Henry Cowell**	**membranophones**
aleatory	**heterophonic**	**metallophones**
chance music	**idiophones**	**pentatonic scale**
chordophones	**indeterminacy**	**prepared piano**
ethnomusicology	**John Cage**	**tone cluster**
gamelan		

Finale

Listen again to Sonata V and compare your impressions now with your notes from your first listening. Do you hear more now than you did before? You should now be able to answer the following questions:

▌ What is the tempo?

▌ What is the meter?

▌ What instrument is playing?

▌ What creates the sounds that are not usually heard on a piano?

▌ What is the mood of the piece?

40 | Influences from India

Music is the universal language of mankind—poetry
their universal pastime and delight.
—POET HENRY WADSWORTH LONGFELLOW
(1807–1882)

Listening Introduction

Listen to the example of music that represents this chapter, *Company,* second movement, by Philip Glass, and make notes about what you hear. Give some attention to the following:

■ Can you guess at the tempo?

■ Can you detect the meter?

■ Can you tell what instruments are playing?

■ Can you hear any repeated melodies?

■ What is the general mood of the piece?

Keep these notes to compare with your impressions about the music after you study the information in this chapter.

Indian Music

The cultural heritage of India is divided between two basic traditions: the Muslim culture of the north and the Hindu tradition of the south. Indian music, too, reflects this cultural split; for example, the two systems use different instruments and different naming systems. Yet they also hold many things in common, including the philosophic premise that music is intimately connected with the spiritual world. In our discussion we generally refer to the music of the southern, Hindu tradition.

The Hindu religion influences many forms of musical expression in India. The majority of Indian songs are devotional, expressing love for the deity. The religious spirit expresses itself throughout a wide range of subjects, from personal and familiar to esoteric, abstract philosophy. Even the songs of erotic love convey the bliss of union with the divine.

The basis for Indian melodies is the ancient religious music of the Aryan-speaking people of West Asia who migrated to India as early as the second or third millennium B.C.E. About 1500 B.C.E. the music began to be recorded in sacred books, or *Vedas* ("knowledge"), containing prayers, chants, hymns, and other religious knowledge. Sung as incantations to the divinities or as sacred sacrificial formulas, the hymns were performed to ensure the order and stability of the universe. The oldest known treatise on classical Hindu musical theory, the *Natya Sastra,* dating from about 200 B.C.E., provides the bridge that connects the ancient musical heritage of India with forms still in use today.

The basic motive force of Indian music has remained constant: Music must reflect the inherent order and majesty of the universe and contribute to a performer's own spiritual development. This deep and sustaining motivation, which anchors Indian music to its mystical, philosophic framework, is reflected in the ordering of the melodic modes known as **ragas.** Each raga is related to a certain time of day or night. Indian historians tell of a musician at the court of the sixteenth-century emperor Akbar who sang a night raga at midday with such power and beauty that "darkness fell on the place where he stood." Each raga is associated also with a definite mood, a color, a festival, a deity, and certain specific natural events. Sexual differentiation of the ragas into male ragas and female *raginis* completes the unification of Indian music with the total surrounding cosmology.

A teacher of Indian music is considered a true guru, responsible not only for his students' musical progress but also for their spiritual development. The guru receives no money for his services. The knowledge and wisdom he imparts are thought to be priceless and far beyond any conceivable financial remuneration. Often, a student binds himself to one guru for a period of ten years or more. During that time he will be expected to memorize more than sixty ragas and rhythmic cycles called **talas.** The memorization is demanded not to ensure perfect reproduction of the ragas as such but to promote the complete familiarity and understanding needed to master the pinnacle of Indian musical art—the art of improvisation.

Raga melodies are based on the Hindu scale that consists of seven tones, each of which is associated with a particular mood. Many notes between those seven tones are played when the basic tones are played flat (lowered), very flat, sharp (raised), or very sharp. Hindu musical instruments allow for a certain amount of pitch fluctuation, including the sliding from one tone to another. To set off the melody of Indian ragas, a harmonic drone is played almost constantly throughout the piece. It serves an extremely important function by providing a harmonic frame of reference for both the audience and the performer.

When playing a raga, the players are free to explore and improvise on their own rhythms, competing with each other in a contest of rhythmic skill. The rhythmic tension is increased only by the requirement that all players reach the *saman,* or first beat of the cycle, exactly together. As the players attempt more and more daring cross-rhythms and yet still manage to come out together on the *saman,* the audience begins to assist the performers by clapping out the beat of the tala.

Listening Guide

"Raga Bhairavi" MASTER DATTOPANT AND GROUP

CD 5
Track 32

Texture: Homophonic

Tempo: Rather fast

Form: The repetition of the raga creates a repeating structure with variations on each repeat.

Instrumentation: *Jalatarang* (a melodic instrument composed of numerous porcelain bowls partially filled with water to produce specific notes when they are struck with wooden sticks), *tabla* (a set of two drums played with the hands), and a *tambura* (a stringed drone instrument).

Duration: 3:06

Special feature: This is an early-morning raga. Hopefully, playing it at another time of day will not upset the solar system by causing the sun to rise.

An Indian musician playing tabla (two small drums).

Indian music has been very influential on the development of new styles of composition in the late twentieth century, particularly through the works of Terry Riley and Philip Glass. They each developed their own individual styles, but the general term for the style they have in common is **minimalism.**

Terry Riley

Composer Terry Riley

Terry Riley was born in 1935 in northern California. He attended San Francisco State College and then transferred to the University of California at Berkeley, where he received a master's degree in composition in 1961. Tape recorders were relatively new in the late 1950s and early 1960s, and they provided musicians with a wealth of new possibilities in the creation and manipulation of sound. Along with other members of the San Francisco Tape Music Center, Riley experimented with tape loops and the multitracking of sounds. To get the effects he wanted, Riley invented some rather unconventional techniques. He described his use of tape loops as follows: "I would take tapes and run them into my yard and around a wine bottle back into my room and I would get a really long loop and then I would cut the tape into all different sizes and I would just run them out into the yard and I would record onto one machine just sound on sound. I would build up this kind of unintelligible layer." In the end, however, he opted for live musicians. "Out of doing all that experimentation with sound I decided I wanted to do it with live musicians. To take repetition, take music fragments and make it live." Riley's most famous piece, *In C*, resulted from that experiment.

In C (1964) was first called "The Global Villages for Symphonic Pieces." The piece is an early example of minimalism, a style in which a minimal amount of musical material is repeated many times, often with gradual changes occurring during the repetitions. It is also an example of aleatory, or chance, music. It consists of 53 short bits of melody all based on a C-major scale. A pianist begins the work by repeatedly playing the top two "C" notes on the piano (an octave) to create a regular beat called the "pulse." Other musicians play all 53 of the melodic patterns in order and in rhythm to the pulse. The aleatoric aspect of the work is that the musicians can play on any instrument they choose as long as it can play the written notes. Each musician can begin playing any time he or she wants, can repeat each pattern as many times as desired, and then must move on to the next pattern. The piece can be as short as ten or fifteen minutes (if the players choose not to repeat the patterns very many times), or it can last for hours.

It should be clear by now that each performance of a work that includes aleatory music, or choices made for a single performance, is different from every other performance of the same work. Aleatoric pieces have been recorded—certainly *In C* has been several times—but recording the piece undermines the purpose of aleatory.

Terry Riley went to India to study with Pandit Pran Nath, a master vocalist. In the 1970s he taught both composition and courses in Indian music at Mills College in Oakland, California. Riley's compositions were greatly influenced by his studies of Indian music. He tuned electric pianos and organs to Indian scales for his composition "Shri Camel" (1978), and "Songs for the 10 Voices of the Two Prophets" (1980) was composed using Hindu vocals accompanied by improvisations on synthesizer. While in Oakland, Riley met members of the Kronos Quartet, who specialized (and continue to specialize) in performing and recording music to expand the string quartet literature. During the early 1980s he worked with them and had them perform with the Indian sitar player Krishna Bhatt. He then went on to compose nine string quartets, along with a keyboard quintet (piano and string quartet), and a concerto for string quartet and orchestra. He still often returns to India and performs as both a vocalist and a *tambura* (an Indian drone instrument) player with his former teacher. Clearly, music for Riley is an expression of Indian spirituality. In one interview Riley said, "This morning I was practicing raga, and at one point I was singing a long tone and I became very peaceful and still. I thought this is really the highest point of music for me is to become in a place where there is no desire, no craving, wanting to do anything else, just to be in a state of being to the highest point. Then you get a little meditated, you get to a place that is really still and it is the best place you have ever been and yet there is nothing there. For me, that is what music is. It is a spiritual art."

Composer Philip Glass

Philip Glass

Another composer whose minimalist works have been inspired by Indian music is **Philip Glass** (born in 1937). Glass was born in Baltimore, where his father owned a record store. He grew up hearing music of all kinds, because his father brought home the records that did not sell, and young Philip would listen to them himself. Glass became acquainted with many styles of modern music and jazz through this listening. He also learned to play both the violin and the flute. He studied Arnold Schoenberg's twelve-tone composition techniques at the University of

Chicago, where he graduated with degrees in mathematics and philosophy. From there he studied composition at the Juilliard School. He changed composition teachers often in an effort to find what he described as "his own voice." In 1960 he went to Paris and studied with Nadia Boulanger, the French composer who taught Aaron Copland and other important twentieth-century composers. It was in Paris that Glass became involved with Indian music, which led him to discover the "voice" he had been looking for in his own music.

Glass was introduced to Indian music when a filmmaker hired him to put music by sitarist Ravi Shankar into a notational system that French musicians could read and play. Energized by this initial experience with music from India, Glass went on to study music from North Africa as well. When he returned to composing his own music, he felt a new sense of freedom from traditional European rhythm patterns. He began to let little "cells" of sound repeat to form hypnotic sound cycles. It is those hypnotic repeating patterns that characterize Glass's work to this day.

Theater had always been an interest of Glass's, and his new style fit well for avant-garde works by Samuel Beckett, Bertold Brecht, and others. After many works for theatrical or dance productions, Glass produced his own masterpiece, the opera *Einstein on the Beach* (1976). The opera has no plot or storyline. Instead, it musically portrays or describes Albert Einstein (1879–1955), the physicist who is famous for his theory of relativity. It came to be seen as a "portrait" of Einstein and was lauded by critics. It was followed by a commission from the Netherlands Opera Company to compose a similar portrait of Gandhi, called *Satyagraha* (1982). Mahatma Gandhi (1869–1948) was a Hindu who used passive resistance (called *satyagraha)* to free India from the British. Finally, Glass was commissioned by the Stuttgart Opera Company to compose a third operatic portrait of the famous Egyptian pharaoh, *Akhnaten* (1984). Akhenaten was an

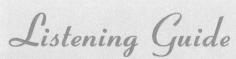
Listening Guide

Company, second movement PHILIP GLASS

CD 2
Tracks 39–40

Year: 1983

Texture: Homophonic

Tempo: 160 beats per minute

Meter: Changes often between duple and triple

Form: Two sections alternate. The first one, A, is a homophonic pounding at a steady beat.
The second, B, is made up of short ascending arpeggios that repeat and then sometimes extend or reverse direction, creating an almost swirling motion over a steady pulse in the bass. The A sections are all five seconds long, but the B sections vary in length.

Instrumentation: String orchestra made up of first violins, second violins, violas, cellos, and basses. (The work can also be played by a string quartet, because the bass part duplicates the cello one and can be done without.)

Duration: 1:55

Special feature: One can see how this movement would fit the story of a person contemplating his life during the swirling arpeggios and then being interrupted by voices in the past when the pounding A sections return.

	Timing		What to listen for
39	0:00	A	Homophonic pounding at a steady beat, forte dynamic level
40	0:05	B	Short ascending arpeggios repeat and change by being extended or reversing direction on some repetitions. Dynamics change abruptly from mezzo forte to piano and back.
	0:28	A	
	0:33	B	
	0:37	A	
	0:42	B	
	1:23	A	
	1:28	B	
	1:32	A	
	1:37	A	Louder with more intensity
	1:42	B	Fades at end

eighteenth-dynasty Egyptian pharaoh who rejected the polytheistic beliefs of his people's past in order to worship a single god, Aten. He was the only pharaoh to have held such beliefs.

Chapter 40
Timeline

Philip Glass

The work by Philip Glass that we will listen to was originally composed for a theater piece called *Company* by Samuel Beckett, although it is also effective as a concert piece. The drama focuses on an old man at the end of his life who hears voices from his past as he prepares himself for death. We will hear the second movement, which is rather fast. The first and third movements are slow, and the fourth is again fast. The influence of Indian music can be heard in Glass's use of changes between duple and triple meters. Many Indian *talas* (metric patterns) are made up of such patterns. This is often called **additive meter** because a pattern of 10 beats, for example, might be made up of 2 beats + 3 beats + 2 beats + 3 beats.

Earlier, we listened to a movement of a string quartet by Haydn. "Hearing the Difference: Haydn's String Quartet, fourth movement, and Glass's *Company*, second movement," compares the two works.

As Philip Glass describes his style, it is "music with repetitive structures," which goes beyond the repetition and slight variation of most minimalism. Glass's music has been an important influence on any number of art rock groups, such as King Crimson, Pink Floyd, and Talking Heads. His CD, *Songs from Liquid Days* (1986), features music that he cowrote with Paul Simon, Suzanne Vega, David Byrne (of Talking Heads), and Laurie Anderson. Linda Ronstadt, the Roches, and many other singers and instrumentalists from the world of rock and pop music perform on the CD. Glass's *Heroes Symphony* (1997) was based on the music of David Bowie and the composer, producer, and rock musician Brian Eno.

Glass has been an effective film score composer as well, having composed twenty-one scores ranging from *North Star* (1977) to *The Baroness and the Pig* (2002). His soundtracks for *Kundun* (1997) and *The Hours* (2002) were both nominated for Academy Awards, and both won Golden Globes. *The Truman Show* (1999) won him a Golden Globe as well. In 2003, Glass composed the score for the Academy Award–winning documentary feature "The Fog of War: Eleven Lessons from the Life of Robert S. McNamara." (McNamara was the U.S. Secretary of Defense during much of the Vietnam War.)

HEARING THE DIFFERENCE
Haydn's String Quartet, fourth movement, and Glass's *Company,* second movement

In comparing these compositions we are comparing two works that were written just over two hundred years apart. Haydn's Quartet was composed in 1781 and Glass's piece in 1984. Haydn's work is based on a clearly organized form that used much repetition and contrast of musical ideas. This type of form was typical of the classical period. Glass's work is also clearly organized with repeating and contrasting sections. Since each style period change (from classical to romantic, and then romantic to the twentieth century) has, in general, rejected many basic characteristics of the previous period, we see these similarities between the classical period and the twentieth century, with the understanding that the romantic period came between them. During the romantic period, musical form was often much less clear and organized. Here we see the structure of the late eighteenth century returning two hundred years later. Of course, Glass's work does not sound classical in other ways—the additive meter of Indian music, and the modern inclusion of much repetition instead of any use of variation create a clearly modern sound—but we still see a return to an earlier interest in formal structure.

	String Quartet, fourth movement	***Company,* second movement**
Tempo	Presto (very fast)	Slightly faster than Haydn's presto
Meter	Duple	Changes from duple to triple
Form	Sonata rondo form (AB-Development AB-Development-A)	Alternating A and B sections have a contrasting effect similar to that of Haydn's quartet movement
Instrumentation	Light sound of four string instruments (two violins, viola, and cello)	If the piece were played by a string quartet, which it can be, it would have the same lightness of Haydn's quartet. This recording is played by a string orchestra, giving it a much larger and heavier sound.
Story line	The second, repeated-note theme is composed to be reminiscent of a bird call	Does not attempt to imitate the sound of any particular thing, but is composed to go with a theatrical work and it does fit the story of that work
Variation	Typically classical in that it is based on short, repeated themes that contrast with one another and then are subjected to variation	Minimalist style also based on short, repeated themes that contrast with one another, but with much more repetition than variation

Summary

Indian music has been very influential on the development of new styles of composition in the late twentieth century, particularly through the works of Terry Riley and Philip Glass. Riley's early works were constructed from the layering of sound on tape. He took ideas from that work and wrote a composition called *In C,* which is an example of both minimalism and aleatory. Minimalism is a style in which a minimal amount of musical material is repeated many times with gradual changes occurring during the repetitions. *In C* is aleatory because Riley composed the piece so that the players can choose the instrument they play and can choose when to change from repeating one pattern to repeating another. Because the players have so many choices, every performance of the work will be different from any other. Riley studied in India and sees his work as a spiritual art.

Philip Glass also composes music in the style of minimalism, and he was also drawn to that style through the study of Indian music. He particularly enjoys working on scores for theatrical works and has had much success as an opera and movie composer. We listened to his *Company* for strings, which was intended to accompany a theatrical production, although it also works well on its own.

New People and Concepts

additive meter	Philip Glass	tala
minimalism	raga	Terry Riley

Finale

Listen again to *Company,* second movement, by Philip Glass and compare your impressions now with your notes from your first listening. Do you hear more now than you did before? You should now be able to answer the following questions:

▌ What is the tempo?

▌ What is the meter?

▌ What instruments are playing?

▌ When do you hear repeating melodies?

▌ What is the general mood of the piece?

Influences from Africa and the Middle Eastern City of Jerusalem

*Every time I open a newspaper, I am reminded that
we live in a world where we can no longer afford not
to know our neighbors.*
—CELLIST YO-YO MA (BORN IN 1955)

Listening Introduction

Listen to one of the examples of music that represents this chapter, *Tehillim*,
part 4, by Steve Reich, and take notes about what you hear. Give some
attention to the following:

▌ Can you detect the tempo?

▌ Can you guess at a meter?

▌ Can you hear any themes that return, even in an altered version?

▌ What types of instruments do you hear?

▌ Can you tell the language of the text, and can you understand any of it?

Keep these notes to compare with your impressions about the music after you
study the information in this chapter.

African Music

Nowhere in the world is music more a part of the very process of everyday living
than in Africa. Almost all communal activities are accompanied by singing,
dancing, and drumming. These three activities are rarely separated; they are in-
terdependent. As a whole, the music is characterized by sophisticated and complex rhythmic structures, a wide range of indigenous instruments, a strong oral
tradition of songs, and a vast store of dances to accompany and celebrate all
aspects of life.

Most African cultures greatly respect the spoken word, which is believed to
be the "life force" and called *nommo* in the Bantu languages. The languages are
often inflective, and common speech assumes musiclike qualities. The musical
sounds produced most often are percussive, and players use bodily gestures to enhance a performance.

Much African music is meant to be heard by the deity. The Dogon people of
Mali believe that music, specifically that played on drums, is the vehicle through
which the sacred word is brought to human beings. More commonly, music is
used to lift up prayers to a divinity. To ensure the delivery of a healthy baby, special songs are sung during the hours of childbirth. After birth, the thankfulness of
the family finds expression in chants and dancing. The naming of the baby, the
loss of a first tooth, and other incidents in the life of the child from infancy
through puberty are celebrated with music.

In addition to marking the stages of life, music deepens and defines African existence. Through songs and dances young men and women are taught the language of the tribe, the traditions of family living, the obligations they will be expected to fulfill, and the "facts of life." Communal holidays and festivals are celebrated through seasonal musical offerings. In some West African cultures, political music is considered so important to the general welfare that singers (the griots, or tribal historians whose connection with blues singers we discussed in Chapter 28) specialize in songs of governmental and social information.

Ewe Drum Ensembles

In our chapter on early jazz, we discussed music from northwestern Africa, because jazz is so clearly rooted in that music. In this chapter we concentrate on Ewe (*ay'-way*) drumming from Ghana. This particular type of drumming has influenced several contemporary composers, particularly Steve Reich, who studied it in Ghana. His music manifests the general characteristics of African music that we discussed earlier: call and response, polyrhythms, and the repetition of individual rhythmic patterns.

For ceremonial occasions it is often customary to bring together large ensembles. Traditional festivals may extend over several days, with different programs of music planned for each day. A festival drum orchestra of the Ewe, who inhabit southeastern Ghana, usually consists of a drum section led by the master drummer, a percussion section (for timekeeping), singers, dancers, and a "master of ceremonies." The drum section consists of three to seven drums of various sizes and tones. The percussion section consists of *gankogui* (two bells that are tapered and joined together to form a handle) and an *axatse* (rattle with a husklike shape, made from a dried gourd covered with nets of beads). These instruments usually act as timekeepers and, in almost every case, play a standard, regular pattern, such as "tap-rest-tap-rest," while other members of the orchestra play contrasting rhythmic parts.

The third part of the orchestra consists of a trained chorus, headed by one or two cantors, which claps as it sings. The drum orchestra is completed by a group

African drum ensemble

of costumed dancers, male and female. The "master of ceremonies" maintains decorum among the dancers and encourages the singers. All of these sections perform in a semicircle facing an open space reserved for dancing. Our listening example was recorded at one of these ceremonies, but is played by a slightly smaller ensemble.

Listening Guide

"Gadzo" ("Kayiboe, The Child is not Matured") MUSIC OF THE EWE OF GHANA

CD 5
Track 33

Tempo: Moderate

Meter: Polyrhythmic

Form: No particular pattern of returning or contrasting sections

Voices: Many voices singing in a "call and response" pattern; some voices are part of the ensemble, and others are from people who are dancing with the music

Language: Ewe, one of many tribal languages in Ghana

Instruments: *Dundun* (drum), *kagann* (congo-like drum), five or six *axatses* (rattles)

Duration: 3:03

Special feature: This is based on a dance for young men, originally a war dance but now a general social dance.

Steve Reich

Composer Steve Reich

The composer previously mentioned as having studied Ewe drumming in Ghana, **Steve Reich** (born in 1936), was born and raised in New York. He studied philosophy at Cornell University and later attended Juilliard to pursue a career as a composer. He moved to northern California and completed his master's degree at Mills College in 1963. He was attracted to Mills College by its faculty, which included two major composers with whom he wanted to study, Darius Milhaud and Luciano Berio. Reich played the piano, but his primary skills and interests were in percussion. When he studied world music at Mills College, he was particularly taken by the music from Indonesia and from Africa. As he said in a 2002 interview, "a number of people became aware that non-Western music was a way of getting to something that we wanted to get to in our own music."

Reich was awarded a grant from the Institute for International Education that allowed him to go to Africa to study drumming at the University of Ghana in 1970. His composition *Drumming* (1971) resulted from that study, and much of his music that followed also was affected by African drumming styles. He pursued his interest in Indonesian gamelan music by attending the American Society for Eastern Arts back in Berkeley, California, where he concentrated on Balinese gamelan music. In discussing his *Music for Eighteen Musicians* (1976), he said, "The piece was written so that a conductor would not be necessary. . . . The conducting responsibilities were delegated to the vibraphone player who, every time he played, it was a cue to, 'Get ready, here we (gong) go,' and everybody changes. That was an idea I took directly from Balinese and African music, where the drummers . . . will make the (call)."

Studies in the Middle East

Reich reached back into his family heritage when he returned to New York in 1976 and then went on to Jerusalem to study traditional Jewish chanting of the Hebrew Scriptures. The piece we will listen to resulted from that study and was also very much influenced by his studies of non-Western drumming. *Tehillim* is Hebrew for "Psalms."

Chapter 41
Timeline

Steve Reich

Listening Guide

Tehillim, part 4 STEVE REICH

CD 5
Tracks 34–38

Year: 1981

Tempo: Fast

Meter: Constantly changing from four, five, and seven beats in
   each bar. The changes are dictated by the text.

Form: Theme and variations

Voices: Two sopranos and two mezzo-sopranos

Instrumentation: Two flutes, two oboes, two clarinets, electric
   organs, amplified first violin, amplified second violin, amplified
   viola, amplified cello, amplified bass, percussion, including
   instruments chosen to sound like ones mentioned in the texts of
   the Psalms, such as tambourines without jingles and miniature
   antique cymbals

Language: Biblical Hebrew

Duration: 6:23

Hebrew text	English translation (from the King James Bible, Psalms 150:4–6)
Haleluhu batof umachol,	Praise him with the timbrel and dance:
Haleluhu baminim va-ugav;	Praise him with stringed instruments and organs.
Haleluhu batzil-tzilay shamah,	Praise him upon the loud cymbals:
Haleluhu batzil-tzilay taruah;	Praise him upon the high sounding cymbals.
Kol hanshamah tahalail Yah,	Let all that hath breath praise the Lord,
Haleluyah.	Praise ye the Lord.

	Timing	What to listen for
34	0:00	Two sopranos sing Psalm text accompanied by percussion and long-held orchestral chords
35	0:27	Variation 1: Psalm text sung by two voices canonically
36	0:55	Variation 2: Psalm text sung by four voices canonically
37	2:39	Variation 3: Two singers joined by clarinets and then drums
	3:22	Strings and electric organ play new music
38	3:57	Variation 4: Voices sing new melody
	4:51	"Halleluyah" repeated many times accompanied by electric organ and bells
	6:18	Ending with sudden silence

Steve Reich has composed several pieces for the Kronos Quartet, including one that is performed with a tape recording, *Different Trains* (1988). That composition won him a Grammy Award for Best Contemporary Composition in 1990. His theater piece, *The Cave* (1993), composed in collaboration with Beryl Korot, includes the playing of videos on five screens, along with music played by his eighteen-musician ensemble. The story of *The Cave* is based on the story of Abraham, as told in Genesis 22:1–19 in the Bible. In an often-told part of the story, God tests Abraham's loyalty by commanding him to sacrifice his son Isaac. Just as Abraham is about to kill his son, God steps in and allows the boy to live.

When we talked about electronic music in Chapter 35, we defined the term *musique concrète* as sounds that have been tape recorded and then manipulated in a variety of ways. Steve Reich used that technique very effectively in his 1995 composition, *City Life*. He used samples of a great variety of sounds he recorded around New York, including voices, car horns, door slams, air brakes, subway chimes, car alarms, boat horns, and fire and police sirens. The fire and police sirens were recorded on February 25, 1993, during the commotion after a car bomb exploded under the World Trade Center.

Reich continues to compose music that is touched by minimalistic techniques and influenced by world music in a variety of ways. In his own words, "I studied Balinese and African music because I love them and also because I believe that non-Western music is presently the single most important source of new ideas for Western composers and musicians."

Summary

African music has been very influential on the development of new styles of composition in the late twentieth century, particularly through the works of Steve Reich. His style of minimalism was very much influenced by his having studied Ewe drumming in Ghana. He also studied Indonesian gamelan music and Hebrew chanting styles, making his music a very complex combination of styles. Reich, Riley, and Glass have all used world music as an important source of new ideas and have consequently enriched the world with much new music.

New People and Concepts

Steve Reich

Finale

Listen again to *Tehillim*, part 4, by Steve Reich, and compare your impressions now with your notes from your first listening. Do you hear more now than you did before? You should now be able to answer the following questions:

▌ What is the tempo?

▌ What is the meter?

▌ Can you recognize any of the themes when they are varied?

▌ What types of instruments do you hear?

▌ What is the language of the text, and what does it mean?

42 | Fusion of Cultures

Music has always been transnational; people pick up whatever interests them, and certainly a lot of classical music has absorbed influences from all over the world.

—CELLIST YO-YO MA (BORN IN 1955)

Listening Introduction

Listen to the example of music that represents this chapter, "Bebe el agua tranquila de la canción añeja" ("Drink the tranquil water of the old song"), and make notes about what you hear. Give some attention to the following:

▌ Can you guess at the tempo?

▌ Can you detect the meter?

▌ Can you understand the text?

▌ Can you tell what instruments are in the recording?

▌ Can you hear any repeated melodies?

▌ What is the general mood of the piece?

Keep these notes to compare with your impressions about the music after you study the information in this chapter.

Music from Spain

Spain's placement just north of Africa and its separation from France by the Pyrenees mountains allowed some very distinctive musical styles to develop there. Spain was Christianized during the Middle Ages, but as early as 711 African Muslims invaded and took over parts of the Spanish peninsula. Spain also had a large Jewish population, and gypsies (nomadic people who were probably originally from the Middle East) migrated into Spain during the fifteenth century. For centuries, Christians, Muslims, Jews, and gypsies were all close enough to share musical instruments and playing styles. Even when King Ferdinand and Queen Isabella decided to Christianize Spain in 1492, forcing out the Jews and Muslims, many of the North African and Middle Eastern influences remained as part of Spanish culture and style.

A music that developed out of the *cante jondo* (or "deep song") traditions in Andalusia (southern Spain) was particularly influenced by music of the Muslims and the Gypsies who settled there. That music is called **flamenco** today and is dominated by singing, dancing, and guitar playing, with the percussive additions of hand claps, foot stomps, and castanets. Flamenco shares many characteristics with music from the Middle East and from parts of Asia in that singers often slide from one note to another, melodies are usually derived from a fairly small range of

Shown here is a Spanish flamenco group.

Listening Guide

"Flamenco Dance Song"

CD 5
Track 39

Tempo: Moderately fast

Meter: Triple

Form: No regular repeating sections

Instrumentation: A man's voice, guitar, hand clapping, and dance
footwork

Duration: 0:43

Special feature: The words of the song are not understandable
because the singer is not clearly enunciating the words. The
primary feature of this is its energetic spirit and active rhythm.

Chapter 42
WebQuest

Fusion of
Cultures

notes (not more than the interval of a sixth), and many ornaments (melodic turns)
are added to decorate the melodies. "Flamenco Dance Song" is an example.

Even though *cante jondo* music was heavily influenced by Muslim and Middle Eastern traditions of the past, most of the people living in Andalusia today are
Roman Catholic, and the beliefs and traditions of that religion permeate many
flamenco traditions. The next recording is a traditional Andalusian religious song
usually sung by a woman who stands on a balcony overlooking an Easter procession in which an image of the crucified Christ is carried through the streets. The
singer grips the railing firmly and sings with much strained emotion. This song
has been chosen here not for its religious text, but because of the very passionate
style of singing that captures the soul of the *cante jondo* style.

Listening Guide

"Saeta" ("Arrow")

CD 5
Track 40

Tempo: Moderately fast

Meter: No steady beat or meter

Form: No regular repeating sections except the final phrase, which repeats

Voice: A 12-year-old Andalusian girl sings without accompaniment

Duration: 1:11

Special feature: The singer sings with much strained emotion. The melody is highly decorated with short melodic turns.

Spanish text	English translation
¿Quiéns te han clavado, quiéns te han clavado en esa cruz allí?	Who has nailed you, who has nailed you on that cross there?
¿Quiéns te han puesto esas espinas?	Who has put those thorns on you?
¿Quiéns partió este costado?	Who has cut this side?
¿Qué está tu madre, ella divina con el corazón traspasado?	What of your mother, she the holy one with the broken (pierced) heart?
¿Qué está tu madre, ella divina con el corazón traspasado?	What of your mother, she the holy one with the broken (pierced) heart?

George Crumb

American composer **George Crumb** (born in 1929) studied the music and the instruments from a variety of world cultures and combines their sounds in his works. As he has said, "Philosophically, I think of all music as being one thing. . . . I was haunted by the thought that all the many musics of the world are coming together as one. Well, I think that's happened."

Crumb has a particular interest in Spain and its literature and music, and we will hear the influences of Spanish music when we listen to his "Bebe el agua tranquila de la canción añeja" ("Drink the tranquil water of the old song"). The work is one of several that Crumb has composed using texts from poems by the Spanish poet and playwright Federico García Lorca (1898–1936). García Lorca is a sympathetic historical figure because his work is famous for its portrayals of passionate love of life, the sounds of nature, and death. He was shot to death by Fascist soldiers at the beginning of the Spanish Civil War. The actual text used in "Bebe el agua tranquila de la canción añeja" ("Drink the tranquil water of the old song") is a fragment of the longer poem, "Balada de la Placenta" ("Ballad of the Little Plaza"). The song comes from a work called *Madrigals, Books I–IV*. It is the first song in Book II.

Composer George Crumb

Listening Guide

"Bebe el agua tranquila de la canción añeja" ("Drink the tranquil water of the old song")

GEORGE CRUMB

CD 2
Track 41

Year: 1965 (The first two books of madrigals were composed in 1965 and the second two in 1969)

Tempo: Varies

Meter: No steady beat or meter

Voices: Female soprano, alto flute, and percussion

Language: Spanish. The only text is that of the title, sung two times through.

Duration: 1:45

Special feature: The alto flute is larger and deeper sounding than the "standard" flute. The flute imitates the very flamenco-sounding melodic turns sung by the soprano.

Timing	What to listen for
0:00	Introduction played by percussion and alto flute
0:04	Soprano sings flamenco-styled melodic turns on "ah"
0:27	The text (the song title) begins
0:41	Percussion and flute interlude
0:46	Soprano sings in a style reminiscent of her introduction on "ah," but at a pitch level a step higher than the introduction.
0:52	The text repeats, but with a different melody than before
1:18	Percussion and flute closing

(41 appears at the 0:00 row)

George Crumb was born in Charleston, West Virginia. After receiving bachelor's and master's degrees in the United States, he went to Berlin to study before going back to school to complete a D.M.A. from the University of Michigan, Ann Arbor. He taught composition at the University of Pennsylvania from 1965 until his retirement from teaching in 1997. He has won many awards, including a Pulitzer Prize for a piece called *Echoes of Time and the River* (1968), the Cannes Classical Award for "Best CD of a Living Composer" (1998), and a Grammy for "Best Contemporary Composition" for *Star-Child* (2001).

In addition to the obvious Spanish influences in the work we listened to, Crumb has brought the sounds of other cultures into his compositional style. Another work based on the poetry of Garcia Lorca, *Ancient Voices of Children* (1970), includes Tibetan prayer stones hit together rhythmically, frequent pitch bending by the singers and instrumentalists, a harp with paper threaded between the strings, and other folk and commercial instruments including a mandolin and an electric piano. In that work, Crumb required that the mandolin be tuned with one of its sets of strings a quarter-step (half the distance from one note to the next on a piano) lower than the other set. Because the two sets of strings are played at the same time, the instrument has a very dissonant sound. Other percussion instruments in the ensemble include Japanese temple bells, African drums, Latin-American claves (wooden sticks that are hit together), Latin maracas (gourds with rattles in them that are shaken), a marimba, sleigh bells, a glockenspiel, tubular bells, a vibraphone, and an Asian gong. Crumb has, in many ways, done exactly what he set out to do in bringing many musics of the world together.

"Hearing the Difference: Glass's *Company*, second movement, and Crumb's "Bebe el agua tranquila de la canción añeja" compares these two works.

HEARING THE DIFFERENCE

Glass's *Company*, second movement, and Crumb's "Bebe el agua tranquila de la canción añeja" ("Drink the tranquil water of the old song")

These compositions were both written during the second half of the twentieth century, but they are quite different from one another. Twentieth-century music has developed into a very great variety of sounds and styles, at least partly because of the many different world cultures that have influenced composers of the era. While we are listening here to two works by American composers of the same time period, we are also hearing the additive meter of Indian musical traditions and comparing it with music much influenced by Spain and other cultures.

	Company, second movement	"Bebe el agua tranquila de la canción añeja"
Tempo	Steady, 160 beats per minute	Varies
Meter	Beat remains steady, but meter changes often from duple to triple and back to duple; influence of Indian additive meters is obvious	No steady beat or meter
Form	Sectional, with two main sections alternating throughout and an intense repetition of the beginning section at the end	No regular sections that repeat or contrast
Instrumentation	All bowed string instruments including first violins, second violins, violas, cellos, and basses	For soprano singer, alto flute, and percussion; language is Spanish

Summary

The music of Spain is multicultural in itself because the country has a long history of Christians, Moslems, gypsies, and Jews all living on the same peninsula and sharing musical practices and instruments. Flamenco music with its high level of energy and passion developed out of the influences of all of those traditions.

American composer George Crumb studied the music and instruments from a great variety of world cultures and combined many of those instruments and vocal styles in his works. The one we heard, "Bebe el agua tranquila de la canción añeja" ("Drink the tranquil water of the old song"), has a very Spanish character, which is appropriate because it is based on fragments of poetry by the Spanish poet and playwright Federico García Lorca.

New People and Concepts

flamenco   **George Crumb**   **microtones**

Finale

Listen again to "Bebe el agua tranquila de la canción añeja" ("Drink the tranquil water of the old song"), and compare your impressions now with your notes from your first listening. Do you hear more now than you did before? You should now be able to answer the following questions:

▌ What is the tempo?

▌ What is the meter?

▌ What is the text about?

▌ What instruments are in the recording?

▌ Where do you hear melodies repeat?

▌ What is the general mood of the piece?

Characteristics of Non-Western-Influenced Music in the West

Texture	Both homophonic and polyphonic textures employed; variety of textures within a single composition; some uses of heterophonic (a single melody improvised on by two or more parts at the same time) texture
Tonality	Major-minor system employed in minimalism; atonality or a constantly changing tonality used by some composers; pentatonic and other non-Western scales commonly used; microtones used in non-Western and non-Western-influenced music
Rhythm	Very complex rhythms used in some music; repetitious rhythm patterns set to a steady beat in minimalism
Form	Some works with repeating and contrasting sections, others with no clear-cut sections but with gradual continuously evolving structures
Tone color	Non-Western instruments provide new sounds for use by Western composers; percussive sounds on "prepared" pianos; pianos and other traditional musical instruments played in nontraditional ways to create new sounds
Musical instruments	Non-Western instruments from many cultures used by Western composers; electronic instruments and manipulated tapes are used as musical instruments by themselves or in ensembles with other instruments

Glossary

Absolute music Music that is entirely free of extra-musical references or ideas.

A cappella Choral music without instrumental accompaniment.

Accent A stress on a particular beat, note, or chord.

Acoustic Non-electric, as in an instrument that has its own sound box and can be heard without the use of an amplifier.

Act A large section of a play or an opera. An act can be complete in itself, or it might be composed of several scenes.

Ad libitum Music to be played freely or even omitted depending on the performer's wishes.

Adagio A leisurely tempo, literally, "at ease."

Aerophones A general term for wind instruments in world music.

Aleatory Music in which some aspect is decided by performers or someone else other than the composer, guaranteeing that every performance of the work will be different from any other performance. See also "chance music" and "indeterminacy."

Allegretto A moderately fast tempo.

Allegro A fast tempo, faster than Allegretto.

Allegro assai Very fast and cheerful.

Allegro con brio Fast, with vigor and spirit.

Allegro moderato Moderately fast.

Allemande A Renaissance and baroque dance that is fairly fast and in duple or quadruple meter.

Alternative rock Late eighties and early nineties rock music that served as an alternative to the pop music commonly promoted on such places as MTV.

Alto A low, female voice (also called *contralto*), or an instrument that is lower than a soprano instrument and higher than a tenor instrument.

Andante A moderately slow tempo: literally, at a "walking" pace.

Andante con moto A tempo that is a walking pace, with a sense of motion (con moto).

Anthems Sacred choral compositions.

Arch form A composition that comprises an odd number of sections, usually five, in which the first and last are related, the second and second to last are related (more if there are more than five), and the middle section stands alone, like the head stone of an arch.

Aria A composition for solo voice and instrumental accompaniment.

Arioso A vocal style midway between recitative and aria. Its meter is less flexible than that of recitative, but its form is much simpler and more flexible than that of an aria.

Arpeggio A "broken" chord in which the tones are played one after another in rapid succession rather than simultaneously.

Articulation The type of attack and release or decay of the sound of an individual note or chord.

Art rock Rock music that has some characteristics also common in classical music. Some types of art rock have rock bands playing with orchestral instruments; other types have rock musicians playing large-scale multisectional works, such as those common in classical music.

Art song A musical setting of a poem for solo voice and piano. The German words for song and songs, *lied* and *lieder* (plural), became the standard terms for this type of song.

Atonal Lacking a recognizable tonal center or tonic.

Avant-garde Very current, modern, and experimental.

Ballad (vocal) A narrative poem set to music.

Ballade (instrumental) A relatively large, free-form work. The term was apparently used first by Chopin.

Ballad opera A dramatic work with spoken dialogue and popular songs that began in England during the middle 1700s. Ballad operas were the first musicals.

Ballett A simplified version of a madrigal.

Baritone A male voice or a musical instrument with a range below the tenor and above the bass.

Bass The lowest male voice, or musical instruments that are low in pitch.

Bass clarinet A large and low-sounding clarinet.

Bass drum A large, low drum that produces an indefinite pitch.

Basso continuo Continuous bass. A bass part performed by (1) a chordal instrument such as a keyboard instrument or a lute, and (2) a bass instrument such as a cello, viola da gamba, or bassoon that reinforces the bass line.

Bassoon A low-sounding woodwind instrument that uses a mouthpiece with a double reed.

Beat Regularly occurring pulsations that create the basic units of musical time.

Bebop A jazz style that emphasizes small ensembles playing very active and complex music.

Bel canto "Beautiful song." A vocal technique emphasizing beauty and purity of tone and agility in executing various ornamental details.

Binary form A basic musical form consisting of two contrasting sections (AB), both sections often being repeated (AABB).

Blue notes In blues and jazz, any of the notes produced by flatting the third, fifth, or seventh notes of a major scale.

Blues A lamenting, melancholy song characterized by a three-line lyrical pattern in AAB form, a twelve-bar harmonic progression, and the frequent use of "blue notes."

Bongos A pair of attached small drums that produce indefinite pitches.

Bridge (1) In a musical composition, a section that connects two themes. (2) In popular music, the bridge is a section between repetitions of the main melody (AABA form, the "B" is the bridge).

British invasion A term for rock music from Britain that first became enormously popular in the United States in and after 1964. The Beatles and the Rolling Stones led the "invasion."

Cadence A point of rest at the end of a passage, section, or complete work that gives the music a sense of convincing conclusion. Also, a melodic or harmonic progression that gives the feeling of conclusion.

Cadenza A section of music, usually in a concerto, played in an improvisatory style by a solo performer without orchestral accompaniment.

Call and response A song style (found in many West African cultures and African American folk music) in which phrases sung by a leader alternate with responding phrases sung by a chorus.

Canon A contrapuntal technique in which a melody in one part is strictly imitated by another voice or voices.

Cantata A choral work, usually on a sacred subject and frequently built upon a chorale tune, combining aria, recitative, chorus, and instrumental accompaniment.

Castrato A male singer who was castrated before puberty so that his voice would remain high. Castratos often sang hero roles in baroque operas and were hired by the Catholic Church, which did not want women to sing in the church services.

Celesta A keyboard percussion instrument that strikes tuned steel bars and looks something like a small upright piano.

Cello A large and fairly low-sounding member of the family of bowed string instruments. Because of its size, it rests on an end pin that sits on the floor. The instrument is held upright between the player's knees. Also called *violoncello*.

Chamber music Music written for a small group of instruments, with one player to a part.

Chance music See "aleatory."

Chanson French for "song." A type of Renaissance secular vocal music.

Character pieces Works portraying a single mood, emotion, or idea.

Chimes A set of tuned metal tubes suspended vertically in a frame, and played by being hit with mallets. Their sound resembles that of church bells. Also called *tubular bells*.

Choir A vocal ensemble consisting of several voice parts with four or five or more singers in each section. Also, a section of the orchestra comprising certain types of instruments, such as a *brass choir*.

Chorale A German hymn, often used as a unifying theme for a cantata.

Chorale prelude An organ composition based on a German hymn.

Chordophones A general term for stringed instruments in world music.

Chord progression A particularly distinctive series of harmonies, or chords.

Chorus, choir A vocal ensemble consisting of several voice parts with four or five or more singers in each section. Also, a section of the orchestra

comprising certain types of instruments, such as *brass choir*.

Chromatic Designating melodic movement by half steps.

Chromatic scale The scale containing all twelve tones within the interval of an octave.

Church modes A system of eight scales forming the tonal foundation for Gregorian chant and for polyphony up to the baroque era.

Clavichord A stringed keyboard instrument in common use during the Renaissance and baroque periods. It is softer than a harpsichord because its strings are hit with a tangent to sound instead of being plucked.

Clarinet A high-sounding woodwind instrument that uses a mouthpiece with a single reed.

Clavier A generic term for a keyboard instrument.

Coda The concluding section of a musical work or individual movement, often leading to a final climax and coupled with an increase in tempo.

Codetta The closing theme of the exposition in a sonata-form movement.

Collective improvisation Several musicians improvising at the same time, creating a complex, polyphonic texture, often done in early New Orleans jazz.

Concertino The solo instrument group in a concerto grosso.

Concert overture A one-movement self-contained orchestral concert piece, often in sonata form.

Concerto A work for one or more solo instruments and orchestra.

Concerto grosso A multimovement work for instruments in which a solo group called the *concertino* and a full ensemble called the *ripieno* are pitted against each other.

Conductor A person who directs a musical ensemble and who is responsible for all aspects of the performance of the ensemble.

Congas Long, single-headed Afro-Cuban drums that produce indefinite pitches.

Consonance A quality of an interval, chord, or harmony that imparts a sense of stability, repose, or finality.

Consort A small group of Renaissance instruments. For example, a "recorder" consort is made up of recorders of various sizes, and a "viol" consort is made up of viols of various sizes. A "mixed" consort includes instruments of more than one instrumental type or family.

Continuo See "basso continuo."

Contrabassoon A very low-sounding woodwind instrument that uses a mouthpiece with a double reed.

Contrast Something different from what came before.

Cool jazz A restrained, controlled jazz style that developed during the late 1940s.

Council of Trent A series of meetings of leaders of the Roman Catholic Church (1545–1563) to discuss church reforms following the Reformation. The decisions generated the Counter-Reformation (Catholic-Reformation).

Counterpoint A musical texture consisting of two or more equal and independent melodic lines sounding simultaneously. See also "polyphony."

Counter-Reformation See "Council of Trent."

Countersubject (of a fugue) In a fugue, new melodic material stated in counterpoint with the subject.

Counter tenor A male singer who develops his high vocal range (falsetto range) to be able to sing parts otherwise appropriate for a castrato or a woman.

Country rock A rock style that began in the late 1960s that added country-styled vocals and instruments to what was otherwise a rock band.

Courante A Renaissance and baroque dance with a moderate tempo and triple meter.

Cover recording A recording made subsequent to the original recording of a particular song.

Crescendo Music gradually gets louder.

Cue sheet Musical directions used by early film directors to tell musicians when to play what music in order to fit music to the actions in the film.

Cyclic form A unifying technique of long musical works in which the same thematic material recurs in succeeding movements.

Cymbals Circular metal plates that can be hit together or can be suspended and hit with a beater. They produce an indefinite pitch.

Da capo aria An aria in ABA form; the original melody of A may be treated in a virtuosic fashion in the second A section.

Decrescendo Gradually softer (same as diminuendo).

Development In a general sense, the elaboration of musical material through various procedures. Also, the second section of a movement in sonata form.

Dies irae "Day of wrath." A chant melody from the Middle Ages that represents death in music.

Diminuendo Gradually softer (same as decrescendo).

Dissonance A quality of an interval, chord, or harmony that gives a sense of tension and movement.

Dixieland A jazz style based on the original "hot" jazz from New Orleans.

Dodecaphony See "twelve-tone."

Double bass The largest and lowest-voiced member of the bowed string family of instruments. Also called *string bass*. Because of its size, the player sits on a stool or stands.

Downbeat The first, and often stressed, beat of a metric pattern of beats.

Drone A long-held note or notes over or under which other music is played.

Duet A piece of music for two players or singers.

Duple meter A meter with two beats in each measure.

Dynamics Relative degrees of loudness or softness.

Electronic Music produced by such means as magnetic tape, synthesizer, or computer.

Embellished A musical line that has been decorated by added notes or ornaments.

Embellishment The practice of decorating musical lines by adding notes or ornaments.

English horn A woodwind instrument with a pitch range between the oboe and the bassoon, and that uses a mouthpiece with a double reed.

Episode In a fugue, a transitional passage based on material derived from the subject or based on new material, leading to a new statement of the subject.

Ethnomusicology The study of non-Western (or "world") music.

Étude A study piece concentrating on a single technical problem.

Exposition The first section in sonata form, containing the statement of the principal themes. Also, the first section in a fugue, in which the principal theme or subject is presented imitatively.

Expressionism An artistic school of the early twentieth century that attempted to represent the psychological and emotional experience of modern humanity.

Fantasia An improvised piece characterized by virtuosity in composition and performance; popular during the Renaissance and baroque eras.

Fantasy overture A single-movement orchestral piece based on a literary story, also called a concert overture.

Fermata (⌢) A notational symbol indicating that a note is to be sounded longer than its normal time value, the exact length being left to the discretion of the performer.

Field hollers Singing by African American field workers that influenced the development of early country blues styles.

Figured bass A shorthand method of notating an accompaniment part. Numbers are placed under the bass notes to indicate the intervals to be sounded above the bass notes. See also "basso continuo."

Flamenco A style of music, dance, and singing that originated with the Gypsies in southern Spain.

Flute A high-sounding woodwind instrument that is played by blowing across a mouthpiece on the side of the instrument. Modern flutes are usually made of metal, but early ones were made of wood.

Folk-rock Folk singing accompanied by amplified instruments and drums as they are generally used in rock music.

Form The aspect of music involving the overall structuring and organization of music.

Forte (f) A loud dynamic level.

Fortissimo (ff) A very loud dynamic level.

Free jazz A post-bebop jazz style that freely changed rhythmic patterns and disposed of repeating melodies in favor of free-flowing, improvised playing.

French horn A medium-ranged, mellow-sounding brass instrument.

French overture A popular type of introductory movement in baroque music that begins with a stately section using dotted rhythms (very long followed by very short notes) followed by a faster fugal section. Sometimes the dotted rhythms return at the end.

Front line In jazz bands, the instruments that carry the melodic material.

Fuging tunes Psalm or hymn melodies that are sung as canons or written to contain imitation, popular in Britain and the U.S. during the 1700s.

Fugue A composition that uses imitative polyphony and is organized around the returns of a theme or subject and a countermelody (countersubject) that often appears with it. Fugues can have more than one subject, but a single one is more common.

Funk A polyrhythmic form of rock music in which rhythms are much more important than the melodies sung or played with them.

Fusion A style of jazz developed in the late 1960s that has been influenced by rock music through the inclusion of amplified instruments, short riffs (repeating melodies), and even beat subdivisions.

Gamelan An Indonesian musical ensemble usually consisting of idiophones, metallophones, and sets of knobbed gongs. Membranophones, chordophones, aerophones, and voices can also be included.

Gangsta rap Rap singing that stresses gang violence.

Gavotte A baroque dance in duple meter danced to a moderate tempo.

Gigue A Renaissance and baroque dance with a fast tempo and, usually, a sextuple meter.

Glissando A rapid sliding up or down the scale.

Glitter rock A theatrical style of 1970s rock music that stressed glamorous outfits and androgynous dress by male performers.

Glockenspiel A percussion instrument with two rows of steel bars, each of which produces a definite pitch when struck by a mallet.

Gong Large Asian metal percussion instrument that produces an indefinite pitch.

Grand opera A type of Romantic opera that concentrated on the spectacular elements of the production.

Grave A slow and solemn tempo.

Gregorian chant A body of music to which the medieval Roman Catholic liturgy was sung, consisting of monophonic, single-line melodies sung without instrumental accompaniment.

Griots African singers who memorized their tribe's history through their songs.

Ground bass A bass line that constantly repeats a short melody.

Grunge rock A punk-related style of rock music of the 1980s and 1990s based in Seattle, Washington.

Guitar A plucked stringed instrument with a fingerboard that exists in both acoustic and electric versions.

Hard bop A late bebop jazz style popular during the middle 1950s.

Hard rock A blues-based rock style popular in the 1970s and after that uses repeating riff patterns in the bass and fuzztone guitar timbres but that is not as powerful as heavy metal.

Harmony A composite sound made up of two or more notes of different pitch that sound simultaneously.

Harp A plucked string instrument with strings stretched vertically in a triangular frame.

Harpsichord A plucked stringed keyboard instrument in common use

during the Renaissance and baroque periods. The sound of plucked strings is much crisper than that of other keyboard instruments that produce their tones by tangents or hammers hitting the strings.

Heavy metal A blues-based rock style popular in the 1970s and after that uses repeating riff patterns in the bass, fuzztone guitar timbres, and stage sets and performer images that stress power or horror.

Heterophony Performance of a single melody by two or more individuals who add their own rhythmic or melodic modifications.

Homophony Music in which a single melody predominates, while the other voices or instruments provide harmonic accompaniment.

Hymn Religious songs that usually praise God.

Idée fixe A single, recurring motive; e.g., in Berlioz's *Symphony fantastique*, a musical idea representing the hero's beloved that recurs throughout the piece.

Idiophones A general term for solid percussion instruments in world music that are struck together, shaken, scraped, or rubbed to create their sound.

Imitation The repetition, in close succession and usually at a different pitch level, of a melody by another voice or voices within a contrapuntal texture.

Impressionism A late nineteenth-century artistic movement that sought to capture the visual impression rather than the literal reality of a subject. Also, in music, a style belonging primarily to Claude Debussy, characterized by an emphasis on mood and atmosphere, sensuous tone colors, elegance, and beauty of sound.

Improvisation The practice of "making up" music and performing it on the spot without first having written it down.

Incidental music Music written to accompany a play.

Indeterminacy, aleatory, or chance music Music in which the composer sets out to remove the decision-making process from his or her own control.

Chance operations, such as throwing dice, are employed to obtain a random series of musical events.

Industrial rock A 1980s and after rock style that expresses anger at an industrial society. It is usually very loud and includes synthesized sounds and distorted vocals.

Interval The distance in pitch between any two tones.

Jazz Improvisatory music based on African American musical traditions. Jazz developed into many styles through the twentieth century and beyond and has come to be widely popular all over the world.

Jazz rock Music played by rock bands that include horn sections that play in a swing jazz style.

Jongleurs Medieval street musicians who sang, played instruments, and sometimes acted in plays.

Key Tonality; the relationship of tones to a central tone, the tonic.

Key signature The group of sharps or flats placed at the beginning of each staff to indicate which notes are to be raised or lowered a half step. The particular combination of sharps or flats indicates the "key" of a composition.

Largo A very slow and broad tempo.

Legato "Linked, tied," indicating a smooth, even style of performance, with each note connected to the next.

Leitmotif "Leading motive." A musical motive representing a particular character, object, idea, or emotional state. Used especially in Wagner's operas.

Lento A slow tempo.

Libretto The text of an opera or similar extended dramatic musical work.

Lied (Lieder, plural) German for "song." See "art song."

Lining out A way of leading Protestant hymn singing by having a leader, often the minister, sing or speak a line, which is then repeated by the congregation.

Liturgy The text of the Roman Catholic Mass (reenactment of the Last Supper) service, also used by some Protestant religions.

Lute A stringed instrument with a fingerboard and bowl-shaped body

popular during the Renaissance and baroque periods in Europe.

Lyric opera A type of French Romantic opera that relied on beautiful melodies for its effect.

Madrigal A polyphonic vocal piece set to a short poem; it originated during the Renaissance.

Major scale A scale having a pattern of whole and half steps, with the half steps falling between the third and fourth and between the seventh and eighth notes of the scale.

Marimba A percussion instrument with tuned wooden bars that produce a hollow sound when struck by mallets and resonators under each bar.

Mass The most solemn service of the Roman Catholic Church. The parts of the Mass most frequently set to music are the Kyrie, Gloria, Credo, Sanctus and Benedictus, and Agnus Dei.

Mazurka In Romantic music, a small piano piece based on the Polish dance form. Prominent in the works of Chopin.

Measured rhythm Regulated rhythm in which precise time values are related to each other.

Measures Units of time organization consisting of a fixed number of beats. Measures are separated from one another by vertical bar lines on the staff.

Melisma Several notes sung to a single syllable of text.

Melismatic Designating a melodic phrase in which one syllable of text is spread over several notes.

Melody A basic musical element consisting of a series of pitches of particular duration that sound one after another.

Membranophones A general term for drums in world music.

Mensural notation A system of notating the length of time a given note is to be held.

Metallophones An idiophone with a row of tuned metal bars that are struck with mallets.

Meter The organization of rhythmic pulses or beats into equal, recurring groups.

Mezzo forte (mf) A moderately loud dynamic level.

Mezzo piano (mf) A moderately soft dynamic level.

Mezzo soprano A female voice between the ranges of soprano and alto.

Microtones Intervals smaller than a half step.

Minimalism A late-twentieth-century movement that seeks to return music to its simplest, most basic elements. It is characterized by a very steady beat and gradually changing repeating figures.

Minnesingers Medieval German poet-singers.

Minor scale A scale having a pattern of whole and half steps, with the half steps falling between the second and third and between the sixth and seventh tones of the scale.

Minstrels Medieval wandering street musicians and entertainers.

Minuet and trio A form employed in the third movement of many classical symphonies, cast in a stately triple meter and ternary form (ABA).

Moderato A moderate tempo.

Modified-strophic form A song structure that varies the regularity of the repeated melodies of strophic form by having some verses sung to a new melody.

Modulation Gradual or rapid change from one key to another within a composition.

Monody A type of accompanied solo song that evolved in Italy around 1600 in reaction to the complex polyphonic style of the late Renaissance. Its principal characteristics are (1) a recitative-like vocal line and (2) an arioso with basso continuo accompaniment.

Monophony A musical texture consisting of a single melodic line without accompanying material, as in Gregorian chant.

Motet A polyphonic choral work set to a sacred text.

Motive A short melodic or rhythmic theme that reappears frequently throughout a work or section of a work as a unifying device.

Movement Independent section of a longer composition.

MTV Cable Music Television.

Musicals Dramas that are told through a series of songs, usually with spoken dialogue between the songs.

Music drama Richard Wagner's term for his operas.

Musique concrète "Concrete music." A musical style originating in France about 1948; its technique consists of recording natural or "concrete" sounds, altering the sounds by various electronic means, and then combining them into organized pieces.

Mute A device used to soften or change the tone quality of an instrument. Mutes can be clamped to the bridge of bowed string instruments. Mutes for brass instruments are cone shaped and fit into the instrument's bell.

Naturalism A literary movement of nineteenth-century France that realistically depicted the lives of working-class people.

Neoclassicism In music of the early twentieth century, the philosophy that musical composition should be approached with objectivity and restraint. Neoclassical composers were attracted to the textures and forms of the baroque and classical periods.

New Orleans jazz The first jazz to be recorded and, therefore, the root of later jazz styles.

Nonet Chamber music for nine players.

Note A symbol used to notate a pitch and its duration. "Note" is also used to identify a pitch or a tone.

Oboe A high-sounding woodwind instrument that uses a mouthpiece with a double reed.

Octave An interval between two pitches in which the higher pitch vibrates at twice the frequency of the lower. When sounded simultaneously, the two pitches sound very much alike.

Octet Chamber music for eight players.

Opera A drama set to music and made up of vocal pieces such as recitatives, arias, duets, trios, and ensembles with orchestral accompaniment, and orchestral overtures and interludes.

Scenery, stage action, and costuming are employed.

Opera buffa Italian comic opera.

Opera comique A type of French Romantic opera distinguished by its use of spoken dialogue rather than sung recitative. Though called "comique," many operas in this form had serious plots.

Opera seria Italian opera with a serious (i.e., noncomic) subject.

Operetta Short, small-scale operatic works popular during the 17th and 18th centuries.

Opus "Work." The term is usually followed by a number that identifies the particular work in the catalogue of music by a composer.

Oratorio An extended choral work made up of recitatives, arias, and choruses, *without* costuming, stage action, or scenery.

Orchestra An ensemble of instruments consisting mainly of strings, but also usually including woodwinds, brass, and percussion. The size and particular instrumentation of an orchestra depends on the needs of the composition to be performed.

Orchestration The arrangement of a musical composition for performance by an orchestra. Also, utilization of orchestral instruments for expressive and structural purposes.

Ordinary (of the Mass) The sections of the Mass that stay the same throughout the church year. They are the Kyrie, Gloria, Credo, Sanctus, and Agnus Dei.

Organ Originally a wind instrument in which sets of pipes are controlled by a keyboard that sends air from a blower into the pipes. Electronic organs that can imitate the sound of pipe organs are also common in the twenty-first century.

Organum The earliest type of medieval polyphonic music.

Overture The orchestral introduction to a musical dramatic work.

Passion A musical setting of the story of the suffering and crucifixion of Jesus Christ.

Pedal board The organ keyboard for bass lines played by the organist's feet.

Pentatonic scale A five-tone scale. Various pentatonic scales are commonly employed in non-Western music.

Phrase A portion of a melody that can sound complete or incomplete. An incomplete-sounding phrase makes the listener want to hear another phrase that completes the melody.

Phrasing Musical units consisting of several measures.

Pianissimo (pp) A very soft dynamic level.

Piano A stringed instrument played by a keyboard that causes hammers to hit the strings.

Piano (p) A soft dynamic level.

Pianoforte An eighteenth- or early-nineteenth-century piano.

Piano, four hands Two players playing one piano at the same time.

Piano quartet Usually, a work for one piano and strings. Can be four pianos, but that is rare.

Piano quintet Usually, a work for one piano and strings. Can be for five pianos, but that is rare.

Piano trio Usually, a work for one piano with violin and cello. Can be for three pianos, but that is rare.

Piccolo A small, high-pitched flute.

Pitch The highness or lowness of a musical tone, determined by the frequency of vibration of the sounding body.

Pitch range The span from low to high pitches that an instrument or a voice can produce.

Pizzicato A performance technique in which stringed instruments, such as the violin, are plucked with the fingers instead of bowed.

Plainchant See "Gregorian chant."

Polonaise In Romantic music, a small piano piece based on the Polish dance form.

Polyphony Many voices. A texture combining two or more independent melodies heard simultaneously; generally synonymous with counterpoint.

Polyrhythms Two or more contrasting and independent rhythms used at the same time.

Polytonality The simultaneous use of two or more different keys.

Prelude A free-form piece that may introduce another piece or stand alone.

Première The first or most eminent performance of a work.

Prepared piano A piano with the sound altered by the insertion of items such as bolts, screws, pencils, cloth, and even paper on or between the strings.

Prestissimo A tempo that is as fast as possible.

Presto A very fast tempo.

Primitivism In music, the use of frenzied, irregular rhythms and percussive effects to evoke a feeling of primitive power, as in Stravinsky's *The Rite of Spring.*

Program music Instrumental music associated with a nonmusical idea, this idea often being stated in the title or in an explanatory program note.

Program symphony A symphony with a story line or other type of program.

Proper (of the Mass) The sections of the Catholic Mass that change with the church year. The proper is generally not set to music because each text is used so seldom.

Protestantism Religions that "protested" against the Church of Rome (later called the Roman Catholic Church) during the Renaissance and broke away from it in what was called the Reformation.

Psalms The sacred poems from the book of Psalms in the Bible.

Punk rock An angry and rebellious rock style that began in New York and Detroit during the late 1960s and moved on to London and then the rest of the United States; characterized by a fast, throbbing pulse and monotone shouted vocals.

Quadruple meter A meter in which each measure has four beats.

Quadruple stops Bowed stringed instruments played to sound all four strings together.

Quartet Chamber music for four players.

Quintet Chamber music for five players.

Quintuple meter A meter in which each measure has five beats.

Raga An ancient melodic pattern employed in Indian music.

Ragtime A composed music of the 1890s, usually for piano.

Rap A style of contemporary popular music that employs a rhythmically spoken text delivered over a funk or related musical background.

Realizations Keyboard or lute parts that have been taken from figured bass lines to play basso continuo parts in baroque music.

Recapitulation The third section of sonata form, which restates the themes from the exposition.

Recitative A form of "singing speech" in which the rhythm is dictated by the natural inflection of the words.

Recorders A wooden end-blown flute-type instrument common during from the Middle Ages through the baroque.

Repetition Music is played again, or repeated.

Refrain Text and/or music that is returned to or repeated within a larger piece of music.

Registration (on an organ) The combination of stops or registers chosen by an organist for the performance of a work.

Rhythm The element of music that encompasses all aspects of musical time.

Rhythm and blues A form of African American popular music that blends elements of jazz and the blues.

Rhythm section In jazz or rock bands, the instruments that supply the harmonic and rhythmic accompaniment.

Ripieno The full ensemble in a concerto grosso.

Ritornello "Return." A characteristic form for the first and sometimes the last movement of the baroque concerto grosso. The thematic material given to the ripieno returns between the passages played by the soloists.

Rockabilly A 1950s rock style that combined elements of "hillbilly" country music with rock music. It is characterized by a strong back beat (accenting of beats two and four in a four-beat pattern), a slapping bass, and an energetic tempo.

Rondo An extended alternating form often employed in the fourth movement of classical symphonies; generally spirited and playful in character.

Round A contrapuntal technique in which a melody in one part is strictly imitated by another voice or voices. See also "canon."

Rubato "Robbed." A term indicating that a performer may treat the tempo with a certain amount of freedom, shortening the duration of some beats and correspondingly lengthening others.

Sarabande A Renaissance and baroque dance that is fairly slow and in triple meter, often using dotted rhythms (long, short, long, short note values).

SATB chorus A four-part group of singers that include sopranos, altos, tenors, and basses. The chorus can include women on the higher two parts and men on the lower ones, or it can be all men or men with boys singing the high parts.

Saxophone A woodwind instrument that uses a mouthpiece with a single reed and is made of brass. Saxophones come in many sizes and pitch ranges.

Scat singing A jazz vocal style in which the singer uses nonsense syllables in the place of words.

Scene A subsection of an act in a play or opera.

Scherzo Literally, "joke." A sprightly, humorous instrumental piece, swift in tempo; developed by Beethoven to replace the minuet.

Secular Nonreligious

Septet Chamber music for seven players.

Sequence The repetition of a motive or melody at different pitch levels.

Serialism See "twelve-tone."

Sextet Chamber music for six players.

Sextuple meter A meter in which each measure has six beats.

Side drum A drum with two heads, the bottom of which has snares or metal wires that can be tightened to rattle against that head when the upper head is hit. Also called a "snare drum."

Sight sing Sing by looking at musical notation instead of having memorized the music in advance.

Sinfonia A short instrumental introduction to a baroque choral work.

Singspiel German comic opera that employed spoken dialogue.

Solo concerto A multimovement baroque work that differs from concerto grosso in that the concertino consists of only one instrument.

Solo sonata A sonata for one instrument with continuo accompaniment.

Sonata An instrumental work consisting of three or four contrasting movements.

Sonata da camera "Chamber sonata." A baroque instrumental work, essentially a dance suite.

Sonata da chiesa "Church sonata." A baroque instrumental work in four movements (slow-fast-slow-fast).

Sonata form A musical form encompassing one movement of a composition and consisting of three sections—exposition, development, and recapitulation—the last often followed by a coda.

Sonata rondo The form of a movement that shares characteristics of both the sonata and the rondo forms. It usually has an A section that returns as it would in a rondo, but it also has a development section such as that found in a movement in sonata form.

Song cycle A series of art songs that tell a story.

Soprano A high, usually female, voice. Also, the high instrument in an instrumental family.

Soul music A 1960s term for music based on African American gospel singing styles.

Southern rock A 1970s style that stressed the blues, along with elements of country music and texts about pride in the American South.

Sprechstimme Literally, "speech voice." A vocal technique in which a pitch is half sung, half spoken. Developed by Arnold Schoenberg.

Staccato "Detached." Indicating a style of performance in which each note is played in a short, crisp manner.

Staff A graph-like structure consisting of five lines and four spaces. Each line and each space represents a different pitch.

Stops (on an organ) Rows of organ pipes that are activated by the player pulling the knob that opens them and then playing the keyboard.

String quartet A chamber ensemble consisting of a first and a second violin, a viola, and a cello; also, the form which is a sonata for these instruments.

Strophic Designating a song in which all verses of text are sung to the same music.

Swing A big-band jazz style particularly popular for dance music during the 1930s through the middle 1940s.

Subject (of a fugue) In a fugue, the principal theme, introduced first in a single voice and then imitated in other voices, returning frequently during the course of the composition.

Suite A series of instrumental movements, each based on a particular dance rhythm.

Syllabic Designating a musical phrase in which each syllable of text is given one note.

Symbolism A subtle French poetic style from the late nineteenth century that stressed the sound and color of the words and suggested rather than clearly outlined the meaning or story behind the text.

Symphonic poem See "tone poem."

Symphony A sonata for orchestra.

Syncopation A deliberate disturbance of the normal metrical pulse, produced by shifting the accent from a normally strong beat to a weak beat.

Synthesizer An electronic instrument that can duplicate almost any sound and can be used to create entirely new sounds.

Tala One of the ancient rhythmic patterns employed in Indian music.

Tambourine A single-headed drum with metal discs loosely set in the frame. The instrument is hand-held and shaken or struck to produce an indefinite pitch.

Techno A highly electronic rock style that developed out of disco and hip-hop, popular during the 1980s and after.

Te Deum A text that praises God.

Tempo The speed at which a piece of music moves.

Tenor A high, male voice, or an instrument that is lower than an alto and higher than a bass instrument.

Ternary form A musical form that consists of three sections, ABA, in which the final section (A) is a repetition of the first section (A), and the middle section (B) contrasts with A.

Texture The relationship between the melodic and harmonic aspects of a piece of music. The principal classifications in most Western music are monophony, homophony, and polyphony.

Theme A musical idea that serves as a starting point for development of a composition or section of a composition.

Theme and variations form A form based on a single theme and its subsequent repetition, with each new statement varied in some way from the original.

Theme transformation The practice of varying a single theme or melody through the different sections of a piece; this procedure was used especially in Romantic tone poems.

Through-composed form A term applied to songs in which new music is used for each successive verse.

Timbre The characteristic tone quality of a musical sound as produced by a specific instrument or voice, or by a combination of instruments or voices.

Timpani Tuned drums each of which has a single head stretched across a kettle-like body. The pitch of each drum is controlled by the player. Also called "kettledrums."

Toccata A baroque keyboard piece full of scale passages, rapid runs and trills, and massive chords.

Tom-tom Cylindrical-shaped drums, usually found in sets of assorted sizes that produce indefinite pitches.

Tonality The relationship of tones to a central tone called the tonic. See also "key."

Tone cluster A chord produced by playing a large group of adjacent notes on the piano with the flat of the hand. The resulting sound is dense and indistinct.

Tone color, timbre The characteristic quality, or "color," of a musical sound as produced by a specific instrument or voice, or by a combination of instruments.

Tone poem, also symphonic poem A single-movement programmatic work, relatively long and very free in form, usually involving a dramatic plot or literary idea.

Tone row See "twelve-tone."

Tonic The tonal center. The tone that acts as a musical home base, or point of rest and finality, in a piece of music.

Transcription An arrangement of a composition for a medium other than that for which it was originally written.

Tremolo Fast repeated notes.

Triad A three-note chord in which each note is the interval of a third from the next closest note.

Triangle A triangular-shaped metal percussion instrument that is struck by a metal bar to produce an indefinite pitch.

Trill A musical ornament in which two adjacent notes quickly alternate between one another.

Trio Chamber music for three players.

Trio sonata A sonata for two instruments with continuo accompaniment.

Triple meter A meter in which each measure has three beats.

Triplet Three notes fitted into the time in which only two of those notes would normally fit.

Trombone A brass instrument that is played with a slide and produces a medium- to low-pitch range.

Troubadours Medieval poet/singers from southern France. They were often people of noble rank who would not perform in public but would sing to family members and friends.

Trouvères Medieval poet/singers from northern France. Like troubadours, they were often people of noble rank who would not perform in public but would sing to family members and friends.

Trumpet A brass instrument with a high-pitch range.

Tuba A large brass instrument with a low-pitch range.

Tutti "All," or the entire ensemble.

Twelve-tone, also serialism and dodecaphony A system of composition developed by Arnold Schoenberg that consists of arranging the twelve pitches of the chromatic scale in a particular order (known as a tone row, series, or set).

Unison Two notes that are the same pitch, or two or more instruments or voices producing the same pitches at the same time.

Upbeat One or more unaccented beats that precede the accented downbeat. Also called "pickup."

Variation A modified version of something previously performed in which some elements of the original remain.

Verismo "Realism." An Italian operatic point of view favoring realistic subjects taken from everyday, often lower-class, life.

Vernacular The everyday spoken language.

Vibrato A slight fluctuation in pitch that increases the "warmth" of a tone.

Viola A bowed string instrument slightly larger and lower-sounding than the violin.

Violin A high-sounding bowed string instrument, the neck of which is held by the player's left hand, and the tail rests beneath the player's chin.

Viols Fretted, bowed string instruments commonly used during the Renaissance and Baroque periods.

Virtuoso A performer with complete technical control of the playing of his or her musical instrument.

Vitaphone A recording system invented during the mid-1920s to allow previously recorded music to play simultaneously with a film.

Vivace A fast and "vivacious" tempo.

Volume (dynamics) Relative degrees of loudness or softness.

Wind ensemble An orchestral type of concert band made up primarily of woodwind, brass, and percussion instruments. Also called "symphonic band" or "concert band."

Word painting Representation of the literal meaning of a text through musical means.

Work songs Rhythmic songs sung by African American workers while they worked. This type of singing was influential on the development of country blues styles.

Xylophone A pitched percussion instrument with tuned wooden bars that produce a hollow sound when struck by mallets.

Credits

Text

pp. 246–247, Used by permission of Belmont Music Publishers, Pacific Palisades, CA 90272. **p. 267,** "Lost Your Head Blues," by Bessie Smith. © 1926 (Renewed) FRANK MUSIC CORP. All Rights Reserved. **p. 271,** "It Don't Mean a Thing, If It Ain't Got That Swing" from *Sophisticated Ladies.* Music by Duke Ellington, words by Irving Mills. Copyright © 1932, Renewed 1960 EMI MILLS MUSIC, INC., & FAMOUS MUSIC CORPORATION in the USA. Rights for the world outside the U.S.A. Controlled by EMI Mills Music Inc. (Publishing) and Warner Bros. Publications Inc. (Print) International Copyright Secured. All Rights Reserved. Used by permission Warner Bros. Publications U.S. Inc., Miami, Florida 33014. **pp. 304–305,** "America" by Stephen Sondheim © 1957, renewed 1991 by Leonard Bernstein Music Publishing Company, LLC administered by Universal-Polygram International Publishing, Inc./ASCAP. Used by permission. International Copyright Secured. All Rights Reserved. **p. 347,** © Copyright 1981, 1994 by Hendon Music, Inc., a Boosey & Hawkes company. Reprinted by permission. **p. 352,** Music from *Ancient Voices of Children,* by George Crumb, first movement. © 1970 by C.F. Peters Corporation. Text excerpted from "Selected Poems" by Federico García Lorca. © 1955 New Directions Publishing Corporation.

Photos

p. 2 (bottom), R. May 2001 © ArenaPal/Topham/The Image Works. **p. 2 (top),** Odile Noel/Lebrecht/The Image Works. **p. 3,** Ilian Iliev/ Lebrecht/The Image Works. **p. 17,** ArenaPal/Topham/The Image Works. **p. 19 (bottom left),** Chris Stock/ Lebrecht/The Image Works. **p. 19 (bottom right),** Royalty-free/Corbis. **p. 19 (top),** Chris Stock/Lebrecht/The Image Works. **p. 20,** ArenaPal/Topham/The Image Works. **p. 21 (bottom left),** Chris Stock/Lebrecht/The Image Works. **p. 21 (bottom right),** Chris Stock/Lebrecht/The Image Works. **p. 21 (top),** Chris Stock/Lebrecht/The Image Works. **p. 22 (bottom),** Chris Stock/Lebrecht/The Image Works. **p. 22 (top),** Chris Stock/Lebrecht/The Image Works. **p. 23,** Odile Noel/Lebrecht/The Image Works. **p. 25,** Lawrence Manning/Corbis. **p. 30,** Cimabue (1240–1302), *Madonna of the Holy Trinity.* Uffizi, Florence, Italy. Scala/Art Resource, NY. **p. 31 (left),** *Poseidon (Zeus).* Bronze figure from the Artemisius at Cape Sounion. 460 BCE. H: 1.95m. Inv. 15161. National Archaeological Museum, Athens, Greece. Photo: Erich Lessing/Art Resource, NY. **p. 31 (right),** *Apollo Belvedere,* 3/4 view. Roman copy after Greek original, c. 350–320 BCE. Museo Pio Clementino, Vatican Museums, Vatican State. Photo: Scala/Art Resource, NY. **p. 34,** Manetti, Rutilio (1571–1639), *Saint Gregory the Great.* Coll. Monte dei Paschi, Siena, Italy. Photo: Scala/Art Resource, NY. **p. 36,** Bridgeman Art Library. **p. 40,** Heidelberg University Library. **p. 41,** Lebrecht Music Collection. **p. 46,** Raphael, *Madonna del Granduca.* Alinari/Art Resource. **p. 47,** Royalty-free/Corbis. **p. 50,** Lebrecht Music Collection. **p. 53,** Lebrecht Music Collection. **p. 57,** The Pierpont Morgan Library/Art Resource. **p. 60,** Caravaggio, *Conversion of St. Paul.* S. Maria del Popolo, Rome, Italy. Photo: Scala/Art Resource. **p. 61,** Bernini, *David.* Marble, 1623–1624. Frontal view. Post-restoration. Galleria Borghese, Rome, Italy. Photo: Scala/Art Resource. **p. 62 (bottom),** Hogarth, William (1697–1764), *A Rake's Progress (plate 3): The Tavern Scene.* 1735. Etching and engraving on paper, 318 × 387 mm.

Transferred from the reference collection, 1973.Tate Gallery, London, Great Britain. Photo: Tate Gallery, London/Art Resource, NY. **p. 62 (top),** Le Nain, Louis (1593–1648), *Peasant family in an interior.* Louvre, Paris, France. Photo: Erich Lessing/Art Resource, NY. **p. 65,** Scala/Art Resource. **p. 66,** AKG London. **p. 67,** Amigoni, Jacopo (1675–1752), *The singer Carlo Broschi, called Farinelli (famous castrato).* National Museum of Art, Bucharest, Romania. Photo: Cameraphoto/Art Resource, NY. **p. 70,** Bridgeman Art Library. **p. 75,** Paul Joseph Delcloche, *Court Concert at Prince Bishop of Lueltich at Seraing.* Bayerisches National Museum. Photo: AKG London. **p. 79,** AKG London. **p. 82,** AKG London. **p. 84,** Stock Montage Inc. **p. 92,** Lebrecht Music Collection. **p. 94,** Lebrecht Music Collection. **p. 100,** Portrait of Vivaldi. Civico Museo Bibliografico Musicale Rossini, Bologna, Italy. Scala/Art Resource. **p. 104,** Fragonard, Jean-Honore (1732–1806), *The Bathers.* Oil on canvas, 64 × 80 cm. Louvre, Paris, France. Photo: Erich Lessing/Art Resource, NY. **p. 105,** Gérard Blot/Réunion des Musées Nationaux/Art Resource, NY. **p. 106,** David, *The Death of Socrates.* The Metropolitan Museum of Art, New York. Gift of Catherine Lorillard Wolfe Collection, Wolfe Fund, 1931 (31.45). Photograph © The Metropolitan Museum of Art, New York. **p. 107,** Lefevre, Robert (1755–1830), *Portrait of Napoleon Bonaparte,* Premier Consul. Oil on canvas, 158 × 114 cm. Chateaux de Versailles et de Trianon, Versailles, France. Photo: Gérard Blot/Réunion des Musées Nationaux/Art Resource, NY. **p. 109 (left),** James Davis/Corbis. **p. 109 (right),** Joseph Sohm/Corbis. **p. 112,** Jon Feingersh/Corbis. **p. 113,** Lebrecht Music Collection. **p. 120,**

Performance Information for 2-CD Set

Disc 1

1 Chant: "Salve, Regina" ("Hail, Holy Queen")
   Niederaltaicher Scholaren; Conrad Ruhland, dir.
   Courtesy of Sony BMG Music Entertainment

2 Mauchat: "Agnus Dei" ("Lamb of God") from
   Messe de Nostre Dame (Mass of Our Lady)
   Oxford Camerata; Jeremy Summerly, dir.
   Naxos of America Inc.

5 Beatriz of Dia: "A Chantar" ("It is Mine to Sing")
   Mara Kiek, voice; Steven Wishart, dir.
   1991 Hyperion Records Limited, London.
   Courtesy of Hyperion Records Limited

6 Josquin: "Ave Maria" ("Hail, Mary")
   Capella Nova; Richard Taruskin, dir.
   Musical Heritage Society

8 Farmer: "Fair Phyllis"
   Oxford Camerata; Jeremy Summerly, dir.
   Naxos of America Inc.

9 Praetorius: Three Dances from *Terpsichore*
   Ensemble Bourrasque; Lena Hellstrom-Farmlof
   Naxos of America Inc.

13 Purcell: "When I am laid in earth," from *Dido and Aeneas*
    The Scholars Baroque Ensemble
    Naxos of America Inc.

    Handel: *Messiah*
14 Recitative: "Comfort ye"
15 Aria: "Ev'ry Valley"
16 Chorus: "Hallelujah"
    Scholars Baroque Ensemble
    Naxos of America Inc.

17 Bach: "The Little Fugue in G Minor"
    Julia Brown, Organ
    Naxos of America Inc.

18 Vivaldi: "Spring," I, from *Le Quattro Stagione (The Four Seasons)*
    Accademia Ziliniana; Jindrich Pazdera,
    Frantisek Figura
    Naxos of America Inc.

23 Mozart: Symphony no. 40 in G Minor,
    I Capella Istropolitana; Barry Wordsworth
    Naxos of America Inc.

29 Haydn: String Quartet op. 33, no. 3 ("The Bird"), IV
    Kodaly Quartet
    Naxos of America Inc.

37 Mozart: "Non più andrai" ("No more will you")
    from *Le Nozze di Figaro (The Marriage of Figaro)*
    Vienna Mozart Orchestra, Johannes Wildner,
    Konrad Leitner
    Naxos of America Inc.

43 Beethoven: Symphony no. 5 in C Minor,
    I Zagreb Philharmonic; Richard Edlinger
    Naxos of America Inc.

49 Schubert: "Erlkönig" ("King of the Elves")
    Tamara Takacs, mezzo soprano and Jenno
    Jando, Piano
    Naxos of America Inc.

50 Chopin: Ballade no. 1 in G Minor
    Ivan Szekely
    Naxos of America Inc.

55 Puccini: "Sì, mi chiamano Mimì" ("Yes, they
    call me Mimi") from *La Bohème*, Act I
    Slavic Philharmonic Chorus, Bratislava
    Children's choir, Czecho-Slovak Radio
    Symphony Orchestra (Bratislava); Will
    Humburg Naxos of America Inc.

Disc 2

1 Berlioz: *Symphonie fantastique*, V, "Dream of
   a Witches' Sabbath"
   CSR Symphony Orchestra (Bratislava)
   Naxos of America Inc.

4 Smetana: "The Moldau"
   Slovak State Philharmonic Orchestra; Reinhard
   Seifreid
   Naxos of America Inc.

12 Mahler: Symphony no. 1 in D Major, III
    Polish National Radio Symphony Orchestra;
    Michael Halasz
    Naxos of America Inc.

16 Debussy: Prélude à "L'après-midi d'un faune"
    (Prelude to "The Afternoon of a Faun")
    BRT Philharmonic Orchestra; Alexander
    Rahbari Naxos of America Inc.

21 Billings "When Jesus Wept"
Atlanta Singers
Albany/ACA Digital

22 Beach: "Ah, Love, but a Day"
D'Anna Fortunato, mezzo soprano and Viginia
Eskin, piano
Under License from Northeastern Records

25 Smith: "Lost Your Head Blues"
Bessie Smith
Courtesy of Sony BMG Music Entertainment,
Sony Legacy (P) 1926

30 Parker: "Ko Ko"
Charlie Parker & his Bee-Bop Boys
Courtesy of Savoy

31 Copland: "Fanfare for the Common Man"
Czechoslovak Radio Orchestra; Stephen
Gunzenhauser
Naxos of America Inc.

32 Varèse: "Poème électronique" ("Electronic
Poem")
Riccardo Chailly
Courtesy of Universal Music Enterprises (P) 1998

33 Bernstein: "America" from *West Side Story*
Nashville Symphony Orchestra, Morrison, Eldred,
Cooke, Dean, Sam Giovanni, Kenneth
Schermerhorn
Naxos of America Inc.

37 Cage: Sonata V from *Sonatas and Interludes*
Borris Berman
Naxos of America Inc.

39 Glass: *Company,* II
Ulster Orchestra Takuo Yuasa, dir.
Adele Anthony
Naxos of America Inc.

41 Crumb: "Bebe el agua tranquila de la canción
añeja" ("Drink the tranquil water of the old song")
(P) 1986 New World Recordings

Index

Note: Page references in italics refer to figures. Page references in boldface refer to Listening Guides.